WARSHIP 2012

WARSHIP 2012

Editor: **John Jordan**

Assistant Editor: **Stephen Dent**

CONWAY

Frontispiece:
The cruiser HMS Doris *in the Suez Canal, photographed from a Bibby liner. Between 1914 and 1918* Doris *served in the East Indies, Red Sea, Mediterranean and Dardanelles.*

Visit the Conway website at www.conwaypublishing.com

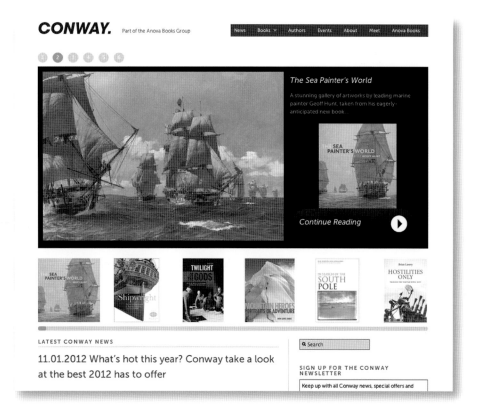

© Conway 2012

First published in Great Britain in 2011 by Conway,
an imprint of Anova Books, 10 Southcombe Street, London W14 0RA
www.conwaypublishing.com

All rights reserved. No part of this publication may be reproduced, stored in a retrieval system, or transmitted in any form or by any means, electronic, mechanical, photocopying, recording or otherwise, without the prior permission of the publisher.

British Library Cataloguing in Publication Data
A record of this title is available on request from the British Library.

ISBN: 9781844861569

Printed and bound by 1010 Printing International Ltd, China
Reproduction by Rival Colour Ltd, UK

CONTENTS

Editorial — 6

FEATURE ARTICLES

Building the Grand Fleet: 1906-1916 — 8
Ian Johnston, **Brian Newman** and **Ian Buxton** look at the industrial infrastructure which underpinned the dreadnought programme in the United Kingdom.

Jules Verne and *Le Gladiateur* — 22
John Jordan focuses on two little-known ships designed during the interwar period to support the Marine Nationale.

TB 191 – A Tasmanian Torpedo Boat — 33
Mark Briggs tells the story of Tasmania's only torpedo boat and details the operation of the spar torpedo, comparing it with the self-propelling Whitehead torpedoes which were also beginning to enter service.

The Loss of the *Giuseppe Garibaldi* — 40
Zvonimir Freivogel recounts the sinking of the Italian armoured cruiser *Giuseppe Garibaldi* in 1915, and of how the wreck came to be discovered by a team of divers in 2008.

Conduite du Tir Part 2: 1900 to 1913 — 52
John Spencer looks at the period prior to the Great War during which the basic principles of fire control were defined and established in the Marine Nationale.

Modern Air-Independent Propulsion Equipped Submarines — 65
Conrad Waters reviews the latest developments in submarine propulsion technmology.

Yahagi: One Light Cruiser at Leyte Gulf — 81
Mike Williams recounts the last of the IJN's massed destroyer torpedo attacks, which took place during the battle of Leyte Gulf, from the perspective of the *Yahagi*, flagship of the 10th Destroyer Squadron.

Russia's 'American' Monitors: The *Uragan* Class — 98
Stephen McLaughlin describes the origins, construction and careers of the American-style monitors built by the Russian Imperial Navy as a result of the suppression of the 1863 Polish revolt.

The Battleship *Gaulois* — 113
Philippe Caresse traces the eventful career of the *Gaulois*, one of three battleships of the *Charlemagne* class.

The Cruiser Family *Talbot* — 136
Keith McBride looks at the origins of the protected cruisers of the *Talbot* class, designed primarily for trade protection, and assesses the ships' merits and deficiencies.

The Battlecruisers of the *Kongô* Class — 142
Hans Lengerer examines the origins of the first IJN battlecruiser to be built abroad.

The Limits of Naval Power — 162
Colin Jones examines the naval campaign during the Franco-Prussian War of 1870-71.

Warship Notes — 169

Naval Books of the Year — 183

Warship Gallery — 202
A selection of photographs taken by **John Jordan** during the period immediately after the 1982 Falklands Conflict.

EDITORIAL

The positive responses to *Warship 2010* and *Warship 2011* have been particularly gratifying. A number of readers have written in to say how much they enjoyed these two annuals, highlighting both the breadth of coverage and the quality of the individual articles. We have also received a number of suggestions and requests for future articles. These are noted, and some of these suggestions have been duly communicated to regular contributors who specialise in a particular field of research and/or are an authority on a particular period or navy. However, the editorial staff rarely 'commission' an article; rather, potential contributors approach us with a proposal, which is then discussed in detail, taking particular account of possible illustration in the form of photographs, plans and schemas before it is agreed. We do not accept everything we are offered; criteria for acceptance include potential interest for *Warship* readers, depth of research and quality of writing. Within these constraints we attempt to achieve a balance of coverage in terms of types of warship, historical period and particular navies. A strong editorial hand is important; however, we try never to lose sight of *Warship*'s primary mission: to provide a forum for the publication of original research into warship history based, where possible, on little-known or recently-available primary source material. The quality of the individual submissions is undoubtedly the key to the success of the annual, and this is possible only if the contributor is committed to, and enthusiastic about his/her chosen subject. Thus, while readers' suggestions and requests for future articles are noted and, where possible, acted upon, the contents of the current and future annuals will continue to be centred around the proposals we receive from both new and established authors. Although many new authors have been introduced to *Warship* over the past few years, we continue to welcome any contact from prospective contributors; style guidelines are available on request.

The weight of this year's articles falls firmly on the period 1860-1918. Stephen McLaughlin follows last year's article on Russia's first ironclads with one on the American-style monitors of the *Uragan* class built during the 1860s to defend St. Petersburg in the wake of the Polish revolt, the brutal suppression of which had provoked considerable hostility towards imperial Russia on the part of Britain and France. Built – or assembled – in Russia's Baltic shipyards, these unusual vessels remained in active service until 1900, when they were stricken.

In a very different article, Colin Jones examines the little-known naval campaign which accompanied the Franco-Prussian War of 1870-71. The Marine Nationale of the period was the second most powerful in the world, but its fleet of ironclads made little impression on the conflict, and failed to make its superiority over the embryonic Prussian Navy count. In so doing it served to reemphasise the peripheral role that even the most powerful navy could play in a continental European conflict in which land armies were the decisive weapon; it defined, as Colin Jones has termed it in his study, 'The Limits of Naval Power'.

The 1880s is the setting for Mark Briggs' article on Tasmania's only Vosper-built torpedo boat, *TB-191*. Mark is a new contributor to *Warship*, and has produced a fascinating and well-researched article which exposes the dilemmas faced by Britain's remote colonies in the South Pacific, vulnerable to the depredations of Russian and French cruisers but with limited economic resources to provide for the defences of key ports and harbours. Faced with a choice between an expensive gunboat and a modern torpedo boat to supplement the fixed defences at Hobart, the Tasmanian authorities opted for the latter, armed first with a McEvoy spar torpedo and subsequently with the self-propelled – and significantly more expensive – Whitehead torpedo.

Moving on to the 1890s, there is an article by Keith McBride on the protected cruisers of the *Talbot* class, typical of the ships built for the late Victorian navy to protect Britain's trade. And Philippe Caresse follows up his earlier articles for *Warship* on the French battleships *Iéna* and *Suffren* with an article on the *Gaulois*, one of a class of three vessels which succeeded the 'singletons' of the *Flotte d'échantillons* (patchwork fleet) of the 1870s and 1880s. Ironically, while during the First World War the more modern battleships of the Marine Nationale were condemned to fruitless patrols in the southern Adriatic as part of a strategy to blockade the Austro-Hungarian Fleet, it was the older French battleships which saw action in the eastern Mediterranean, notably at the Dardanelles. Having survived a shell hit which caused major flooding and resulted in the ship being beached, *Gaulois* was repaired only to be sunk by a German U-Boat while heading back to join the fleet. Philippe has illustrated the ship's eventful career with some stunning photographs.

The period 1900-1918 is the subject of no fewer than four major feature articles. John Spencer (my sincere apologies for referring to him as 'David' in the 2010 Editorial) continues his series on French fire control with an in-depth analysis of the Marine Nationale's thinking immediately prior to the Great War which includes detailed descriptions of the equipment and the tactics developed to ensure that an enemy battle line would be subjected to a withering and constant barrage of shell. The focus of the article by Ian Johnston, Brian Newman and Ian Buxton, entitled Building the Grand Fleet, is on the industrial infrastructure which underpinned the construction of the most powerful fleet of its time, and the changes which had to take place at the shipyards in order to keep pace with the rapid increases in the size and capabilities of the new super-dreadnought battleships and battlecruisers. Hans Lengerer's article on the IJN's *Kongô* class battlecruisers of the same period, the first of which was built by the British company Vickers alongside HMS *Princess Royal*, looks at the innovations which Vickers incorporated into the design and the importance accorded by the Japanese to 'technology transfer', which would lead to major advances in IJN shipyard capabilities and enable a new generation of super-dreadnought battleships to be built in Japan using components manufactured locally.

Finally, in an article held over from last year, Zvonimir Freivogel writes about the loss of the Italian armoured cruiser *Garibaldi*, sunk in 1915 and discovered by a team of divers in 2008. In the process he analyses the tactics employed by the Italian and Austro-Hungarian navies respectively in the Adriatic, and how these tactics had to change to take account of the dangers from mines, motor torpedo boats and submarines in these confined waters. Zvonimir also highlights the undoubted perils of diving on shipwrecks – a fascinating and valuable process but one which is dangerous nonetheless, however advanced the equipment.

From the interwar period there is a single article: the Editor's dual feature on the French submarine depot ship *Jules Verne* and the netlayer *Le Gladiateur*. The vessels built to support the fleets have generally received little coverage in naval journals, but they were often the key to naval operations on distant stations, and the two ships in question were purpose-built designs which showed considerable ingenuity on the part of their designers. The drawings prepared for this article benefit considerably from the decision of the French naval archives to publish their plans online; it is to be hoped that the British and US national archives will eventually be persuaded to follow this lead.

Mike Williams' article on the IJN cruiser *Yahagi* at the Battle of Leyte Gulf focuses on the Japanese tactic of massed torpedo attacks, which were practised exhaustively during the 1930s and were regarded as a potential game-changer in the 'decisive battle' against the US Navy. Although the oxygen-fuelled 'Long Lance' torpedo was a formidable weapon and scored many successes in the night actions of the Solomons in late 1942 and 1943, its employment at long range in daylight proved less decisive than hoped, and in the action at Leyte Gulf not a single torpedo found its mark despite favourable tactical conditions. Mike Williams speculates on the possible reasons for this failure.

Finally, in the latest of his series of articles on modern-day navies, Conrad Waters reviews the latest developments in air-independent propulsion technology for submarines. The ability to remain submerged for long periods has long been a Holy Grail for the submarine service. Nuclear power has resolved the issue for the major naval powers, but the large size and technical complexity of these submarines has placed them beyond the reach of most of the smaller and middle-ranking powers. The competing propulsion technologies developed over the past decade in Sweden, Germany and France have made the AIP-equipped submarine a formidable opponent, particularly in the shallow waters likely to be encountered in littoral operations.

Warship Notes this year is the usual eclectic mix, with contributions on shipbuilding projects for South

The cruiser Venus, *one of the ships featured in Keith McBride's article on pp.136-141.* (World Ship Society, Abrahams Collection)

American navies, on the postwar conversion of the Dutch gunboat *Soemba* to a radar instruction and fighter direction ship, and on the origins of the name of the British cruiser *Curacoa*, which has probably been mis-spelled on more occasions than that of any other RN warship. Following a lean period, Warship Notes is now back to its customary size; again we welcome future contributions to this section of the annual.

It has long been the case that not all high-quality books on naval history have been published in the UK or the USA. We are receiving an increasing number of books for review from publishers in continental Europe, particularly from France and Italy, so in a new departure we now have a review section dedicated to books published in languages other than English. We feel sure that this will be welcomed by our readers, not all of whom have English as their first language.

In this year's Gallery, we look back to the Falklands War, which took place exactly thirty years ago. The focus is not on the war itself, but on the ships that sailed late to reinforce the South Atlantic 'Task Force' and those that returned from the conflict, and on the modifications to close-range armament and livery which were implemented during this period.

Next year Jon Wise will be following his own note on the Chilean prewar cruiser projects with a major feature article on British shipbuilders and the South American export market during the period 1950-70. Other features will include the Australian Modified *Leanders*, a study of the action at Dogger Bank with special attention to the damage sustained by the battlecruisers *Lion* and *Tiger* and the treatment of casualties, the US Navy's 'V'-Boats of the 1920s (which included the giant submarines *Nautilus*, *Narwhal* and *Argonaut*), and the Imperial Japanese Navy's Fourth Fleet Incident of 1935.

Many readers are probably already aware that the new Conway website is now up and running at http://www.conwaypublishing.com, which incorporates various *Warship*-related content. Please note that the current pages are simply a first step. Developments are planned which we are not yet in a position to detail, but which we are sure will be favourably received by readers past and present. Watch this space…!

John Jordan
December 2011

BUILDING THE GRAND FLEET: 1906-1916[1]

The Grand Fleet which contested the North Sea with the German High Seas Fleet in May 1916 was the most formidable force of battleships and battlecruisers ever assembled. **Ian Johnston**, **Brian Newman** and **Ian Buxton** look at the industrial infrastructure which underpinned the dreadnought programme in the United Kingdom.

Much has been written about the Grand Fleet and its epic if inconclusive battle with the High Seas Fleet at Jutland in May 1916. The technical development of dreadnought battleships and battlecruisers, like the Battle of Jutland itself, has been the subject of an entire library of publications, articles and television documentaries. The thirty-seven British dreadnoughts at sea on that day represented an industrial achievement of the highest order, requiring the collective efforts of tens of thousands of persons, millions of tons of material and a significant percentage of the gross national product. Building one battleship was a time-consuming, complex as well as a hugely expensive business. Building fifty-one[2] in little more than a decade required an industrial infra-

Conqueror *going down the ways on 1 May 1911, under the building gantry at Wm. Beardmore's Naval Construction Works, Dalmuir.* (Author's collection)

structure of considerable proportions. The costly and specialised plant for the manufacture of the largest naval guns, gun mountings, armour plate, as well as the provision of shipbuilding and docking facilities were vital elements in the realisation of the battle fleet.

This article considers the impact the creation of the Grand Fleet had on the shipbuilding and armaments industries at their peak in the UK with particular reference to the dreadnought type, and looks briefly at the likely consequence of the post-1918 naval arms race had this not been terminated at the Washington Conference in February 1922.

Inevitably, the ever increasing size of these warships over a short period of time taxed the productive facilities of the shipbuilding industry to the point where some shipyards could no longer physically accommodate them, or may have been unwilling to make the necessary investment in improved yard layout even where topography allowed. Starting in 1906, the year that the battleship *Dreadnought* appeared, a total of eleven shipyards, both private and naval dockyards, were tendering for the construction of battleships and battlecruisers mounting 12-inch guns. Just ten years later, only five of these yards were able to accommodate the latest 15-inch gunned battlecruisers. Had this pattern continued into the era of projected 18-inch gunned vessels, the impact on productive as well as on refit and maintenance facilities would have been significant.

The British Shipbuilding Industry at the End of the 19th Century

Traditionally, most of the Royal Navy's large warships had been built in the Royal Dockyards: principally Portsmouth, Devonport, Chatham and Pembroke. There were exceptions to this, and as early as the 1860s warship contracts had been placed with private yards although these were relatively few in number. *Warrior* (launched 1860) for example was built by the Thames Iron Works with engines by Penn while her half-sister, *Black Prince*, was built and engined by Napier on the Clyde. Commercial shipbuilders were also responsible for the development of specialist warship types such as the Elswick cruisers pioneered by Armstrong or the destroyers pioneered by a number of yards amongst which was Yarrow at the Isle of Dogs. Where these yards undertook research and development activities at their own cost, they were usually rewarded with contracts, as was the case with the examples given above. This tendency increased from the late 1880s onwards, when more reliance was placed on private yards in the context of the growing technical sophistication of warships. Export orders for foreign navies coupled with advances in merchant ship construction and marine engineering gave the private yards a technological lead over the Royal Dockyards. Increasingly, private yards, investing in plant and facilities to maintain or enhance competitiveness, were becoming better equipped than their dockyard counterparts. By the end of the 19th century, a number of private yards had become regular contractors to the Admiralty, building every class of warship. Of these yards, a few of the larger had developed into vast industrial empires with significant investment in armaments and armour manufacture.

It would be the battleship more than any other type of warship that would define the upper limits of a shipyard's physical suitability as well as its level of competence in managing the complexity of the armament, armour, and propulsive systems. It is on this type of warship, its cost and consumption of materials, manpower and constructional facilities, that this article is principally focused. By the early 1900s, the shipyards in the UK which were active in the construction of battleships of the dreadnought type were as follows:[3]

The Royal Dockyards
Portsmouth and Devonport[4]
(While both yards had the capacity to build battleships, they were reliant on private firms for the supply of machinery, armour and armament.)

Private Yards
Armstrong Whitworth, Elswick
Armstrong Whitworth, Walker (from 1912)
Beardmore, Dalmuir (from 1905)
John Brown, Clydebank
Cammell Laird, Birkenhead
Fairfield, Govan
Palmers, Jarrow
Scotts, Greenock
Thames Iron Works, Blackwall
Vickers Son & Maxim, Barrow in Furness

The above shipbuilders strove to win contracts from the Admiralty, as warship work was highly profitable and prestigious with none more so than the battleship, the cornerstone of British imperial defence. For its part, the Admiralty encouraged firms in this competitive process with the result that shipbuilders became eager to provide new production facilities to demonstrate their suitability. As an example, when William Beardmore laid out a new yard at Dalmuir on the Clyde, he was keen to ensure that the Third Sea Lord, Admiral May, and the Director of Dockyards, Sir James Williamson, visited the site before work in building the shipyard had begun; indeed its title was Naval Construction Works.

Of the above firms Beardmore, Charles Cammell, John Brown and Vickers had recently expanded into shipbuilding from a core business of steel and armour production, while in the case of Armstrong shipbuilding capacity had been added from a core business of armament manufacture with its Elswick Ordnance Company many years earlier. Through this process of vertical integration, each of these firms had accumulated capacity across warship production and had further capitalised their works through programmes of investment, resulting in modern yards with excellent facilities.

However, within this group further subtlety existed. The amalgamation of Vickers with Maxim and Armstrong with Whitworth created two integrated armaments companies that had greater influence over warship production than any of the other firms. Both were able to build the hulls, design and manufacture the highly complex gun mountings, guns and armour. However Armstrong did not have an in-house facility to manufacture propulsion machinery, and this portion of the contract was sub-contracted to a number of firms. Nevertheless, Armstrong Whitworth and Vickers Sons & Maxim enjoyed a unique advantage in dealing with the Admiralty. When William Beardmore expanded from his highly successful steel works and forge into shipbuilding, he had every intention of adding heavy gun mounting plant to challenge the monopoly enjoyed by Armstrong and Vickers. However, financial indebtedness to Vickers resulting in a 49% shareholding in Beardmore enabled Vickers to prevent this development, and the former's naval gun mounting activities were limited to mechanisms up to 6-inch. A further and somewhat more successful attempt at breaking the Armstrong and Vickers grip on heavy gun mounting manufacture took place in 1905 when John Brown, Cammell Laird and Fairfield jointly developed the Coventry Ordnance Works to design and manufacture guns and mountings. Thus, at the time when the greatest number of dreadnoughts were under construction, the manufacture of mountings, a highly complex and time consuming activity, was concentrated in the hands of three manufacturers, one of whom was relatively inexperienced.

In the years before the First World War, when the maximum demand was placed on the warship building industry, the manufacture of gun mountings would prove to be a significant bottleneck, as was equally the shortage of skilled labour.

Ever Increasing Size

While it is patently the case that ships had continued to increase in size over the decades since the introduction of iron as a shipbuilding material, the pace of growth in battleships and battlecruisers in the ten years from 1906 to 1916 was wholly extraordinary, particularly in the case

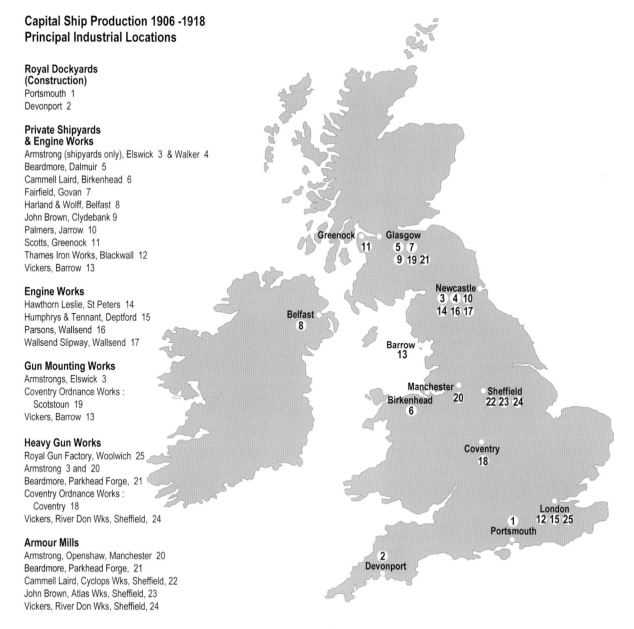

**Capital Ship Production 1906 -1918
Principal Industrial Locations**

**Royal Dockyards
(Construction)**
Portsmouth 1
Devonport 2

**Private Shipyards
& Engine Works**
Armstrong (shipyards only), Elswick 3 & Walker 4
Beardmore, Dalmuir 5
Cammell Laird, Birkenhead 6
Fairfield, Govan 7
Harland & Wolff, Belfast 8
John Brown, Clydebank 9
Palmers, Jarrow 10
Scotts, Greenock 11
Thames Iron Works, Blackwall 12
Vickers, Barrow 13

Engine Works
Hawthorn Leslie, St Peters 14
Humphrys & Tennant, Deptford 15
Parsons, Wallsend 16
Wallsend Slipway, Wallsend 17

Gun Mounting Works
Armstrongs, Elswick 3
Coventry Ordnance Works :
  Scotstoun 19
Vickers, Barrow 13

Heavy Gun Works
Royal Gun Factory, Woolwich 25
Armstrong 3 and 20
Beardmore, Parkhead Forge, 21
Coventry Ordnance Works :
  Coventry 18
Vickers, River Don Wks, Sheffield, 24

Armour Mills
Armstrong, Openshaw, Manchester 20
Beardmore, Parkhead Forge, 21
Cammell Laird, Cyclops Wks, Sheffield, 22
John Brown, Atlas Wks, Sheffield, 23
Vickers, River Don Wks, Sheffield, 24

Ajax in the fitting-out basin at Scotts shipyard, Greenock, in 1913. The Cunard liner Alaunia is in the background. (Author's collection)

of battlecruisers. In physical size *Dreadnought's* 526 feet and 20,000 tons had risen to 640 feet and 31,000 tons in the *Queen Elizabeths*, while *Invincible's* 567 feet and 20,000 tons rose to 860 feet and 42,000 tons in *Hood*. Although heavy armour was widely in use before 1906, the maximum of 13-inch used in the battleships of the *Queen Elizabeth* and *Royal Sovereign* classes was noteworthy because of the amount needed to protect much longer hulls. Gun calibre rose from 12-inch to 15-inch, which apart from other considerations required shipbuilders to utilise craneage of increased capacity to lift the very heavy indivisible loads such as turntables.

In response to this rapid development, the layout and size of shipyards became increasingly important. Scotts' yard at Greenock, which had built *Colossus* and *Ajax*, would not have been able to accommodate the ships under construction at the start of the First World War. After the *Lion* class battlecruisers, Vickers, who built *Princess Royal*, were no longer able to accommodate succeeding classes. In 1912, after the completion of *Thunderer*, the Thames Iron Works closed because the firm was no longer able to make adequate profits from non-naval contracts and suffered from certain Admiralty misgivings over facilities. In late 1914, when it was decided to change the order for a *Royal Sovereign* class battleship (620ft oa) awarded to Palmers to that of a battlecruiser *Repulse* (794ft oa), the contract was transferred to John Brown, the reason being that Palmers did not have a berth long enough. After *Lion* (700ft), Devonport could not accommodate succeeding classes of battlecruiser. Portsmouth built battleships up to the size of the *Queen Elizabeth* class (640ft) but could not have accommodated *Lion*. Added to this were the problems resulting from Fisher's control of warship building from the end of 1914, which demanded unrealistically rapid construction times for vessels (battlecruisers) which, because of his obsession with speed, implied long hulls to reduce drag and to accommodate greater boiler power.

Timing

Either by good fortune or by an uncannily accurate reading of the political situation, the heavy warship building industries in Britain coalesced into a coherent whole at exactly the right time to meet changing events at home and abroad. The expansion of the German fleet from the turn of the 20th century onwards added political edge and, most importantly, the prospect of many lucrative contracts from the Admiralty. Farther afield the USA and Japan also recognised the importance of constructing a battle fleet that appropriately reflected their emerging political and industrial power. At home the evolution of the battleship into the turbine driven, all-big-gun *Dreadnought* of 1906 rendered existing battleships obsolete thereby eliminating, technically at least, British preponderance in numbers. The net effect of all of the above was to provide an unprecedented battleship building opportunity for the armaments companies, naval shipyards and royal dockyards.

Labour Issues

When the reality of the First World War impacted on naval construction, the *Queen Elizabeth* and *Royal Sovereign* class battleships were nearing completion or mid-way through construction, while the battlecruisers *Repulse* and *Renown* were yet to be inserted into construction programmes. However, in relative terms, it was clear that by 1914 Britain had won the race against Germany in capital ship construction, and the focus of attention shifted to immediate requirements as determined by the progress of the war at sea. This meant building large numbers of destroyers and submarines. The construction of merchant ships would later become a priority to make up for losses to U-boats

In April 1916, the Admiralty issued contracts for the construction of four battlecruisers of the 'Admiral' class. The British losses incurred at the Battle of Jutland on 31 May 1916 delayed these contracts while, understandably, an improved scheme of armour and enhanced protection could be worked out. All four were laid down in September/October of that year but it quickly became evident that it would be impossible to devote the necessary manpower levels to these vessels without adversely affecting the production of destroyers and merchant ships. There is no doubt that in late 1916 the C-in-C Grand Fleet, Admiral David Beatty, was in urgent need of these ships to face the threat of German battlecruisers known to be under construction. In the event sufficient labour was available to permit the construction of only one, *Hood*, in the John Brown yard, which employed some 10,000 men during the First World War. Labour became such an issue that one bizarre scheme envisaged recruiting large numbers of miners into the shipbuilding industry. Efforts to manage existing shipyard labour were assisted by the passing of the Munitions of War Act, July 1915, in which shipyards and armaments factories were declared Controlled Establishments. This gave the Admiralty the right to coordinate production, including the power to reallocate labour from one shipyard to another as the need arose.

The Ordnance Industry

By the time dreadnought construction started, the naval ordnance industry in Britain had moved from being a business predominantly controlled by the War Office and centred on the Royal Gun Factory at Woolwich, to largely private manufacturers. By the 1880s the Armstrong company at Elswick near Newcastle had built up a thriving export industry, supplying armaments not only for warships it built in its own shipyard such as the Elswick cruisers, but for ships built for overseas navies – and for armies. Based on its commercial experience of hydraulic machinery for cranes and other heavy engineering products, it had also developed heavy naval gun mountings for battleships for the Admiralty, a product that Woolwich could not manufacture. The only challenger for such mountings was Whitworth of Openshaw near Manchester. The two companies merged in 1897 with Armstrong, Whitworth hoping to become a monopoly supplier. But steel maker Vickers was already making guns and armour at Sheffield, and was eyeing the lucrative market associated with building warships and their gun mountings. That same year, it took over the Naval Construction and Armaments shipyard at Barrow, and set about constructing a gun mounting plant there. It tendered successfully for twin 12-inch mountings in 1898, delivering its first sets from the new shops in 1902. It expanded its ordnance business rapidly, helped by a more progressive management than Armstrong's.

The two companies between them then controlled not only the supply of heavy mountings for the Admiralty but

TABLE 1: HEAVY NAVAL ORDNANCE AND ARMOUR & GUN MOUNTING MANUFACTURE

The ordnance companies able to manufacture 12-inch guns and above, armour plate of 6 inches and above and the capacity to manufacture mountings for battleship main armament, were as follows:

Company	Location
Armstrong, Whitworth	
Ordnance:	Elswick Works, Newcastle, Openshaw Works, Manchester
Armour and Forgings:	Openshaw Works, Manchester
Gun Mountings:	Elswick Works, Newcastle
Vickers	
Ordnance:	River Don Works, Sheffield
Armour and Forgings:	River Don Works, Sheffield
Gun Mountings:	Barrow Works
Beardmore	
Ordnance:	Parkhead Works, Glasgow
Armour and Forgings:	Parkhead Works, Glasgow
John Brown	
Armour and Forgings:	Atlas Works, Sheffield
Cammell Laird	
Armour and Forgings:	Grimethorpe and Cyclops Works, Sheffield
Royal Gun Factory	
Ordnance	Woolwich, London
Coventry Ordnance Works	
Ordnance	Coventry
Gun Mountings:	Scotstoun, Glasgow

also for export, where their only serious competitor was Krupp of Germany. While other British shipbuilders could tender for battleship orders from countries like Japan, they had to get their main armament from Armstrong or Vickers. These two not only quoted high prices to such competitors but often shared export order work amongst themselves. It was to counter this 'duopoly' that John Brown, Cammell Laird and Fairfield developed the small Coventry Ordnance Works (COW), so that it could supply both their own shipyards and the Admiralty with naval ordnance. Substantial investment was required. While Brown and Cammell already produced gun forgings (and armour), new gun manufacturing plant was built at Coventry. This was able to build guns up to 60ft long, wire-wound for radial strength, which was the British practice. A new works was built at Scotstoun in Glasgow to build heavy naval mountings. This included five erection pits into which ammunition hoists, working chamber with training and elevating machinery, turntable onto which gun trunnions and slides were fitted, gunhouse and guns themselves could be assembled and tested prior to installation in a battleship. From 1905 COW were able to design and manufacture smaller calibre guns and mountings. But the Admiralty was reluctant to order heavier guns and mountings until the company had proved itself, as also were export customers. It was not until 1909 that the Admiralty, wishing to extend heavy gun mounting manufacture, as well as to provide a check on Armstrong and Vickers prices, ordered heavy guns from COW.

The heavy guns themselves could be manufactured not only by the three heavy gun mounting manufacturers, but also by the Royal Gun Factory at Woolwich and Beardmore at Glasgow – Armstrong built guns at both its Elswick and Openshaw works. These gun manufacturers tendered to the Admiralty for batches of guns to be issued to a class of battleship (including about 40% as spares), but heavy mountings were ordered for a specific ship. Armstrong and Vickers obtained the lion's share of orders for both guns and mountings. Such contracts were very lucrative. The main armament of a battleship comprised around 25% of its cost (typically about £2m) and took as long to build as the ship itself, two years or more. For example, *Orion's* five 13.5-inch twin mountings, which weighed about 600 tons each (including equipment on the hull such as hydraulic pumping engines), cost about £79,000 each including gunhouse armour, with a further £26,000 for the guns, ordered separately under a different Vote in the annual Navy Estimates.

Post-dreadnought secondary armament consisted of guns of 3-inch to 6-inch calibre ordered by the Admiralty in batches, as they were also used in cruisers and destroyers. As this ordnance came off the production lines, it went into store at Woolwich or the Royal Dockyards, to be issued to ships as required. 'Transferable'

A twin 13.5-inch mounting Mark III destined for HMS Conqueror *in one of the gun pits at the Scotstoun shops of the Coventry Ordnance Works in 1912. (Author's collection)*

mountings such as these were manufactured not only by Armstrong and Vickers, but by other companies including COW and Beardmore.

Guns and mountings were also manufactured for export. In some cases, they were installed in the ship in Britain, such as the Japanese battlecruiser *Kongo* by Vickers. In other cases they were exported to an overseas shipyard, e.g. for the small battleship *España* in Spain. In the case of Italy and Japan, both Armstrong and Vickers helped develop indigenous manufacture by providing designs and investing in factories.

Overall the British industry established prior to the First World War manufactured the majority of the world's battleship armament. For heavy mountings (12-inch and over, mainly twins), that amounted to 230 turrets for the Admiralty from 1906 to 1920, with 48% from Armstrong, 42% from Vickers and 10% from COW. For the 184 15-inch guns for the Admiralty, the split was: 49 Vickers, 37 Beardmore, 34 Elswick, 33 RGF, 19 COW and 12 Openshaw.[5]

As with armour manufacture, ordnance manufacture was highly profitable until 1918. But with both home and export warship markets shrinking post war, COW closed down, selling off its works for other use. Vickers and Armstrong merged in 1928, but continued to build mountings at both Elswick and Barrow. Heavy gun manufacture was reduced to Elswick, Beardmore and Woolwich. But despite the lack of battleship orders, the Admiralty provided some support to maintain a modest capacity until battleship building resumed in 1936.

TABLE 2: NAVAL SHIPBUILDING YARDS & ROYAL DOCKYARDS

The table shows the shipyards that built dreadnought warships and the number built. Shipyards and dockyards that also had Engine Works, i.e. the capacity to manufacture propelling machinery and boilers, are marked*.

Shipyard	Dreadnoughts completed
Royal Dockyards	
Portsmouth	8
Devonport	9
Private Shipyards	
Thames	
Thames Iron Works*	1
[took over the Penn Engine Works in 1899]	
Mersey	
Cammell Laird*	1
Barrow	
Vickers*	5
NE Coast	
Palmers*	3
Armstrong Whitworth	8
Clyde	
Fairfield*	4
John Brown*	6
Beardmore*	3
Scotts*	2
Belfast	
Harland & Wolff*	1
Total	**51**

Armour Plate

There had been major developments in armour plate in the 1890s, first with the introduction of American Harvey steel, then with German Krupp cemented (KC) armour, which had about 2.5 times the resistive power of wrought iron (i.e. a 6-inch KC plate was equivalent to 15 inches of iron). Five British armour plate manufacturers set up new plant licensed to make KC, and remained suppliers throughout the dreadnought era. John Brown, Cammell Laird and Vickers had long been established at Sheffield as had Beardmore in Glasgow, but Armstrong Whitworth only started making armour at Openshaw near Manchester in 1900.

The process of making such armour was complex. A nickel-chrome steel ingot was cast, then rolled down to approximate size and thickness. After trimming, it was ready for cementation, which hardened the face in a special furnace by applying a charcoal mixture to increase carbon content to the outer surface, leaving a relatively tough back. It was then bent to shape if required – belt armour was usually flat, but barbette and some gunhouse armour was curved. The edges were planed and grooved to interlock with adjacent plates. The plate was then hardened by reheating and cooling with water jets. Holes were then drilled and tapped into the back for securing to the hull by armour bolts. After testing the plate was despatched to the shipyard by rail.

This process was expensive, and together with royalty and experimental costs, resulted in the makers charging very high prices for armour. Prices varied according to location in the ship, thickness and shape, but were typically £80-£150 per ton, at a time when mild steel cost around £6-8 per ton. The Admiralty was aware that the armour makers had formed a 'ring' to charge uniform prices, but was prepared to accept this if the industry invested in sufficient capacity and paid for research and development – Vickers had come up with an improved plate by 1910. But the prices charged were highly profitable to the makers, with manufacturing costs only about half selling prices.

The armour quantities required for a dreadnought-era battleship were around 6-8000 tons including gunhouse armour, although the latter was ordered separately with the heavy gun mountings. Armour cost was around 25-30% of total ship, while protection weight formed a similar proportion of displacement. The Admiralty shared the orders for armour approximately equally between the five manufacturers at an agreed price for that year's battleship building programme.

Even though armour resistive power was improving, so was gun power and the capability of armour-piercing projectiles. So while *Dreadnought* had a maximum side belt thickness of 11 inches, it had increased to 13 inches in the *Queen Elizabeth* class less than ten years later. Battleship armour was ordered by weight not thickness, e.g. 360lb (per square foot) was nominally 9 inches thick (actually 8.82 inches as 1-inch plate weighed 40.8 lb/sq ft).

In addition to KC armour, a more ductile non-cemented (NC) armour was used for thinner plates or where glancing blows were expected, e.g. gunhouse roofs. Deck protection remained of cheaper high tensile steel, typically two thicknesses of about 1in, as it was not expected to resist normal impact (at 90° to the plate) at the then-anticipated short battle ranges. It was only after the First World War, with the threat of aerial attack and long-range plunging fire that NC armour was fitted to decks, over magazine and machinery spaces.

By the outbreak of the First World War, the British armour industry was capable of making 50,000 tons a year, although a typical annual output per firm was 5000-10,000 tons. But with no more battleships ordered after 1914 and only a handful of battlecruisers, armour production for capital ships fell off after 1916, although it was still required for cruisers and tanks. Indeed, after the war the industry had to reduce capacity, as export orders had also disappeared, so by the start of rearmament in 1936 there were only three manufacturers left.

Propulsion Machinery

The relationship between the builders of the hulls and the makers of the propulsion machinery was a close one; in the context of dreadnought construction, in most instances the firms were one and the same. There were a few exceptions, but the only truly independent engine builders were Parsons Marine Steam Turbine Co. at Wallsend on the Tyne and Humphrys & Tennant on the Thames.[6] Also on the Tyne was the Wallsend Slipway & Engineering Co., in which the shipbuilder, Swan Hunter, held a simple majority shareholding but which in practice acted as an independent firm. A measure of this independence is evident in the statistic that Wallsend Slipway won contracts for the machinery for five of these vessels, whilst its nominal owner Swan Hunter won none for their hulls.[7] Shipbuilder Hawthorn Leslie, also on the Tyne, wholly owned an engine works at St Peters a few miles upriver, and whilst the shipyard, because of its limited inland penetration, was not in a position to tender for battleships, the engine works were eminently successful in this field, winning contracts for seven sets of machinery for such vessels.

That the shipbuilding firms which owned these engine builders jointly won no contracts for dreadnoughts is an endorsement of their status as effectively the most successful independent engine builders involved in the construction of machinery for these vessels. Such a condition can only have been based on their design competence and facilities, and that they tendered competitively.

A geared turbine set for one of four shafts intended for HMS Furious *with the top casing removed in the shops at Wallsend Slipway. The machinery for the three light battlecruisers of the* Courageous *type were the first large installations to employ reduction gearing, which can be seen to the right. (Author's collection)*

In effect, and in the context of dreadnought machinery, they were independent engine builders whose contracts were secured not on the basis of an interlocked commercial relationship with a shipbuilder but on their proven reputation amongst those in the Admiralty charged with placing orders. That they were able to win far more contracts than the leading exponent of marine turbine design, Parsons Marine,[8] adds further to their achievements in this context.

John Brown & Co. at Clydebank were also successful in supplying other shipbuilders with machinery, six contracts being won; Vickers won two and Fairfield, Scotts, Cammell Laird, and Humphrys & Tennant each supplied one. Scott's turbines were subcontracted to Parsons Marine and Humphrys & Tennant's to John Brown. This is the extent to which the marine engine building industry in Britain cross-contracted to meet the exigencies placed upon it by the Admiralty. Much of this cross-contracting was to provide the seventeen naval dockyard-built hulls with the machinery their builders were not equipped to furnish.

An initial problem facing most of the thirteen engine building firms involved was their relative collective inexperience in constructing steam turbines of high power. These were a development at the leading edge of such technology when *Dreadnought* was conceived, and only Parsons Marine, Wallsend Slipway and Clydebank could claim such experience at that time; some firms also lacked the essential machinery and plant needed specifically for turbine construction. An example of this inexperience as a factor was the otherwise lavishly equipped firm of Harland & Wolff who, after winning the contract to supply the machinery for *Neptune*, sub-contracted the turbines to Clydebank, as they had for the turbines fitted in the Atlantic Liners *Olympic* and *Titanic*.[9]

A further problem was the need to provide specialised machine tools in order to construct the turbines, a not very demanding technical problem, but one which was time consuming and expensive to resolve, and may have accounted for Harland & Wolff sub-contracting such large and important contracts. Another expense was incurred in extending machine and erecting shops to accommodate turbine construction whilst maintaining existing reciprocating steam engine capacity. A particular problem which had to be addressed was the handling of the low-pressure rotors. These were not amenable to dismantling, and so more powerful overhead cranes were required in erecting shops than would normally be provided for reciprocating engine construction. For dreadnought construction this was paralleled in boiler shops where, despite being considerably lighter than the typical 'Scotch' boiler which predominated in contemporary merchant vessels, the boilers carried in large numbers by dreadnoughts (*Invincible* had 31, *Lion* 42) demanded greatly increased assembly space. As a result, a spate of new workshops and extensions to existing ones was a characteristic of the principal marine engine building firms in Britain in the decade before 1914.

The Yarrow boilers for Conqueror, complete with funnel uptakes, in the boiler shop at Dalmuir. (Author's collection)

The technology of engine construction was identical, whether it was for the 23,000shp of the early dreadnoughts or the 112,000shp of *Renown* and *Repulse*. Higher power demanded only more boiler capacity, and rotors with more blades to drive higher pitch and larger diameter propellers, and had little if any effect on the facilities required for construction. This changed with the adoption of geared turbines for the light battlecruisers *Glorious*, *Courageous* and *Furious*. The relative precision required in building turbines in comparison with reciprocating machinery represented another learning curve for builders, and this was greatly complicated by the advent of reduction gearing.

A largely neglected area of study is that of the boilers which supplied the steam to the turbines. Large tube designs by Yarrow and Babcock & Wilcox were specified exclusively for dreadnought battleships and battlecruisers until the advent of the light battlecruisers when the change to lighter, small-tube boilers was made. The persistence with large-tube boilers reflected a conservative attitude by an Admiralty obsessed with reliability above efficiency.

It should also be noted here that all of the engine builders involved had to fulfil other equally demanding contract obligations both for the Admiralty and for commercial owners, and that battleship machinery was a more occasional activity than discussion here would suggest.

Fitting Out

The parallel processes of ship and engine building coalesced in a further activity defined as fitting out, a process which had evolved from the practice of shipping the heaviest loads in ship construction – the engines and boilers – after launch, so that a single large-capacity crane could serve any number of vessels which could be brought alongside it, even vessels built by other firms in the locality. Whilst engines could be dismantled in order to reduce their shipping weight to accommodate the capacity of a given fitting-out crane, boilers could not, and so for the second half of the 19th century the weight of boilers generally defined the lifting power of fitting-out cranes. Such cranes were commonly of the sheerlegs type,[10] and of between 40 tons and 80 tons capacity.

Around the turn of the 20th century the Admiralty installed a number of 100-ton steam sheerlegs in the principal naval dockyards[11] in order to meet the new operational agenda being driven by the turret-mounting of the main armament in battleships, either during construction or repair. Between the installation of the first of those sheerlegs in 1898 and the shipping of the five 100-ton turntables by the Portsmouth sheerlegs aboard *Dreadnought* in 1906 two revolutions in shipbuilding technology had taken place.

Firstly, in October 1898, a new form of fitting-out crane was completed in Germany: the hammerhead crane. Secondly, the steam turbine had been adopted as the motive power for vessels of the greatest size and highest speed. The hammerhead crane,[12] and its British equivalent, the Giant cantilever crane, made possible the safer

TABLE 3: SHIPYARDS AND ENGINE BUILDERS

Ship names in [ ] indicates ordered but subsequently cancelled.

Armstrong Whitworth
Invincible, Superb, Monarch, Agincourt, Malaya, Canada, Courageous, Furious, [Anson]
(Main machinery contractor/turbine builder as listed above: Humphrys & Tennant/John Brown, Wallsend, Hawthorn Leslie, Vickers, Wallsend, John Brown, Parsons, Wallsend)

Beardmore
Conqueror, Benbow, Ramillies

John Brown
Inflexible, Australia, Tiger, Barham, Repulse, Hood

Cammell Laird
Audacious, [Howe]

Fairfield
Indomitable, New Zealand, Valiant, Renown, [Rodney]

Harland & Wolff
Glorious

Palmers
Hercules, Queen Mary, Resolution
(Engines for *Queen Mary* by John Brown)

Scotts
Colossus, Ajax

Thames Iron Works
Thunderer. (Turbines subcontracted to Parsons)

Vickers Son & Maxim
Vanguard, Princess Royal, Emperor of India, Erin, Revenge

Portsmouth DY
Dreadnought, Bellerophon, St Vincent, Neptune, King George V, Iron Duke, Queen Elizabeth, Royal Sovereign
(Main machinery contractor/turbine builder as listed above: Vickers/Parsons, Fairfield, Scotts/Parsons, Harland & Wolff / John Brown, Parsons, Cammell Laird, Wallsend, Parsons)

Devonport DY
Temeraire, Collingwood, Indefatigable, Orion, Lion, Centurion, Marlborough, Warspite, Royal Oak
(Machinery as listed above: Hawthorn Leslie, Hawthorn Leslie, John Brown, Wallsend, Vickers, Hawthorn Leslie, Hawthorn Leslie, Hawthorn Leslie, Hawthorn Leslie)

and more efficient shipping of those costly, heavy, yet relatively fragile loads essential to the construction of the battleships of that era: the low-pressure rotors of the engines and the turntables of the gun mountings.

In the context of the fitting-out of dreadnought vessels, the turntable which carried the entire revolving weight of the mounting was invariably the heaviest item to be shipped, followed by the low-pressure rotor in those vessels with direct drive – which was the entire battle fleet apart from the battlecruisers *Courageous*, *Glorious* and *Furious* (the geared turbines of the latter greatly reduced the weight and size of the rotors).

A 12-inch turntable for the pre-dreadnought *Lord Nelson* weighed 102 tons,[13] that for the battlecruiser *Tiger* 160 tons, but the latter was probably shipped in a more complete condition than was typical with such components.

The maximum lifting capacity available to contemporary hull-building firms was:

- Armstrong: 150-ton hydraulic portal crane
- Beardmore: 150-ton hammerhead crane
- John Brown: 150-ton derrick and 150-ton Giant Cantilever cranes
- Cammell Laird: 150-ton hammerhead derricking crane
- Devonport Naval Dockyard: 100-ton sheerlegs until 1908, then 160-ton Giant cantilever crane
- Fairfield: 120-ton sheerlegs until 1911 then 200-ton Giant cantilever crane
- Harland & Wolff: 150-ton floating crane
- Palmers: 120-ton sheerlegs crane
- Portsmouth Naval Dockyard: 100-ton sheerlegs until 1912, then 250-ton Giant cantilever crane
- Scott's: 100-ton derrick crane
- Thames Iron Works: 150-ton floating crane
- Vickers, Barrow: 150-ton hammerhead and 150-ton Giant cantilever cranes

Other fitting-out cranes capable of handling the heaviest loads available at the centres where such vessels were constructed were concentrated on the Tyne in the form of *Titan*, a 140-ton floating crane owned by Swan Hunter, and 150-ton Giant cantilever cranes at North Eastern Marine from 1909 and at Wallsend Slipway from 1910. Although there is no evidence that the latter pair were involved in dreadnought fitting-out, the North Eastern Marine crane almost certainly shipped the turntables for the 15-inch monitors *Marshal Ney* and *Marshal Soult*. *Titan* was photographed alongside a number of dreadnought vessels installing engines and boilers, but of those vessels built on the Tyne it is probable that most received their main armament at the Elswick crane.

Whilst the maximum capacity of a given fitting-out crane was to some extent a measure of its capability, for the fitting-out of battleships and battlecruisers an additional operational factor unique to such vessels had to be accommodated. The fitting of armour plate, particularly side armour, was a time-consuming process which

One of 24 Yarrow small-tube boilers destined for A boiler room being lowered into HMS Hood through the main (protective) deck. The boiler, weighing about 30 tons, is being manipulated over the opening in the deck by two wooden sheerlegs stepped on either side of the hull. (Author's collection)

demanded a lifting capacity in a crane below that of the maximum but well beyond the capacity of typical shipyard or dockside cranes at that time. Fitting-out cranes were commonly fitted with a range of hoists in order to handle loads economically and rapidly according to their weight. Thus side armour would usually be handled by an auxiliary hoist of about twenty to forty tons capacity. Whilst fitting the armour the crane was unavailable for other duties for considerable periods, this in general being one of the factors which account for the long construction time typical of the fitting-out of these vessels. Some builders utilised temporary sheerlegs mounted at deck level to hold up the armour plate during the bolting-through operations, thus releasing the fitting-out crane for other duties.[14]

In 1912, Armstrong made much of its achievement in shipping complete the five twin 13.5-inch mountings for the battleship *Monarch* in three days with their 150-ton hydraulic crane. They claimed[15] that 250 lifts were involved and that the maximum was 145 tons – this no doubt representing the turntables, with a total of 2800 tons for the cumulative weight shipped.

The weight of the turntables for the twin 15-inch mountings of the *Queen Elizabeth* and *Royal Sovereign* classes as well as *Renown, Repulse, Glorious, Courageous, Furious*[16] and *Hood* was about 150 tons. Such weights were successfully managed in constructing these ships. The classes of battlecruiser and battleship proposed in the belief that a naval arms race in the Pacific between Britain, Japan and the United States was imminent would have challenged the fitting-out facilities infrastructure in Britain. The weight of the triple 16-inch turntables for the new 'G3' battlecruisers was estimated at 185-tons, but this was probably an overestimation.[17] The 18-inch triple mounting proposed for a later class of battleship represented a handling problem that could probably not have been resolved within the existing capacity of fitting-out cranes owned by the presumed builders of these vessels,[18] since the turntables of such mountings would have weighed at least 250 tons. Whilst this was not an insurmountable problem it would have involved considerable expense in providing such a capacity at all of the yards charged with the fitting-out of such vessels.

The fitting-out of a battleship was not complete until it had been dry-docked for propellers and underwater fittings to be checked and the application of an anti-fouling coating. By 1914 both the Clyde and Tyne lacked dry docks capable of docking the largest ships, which had to go to Belfast, the Mersey or a Royal Dockyard before they could run their trials and be accepted by the Admiralty.

The battleship Conqueror *in the fitting-out basin at Dalmuir on 17 May 1911 with the cruiser* Falmouth *alongside. The ring bulkhead for one of the barbettes has been prefabricated and is lying on the quayside waiting to be lifted on board. The 150-ton hammerhead fitting-out crane was designed and built by the German Benrather Maschinenfabrik AG in 1903-04 and was similar to one built at Barrow by the same company. However, from this time onwards fitting-out cranes erected in British yards were of British manufacture.* (Author's collection)

Rosyth was completed as a Royal Dockyard in 1916 with the principal aim of maintaining the ships of the Grand Fleet. In this photograph, taken sometime after May 1917, a battleship of the Bellerophon *class is under the recently-completed 250-ton British-built Giant cantilever crane. The 150-ton floating crane off her starboard side is the former Thames Ironworks Crane transferred to the Admiralty after the closure of the former. The 14-inch Mark I guns lying on the quayside are probably spares for HMS Canada, the only battleship in the Grand Fleet so fitted. The battlecruiser in the background is* Indomitable. (IWM)

Benbow *during trials on the Clyde in October 1914 prior to handing over to the Navy.* (Author's collection)

TABLE 4: A GRAND FLEET: COST TO THE NATION

The following estimates, given as a very approximate guide only, have been derived from a variety of published sources. Figures for cost and material are averaged from the fifty-one capital ships built or laid down from 1906 to 1916.

Man-effort

According to *The Naval Annual* of 1913,[1] 5000 men were required working continuously for two years to build a battleship. Of this figure approximately 2,500 were shipyard trades employed on the hull and about 750 engine trades employed in constructing machinery and boilers. The remainder were employed in armour and ordnance works, as well as numerous other works making all manner of items. During the period in question, a five and a half day working week was worked for say, a 50 week working year. Thus, 51 (ships) x 2 (years) x 50 (weeks) x 5.5 (days) x 5000 (men) equals a total of **140,250,000** man days.

Cost

In very broad terms, the price of 51 capital ships from *Dreadnought* to *Hood* was £111 million.[2] Taking 1916 as the year of calculation and using a price inflation calculator[3] returns a figure of **£8,389,000,000** in today's money.

Notes:
1. See pp.5-7.
2. A rounded figure based on RA Burt's *British Battleships of World War One*.
3. http://www.thisismoney.co.uk/historic-inflation-calculator

Conclusion

By the end of the First World War, the British armaments companies were at their peak in terms of scale, manufacturing capacity and numbers employed. Considerable investment had been made in plant and facilities during the war, some of it by the Admiralty. The industry had coped with the remarkable development of the capital ship which, in the ten-year period 1906-1916, had increased by more than 63% in length and 100% in displacement. While industry had coped during peacetime, the pressures applied during the war precluded the construction of three of the four 'Admiral' class battlecruisers in favour of urgently-needed smaller warship classes and merchant ships. The choke point was not the physical capacity to build but the shortage of skilled labour.

At the end of the war the Admiralty had to refocus on the major construction plans in hand by the American and Japanese navies. British designs envisaged *Hood*-sized ships mounting 16 and 18-inch guns. In the event, the conclusion of the Washington Conference in 1922 ensured that none of these ships were laid down, although four had been ordered. The armour, ordnance and shipbuilding industries that had been nurtured and encouraged by the Admiralty in the years leading up to and including the First World War and which, in turn, had taken full advantage of the profits to be made, languished after 1920, reaching a state of near collapse by the late 1920s. When rearmament began in earnest in 1936, much of this capacity was gone for ever, including the great Beardmore and Palmers yards on the Clyde and the Tyne.

Footnotes:
1. Including all ships ordered until 1916.
2. *Dreadnought* to *Hood*. Strictly speaking this figure should be fifty-four to include the three 'Admiral' class battlecruisers ordered in April 1916, but subsequently cancelled, all of which were fully part of the shipbuilding programme allowed for under the naval estimates. Although not relevant to the Grand Fleet, a further three ships built by Armstrongs and Vickers for the export market should be added to give a true reflection of capital ship construction in the UK between 1906 and 1916.
3. This list does not include all the shipbuilders who had the physical capability to build battleships. Harland & Wolff and Swan Hunter & Wigham Richardson had the productive capacity but either did not tender for battleship contracts or were unsuccessful in winning them.
4. Pembroke and Chatham Dockyards took no further role in battleship construction after the *Majestic* class and *King Edward* class respectively – their facilities were too limited.
5. *Warships No.67*, World Ship Society, 1981.
6. The firm constructed the machinery for *Invincible* but went into liquidation immediately afterwards.
7. Swan Hunter did not pursue contracts for these vessels with the vigour typical of the more successful firms in this contest.
8. Parsons Marine supplied the engines for *Dreadnought* as a sub-contract from Vickers, who supplied the boilers.
9. *Ships for a Nation*, I Johnston, West Dunbartonshire Libraries and Museums, 2000, p.125.
10. A small number of derrick, Fairbairn, and single-plane slewing cranes were also employed for fitting-out in Britain during the 19th century.
11. Devonport (1898), Haulbowline (1898), Malta (1898), Portsmouth (1900).
12. Only three British firms were equipped with hammerhead cranes during the period in question: Beardmore at Dalmuir, Vickers at Barrow, and Cammell Laird at Birkenhead whose crane, while having a hammerhead mounting, differed significantly in other respects from the previous two examples. Each of these cranes was designed and built in Germany.
13. This was probably the weight of most of the 12-inch turntables throughout the fleet.
14. Side armour was fitted to vessels in dry dock by means of 35-ton travelling cranes at Devonport on both *Temeraire* and *Collingwood*. *The Shipbuilder*, Vol 3, No 11, Winter 1909, p.156.
15. *Engineering*, 4 August 1911, p.174.
16. The planned forward 18-inch mounting was not fitted.
17. Glasgow University Archives. UCS1/107/81: the actual weight of the triple 16-inch turntables for the battleship *Nelson* in 1926 was 165 tons.
18. There was a 250-ton capacity Giant cantilever crane at both Portsmouth (1912) and Rosyth (1917) naval dockyards but none of the commercial British yards had such a capacity until 1931, the first being for Vickers Armstrong at their Walker Naval Yard on the Tyne.

JULES VERNE AND LE GLADIATEUR

Using official plans published on the SHD website, **John Jordan** focuses on two little-known ships designed during the interwar period to support the Marine Nationale.

Little has been published about these two auxiliary vessels, built for quite distinct purposes for the interwar Marine Nationale. However, the plans published the website of the *Service Historique de la Défense* reveal well-thought-out designs with a number of interesting features. These plans have been selectively redrawn by the author to form the basis of this article.

Both ships were built to support overseas deployments by French surface ships and submarines despatched to provide security for the French Empire, which like that of Britain extended across the world, from North Africa and the Middle East through the Indian Ocean to Southeast Asia and the Pacific. Although the Marine Nationale, unlike the Royal Navy, at no time envisaged the deployment of a battle fleet to distant waters, a threat to any of the French colonies would have prompted the despatch of one or two division of submarines, cruisers or *contre-torpilleurs*, to bolster the small but capable naval forces already in place.

Jules Verne

Following the Washington Conference of 1921-22, the French embarked on a major construction programme which aimed to deliver 90,000 tonnes of submarines by 1932. The first stage, the *Statut Naval* of 1922, comprised nine ocean-going submarines of the *Requin* class and twelve 600-tonne coastal boats. The latter were intended to protect the coasts of metropolitan France and to provide local area defence for the key colonial ports of North and West Africa. However, they had limited endurance, and required considerable support in order to operate from overseas bases. Of these bases only Bizerte (Tunisia) had the facilities required to support and maintain a squadron of submarines, so in the mid-1920s the Marine Nationale proposed the construction of two *ravitailleurs* (lit. re-suppliers) *de sous-marins* to serve as mobile bases for up to six submarines. Only the first, designated 'R1', was authorised; the second was never built due to

The submarine depot ship Jules Verne *in her original configuration, shortly after completion in 1931. Note the single 90mm guns visible aft.* (Courtesy of Gérard Prévoteaux)

budgetary constraints. *Jules Verne* was authorised under the 1926 Programme. The order was placed with Lorient Naval Dockyard, but due to production bottlenecks the keel was laid only in June 1929. In the interim an elderly sloop, the *Vitry-le-François*, was converted as a submarine support ship; she would serve in this role until 1934, handing over to the recently-completed *Jules Verne* in August of that year.

When first completed *Jules Verne* took part in the salvage operations for the submarine *Prométhée*, lost off Cherbourg on 8 July 1932. She then embarked on her *traversée de longue durée* (shakedown cruise) from Lorient to Cherbourg, accompanied by three 1500-tonne submarines: *Phénix*, *Pasteur* and *Poncelet*. She entered service with the 2nd Escadre at Brest in September of the same year, and on 10 July 1935 became flagship of the 2nd Submarine Flotilla, comprising one squadron (*escadrille*) of 1st class (4ᵉ ESM) and another of 2nd class boats (2ᵉ ESM) under the command of Rear-Admiral Devin. An *escadrille* normally comprised between two and four submarine divisions (*Divisions de sous-marins*, or DSM), each of four boats. In exercises *Jules Verne* was frequently deployed with her cohort of submarines to ports in North and West Africa.

In the Spring of 1939, with international tensions rising, *Jules Verne* deployed with the 2ᵉ ESM to Oran to join the 6ᵉ Escadre, one of the three divisions of 2nd class (coastal) submarines being detached to Casablanca. On 17 February 1940 she returned to Brest. Shortly afterwards the French *Amirauté* received a request from the British Admiralty for a force of six or seven submarines, accompanied by a depot ship, for surveillance of the Dutch coast. The force was to be based at Harwich and to be under the direct control of the Admiralty. The French promptly acceded to this request and *Jules Verne*, flying the flag of Capitaine de Vaisseau (CV) Belot, who had been appointed to command of the group, departed Brest accompanied by three submarines of the 16ᵉ DSM. They arrived at Harwich on 22 March, being subsequently joined by the 13ᵉ DSM from Bizerte and by the fourth boat of the 16ᵉ DSM, *Orphée* (see table for the complete list). Once this force was complete it would serve as the 10th Submarine Flotilla under the British Flag Officer Submarines, Vice-Admiral Max Horton.

Following the German occupation of the Netherlands the 10th Flotilla was transferred first to Rosyth and then to Dundee (25 May), where it was joined by the 1500-tonne submarines *Casabianca* and *Sfax*, and the minelayer *Rubis*. However, with the deteriorating situation in Belgium and Northern France and the threat of Italy entering the war, the French *Amirauté* requested that all the submarines serving with the British be transferred to the Mediterranean. Only the *Rubis* remained in the UK; *Jules Verne* and her consorts departed Dundee on 4 June, arriving in Brest five days later. With the German panzer divisions fast approaching, she left for Casablanca with the *Groupe des sous-marins de l'ouest* – five DSM with fourteen submarines – on 18 June, arriving on 23 June.

When the Armistice was signed in late June it was decreed that *Jules Verne* be placed in care and maintenance with a reduced crew (*en gardiennage*) at Bizerte, but following the British attacks on Mers el-Kebir and Dakar

NORWEGIAN CAMPAIGN MARCH-JUNE 1940:

Groupe *Jules Verne*
Harwich: 22 March – 16 May
Dundee: 25 May – 4 June

Jules Verne (CV Belot – from Brest)

16ᵉ DSM	13ᵉ DSM
(from Brest, arrived 22 March)	(from Bizerte, arrived 14-17 April)
Sibylle	Doris
Antiope	Thétis
Amazone	Circé
Orphée	Calypso

Note:
Once in UK waters, this grouping served under Flag Officer Submarines, Vice-Admiral Max Horton as the 10th Submarine Flotilla. On 26th May the group was joined by three French submarines already based at Dundee: the 1500-tonnes *Casabianca* and *Sfax*, and the small minelayer *Rubis*.

Source: CF Caroff, *La campagne de Norvège 1940*, Service Historique de la Marine 1955.

the Marine Nationale was permitted to mobilise a small force of submarines to defend Dakar. The *Groupe des sous-marins de l'AOF*[1] was formed in February 1941, and *Jules Verne* was duly activated to provide support, arriving the following month.

Following the liberation of French North Africa *Jules Verne* served first as a floating base for 295 Wing, Coastal Command, at Port-Etienne (Mauritania), returning to Dakar before undergoing a major refit at Algiers from December 1943 September 1943, when she was rearmed with seven single 40mm guns and eight single 20mm Oerlikons. After three rotations between Algiers and Toulon, she was again refitted at Algiers, returning to Toulon in August 1945 to be fitted out as a repair ship (*navire atelier*) for the amphibious forces in Indochina. A new light lattice mast was built atop the bridge structure to carry a modern outfit of electronics, and the ship was painted in the standard two-tone colour scheme of the period. She returned to metropolitan France in 1955 and for the next four years supported amphibious forces at Toulon. Decommissioned in 1959, she was stricken 1st August 1961 and scrapped at Toulon the following year.

General Configuration
Unlike her Royal Navy contemporary, HMS *Medway*, which was a much larger vessel built to warship standards,[2] *Jules Verne* was an adaptation of a mercantile freighter; her only visible military feature was her powerful anti-aircraft armament of four 90mm guns and four single 37mm guns.

Jules Verne had a conventional mercantile-type bridge structure amidships with a single funnel housing the uptakes for her diesel engines, and specially-configured holds fore and aft, served by hinged cargo derricks fixed to each of the two masts. The foremast had two derricks each with a 2.5-tonne capacity on its after side; the mainmast had two similar derricks on its after side and a heavy-lift

JULES VERNE: BUILDING DATA & GENERAL CHARACTERISTICS

Name	Builder	Laid down	Launched	In service
1926 Programme				
Jules Verne	Arsenal de Lorient	03.06.29	03.02.31	26.09.32

Displacement:	4347 tons standard; 6340 tonnes full load		
Length:	115.06m pp, 122m oa		
Beam:	17.2m		
Draught:	6.75m max.	Armament:	4 – 90mm/50 Mle 1926 [4 x I]
Machinery:	two-shaft diesel; two Sulzer diesel 7000bhp = 16kts		4 – 37mm/50 Mle 1925 [4 x I]
Diesel Oil:	950t max. (350t for S/M)		9 – 8mm MG [9 x I]
Endurance:	12,000nm @ 15kts; 18,500nm @ 11kts	Complement:	12 officers + 292 men

Jules Verne:
Profile and Plan Views

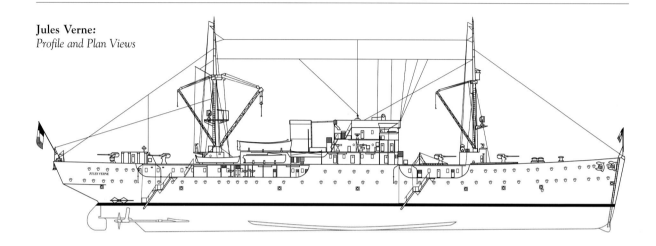

Inboard Profile

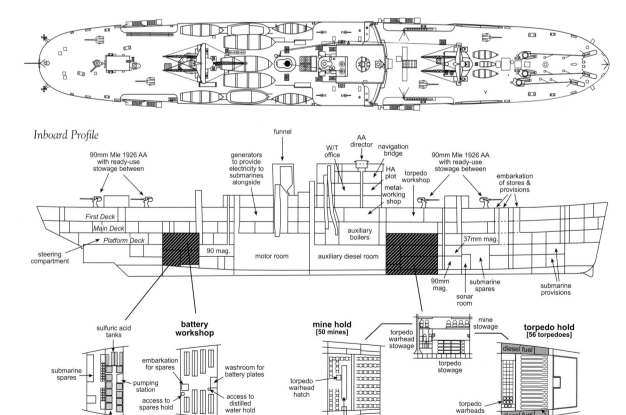

derrick with a 7.5-tonne capacity on its forward side to handle the ship's boats.

The hull was of traditional riveted transverse construction with 1-metre spacing between the frames. The seven main transverse bulkheads, which extended from the keel to the First Deck, divided the ship into eight watertight compartments. Damage control was to warship standards. There was a 120mm fire main (reducing to 90mm at the ends of the ship), a fire extinguishing system using foam (*mousse carbonique*), and the customary battery of pumps for fighting fires and for extracting water – the damage control station was in the bridge structure. Because the ship was intended to be deployed to North and West Africa, where high temperatures were the norm, all messdecks were isolated from the outer hull plating by 'aerocellular' insulating blocks plus a void space (*lame d'air*).

It was envisaged that the ship would generally be moored in an open anchorage, with up to four of her submarines alongside, so the anchor and cable outfit was unusually heavy, on a par with contemporary French Treaty cruisers. There were three 6-tonne bower and sheet anchors of the Byers type in hawsepipes, a stern anchor of 1900kg, and two substantial kedge anchors of 1400kg and 1140kg respectively. Mooring in an open anchorage also required a cruiser-standard outfit of boats, which included three 11-metre pinnaces (two motor, one pulling), a 9-metre steam pinnace, two 9-metre cutters (one motor), a 9-metre petrol-driven motor boat, and two 8.5-metre whalers. All except the two whalers, which were on davits, were handled by the 7.5-tonne boat crane on the forward side of the after mast.

Armament
The four 90mm Mle 1926 guns – the same model fitted in the cruisers *Colbert* and *Foch* – were located on the upper deck fore and aft, and were mounted *en echelon* so that all four guns could fire on either beam. The four single 37mm Mle 1925 guns were mounted on the lower bridge deck to port and starboard. A total of 1600 rounds (a mix of time-fuzed HE, tracer and starshell – 400rpg) were provided in below-decks magazines for the 90mm mountings; and 4000 rounds (1000rpg) for the 37mm guns. There were lockers for ready-use rounds close to each of the HA mountings, those for the 90mm guns being located in prominent deckhouses between the guns. Fire control was provided by an HA director equipped with a 3-metre rangefinder atop the bridge, the associated calculating position being located at the forward end of the bridge structure. For night firing there were 75cm searchlight projectors fore and aft, on platforms projecting from the masts.

During the refit at Algiers 1943-44 the four 37mm Mle 1925 guns were removed and seven single Bofors 40mm Mk III were fitted. Three were mounted in tubs on the foredeck, two (also in tubs) atop the after deckhouse, and two on the lower bridge deck in positions formerly occupied by the 37mm guns. There were also eight 20mm single Oerlikon guns, likewise disposed fore, aft and amidships. The number of 20mm guns was reduced to four during the postwar era.

Machinery
Like the British *Medway*, the *Jules Verne* was powered not by steam turbines but by diesel engines. The main propulsion diesels were 8-cylinder, 2-stroke models each with a nominal rating of 4000bhp, built by the *Compagnie de Constructions Méchaniques*. They drove two shafts with propellers 3.4 metres in diameter.

In addition to the fuel economy at cruise speed and the impressive deployment range conferred by diesel propulsion – 18,500nm at 11 knots – there were major advantages associated with the adoption of the same motive power as the submarines the ship was intended to service and support. There was no need to provide accommodation for large numbers of stokers,[3] thereby maximising the space available to accommodate submarine crews. Commonality of machinery meant a common fuel, so although there was a notional division between the diesel

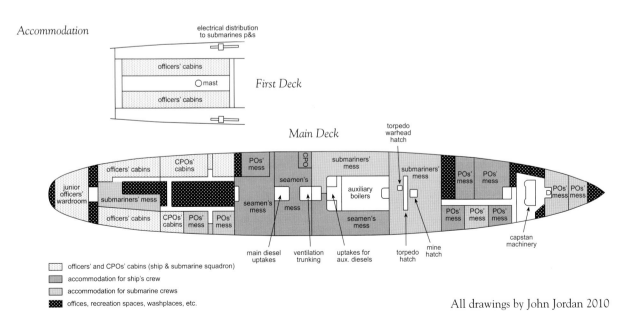

All drawings by John Jordan 2010

fuel carried for the ship and for the submarines in terms of the bunkerage and pumping arrangements, in practice the fuel could be used by either. And the specialists needed to maintain and repair the diesels of the submarines could repair the ship's own engines.

In theory the adoption of diesel propulsion for the *Jules Verne* should also have reduced the number of spare parts which needed to be carried. However, this proved difficult to achieve due to the failure to adopt a common 'standard' type of diesel for submarines.[4] Both the *Requin* and the *1500-tonnes* types were fitted with either Sulzer or Schneider diesels, while the coastal submarines of the *600-tonnes* and *630-tonnes* types had a mix of Sulzer, Schneider and Normand-Vickers models.

In addition to the main diesel propulsion motors there were four diesel-generator groups to provide power for the ship's own services and for the submarines lying alongside when at anchor, and small oil-fired auxiliary boilers to provide on-board services to the ship while underway. The auxiliary diesel room was forward of the main motor toom with the auxiliary boiler room directly above it. Each generator group comprised a Q45 6-cylinder diesel rated at 1130hp driving a 765kW dynamo. The main generating station distributed the current via a 235V circuit to seven different sectors from two switchboards. There were also two 150kW diesel-generators specifically for submarine battery recharging (First Deck to starboard), with electrical distribution points on either side of the ship immediately abaft them beneath the boat deck (see plan view of accommodation).

Three compressors produced a 250kg/cm^2 compressed air supply, and there were ten 160-litre bottles as a reserve. A high-pressure circuit supplied the optics and torpedo workshops and the compressed air bottles used to start the main diesels and generators; there were eight take-off points for the submarines. A low-pressure (8kg/cm^2) circuit fed by a single compressor supplied compressed air to the metal working shop, the tools and the main diesel compartment.

Workshops, Stores & Magazines
It was initially envisaged that *Jules Verne* would support nine submarines; this figure proved too ambitious given the relatively small size of the hull, and it was subsequently revised downwards to six, with on-board accommodation for 15 officers and 250 men.[5] However, at the height of the Norwegian Campaign the ship was supporting two *1500-tonnes*, six *600/630-tonnes* and the minelayer *Rubis*.

Forward of the bridge, and served by the twin derricks of the foremast, was a capacious hold with accommodation for both reserve torpedoes and mines (see inboard profile). Reserve torpedo bodies were stowed four high and 14 abreast on racks in the lower section of the hold, for a total of 56. The warheads were stowed vertically in racks in a separate section of the hold, at its after end. The mines were stowed on rails in the upper section of the hold. There was accommodation for 50 mines; a further fourteen reserve torpedoes could be substituted in place of the mines if required. The mines, torpedoes and torpedo warheads were embarked (or disembarked) via hatches in the upper deck using the ship's derricks (see inboard profile). The torpedo maintenance workshop was above the hold on the First Deck. Abaft it on the same level, immediately below the bridge, were a foundry and metal-working shop capable of conducting a variety of mechanical repairs. Other workshops included an armourers, and an optics maintenance shop – in a deckhouse on the port

Jules Verne *as an amphibious support ship in 1948. She still has the two-tone colour scheme applied during the late war period. She has a new lattice mast atop the bridge structure for an American SF-1 surface surveillance radar. The anti-aircraft armament fitted in 1943-44 is particularly prominent. The original 90mm single mountings have been fitted with shields, and there are seven 40mm Bofors guns, of which the three on the forecastle and the two aft are in prominent tubs. There are 20mm single Oerlikon guns disposed in pairs beneath the foremast (2x1) and mainmast (4x1), and in the bridge wings (2x1). (Marius Bar, courtesy of Gérard Prévoteaux)*

side of the boat deck – which could accommodate four complete submarine periscopes.

Immediately forward of the torpedo hold was the forward 90mm magazine, with the 37mm magazine above it. There was a second 90mm magazine, for the after guns, just above the propeller shafts. All three magazines were served by vertical hoists which carried the ammunition to the upper deck close to the mountings.

On the upper deck forward of the mainmast were hatches for the embarkation of stores and provisions. The adoption of a broad, deep mercantile hull made it possible to accommodate large store rooms for submarine spares and provisions on the lower platform deck and in the hold, with the ship's own stores, provisions and cold rooms on the platform deck above. There was sufficient stowage for 30 days' provisions for nine submarines.

In the after part of the ship, abaft the 90mm magazine and served by the derricks of the after mast, there were deep full-width holds for the maintenance and repair of submarine batteries. At the upper level was the battery workshop, which was capable of accommodating a complete submarine battery for maintenance plus one half-battery (160 elements) as a spare. It was served by two travelling cranes with a 1-tonne capacity (see inboard profile). Beneath it were tanks for distilled water (25 tonnes) and sulphuric acid (8 tonnes in 400-litre tanks), together with a second large store room for submarine spares. To port of the 90mm magazine there was a powder magazine and a shell room for the 100mm deck guns which were originally to have been fitted in all French submarines – the 100/40 Mle 1925, which fired separate ammunition, was replaced by the 75/35 Mle 1928 in the smaller coastal boats and minelayers.

Accommodation

Accommodation had to be provided not only for a ship's crew of just under 300 officers and men, but also for the crews of up to six submarines. Most of this accommodation was on the Main Deck, although many of the officers' cabins were on the First Deck above. Commissioned officers and Chief Petty Officers had single or twin-berth cabins, while Petty Officers and Seamen had traditional open messes where they slept and ate.

The accompanying deck plans show the layout of the accommodation. On the original plans no differentiation is made between the cabins for officers of submarines and the ship's own officers, who shared the same wardrooms and other facilities; the other accommodation spaces are clearly differentiated (see drawing). The only accommodation on the First Deck was the officers' cabins aft; forward of these were the galleys, followed by the large workshops (metal-working and torpedo maintenance) beneath the bridge, with the bow section given over to the heads and washplaces for the crew. At the after end of the First Deck, abaft the officers' cabins, was a large, well-appointed 12-bed hospital, with a sick-bay, isolation room, consultation room, operating theatre and medical store.

On the Main Deck the officers' cabins occupied the traditional location aft, with the CPOs' cabins just forward of them. The broad midships section was given over to the large messes for the seamen and submariners, while the smaller messes for the Petty Officers were fitted into the tapering bow section.

The internal layout of the ship was rational and showed considerable ingenuity on the part of designers who were faced with cramming the customary quart into a pint pot.

Le Gladiateur

During the late 1920s there was considerable interest in purpose-built netlayers designed to provide protection against submarines and torpedoes in exposed anchorages or undefended harbours. During the First World War such nets had had to be laid in small sections by a multitude of converted mercantile ships, but the new naval units would be equipped to lay (and retrieve) an entire net system defended by mines and explosive devices attached to the nets themselves.

The IJN's *Shiratake* (1923 Programme, launched and completed 1929) was a dual-purpose ship capable of stowing mines instead of nets in her holds and laying both from the flat expanse of her after upper deck. The British *Guardian* (1930 Estimates) and *Protector* (1934 Estimates) were single-purpose netlayers[6] similar in conception, size and capabilities to *Le Gladiateur*. They were slightly shorter but much broader in the beam (16.2m vs 12.7m), which resulted in a standard displacement in excess of 2800 tons.

Laid down at Lorient as a *mouilleur de filets* (netlayer) and completed in January 1935, *Le Gladiateur* had a relatively short career. Based at Toulon as part of the Mediterranean Squadron (later Fleet), she was despatched to the Eastern Mediterranean as part of Force 'X' in 1940. She was at Beirut when the French squadron of Rear-Admiral René-Emile Godfroy was impounded in Alexandria as part of Operation 'Catapult', and subsequently returned to Toulon, where she was placed in care and maintenance (*en gardiennage*) under the terms of the Armistice. She was scuttled while moored quayside in the Darse des Sous-Marins on 27 November 1942.

General Configuration

Unlike *Jules Verne*, *Le Gladiateur* was a military vessel in every respect, with a long, slim hull designed around her primary netlaying mission. The nets, attached to their sinkers, and the mines intended to form an outer defensive barrier were readied on a large, flat expanse of upper deck inset with sets of rails parallel to the ship's axis, and launched from an inclined ramp above the stern. There were raised deckhouses to port and starboard amidships, the port-side deckhouse accommodating the uptakes for the propulsion machinery, and a raised deckhouse for the after gun mounting spanned the mine/net tracks aft. There were whalers on davits abeam this deckhouse, while the remainder of the ship's boats were divided between the forward end of the upper deck and the after end of the raised forecastle, where they were served by twin boat cranes.

Atop the raised deckhouses to port and to starboard were rows of smoke pots which allowed the ship to lay a smokescreen to cover her netlaying work under enemy fire. The sides of the upper deck between the raised deckhouses

LE GLADIATEUR: BUILDING DATA & GENERAL CHARACTERISTICS

Name	Builder	Laid down	Launched	In service
1929-30 Programme				
Le Gladiateur	Arsenal de Lorient	01.02.32	10.04.33	20.12.35

Displacement:	1858tW standard; 2330 tonnes full load
Length:	106m pp, 113m oa
Beam:	12.7m
Draught:	4.03m max.
Machinery:	two-shaft geared steam turbines; two Indret boilers, two sets of Parsons turbines, 6000shp (7700 max.) = 18kts
Oil fuel:	400 tonnes
Armament:	4 – 90mm/50 Mle 1926 [2 x 2]
	4 – 13.2mm/76 Mle 1929 MG (2 x 2)
	6 – 8mm MG [6 x I]
Complement:	132

were lined with hatches which gave access to the net stowage holds, served by derrick-style cranes. The mines and sinkers were raised by two centre-line hoists at the forward end of the upper deck in line with the boat cranes, which were also used for embarkation of these items.

Forward there was a *torpilleur*-type enclosed bridge, topped by a pole mast (*mat de flêche*) of similar design to that in the contemporary *Le Fantasque* class. The small centre-line funnel abaft the bridge housed the uptakes for the auxiliary boilers, which together with the generators and the switchboard were located at upper deck level at the after end of the forecastle.

Armament

Le Gladiateur was designed two/three years after *Jules Verne*, and the advances in the anti-aircraft armament reflect those on contemporary French cruisers. The 90mm guns, located on the forecastle and atop the after deckhouse, were in the twin Mle 1930 mounting adopted for the last of the *Suffren*-type treaty cruisers, the *Dupleix* (see *Warship 2006*), and for the six post-London light cruisers of the *La Glaissonnière* class (see *Warship 1995*). This appears to have been a particularly successful mounting, and when in 1940 it was decided to revise the armament of the battleships *Richelieu* and *Jean Bart* to incorporate a battery of dedicated HA guns, a shortage of suitable mountings led to a proposal to remove the 90mm twins fitted in *Le Gladiateur* for installation on the *Jean Bart*. The hasty departure of the latter from Saint-Nazaire precluded this, and the mountings remained aboard the netlayer until she was scuttled at Toulon in November 1942.

As in *Jules Verne* the 90mm guns were controlled by an HA director equipped with a 3-metre rangefinder located atop the bridge. Beneath it, at the lower bridge level, was a fully equipped HA calculating position which provided bearing, elevation, range and deflection data to the guns. However, whereas in *Jules Verne* the guns were trained and elevated manually, in *Le Gladiateur* remote control power (RPC) was provided for the mountings, the associated

Le Gladiateur *shortly after her completion on 6 June 1935. Note the angled ramp at the stern and the platform for the after twin 90mm HA mounting, which straddled the three mine/netlaying tracks.* (Marius Bar, courtesy of Gérard Prévoteaux)

JULES VERNE AND LE GLADIATEUR

Le Gladiateur:
Profile and Plan Views

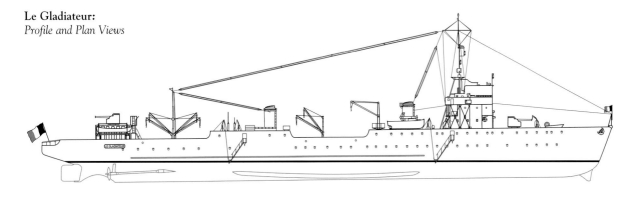

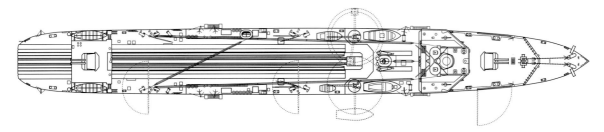

Inboard Profile

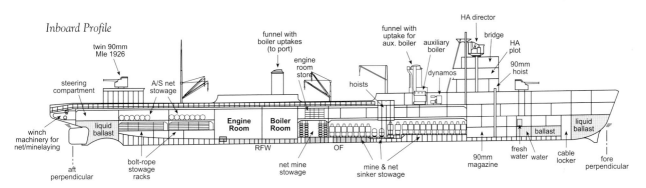

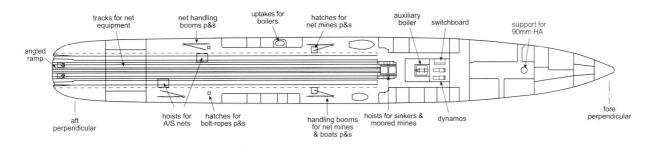

Main and hold decks

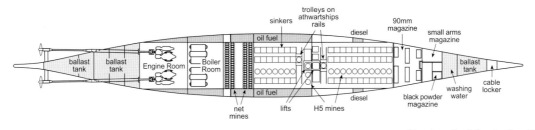

Drawings by John Jordan 2009

A later view of Le Gladiateur *taken on 8 February 1938. She is flying the flag of a rear-admiral at the foremast. The funnel immediately abaft the bridge structure (on the centre-line) housed the uptakes for the auxiliary boiler; the one farther aft to port the uptakes for boilers for the main propulsion machinery. (Marius Bar, courtesy of Gérard Prévoteaux)*

The service career of Le Gladiateur *was cut short by the scuttling of the fleet at Toulon on 27 November 1942. The photo shows her heeled over onto her starboard side. (Courtesy of Gérard Prévoteaux)*

Le Gladiateur:
Mine and Net-Laying Arrangements

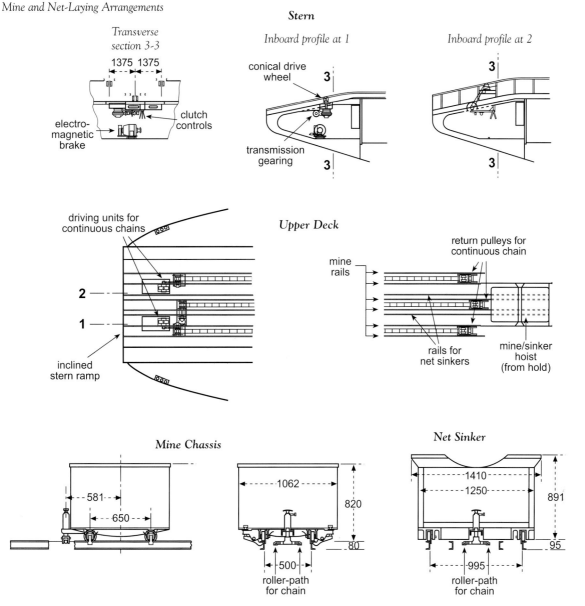

© John Jordan 2010

Ward-Leonard servo-motors and converters being located to port and starboard of the HA plot (see bridge deck drawings). Close-range AA fire was provided by twin 13.2mm Hotchkiss MG Mle 1929 in the bridge wings. Fire control for the latter was provided by two one-metre rangefinders located at the forward corners of the upper (open) bridge.

One of the limitations of the design was that there was only a single magazine forward for the 90mm mountings. This was located in the hold directly beneath the bridge, with a single hoist which brought the cartridge ammunition to the forecastle deck behind the forward gun mounting. The after mounting fired using ammunition stowed in ready-use lockers atop the after platform, and this was replenished using trolleys and rails on the upper deck.

Machinery

Unlike *Jules Verne*, *Le Gladiateur* was driven by conventional two-shaft geared steam turbines. The installation was relatively compact in order to maximise the internal volume available for net and mine stowage. There were two Indret boilers providing steam for two sets of Parsons steam turbines; total horsepower was a nominal 6000shp, 7700shp with forcing. The slim hull, which had a maximum beam of only 12.7m, had more favourable resistance characteristics than that of *Jules Verne* or her British counterparts, and maximum speed was in excess of 18 knots. The propulsion machinery spaces were aft of amidships, which reduced shaft weight but required the offsetting of the funnel housing the boiler uptakes to port.

In order to provide power for on-board services there was a large auxiliary boiler on the centre-line forward, directly beneath the fore-funnel, and this provided steam for two turbo-generators in an adjacent compartment, the dynamos being offset to starboard with the main switchboard to port.

Internal Arrangements
The allocation of much of the Main Deck to net and mine handling and the associated tracks resulted in a relatively shallow hull in which access to the single Boiler and Engine Rooms was from the upper deck. In normal condition the hull trimmed by the stern to assist the laying of both mines and nets (see inboard profile). Fore and aft of the propulsion machinery spaces were capacious holds for the netlaying gear and the mines. The two after holds accommodated the nets and the buoys, while the two forward holds housed the mines and the sinkers. The nets and buoys were raised to the upper deck via large rectangular hoists served by the after handling derricks. The mines and sinkers were moved from their stowage racks onto trolleys which ran on athwartships rails. From these they were transferred to one of the two square centre-line hoists which raised them to the upper deck; they were then moved aft on the upper deck rails, the sinkers being connected to the nets with bolt-ropes before the nets were laid over the stern.

The Hautter-Sarlé H5 mine entered service in 1928; it was a traditional moored mine activated by contact with its horns, and had a 220kg TNT charge. The deck plan of *Le Gladiateur* suggests stowage space for twenty H5 mines: eleven in the forward hold and nine in the after hold. These would have been laid in a protective line outside the net system. A fifth hold, located just forward of the boiler room, had racks for mines which would have been fixed to the nets, so that a submarine which became entangled in the nets would detonate one or more mines. These mines were relatively small, and were stowed in four athwartships racks six deep; they were lifted by the derricks through small square hatches forward of the deckhouses port and starboard.

Unusually all accommodation was concentrated in the fore part of the ship, the after part of the hull being occupied by the steering compartment, the propulsion machinery spaces, and the holds for the netlaying gear and mines. The officers' cabins and wardroom were on the Main Deck forward of the bridge. Most 'services' were also located on this deck: the sickbay, shop, etc. in the bow section, and the heads and galleys on either side of the auxiliary boiler and dynamo rooms beneath the bridge structure (see deck plans). The main accommodation deck was the Lower Deck, with cabins, messes and washplaces for the remainder of the crew extending above the mine and sinker stowage hold, virtually to the midships point. Stores and provisions were stowed at the forward end of this deck and on the platform deck below.

Acknowledgements:
The author wishes to thank Robert Dumas, Gérard Prévoteaux and Jean Moulin for their help with material for this article.

Sources:
Plans held by the Centre d'Archives de l'Armement (CAA), Châtellerault, published on the Service Historique de la Défense website at: www.servicehistorique.sga.defense.gouv.fr/02fonds-collections/banquedocuments/planbato/planbato/central.php.

Jean Moulin: '*Le ravitailleur de sous-marins* Jules Verne', Marines et Forces Navales no.93 (October 2004).

Footnotes:
[1] *Afrique Occidentale Française*, or French West Africa
[2] *Medway* was authorised under the 1926-27 Estimates and completed in 1929. Designed to support 18 large patrol submarines of the 'O' and 'P' classes, she carried 144 spare torpedoes and three spare 4in/40 deck guns, and was designed to provide not only accommodation, stores and maintenance but also heavy repair capabilities, being fitted with a multitude of workshops for the purpose. She had a 1.5in protective deck amidships over her torpedo stowage holds and magazines, and a liquid-loaded underwater protection system 13ft deep based on that of the contemporary battleships of the *Nelson* class.
[3] Stokers were needed only for the small auxiliary boilers employed to provide on-board services while the ship was underway.
[4] The coastal submarines of the *600-tonnes* type and their successors of the *630-tonnes* type were built by three private shipyards to competitive designs. A full account of French submarine development between the wars by the same author was published in *Warship* 1991, pp.59-80.
[5] Official complements of French submarines were as follows: *Requin* class 51; coastal boats (including minelayers) 41-42; *1500-tonnes* 61.
[6] *Guardian* also had an ancillary role as a target towing ship, for which purpose she had a gunnery photographic cabin straddling the open net-handling deck aft.

TB 191 – A TASMANIAN TORPEDO BOAT

Using documentation from the Tasmanian archives and contemporary journals, **Mark Briggs** tells the story of Tasmania's only torpedo boat. The author's account details the operation of the spar torpedo and compares it with the self-propelling Whitehead torpedoes which were then beginning to enter service.

The city of Hobart lies at the southern end of the island of Tasmania along the banks of the Derwent River, which flows south into the vastness of the great Southern Ocean. In the 1880s this small, isolated city boasted among its defences a torpedo boat, one of the newest weapons among the world's navies. Torpedo boats had made their debut only a few years earlier with the *Lightning*, built by John Thornycroft for the Royal Navy in 1876. Tasmania's torpedo boat, *TB 191*, was also the work of John Thornycroft, and arrived in Tasmania aboard the steamer *Abington* in May 1884.

Tasmania had become a self-governing colony of the British Empire in 1856. The mid-nineteenth century was a period when governments in Britain were always on the lookout for ways to reduce the cost burden of military and naval defence, and British garrison forces were withdrawn from the Australian colonies during the 1860s. A British naval squadron based at Sydney remained, but the ships of the Australian squadron were generally recognised as obsolete and virtually useless in any major naval operation against an enemy.[1] It was up to the individual colonies to provide for their local defence, protect their coastal cities from raids by enemy warships, and provide safe harbours for British shipping. For the most part this meant fortifications to deter attacks by an enemy cruiser or steam corvette that had evaded the ships of the Royal Navy, but the Colonial Naval Defence Act of 1865 also allowed the colonies to build 'floating defences' to support their harbour fortifications.

The Franco-Prussian War of 1870 and antagonism between Britain and Russia alarmed the colonies, and they looked for help on how to improve their local defences. In 1876 Major-General Sir William Jervois was appointed to report on local defence needs. Jervois was an engineer with a particular interest in fortifications. Before becoming governor of the Straits Settlements in 1875 he

The Queensland torpedo boat Mosquito, a sister ship to TB 191. *The spar torpedo is visible along the centre line. (Australian War Memorial 300018)*

had served as Lieutenant-General and Director of Works for Fortifications. He completed his report in 1878, suggesting that Hobart's existing defensive works be strengthened by the addition of heavy gun batteries on both sides of the Derwent and, more imaginatively, the deployment of a mine field across the river. Although Hobart is some twenty kilometres from the sea, the Derwent is still a kilometre wide and the minefield was meant to deter an enemy warship from racing upstream to a position from which it could bombard the town beyond the reach of the shore batteries.

Jervois was assisted in producing his report by Lieutenant Colonel Peter Scratchley. Scratchley was also an engineer and had served with distinction in both the Crimean War and in India. The implementation of Jervois' proposals was largely left to Scratchley, who became Commissioner of Defences for the Australasian colonies following Jervois' appointment as Governor of South Australia in 1878. In 1882 Scratchley produced an updated report on the defensive needs of Hobart. Although using the Jervois report as a starting point, Scratchley went farther. Jervois had based his recommendations on a possible attack by an unarmoured vessel which could 'under threat of bombardment, or after actually firing into the place, levy a heavy contribution upon the Colony.'[2] Hobart, Scratchley now argued, needed to be able to fight off an attack by an armoured cruiser or ironclad. He suggested the land based guns recommended by Jervois be supported by 'sea-going war vessels capable of co-operating with fixed defences to defeat an attempt at invasion.'[3] Scratchley put forward two options.

The first was a gunboat of the *Alpha* type. Designed by George Rendel, chief naval architect for the armaments manufacturing firm of Sir William Armstrong, the *Alpha* (later renamed *Lung Hsiang*) was the first of nearly a dozen so-called 'flatiron' gunboats built for China in the 1870s. With a length of 120ft and a beam of 27ft, the 320-ton *Alpha* had a single 11-inch muzzle-loading rifled gun forward, fixed to fire over the bows, and two single 3-inch breech-loading rifles aft. Training the main armament was by moving the whole vessel, and the *Alpha* had twin propellers to help in this. With a top speed of ten knots and no armour, it was hoped *Alpha*'s small size would make her a difficult target while her main armament posed a threat to even large, armoured vessels. Gunboats similar to the *Alpha* were purchased by Victoria and Queensland, with Victoria and South Australia also buying larger versions. The South Australian *Protector* was 188ft overall and 960 tons. Although shallow-drafted gunboats along the lines of the *Alpha* were unsuited to anything but smooth water, and even then were unstable platforms for their big guns, an *Alpha* type gunboat would have made a formidable addition to the defence of the Derwent. The drawback was the price; Scratchley estimated the cost at £27,650.[4] The 360-ton *Albert*, completed for Victoria early in 1884, and her sister ships *Gayundah* and *Paluma* built in the same year for Queensland cost £30,000 each.[5] This was well beyond the means of little Tasmania, which in 1880 had only 100,000 people.

Scratchley's second option was much more modest: a torpedo boat. 'Besides gunboats,' he told the Tasmanian Legislative Council, 'torpedo boats are now considered necessary for harbour defence; and where the choice has to be made, they should be provided before the gunboats.'[6] This must have been music to the ears of the Legislative Councillors, for at around £3,000 a torpedo boat was a tenth the cost of a gunboat. Scratchley suggested that the boat best suited to Hobart's needs was a 17-knot vessel around 67ft in length armed with both a spar torpedo and Whitehead self-propelled torpedoes. Thornycroft was named as the recommended builder, and when not called upon to defend the city the vessel could be used in government harbour service.

John Thornycroft had built his first torpedo boat for the Royal Navy in 1876. The *Lightning* was based on Thornycroft's fast steam launches and betrayed her origins in the 'coach roof' cabin aft. *Lightning* was 87ft overall and displaced 32½ tons. She was followed by ten more improved *Lightnings* by Thornycroft as well as a number of similar vessels by other builders. All were 80 to 90 feet or so in length with top speeds of around 20 knots. They were armed with dropping gear for a Whitehead torpedo on either side amidships and a spar torpedo in the bow.

Alongside these vessels there were also smaller torpedo boats that could be carried aboard larger warships. Small torpedo boats had made a name for themselves in the 1877 war between Russia and Turkey. On 26 May 1877 four Russian torpedo boats had launched a daring attack against two Turkish monitors lying at anchor off Matchim on the south bank of the River Danube. It was a dark and rainy night, and two of the torpedo boats were able to strike the Turkish monitor *Duba Saife* with their spar torpedoes, sending her to the bottom. The torpedo boats had been carried into action aboard the converted steamer *Grand Duke Constantine*.[7] Inspired by this success the world's navies temporarily shunned the large torpedo boats of the *Lightning* type and began building small, so-called 2nd class boats. The Royal Navy placed orders with all the major builders – Thornycroft, Yarrow and White – and torpedo boats became a standard feature on the decks of British battleships. A specialist torpedo boat carrier, the *Vulcan*, was even built, distinguished by a pair of large 'goose neck' cranes to raise and lower her six-strong flotilla. The citizens of Hobart had the chance to see these deadly new weapons for themselves when a Russian squadron visited the city early in 1882. The success of the Russian torpedo boats at Matchim had been widely covered in the Tasmanian press, so the presence of two torpedo boats aboard the 1,300-ton steam-powered and iron-hulled sloop *Vyestnik* caused much interest among the people of Hobart and the official guests, including Colonel Scratchley, who were shown over the Russian ships.[8]

The government of Tasmania ordered *TB 191* from Thornycroft late in 1882. It has been claimed that this was a panicked response to the visit of the Russian squadron in January. The three Russian ships called at Auckland, Sydney, Melbourne and Adelaide as well as Hobart. In Melbourne the visit led to a hysterical outcry in some of the local press with claims that the Russians were planning to hold the colonial capitals to ransom, and that on their way up Tasmania's east coast they had been on the lookout for a suitable location for a secret base from which to mount their attacks.[9] The Tasmanian papers, however, were decidedly more relaxed about the visit and give no indication that the colony was in any way rattled by the Russian ships. Rather than a panicked response to the Russian visit, the purchase of a torpedo boat should be seen as part of the government's determination to act on Colonel Scratchley's proposals to update Hobart's defences. The need for modern coastal defences had been highlighted by events in Egypt, where in July Britain's Mediterranean fleet had easily demolished those of Alexandria. The burden of updating Hobart's defences, the town's leading newspaper argued, could only be avoided by 'consenting to be held up to ridicule in the other Colonies'.[10]

The Torpedo Boat TB 191

TB 191 was designed at the Thornycroft offices in London in 1880 and built in 1883 at Chiswick on the Thames. Typical of the large number of 2nd class torpedo boats built for the Royal Navy in the 1880s, *TB 191* had the same overall characteristics as the Thornycroft torpedo boats bought by Victoria (2), Queensland (1) and New Zealand (4). Displacing 12.94 tons, *TB 191* was 63ft (19.2m) on the waterline with a beam of 7ft 6in (2.28m) and a draft of 2ft 2in (660mm) forward and 3ft 4in (990mm) aft. Speed was a key consideration in her design and she was lightly built, her hull made of $\frac{1}{16}$ inch galvanised steel lap jointed for the longitudinal seams on the outside of the vessel and flush riveted over the deck. During six trial runs over a measured mile she averaged 17.22 knots.[11] Like so many late nineteenth century warships, *TB 191* had a pronounced ram bow and turtleback upper deck. There was a single, slightly raked, funnel on the starboard side about a third of the way from her stem. A single starboard funnel was a feature she shared with the other Australian boats, while the four New Zealand boats had twin funnels.

Behind the funnel was a locomotive type boiler with a pressure of 130psi driving an inverted, directly acting, compound engine of 170ihp, with one high and one low pressure cylinder with a surface condenser, air pump (worked off the low pressure cylinder) and a bilge pump worked off the crankshaft by means of a worm and wheel. The bilge pump had six ejectors: one of 45 tons capacity and the others of 20 tons. There was also a fan engine to supply air to the boiler.

Immediately astern of the engine room was a conning tower, oval in plan, which served as the bridge and control centre. It was connected by telegraph to the engine room and also housed the winch for operating the spar torpedo. In keeping with Colonel Scratchley's suggestion that the boat could be used for harbour duties when not needed for military service, there was cabin accommodation fore and aft of the conning tower which Hobart's leading newspaper, *The Mercury*, described as 'elaborately fitted throughout.'[12]

The Spar Torpedo

When *TB 191* arrived in Hobart her only armament was a spar torpedo. This comprised a hollow steel pole 42 feet

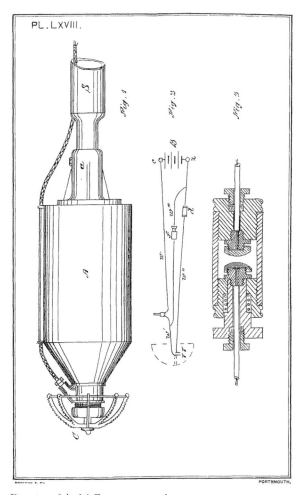

Drawing of the McEvoy spar torpedo.

(12.7m) in length and 6 inches (152mm) in diameter tapering to 5 inches (127mm) at the forward end. When not required the spar was carried in a gutter that was fitted on the centre line beginning about 12 feet (3.6m) from the bow and extending almost to the conning tower. In front of this, about 6 feet (1.8m) from the bow was an iron frame, tapering inward, that could be pivoted upwards. A similar frame was fitted on the boat's stem. At the top of each was a pair of rollers, and as the torpedo boat approached its intended target the spar could be run out between these rollers and plunged into the water in front of the boat at an angle of about forty degrees.

At the end of the spar was attached the 'torpedo' from which the boats took their name. The McEvoy torpedo that armed *TB 191* was a bullet shaped iron canister, filled with 37 pounds of wet guncotton with a further 2½ pounds (1.2kg) of dry guncotton packed around an electrically activated detonator that was connected by a line running back inside the hollow spar to a battery in the conning tower. As the torpedo boat closed her target the spar would be run out through the use of a hand operated winch in the conning tower, the weight of the torpedo causing it to drop into the water until it was at least ten feet below the surface and at least 33 feet in front of the boat. When the torpedo was in contact with the enemy vessel's side below

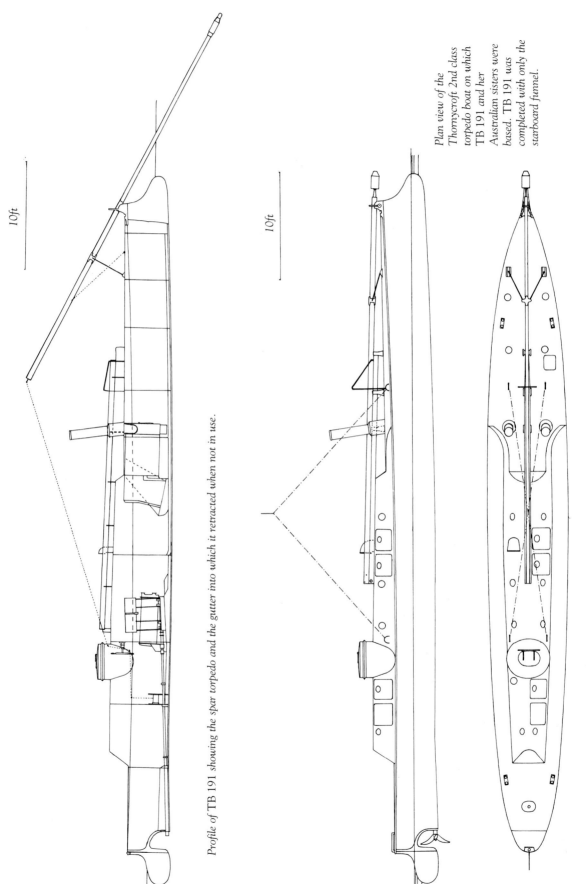

Profile of TB 191 showing the spar torpedo and the gutter into which it retracted when not in use.

Plan view of the Thornycroft 2nd class torpedo boat on which TB 191 and her Australian sisters were based. TB 191 was completed with only the starboard funnel.

(Drawings by Ian Sturton)

the waterline, the torpedo boat's engines would be thrown into reverse and the torpedo detonated. The torpedo boat would then make a desperate attempt to escape to a safe location where the remains of the shattered spar could be removed, a new spar torpedo rigged and, if needed, a second attempt made on the enemy ship.[13]

Trying to sink an enemy warship by jabbing it with a large bomb at the end of a long pole was clearly an extreme, even suicidal strategy and contemporary accounts attest to the dangerous and unpredictable nature of this method of attack. Nevertheless the spar torpedo had been used to effect in both the American Civil War of the 1860s and the Russo-Turkish War of 1877-78. In February 1864 the semi-submersible *H L Hunley* had used a spar torpedo to sink the 1,934-ton Union screw sloop *Housatonic* outside Charleston harbour, albeit with the loss of all her crew. Eight months later the Confederate ironclad ram *Albemarle* had also fallen victim to a spar torpedo in a daring night attack led by 21-year-old Lieutenant William B Cushing aboard a small steam launch. The success of Russian torpedo boats in using spar torpedoes to sink the Turkish monitor *Duba Saife* has already been mentioned.

The Whitehead Torpedo

By the time the Tasmanian government ordered *TB 191* a number of different self-propelled torpedoes had come onto the market. The first and most successful was the torpedo developed by Robert Whitehead, a British engineer working in Austria. The Whitehead torpedo was a revolutionary weapon. It did not require the attacking vessel to make direct contact as the spar torpedo did; rather it was an entirely self-contained and self-propelled weapon system that used an engine driven by compressed air to propel it to the target. Britain had paid £15,000 for the rights to produce this device in 1870, and France, Italy and Germany had quickly followed suit.[14] Most Royal Navy torpedo boats were equipped to operate Whitehead torpedoes and many larger warships had also been fitted to fire them.

Tasmania's decision to opt for a torpedo boat armed only with the more difficult and dangerous-to-use spar torpedo was most likely due to cost. *TB 191* cost £3,300, whereas Whitehead torpedoes were selling at between £300 and £400 each. It should also be borne in mind that in the early 1880s the Whitehead torpedo was still in its infancy. It was not the formidable weapon of later years. The first Whitehead torpedo to be fired in anger was in 1877 by the Royal Navy frigate *Shah* during an action against the rebel Peruvian ironclad *Huáscar*. It missed. The following year Russia had used Whiteheads in their war with Turkey, also with mixed success. The Whitehead torpedo had claimed its first victim, the small Turkish steamer *Intikbah* sunk by torpedo boats off Batum, but an attack against the Turkish ironclad *Mahmoudieh* had failed despite two torpedoes being launched at a range of only 60 yards. Problems with accuracy were such that Alfred von Tirpitz, the German Grand Admiral and Navy Secretary who was a torpedo specialist in his early career, caustically recounted in his memoirs: 'When I gave a demonstration of the Whitehead torpedo before the Crown Prince in 1879, in spite of many weeks of preparation, it was still a toss-up whether they would reach the target or dash wildly out of their course.'[15] While the two Victorian 2nd class torpedo boats, *Nepean* and *Lonsdale*, ordered at the same time as *TB 191*, were fitted with a trough forward and steam ejection gear for Whitehead torpedoes, the Queensland boat and the four New Zealand vessels carried only spar torpedoes.

Within a year of *TB 191* arriving in Hobart, however, the Tasmanian government was persuaded to refit her to launch Whitehead torpedoes. The pressure came from Lieutenant-Colonel William Legge. Legge was a native born Tasmanian who had joined the Royal Artillery, serving in Victoria and Ceylon where he had earned a measure of fame in writing a history of the island's bird life. In 1883 he was appointed to command Tasmania's army volunteers who were responsible for manning the Derwent's defences, which included *TB 191*. Legge had completed the torpedo course at HMS *Vernon*, the Royal Navy's torpedo school at Portsmouth, and in a report on Tasmania's defences in April 1885 urged the government to arm *TB 191* with Whitehead torpedoes.[16] It was advice supported by a regular flow of cuttings from British newspapers extolling the power of the Whitehead torpedo provided to Tasmanian government ministers from London.

Legge's advice was adopted, and *TB 191*'s spar torpedo was removed and dropping gear for Whitehead torpedoes fitted. Two torpedoes were carried, one on each side of the boat, in a light frame, the torpedoes being held in position by a pair of clip tongs at each end. Davits lowered the torpedo into the water where its engine was started and it was released to speed away towards the target. The dropping gear was fitted to *TB 191* in Tasmania at a cost of £13.12.6.[17] The standard British-manufactured Whitehead torpedo of the time was 14 inches (356mm) in diameter and 14ft 6in (4.4m) in length, weighing about 650lbs (295kg). It had a maximum range of around 600 yards (548m) and carried a 60lbs (27kg) warhead.[18]

Tasmanian Service

TB 191 arrived in Hobart on 1 May 1884. While being unloaded from the SS *Abington* the torpedo boat collided with some gear which kinked her hull amidships on the port side, leaving her with a bulge and leaking seams, problems which were never overcome.[19] After this traumatic beginning, *TB 191* was towed to the Battery Point shipyards of John Lucas where her machinery and propeller were fitted. Being of galvanised steel *TB 191* was kept out of the water when not in use, and she remained at the shipyards until April 1885 when a purpose-built boatshed was completed on the foreshore, about a kilometre up river from the Hobart CBD.[20] She was manned and maintained by a group of volunteer militia, initially under the command of Captain James Mathieson, a former Royal Engineer. A visit in October 1884 by the armoured cruiser HMS *Nelson*, flagship of the Australian Squadron, which carried two torpedo boats of her own, was the first opportunity for *TB 191* to show off her capa-

The only known photograph of TB 191, taken late in the vessel's career. The spar torpedo has been removed and the dropping gear for Whitehead torpedoes can be seen immediately abaft the funnel. (Tasmanian Archives ph30-1-5630).

bilities to the people of Hobart. After assisting the Tasmanian volunteers to give *TB 191* her first run on the Derwent, the crew of HMS *Nelson* set sail for New Guinea to proclaim a British protectorate over the south eastern segment of the island.[21] Thereafter *TB 191* settled into a truly uneventful career of occasional training cruises interspersed with general harbour duties and some survey work. She never saw any action and this was probably just as well. Although she was fitted with dropping gear for Whitehead torpedoes, the Tasmanian government was reluctant to allow practice for these expensive weapons.

By the 1890s the little second-class torpedo boats had drifted out of fashion. Lightly constructed, they were fragile and expensive to maintain. As early as 1887 *The Times* claimed they were a type which was now totally discredited. 'Everything was sacrificed for speed,' *The Times* explained, 'and in consequence they were very wet, very crank, very weak and indifferent in manoeuvres.'[22] The year 1887 also saw the signing of an agreement between Britain, the Australian colonies and New Zealand to subsidise an additional force of Royal Navy warships to be stationed in Australian waters. Reassured by this extra protection and with the colony paying a hefty annual contribution toward its upkeep there was little incentive left for Tasmanian governments to continue with their own 'floating defences'. Despite the regular arrival of promotional material for their latest offerings from torpedo boat builders such as Thornycroft and Yarrow, *TB 191* was to be Tasmania's only warship. The little torpedo boat had added interest and colour to the waters of the Derwent, but by the turn of the century she had disappeared from Tasmanian records.

Footnotes:

[1] John Bach, *The Australia Station: A History of the Royal Navy in the South West Pacific 1821-1913*, Sydney 1986, p.186.

[2] 'Memorandum by His Excellency Major-General Sir W.F. Drummond Jervois, K.C.M.G., C.B.' (the Jervois Report), 5 February 1878, *Journals of the Legislative Council* (Tasmania), Vol. XXXV, No. 37.

[3] Memorandum by Colonel Scratchley, 15 June 1882, *Journals of the Legislative Council* (Tasmania), Vol. XXXIII, No. 64.

[4] Scratchley memorandum, 15 June 1882.

[5] Colin Jones, *Australian Colonial Navies*, Canberra 1986, p.61.

[6] Scratchley memorandum, 15 June 1882.

[7] C. W. Sleeman, *Torpedoes and Torpedo Warfare*, Portsmouth 1880, p.197.

[8] *Tasmanian Mail*, 21 January 1882.

[9] Jones, *Australian Colonial Navies*, p.44.

[10] *The Mercury* (Hobart), 12 August 1882.

[11] Colonial Office to N. J. Brown, Minister for Lands and Works, 5 February 1884, Tasmanian Archive and Heritage Office (TAHO), TRE 1/1/1387.

[12] *The Mercury* (Hobart), 2 May 1884.

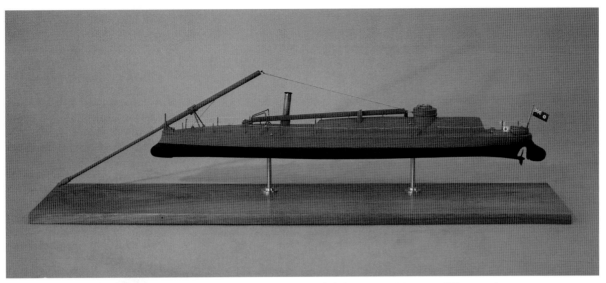

Model of TB191 as she was completed with the spar torpedo fully extended. (Maritime Museum of Tasmania).

Model of TB 191 from astern. Note the single starboard funnel and enclosed oval conning tower. (Maritime Museum of Tasmania).

13. G. E. Armstrong, *Torpedoes and Torpedo-Vessels*, London 1896, pp.73-76.
14. Mark Briggs, 'Innovation and the Mid-Victorian Royal Navy: The Case of the Whitehead Torpedo', *The Mariner's Mirror*, Vol. 88, No. 4, November 2002, pp.447-455.
15. Alfred von Tirpitz, *My Memoirs*, London 1919, Vol. I, p.37.
16. Report on Tasmania's Defences by Lieutenant-Colonel William Legge, 8 April 1885, TAHO, TRE 1/1/1429.
17. John Clarke, Office of the Inspector of Machinery, to Chief Secretary of Tasmania, 20 September 1886, TAHO, TRE 1/1/1399.
18. Edwyn Gray, *The Devil's Device: Robert Whitehead and the History of the Torpedo*, Annapolis 1991, p.269.
19. *The Mercury* (Hobart), 19 May 1885; TAHO, TRE 1/11399.
20. TAHO, TRE 1/11399; *The Mercury* (Hobart), 2 June 1884; Jack Millar, 'Tasmania's only warship – A Navy manned by the Army', *Saturday Evening Mercury* (Hobart), 8 January 1966.
21. *The Mercury* (Hobart), 13 October 1884.
22. *The Times* (London), 28 October 1887.

THE LOSS OF THE *GIUSEPPE GARIBALDI*

Zvonimir Freivogel sets the loss of the Italian armoured cruiser *Giuseppe Garibaldi* in the context of naval warfare in the northern Adriatic in 1915, and tells how the wreck came to be discovered by a team of divers in 2008

On the evening of 17 July 1915, a strong naval detachment under the Italian Rear-Admiral Eugenio Trifari left Brindisi, with the task of disrupting communications between Ragusa and the Bocche di Cattaro on the Austrian Adriatic coast. The bombardment was to be executed in the early morning hours of the following day by the Italian 5th Division, comprising the armoured cruisers *Giuseppe Garibaldi* (Flagship), *Francesco Ferruccio*, *Varese* and the older *Vettor Pisani*, escorted by the destroyers *Ardente*, *Ardito* and *Strale*, and the torpedo-boats *Astore*, *Cigno*, *Centauro*, *Calliope*, *Clio*, *Airone*, *Alcione* and *Arpia*. There were also two supporting groups, commanded by Rear-Admiral Enrico Millo, with the Italian light cruisers *Quarto* and *Marsala*, Italian destroyers *Animoso*, *Irrequito*, *Intrepido*, and the French destroyers *Commandant Rivière*, *Cdt. Bory*, *Bouclier*, *Bisson*, *Magon* and *Protet*. The armoured cruisers were to shell the railway line above Ragusa Vecchia (modern-day Cavtat in Croatia), and the cruiser *Marsala* with several destroyers was to attack the railway line and the station near Gravosa, to the west of Ragusa. The destroyers from the *Quarto* group were to land a detachment of two officers and fifty sailors on Sipan, and to destroy military installations on this island to the west of Ragusa.

For the Allied warships it was not the first operation of this kind in the waters of Ragusa. Already on 5 June, the 5th Division had shelled railway lines near Ragusa, being supported by the British light cruiser HMS *Dublin* and the Italian cruisers *Quarto* and *Nino Bixio*, and escorted by most of the Italian and French destroyers mentioned above. The attack on 18 July was seen as retaliation for Austro-Hungarian bombardments of the Italian coast in May, June and July of 1915.

Historical Background

Italian entry into the war on the side of the Entente on 24 May 1915 brought a new enemy for the Central Powers and severe pressure on the strained human and material reserves of the Austro-Hungarian Empire, already engaged on two fronts against Russia and Serbia/Montenegro. The Italian Army made a swift move to Gorizia, north of Trieste, but the offensive was checked by Austro-Hungarian fortifications in the Tyrol. There followed numerous battles – resulting in a bloody stalemate with heavy losses on both sides – in the Karst and on the slopes of Alpine mountain ranges, culminating in the battles of Caporetto and Vittorio Veneto in 1917 and 1918, which were Austrian and Italian victories respectively.

The armoured cruiser Giuseppe Garibaldi *at Toulon in 1905.* (Dr. Achille Rastelli Collection)

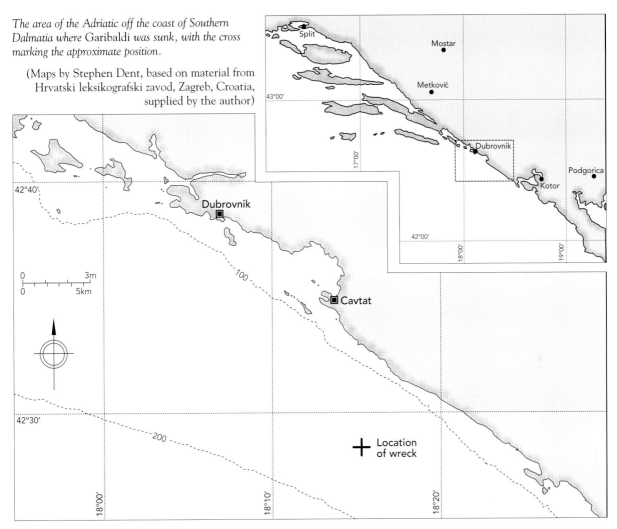

The area of the Adriatic off the coast of Southern Dalmatia where Garibaldi *was sunk, with the cross marking the approximate position.*

(Maps by Stephen Dent, based on material from Hrvatski leksikografski zavod, Zagreb, Croatia, supplied by the author)

The situation at sea was even more frustrating for Italy and the Allies: already in the early morning hours of 24 May, the day that hostilities were to commence, the Austro-Hungarian battle fleet from Pola bombarded Ancona and other harbours on the Italian Adriatic Coast, almost unopposed by the Royal Italian Navy. Some Italian torpedo units were engaged in skirmishes with Imperial and Royal light naval forces, others were supporting the capture of the border-guard installations in the lagoons between Venice and Trieste, and several submarines were sent to patrol the Southern Adriatic, encountering no enemy forces.

Even after this moral defeat, there followed no great Italian naval operations, except the landing on the small island of Pelagosa. This was conducted on 11 July 1915, but the island had little strategic significance, and the landing was to serve as the first step for the envisaged occupation of Lagosta, where a submarine base was to be established. Combined operations against Ragusa and Spalato were contemplated too, but were vetoed by the Italian Navy Minister and Chief-of-Staff and later cancelled.

The Royal Italian Navy was strong enough to hold the enemy fleet in check, but in spite of this other Allies were asked for help, to include battleships, fast light cruisers (the Italian fleet had only three such units at her disposal),

destroyers and submarines. Great Britain and France were already engaged in the naval operations against Turkey, but during the following months the Royal Navy sent four pre-dreadnought battleships to Taranto – to replace four Italian armoured cruisers of the *Pisa* and *San Giorgio* classes (all four were commonly referred as the *Pisa* class), which were transferred from Brindisi to Venice – and several light cruisers and old 'B' class submarines to the Italian Adriatic naval bases at Brindisi and Venice. The French Marine Nationale dispatched several destroyers and modern submarines to the Adriatic to help its new ally.

Allied naval operations were hampered by the activities of the Austro-Hungarian submarines. Already on 21 December 1914, the French battleship *Jean Bart* had been damaged in the southern Adriatic near the island of Saseno by a torpedo fired from the submarine *Ub.12* (*Linienschiffsleutnant/LSLt* Egon Lerch). After this none of the larger French units was sent to the Adriatic. Shortly before Italy entered the war, on 27 April 1915, the submarine *Ub.5* (*LSLt* Georg von Trapp) sank the French armoured cruiser *Léon Gambetta* (12,550t) south of the Otranto Straits, with heavy losses among her crew. The cruiser was on patrol without escorts, and the rescue came too late for many of her sailors and all of her officers, including Rear-Admiral Sénès, Flag Officer of the French

2nd Light Division. From this time no French cruisers were to operate north of Cephalonia, except for specific important operations conducted at high speed and with a heavy escort.

In the meantime the first German submarines were arriving in the Mediterranean: U21 (*Kapitänleutnant* Otto Hersing) rounded Western Europe, making a stop in the Bocche di Cattaro, the southernmost Austro-Hungarian naval base, on her way to the Dardanelles, where she would sink the British battleships *Triumph* and *Majestic*. She would soon be followed by other fleet submarines. Small coastal submarines of the UBI Type were transported overland in sections to Pola, assembled there, and sent to the Dardanelles. Five more units of this diminutive type were sold to Austria-Hungary and remained on the Adriatic. They were very active during trials following their assembly and *Ub.11* (ex-German *UB15*), still with a German crew and under a German CO, *Oberleutnant zur See* (*OltS*) Heino von Heimburg, sank the Italian submarine *Medusa* off Venice on 10 June 1915. Two weeks later, on 26 June, *Ub.10* (ex-*UB1*), also during trials with her German crew and under *OltS* Franz Wäger, sank the Italian torpedo-boat *5PN* not far from the position where *Medusa* was lost.

Bigger losses were to follow. On 7 July the Italian armoured cruiser *Amalfi* (10,000t), supporting a sweep by Italian destroyers near Venice while escorted by only two torpedo-boats, was torpedoed and sunk by the German *UB14*, again commanded by von Heimburg. Because Italy and Germany were not yet officially at war, the submarine operated under the Austrian flag and the designation *Ub.26*.

French destroyers carried out an aggressive and close reconnaissance of Lagosta on 11 July, the day of the Italian landing at Pelagosa, and more raids were contemplated after the landings on Lagosta and Ragusa were cancelled. The railway between Ragusa and Cattaro was shelled and put out of action on 6 June, but the line was restored and another attack was to be carried out on 18 July.

The light cruiser HMS *Dublin*, under Captain John Kelly, demolished the Austro-Hungarian signal station at Lissa on 1 June, in company with the Italian *Quarto*, and on 5 June she took part in the raid against the lighthouse at Glavat. On 8 June *Dublin* left Brindisi again, escorted by three French and four Italian destroyers, for a sweep off the Albanian coast. Afterwards she met the Italian cruiser *Nino Bixio* with a further six destroyers, and the group was steaming back to Brindisi on 9 June, zigzagging at 18 knots, when the ships were intercepted by the Austro-Hungarian submarine *Ub.4* (LSLt Rudolf Singule), on the last leg of her patrol. Singule waited patiently for the French destroyers at the head of the formation to pass, fired a salvo from both tubes, and one of his torpedoes heavily damaged the British cruiser. Her well-trained crew saved the ship from sinking, and *Dublin* finally reached Brindisi under her own power, to be repaired during the following months; *Ub.4* escaped unmolested and returned to the Bocche di Cattaro.

Even these incidents were not enough to persuade Allied naval commanders of the fact that the days of bigger vessels, including armoured cruisers, were over, at least in the Adriatic. And there was now another bombardment group, steaming from Brindisi on the night of 17/18 July, to shell the relatively unimportant railway line near Ragusa Vecchia, regardless of the submarine danger.

Setting the Scene

On 17 July there were other movements, starting with an Austro-Hungarian air attack. The seaplanes *L43*, *L45* and *L49* were sent from Sebenico to bombard Bari, and afterwards *L43* proceeded to Barletta, but after suffering engine failure the plane was compelled to land on the water. Her crew destroyed the aircraft and was captured by Italian Customs officers. *L49* was damaged by anti-aircraft fire and later scuttled, but *L45* rescued the crew and flew

A starboard-side view of Giuseppe Garibaldi *taken later during her career.* (Dr. Achille Rastelli Collection)

THE LOSS OF THE *GIUSEPPE GARIBALDI*

TABLE: BUILDING DATA AND CHARACTERISTICS

	Builder	Laid down	Launched	Completed
Giuseppe Garibaldi	Ansaldo di Genova (Sestri)	08.06.1898	29.06.1899	01.01.1901

Type: armoured cruiser (*Incrociatore corazzato*; *Nave di battaglia di 2ª classe*)

Other Ships of Class: *General Garibaldi* (LD 1894, Argentina); *General San Martin* (LD 1895, Argentina); *General Belgrano* (LD 1896, Argentina); *Pueyrredón* (LD 1896, Argentina); *Cristóbal Colón* (LD 1897, Spain); *Varese* (LD 1898, Italy); *Francesco Ferruccio* (LD 1899, Italy); *Kasuga* (LD 1902, Japan); *Nisshin* (LD 1903, Japan)

Characteristics:

Displacement:	7,350 tonnes normal, 8,100 tonnes full load
Length:	111.8m oa, 104.9m pp
Beam:	18.2 m
Draught:	6.9m-7.30m
Machinery:	two vertical triple-expansion steam engines, 14,000 ihp; 24 Niclausse (*Garibaldi* & *Varese*) or Belleville type (*Ferruccio*) watertube boilers; two shafts
Speed:	20 knots designed (trials 1900: only 19.7 knots at 7,359t with 14,713 ihp)
Coal:	620t/1,200t; endurance 5500 nm at 10 kts
Armour:	belt 150mm, tapering to 80mm forward and aft; deck 38mm; turrets, conning tower & casemates 150mm; shields (deck guns) 50mm
Armament:	1 – 254mm (10in) L/40 forward, 2 – 203mm (8in) L/45 aft, 14 – 152mm (6in) L/40, 10 – 76mm (3in) L/40, 6 – 47 mm L/40, 2 Maxim machine guns, 4 – 450mm (17.7in) TT
Complement:	555 (25 officers), 578 as flagship.

back, finally reaching the Bocche di Cattaro in tow of the torpedo-boat 61, after her own engine also failed. The fate of *L43* was unclear, and two Austro-Hungarian submarines received orders from the Flag Officer in the Bocche (who also commanded the 5th Heavy Division: three ironclads of the *Monarch* class) to search for the missing plane. The submarine *Ub.6* under LSLt Nikolaus Halavanja had already sailed on 17 July, returning on 18 July without encountering enemy forces. Shortly after midnight on 18 July, the already mentioned *Ub.4* under LSLt Singule received her sailing orders. She was to leave Bocche at 02.00 and to proceed to Lagosta, Pelagosa, Gargano and back, in search of the missing *L43*. At 01.45, shortly before sailing, Singule received new orders. He was to proceed at higher speed along the ordered route, where enemy warships were now expected. Already on the evening of 17 July, observers from the Radostak station, 1446 metres above the Bocche, sighted enemy forces, still 60 nautical miles away, proceeding towards the Bocche. During the night the signal station Punta d'Ostro, on the Prevlaka peninsula which closed the Bocche from the south-west, reported further enemy movements, and it was presumed that Ragusa Vecchia was the selected target.

The Giuseppe Garibaldi

The armoured cruisers of the *Giuseppe Garibaldi* class were built as an improved version of the *Vettor Pisani* class, with lower freeboard forward and a heavier armament. They were designed by *Tenente Generale del Genio Navale* (Lieutenant-General Constructor) Edoardo Masdea, under the supervision of the Chief Constructor Benedetto Brin. The ships of the *Garibaldi* class were well armed and, with a speed of 20 kts, fast for their time. The design was well received abroad, and no fewer than seven of the ten

Giuseppe Garibaldi *in the harbour of Genoa.* (Dr. Achille Rastelli Collection)

cruisers of this class were sold to the navies of Argentina, Spain and Japan. Only the *Garibaldi* (fourth ship of the series, commissioned in 1901) and the third, *Varese*, together with their sister-ship *Francesco Ferruccio*, flew the Italian flag when completed. The Argentine ships were not to be tested in battle, but the Spanish *Cristóbal Colón* was lost in 1898 off Santiago de Cuba during the Spanish-

Garibaldi underway. (Author's Collection)

American war, and the two Japanese units, *Kasuga* and *Nisshin*, played an active part in the Russo-Japanese War and the First World War.

The Submarine Ub.4

Ub.4 was the first operational and the longest serving Austro-Hungarian submarine. She was built by the Germania shipyard at Kiel, launched on 20 November 1908, towed to the Adriatic, and commissioned at Pola after trials on 29 August 1909. The Austro-Hungarian Navy started late with the build-up of its submarine flotilla, and *Ub.4* was one of six prototypes. Each pair was built by a different shipyard to three different designs: *Ub.1* and *Ub.2* were designed by the American inventor Simon Lake and built under licence at Pola, *Ub.3* and *Ub.4* belonged to the Germania type, and *Ub.5* and *Ub.6* were built at Fiume to a John Holland design. *Ub.4* was commissioned before her sister-boat and the other prototypes, and remained in service until 1918, becoming the Austro-Hungarian submarine with the longest service record. All six boats were of small dimensions: *Ub.3* and *Ub.4* displaced 240t on the surface

Garibaldi in 1915, with a destroyer behind her. (Dr. Achille Rastelli Collection)

THE LOSS OF THE *GIUSEPPE GARIBALDI*

The Austro-Hungarian submarines Ub.3 and Ub.4 at Pola, before both were transferred to the Bocche di Cattaro. (Eng. Franz Selinger Collection)

and 300t submerged, were 43.2 metres long, with a pressure hull width of 3.8m, a beam of 4.6m a draught of 2.95m. Two 300hp petrol engines enabled a surfaced speed of 12 knots, and with two 160hp electric motors the boats attained a maximum speed of 8.5 knots under water. Diving depth was 50 metres, and range 1200nm at 8 knots on the surface or 40nm submerged at 3 knots. The Germania boats were armed with two 450mm torpedo tubes and carried three torpedoes: two in the tubes with one spare. Their complement comprised three officers and 18 ratings. *Ub.3* was lost during the war, and *Ub.4* was assigned to France after the war and scrapped shortly thereafter.

Singule strikes again

After leaving Bocche di Cattaro, *LSLt* Singule sighted at 03.20 to the south of the Molunat Peninsula conspicuous smoke columns between Bocche and Ragusa. Shortly thereafter, at 03.35, he recognised enemy warships headed for Ragusa, including four armoured cruisers (according to Singule: 'three of the *Garibaldi* class and the fourth probably of the *Vettor Pisani* type) and several destroyers behind them. Singule ordered the engines stopped – the petrol engines of the Germania boats produced clouds of white smoke and were sometimes noisy – and waited on the surface for the enemy. At 03.55 the Allied warships

The Austro-Hungarian submarine Ub.4 *underway. (Eng. René Greger Collection)*

When cold, the petrol engines of Germania-type submarines (Ub.3 is seen here), produced clouds of white smoke. (Eng. Franz Selinger Collection)

changed their course to the south-east, parallel to the coast, and at 04.00 started to shell the railway line. *Ub.4* dived to periscope depth at exactly the same time, and began to approach her targets.

At 04.37 lookouts from the armoured cruiser *Vettor Pisani*, the last ship in the line, spotted a periscope, and the ship opened fire against the submerged submarine with her light guns. The Italian flagship joined the barrage with her own guns and started zigzagging to escape suspected torpedoes. But it was already too late: at 04.38 Singule launched two torpedoes, at a distance of 600 metres from his target, the cruiser in the van of enemy formation, estimating her speed at 10 knots. According to Italian sources, the range was only 400m, but in spite of this, one of the torpedoes missed the stern of *Giuseppe Garibaldi*, passing through the gap between the flagship and the second-in-line, the armoured cruiser *Varese*. Another torpedo hit *Garibaldi* 30 seconds after being launched, on the starboard side near the transverse coal bunkers and close to the after boiler rooms. The mortally wounded warship took a 10° list to starboard. With the flooding of the coal bunkers her draught deepened and the list was temporarily checked. *Garibaldi* returned to an even keel, but started to sink by the stern, and disap-

Giuseppe Garibaldi *sinking after being torpedoed by Ub.4 on July 18, 1915. (Dr. Achille Rastelli Collection)*

peared under the waves some six minutes after being torpedoed (only three minutes according to some sources), her bow pointing skywards. Despite the speed with which she sank, only 53 seamen perished with their ship, and – probably thanks to the warm July weather – 525 crew members were rescued by the escorts, including her Commanding Officer *Capitano di vascello* (Captain) Franco Nunes and Rear-Admiral Trifari.

After launching her torpedoes, *Ub.4* dived to a depth of 20 metres and headed for the coast. All enemy warships, including those from the other two groups, were called off; they ceased their attacks and retreated to their base. Three Italian destroyers remained on the scene, salvaging survivors from the waters and at the same time – while flying Red Cross flags! – trying to ram the submarine, which returned to inspect the results of her attack. Singule ordered one of the tubes to be loaded with the third torpedo, but decided against launching; the torpedo was set for greater depth for use against capital ships, and the contact exploder was inefficient against shallow-draught destroyers. Singule also respected their Red Cross flags. Finally all the seamen were rescued and the destroyers left the scene. Despite engine problems *Ub.4* resumed her patrol and the search for the missing seaplane. She returned to the Bocche on 19 July, and in the meantime the Austro-Hungarian torpedo-boats *13* and *15* searched the site of the sinking and found jetsam and flotsam, including a desk with confidential Italian papers and codes.

LSLt Singule was afterwards allegedly reprimanded by Admiral Anton Haus, C-in-C of the Austro-Hungarian Fleet, because he had sunk only one armoured cruiser despite having three torpedoes at his disposal! According to some memoirs written by former Austro-Hungarian submarine officers, Admiral Haus showed a lack of understanding of the submarines' capabilities; however, earlier during his career he was always open to new ideas, and it is possible that he was not on good terms with some of his subordinates, which resulted in 'bad press' after his death. Despite this unjustified criticism from his superior, for his exploits – damaging a British cruiser and sinking the *Garibaldi* – *LSLt* Singule became a Knight of the Military Maria Theresia Medal, the highest Austro-Hungarian order for military achievement.

The Consequences

After the loss of *Garibaldi*, all Allied plans for landings on the Austrian Adriatic coast and islands – including Lagosta – were cancelled. Shortly thereafter – after the Italian submarine *Nereide* was sunk by *Ub.5* (vonTrapp) off Pelagosa, and the only fresh water tank available to the Italian troops on the island was destroyed during an Austro-Hungarian naval bombardment – Pelagosa was evacuated too, remaining unoccupied until the end of the war. For the Italian side the material and human losses – one old cruiser and 53 crew members – were smaller than the moral effect – losing the ship named after the country's national hero Giuseppe Garibaldi. This incident came shortly after the loss of *Amalfi*, and there would be no more bombardments by heavy Allied fleet vessels against the enemy coast. Only light forces, submarines, light cruisers, destroyers, torpedo boats and motor torpedo boats were to operate successfully in this theatre, and Italian and British monitors and floating batteries were used for bombardments in the lagoon theatre during operations in the Northern Adriatic.

Admiral Trifari and Captain Nunes were cleared of all charges during the investigation of the loss, led by Vice-Admiral Leonardi Cattolica, and praised for the calm and responsible conduct of the crew during the sinking. One charge remained: allegedly an Austro-Hungarian seaplane overflew the Italian naval force after leaving Brindisi on 17 July, and Admiral Trifari was criticised for not having cancelled the operation after being detected. Austro-Hungarian sources do not mention this incident, but the failure of *L43* to return to base started a search for the plane that culminated in the discovery of the Italian 5th Division and the sinking of *Garibaldi*. There was indeed a sighting of Italian warships, but by observers high in the mountains above Bocche.

Rudolf von Singule – a Short Biography

Rudolf Singule was born on 8 April 1883 at Pola, the son of a factory clerk from Brno. He went to the Naval Academy at Fiume in 1897, graduating in 1901, the same year that *Giuseppe Garibaldi* was completed. Afterwards he

Lieutenant Rudolf Singule as a submarine commander.
(Oliver Trulei Collection)

served on several warships, including the small cruiser *Aspern*, was promoted on 1 May 1906 to the rank of *Fregattenleutnant*, and was sent in 1908 to the newly-established submarine base at Pola, serving as the second in command of *Ub.4*. In 1911 he was promoted to the rank of *Linienschiffsleutnant*. In 1912/13 and from 9 April 1915 to 30 November 1917 Singule was in command of *Ub.4*. In addition to the above-mentioned successes against warships, during the course of the war Singule sank 15 merchantmen of 11,127grt and damaged two more. From 1 December 1917 onwards he served as an instructor for future submarine commanders at Pola.

After the war Singule lived and worked at Brno as an insurance clerk. He was subsequently mobilised during the Second World War – because of his German nationality – to serve in the German Kriegsmarine. Again he instructed U-boat commanders, this time at Kiel, being attached to the 3rd and 5th U-Boat-Flotillas. From October 1941 to April 1942 he commanded the training boat *UD-4*. He was promoted to the rank of *Korvettenkapitän* (Lieutenant Commander), but was soon put on the reserve list, at first with the 5th Flotilla and later with the German U-boat Command in Italy. He was pensioned off on 31 August 1943, shortly before the Italian armistice. Singule's wife Dora died in 1943, and he came back to Brno, marrying again shortly thereafter. In the last days of the war, when he was 62, he was shot in the street on 2 May 1945 by Russian soldiers, while trying to defend a woman from molestation. He was clandestinely buried in his wife's grave at Brno, and later his remnants were transferred to the family grave. In 2005 the tomb was restored through the initiative of historians, remembering his deeds during the Great War.

The Search

The position of the wreck of the *Garibaldi*, 42°28'7N/18°15'7E – five nautical miles away from the former Yugoslav coast near Cavtat – was well known and documented by the Austrians, but the depth, 120 metres beneath the surface, prohibited diving on the wreck during the 20th Century. Moreover, the Yugoslav authorities showed no interest in organising and financing an expedition to an Italian warship sunk by 'Austro-Hungarian occupiers' during a 'long-forgotten war'. After the fall of the Iron Curtain and the crumbling of the Yugoslav Federation, independent and free states such as Croatia and the Czech Republic became interested in their roots and history. At the same time, technical developments made diving to greater depths possible. At first the wreck of the Austro-Hungarian dreadnought *Szent István* was dived on near Premuda, at a depth of almost 70 metres. This was followed by a search for the Italian ironclad *Re d'Italia*, found off Lissa in 2005 by a Franco-Italian expedition aboard the research ship *Janus* from Marseille. This wreck, lying 120 metres deep, was inspected and filmed by a Remotely Operated Vehicle (ROV) and by the small submersible *Remora*.

In April 2008 the position of the wreck of the *Garibaldi* was established near the official one by a Czech expedition led by the diver Zdeněk Partyngl, but only in September of the same year was it possible to organise an expedition, which ended in tragedy. The search by the divers' mother ship *Agramer* on 9 September, to confirm the established position, lasted longer than envisaged. Two divers were scheduled to secure a floating buoy to the wreck during the first dive, and they waited long in their scuba suits, suffering in the heat of the day. One of the divers returned prematurely, but another descended and fastened the rope to the middle part of the hull, near one of the 152mm casemate guns. Czech historian Boris Gol, who took part in the expedition, asserted that the wreck was lying on its side – this was not confirmed by later expeditions – and the shallowest part of the hull was found at a depth of 113m. The position of the find was given as 42°28'362N, 18°16'758E.

The exploration of the wreck was scheduled for 10 September. After descending to a depth of 90 metres one of the divers, Jan Otys, signalled that he was having problems, and both divers started a controlled return to the surface. At 50 metres Otys stopped communicating, and the ascent was quickened. At 6 metres he became unconscious, and after being brought to the surface he was transported by speedboat to Cavtat, but after 20 minutes of resuscitation by the medical team he was pronounced dead. His equipment was checked and found to be functioning normally, but one of the four oxygen tanks was found to be empty for unknown reasons.

The police and the Harbour Master began an investigation and finally found the Czech divers guilty of not informing authorities such as the Ministry for Culture about their plans. They were accused of breaking archaeological laws, as underwater monitoring of protected objects of historical value required a special permit from the Ministry. Additionally they were charged with exceeding the depth of 40 metres that scuba divers are permitted to dive. The leader of the diving team was imprisoned, but released the following day after a fine was paid. All divers of the group were expelled from Croatia and forbidden to dive there again. In fact, sport scuba divers using compressed air are prohibited from diving more than 40 metres below the surface, but this rule is not applicable to technical divers with other breathing-gas mixtures. The team had a permit for diving on the histor-

The team of the first successful expedition to the wreck of the Garibaldi *during preparations for diving. In the second row, first from the right is Drazen Goricki.* (Drazen Goricki)

The Dragor Lux team at Cavtat, before the first expedition, August 2009. (Drazen Goricki)

The small submersible that took part in the November 2009 expedition to the wreck of the Giuseppe Garibaldi. *(Eng. Danijel Frka Collection)*

ical wrecks of the Adriatic, but only to visit the wreck of *Szent István*, lying in the Northern Adriatic. Czech divers argued that the existing laws applied only to wreck sites already registered, and not to new discoveries. However, *Giuseppe Garibaldi* was officially designated as a War Grave and was therefore protected from 'uncontrolled diving' and 'souvenir hunting', which was what the Czech divers were accused of.

In 2009 the wreck of the *Garibaldi* was rediscovered again by Croatian divers from the Dragor Lux Diving Club from Zagreb, led by Drazen Goricki. His team included CCR diver Damir Mlinaric, Trimix divers Dinko Jovic and Uros Jelic, scriptwriter and journalist Marijan Vrdoljak, and cameraman and producer Ivan Cvirn, and their first dive followed on 27 August 2009. *Giuseppe Garibaldi* was finally sighted at a depth of 122 metres, and two divers, Goricki and Damir Mlinaric, photographed and filmed the wreck. Several records were broken: *Giuseppe Garibaldi* is the deepest lying wreck found on the Croatian side of the Adriatic, and the deepest visited by scuba divers.

Garibaldi is lying upside down, and her symmetrical superstructure with its two characteristic funnels and single mast with its fighting top are mostly crushed under the hull. In spite of this, it was possible to dive under the overhanging parts of the hull and to photograph some details inside and outside of the ship, such as the conning tower, some ventilator cowlings and secondary guns. Typical of the cruisers of the *Garibaldi* class was the sharp underwater ram, an inheritance of the 19th Century's belief in the efficacy of this antique device, renewed after the Battle of Lissa in 1866, when *Re d'Italia* was sunk through ramming by the Austrian flagship *Erzherzog Ferdinand Max*.

The next expedition took place in November of 2009. This research was of an international character and was organised by the Croatian Ministry of Culture. Some experienced and well-known Croatian divers and wreck specialists were in the team, including Marino Brzac and Danijel Frka. Several Croatian and foreign archaeologists and historians participated in the enterprise, and it was possible to use a small submersible of German origin to stay longer in the vicinity of the remains of the cruiser. The unlucky Czech team was invited too, as a compensation for the loss of their comrade and the misunderstandings of the previous year. The problem with the submersible was the slow response of the boat when details were to be filmed slowly and continuously, but more of the wreck was sighted and discovered this time.

In May 2010 *Garibaldi* was visited again by Goricki's team, and more photos were taken and videos made. Later additional scenes were filmed for a documentary on the loss and the finding of the ship, with interviews with participants, enthusiasts and historians, including the author of this article. The film should be released for television in 2011.

Conclusion

Giuseppe Garibaldi was lost during an era when submarines, light attack craft and mines made the operation of armoured ships in narrow seas almost impossible. She represented the 19th Century's belief in the predominance of the big gun against shore targets, which was shattered at almost the same time during the ventures of the French and British Fleets against the fortifications of the Dardanelles. The use of torpedoes by submarines and fast attack craft made all armoured ships vulnerable, and

The submersible underway to the wreck of the Garibaldi. *(Eng. Danijel Frka)*

Garibaldi was but one of several warships sunk by enemy submarines in the Mediterranean. Later during the war, the Austro-Hungarian ironclad SMS *Wien* was lost in the harbour of Muggia near Trieste, and the newest of the Austro-Hungarian dreadnoughts, SMS *Szent István*, was sunk in open seas by torpedoes, in both cases fired from small motor torpedo boats – which were, incidentally, commanded by one and the same person, the Italian naval officer Luigi Rizzo.

The expeditions to the wreck of *Garibaldi* have other symbolic meanings, making the search for our common history an international issue, and showing the possibilities and dangers of modern diving techniques. We should also respect the victims of the wars and of the exploration of our heritage, in the hope that a belief in the 'supremacy of technology' does not obscure our perception, one of the causes that led to the loss of *Giuseppe Garibaldi* and of one of the divers searching for the wreck.

Sources:

Wladimir Aichelburg, *Die Unterseeboote Österreich-Ungarns*, Parts 1&2, Akademische Druck- u. Verlagsanstalt, Graz 1981.

Vili A. Bačic, *Poviest Prvog svjetskog rata na Jadranu, I. knjiga, do proljeca 1916*, Hrvatski izdavalački bibliografski zavod, Zagreb 1945.

Rainer Busch, Hans Joachim Röll, *Der U-Boot-Krieg 1939-1945: Die Deutschen U-Boot-Kommandanten*, E. S. Mittler Verlag, Hamburg/Berlin/Bonn 1996.

Roger Chesneau, Eugene M. Kolesnik (Editors), *Kriegsschiffe der Welt 1860 bis 1905, Bd. 3: Frankreich, Italien, Österreich-Ungarn und übrige Marinen* (3rd part of the German Edition of

Detail of the Garibaldi's *deck, photographed during the first expedition.* (Drazen Goricki)

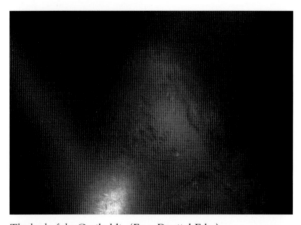

The keel of the Garibaldi. (Eng. Danijel Frka)

Drazen Goricki inside the wreck of the Garibaldi; *1st expedition of the Dragor Lux team.* (Drazen Goricki)

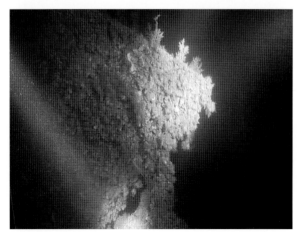

The sharp underwater ram of the bow of Garibaldi. (Eng. Danijel Frka)

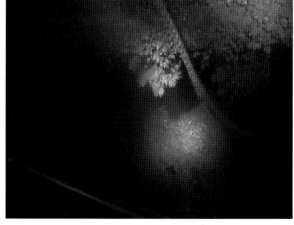

Garibaldi, *showing the deck edge above the bottom.* (Eng. Danijel Frka)

THE LOSS OF THE *GIUSEPPE GARIBALDI*

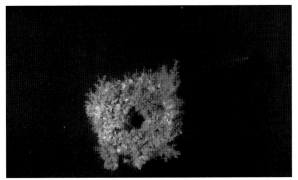

The muzzle of a 152mm gun, overgrown by the maritime flora and fauna. (Drazen Goricki)

A photograph from the 2nd Dragor Lux expedition, May 2010: one of the secondary 152mmn battery guns. (Drazen Goricki)

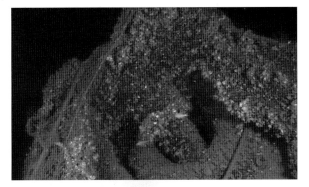

One of the Garibaldi's *bower anchors.* (Drazen Goricki)

Assessing the state of the wreck. (Drazen Goricki)

The bow of the Garibaldi. (Drazen Goricki)

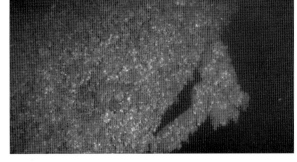

The underwater ram photographed in profile, entangled in fishermen's nets. (Drazen Goricki)

the Conway's All the World's Fighting Ships 1860-1905), Bernard & Graefe Verlag, Koblenz 1985.
Conway's All The World's Fighting Ships 1860-1905, Conway Maritime Press, London 1979.
Aldo Fraccaroli, *Italian Warships of World War I*, Ian Allan, London 1970.
Zvonimir Freivogel, *Austrougarske podmornice u I. svjetskom ratu – Austro-Hungarian Submarines in World War I*, Adamic-Digital Point, Rijeka 2007.
Giorgio Giorgerini, Augusto Nani: *Gli Incrociatori Italiani*, Ufficio storico della Marina Militare, Roma 1964.
Karl Gruber, *Seemacht unter rot weiss roter Flagge*, Österreichischer Milizverlag, Salzburg 2006.
Paul G. Halpern, *The Naval War in the Mediterranean 1914-1918*, Naval Institute Press, Annapolis 1987.
Camillo Manfroni, *Storia della Marina Italiana durante la Guerra mondiale 1914-1918*, N. Zanichelli, Bologna 1925.

Georg Pawlik, Lothar Baumgartner, *S.M. Unterseeboote*, H. Weishaupt Verlag, Graz 1986.
Jacob Rehder, Helmut Sander, *Die Verluste der Kriegsflotten 1914-1918*, J.F. Lehmanns Verlag, München 1969.
Peter Schupita, *Die k.u.k. Seeflieger: Chronik und Dokumentation der österreichisch-ungarischen Marineluftwaffe*, Bernard & Graefe Verlag, Koblenz 1983.
Hans-Hugo Sokol, *Österreich-Ungarns Seekrieg 1914-1918*, Amalthea Verlag, Wien 1933.
Michael Wilson, Paul Kemp, *Mediterranean Submarines*, Crécy Publications, Manchester 1977.

Author's archives
http://www.finnsub.cz/garibaldi/eng/expedition.php
http://www.ceskenoviny.cz/news/index_view.php?id=332830
http://www.shipwreckgaribaldi.com

CONDUITE DU TIR
Part 2: 1900 to 1913

To follow the first part of his article on French fire control published in *Warship* 2010, which covered 19th century developments, **John Spencer** focuses on the period prior to the Great War during which the basic principles of fire control were defined and established in the Marine Nationale.

By 1900, the French led the world in naval gunnery. They had put into place an effective data transmitting system, and with it procedures for engaging targets at around 5000 metres, which was probably twice the effective engagement range of any other navy of the period. From 1900 other navies caught up rapidly, and some even made great advances. However the French, having developed a system, did not rest; progress was made, albeit from quite a different angle.

Gunnery Methods and Practice in 1900

Order transmitters had returned a fighting ship from a platform filled with individual and almost independent guns back into an effective unit of artillery. There was one key observer and one key commander, each with well-defined responsibilities.[1] A system of firing salvos was in place to creep shells onto the target after the initial estimates. Once the range was found, all guns would fire as fast as they could – although this fire was unregulated in that gunners fired at will and at their discretion using gunnery data supplied by the gunnery officer aloft. If the situation was changing rapidly, shells would be targeted into an area that the firing ship knew the target would have to sail through. The system enabled the commander to control the situation more effectively, allowing him to know under which conditions the guns were firing and make rapid judgements (estimates) about any changes required.

Until this time, most gunnery practices involved the use of a measured danger zone around a static balloon, hits

The battleship Danton – the result of lessons learned during gunnery evolutions at the start of the 20th century. She was the first French capital ship to be designed with monostatic (coincidence) rangefinders, not only in raised positions but equally on the roofs of all her turrets. Much effort was made to ensure she carried the largest guns suitable for continuous aim (referring to the 240mm and not the 305mm), the objective being to deliver the largest shells rapidly and effectively (in the knowledge that larger shells would be more effective at longer ranges than smaller ones). (Courtesy of Robert Dumas)

being determined by the number of shells falling into the danger zone. This might sound an easy test, but it involved the ship starting practice at 4000 metres from the target, with the target 30 degrees off the bow. The ship would cruise past the target at 16 knots and practice would finish once the target was 4000 metres and 30 degrees off the stern; the ship would then haul round for a second run. This practice would at first see the range coming down rapidly, although the bearing would not change too much. Then, as the ship reached midpoint of the run, the range would not be changing much, however the bearing would be changing rapidly. As the ship finished its run, ranges would be increasing rapidly but bearings would once more be changing slowly.

Compared to a towed target on a parallel course and direction, where bearing and range would be changing much more slowly, shooting at a fixed balloon is actually harder than it seems. Naturally shooting at such a static target is only suitable for ranges under 5000 metres, at greater distances gunnery practice would become much longer, and the range and bearings would be changing much more slowly.

Despite this, between May 1896 and November 1897, requests for the first towed targets were made. The proposals called a target to be 5 metres high and some 20 to 30 metres long, to be towed at around 5 knots. This was thought to be better than shooting up target balloons and cheaper than shooting up an old ship. Unfortunately nothing came of the proposal at this time on the grounds of cost.

In 1898, a note suggests using the old torpedo boat *Ecureuil* as a target for the Northern Division. The Mediterranean Division wanted to use old torpedo boats for gunnery training against the torpedo boat threat. However, the conversion of old torpedo boats to towed targets was not authorised and undertaken until 1901.

By 1903, the gunnery officers' handbook noted the then-regulatory gunnery practices as follows:

1. Tirs réduits
Exercises used to train individual layers in straightforward aiming. Each gun would take it in turns to fire individually. There were three types of exercise:

- Firing at fixed or towed targets 500m to 1000m away while at anchor.
- Firing at night at 800m on either fixed or towed targets while at anchor.
- Firing at fixed (500 to 1800m) or towed (700m, 6 knots) targets during the day or night while at sea.

2. Tirs d'appréciation
The object of these exercises was to grade each leading and auxiliary gun layer, and to choose which layers would point which guns for the following year. Guns would be required to fire three rounds, switching back and forth between two targets that were spaced apart so as to require re-pointing at 2200m from the anchored ship. Depending on the size of the gun, the layers would be limited in the number of seconds they had to fire rounds (a 164mm would be given 30 seconds, a 100mm only 10).

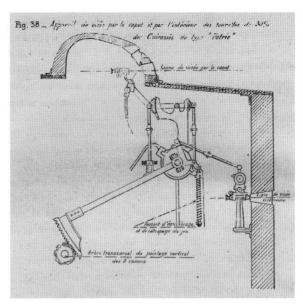

This image shows a typical French pre-dreadnought gun sight arrangement within a turret with two sights: one placed in the hood on the roof, the other in the front of the turret. Movement of the sights themselves was restricted in order to keep the penetrations in the armour to an absolute minimum. All movement was done via mechanical linkages in the form of a parallelogram. There were several mechanical methods either using worms and gears, tooth pinion and gear, spiral and roller method, or via a cam. Each type of ship had – more or less – its own unique turret design and thus sighting method. Later ships finally evolved standard methods which normally involved only cams. (Author's collection)

3. Ecoles de feu
These were general gunnery exercises, testing all aspects of the gunnery system. Exercises could last days, with each ship having several minutes in each daily exercise to perform its practice. Targets might be fixed (in most cases) or towed, and ranges and circumstances would evolve as time went on.

Once range clocks became common use in 1906, tactical plotting exercises began to take place with two ships manoeuvring at distance and plotting the observed ranges at 30-second intervals, while also noting the ranges given by the clocks. At the same time other data such as range rate, inclination, target bearing, firing ship speed and target ship speed were also noted. Other exercises could involve one ship in the division moving out from the line to some point 8000m either directly ahead, astern, or 60 degrees off either the port or starboard quarters, circling round at that distance for some 6500m before coming back again. The next ship in the line would repeat the exercise but on a different quarter.[2]

Contact with British industry and the Royal Navy in the early 1900s brought two factors to French attention. The first was that British turret design allowed British guns to fire at faster rates – almost twice as fast! The second was continuous aim, which allowed the gunner to fire as soon as the gun was ready, rather than waiting for the target to roll through the cross-hairs. As will be seen later, for the French this would lead to a gunnery policy in which the focus was on shooting and hitting faster, as opposed to a policy of more deliberate fire and hitting at ever-increasing ranges. These equally led to a campaign to design and modify turrets so that they could aim continuously.

A Steady Evolution

In 1890, divisional tactics of creating a mêlée which included torpedoing formations was adopted for capital ships and cruisers. By 1900, it was clear that the torpedo was making mêlée tactics with big ships a dangerous proposition. It was also clear that effective fighting and gunnery ranges had increased. Soon the initial ranges available on existing order transmitters were proving insufficient.

In 1903, the 180mm diameter dials of the Germain transmitters (see Part 1) were scaled between 500m and 4500m; by 1907 the same dials were being fitted with screens ranging from 2000m to 6000m. Even this was quickly found to be insufficient, as in 1905 it was recommended that the 180mm-diameter dials be replaced by 250mm models. The range markings would be between 1500m and 7500m. In 1910 the 250mm dial had a new face with ranges from 2000m to 14,000m, which was about as far as the main guns of the battleships currently in service could then shoot.

The cost of fitting Germain transmitters was fairly cheap, around 4000 francs or one third the cost of an electrical system. However, there were problems: air had to be bled out before use, tubes running though the engine spaces were subject to heat which could cause the liquid to expand, but more importantly tubes would corrode and become unusable. For example, in 1908 an order was placed for 1300m of new tubes for the armoured cruiser *Jeanne d'Arc* to replace 1100m that were unusable.

The limits of hydraulic systems were becoming apparent. Increased ranges would eventually demand a greater range of values at smaller and finer increments. The French were already aware of Barr & Stroud's data transmitters in the early 1900s. The earliest mention in the French Archives is May 1906, although they were certainly aware of them before then. These devices were given serious consideration between 11 July 1907 and 23 January 1908 for the recently completed *Patrie* and *Démocratie* class, and again in August 1909 during discussions in the design of the FC system for the new semi-dreadnoughts of the *Danton* class and the armoured cruiser *Waldeck Rousseau*; however the decision was put off until March 1910.

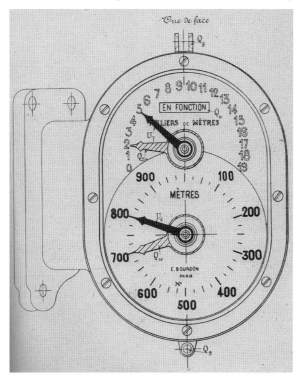

A frontal view of a transmetteur d'ordres Lecomte-Aubry. This one is for range. The upper dial gives ranges to the nearest 1000 metres. The lower dial shows finer graduations (100s marked, down to the nearest 25 metres in fine graduations). By the end of the First World War, nearly all older transmitter types had been replaced by these in all major ships for all gunnery data. (Author's collection)

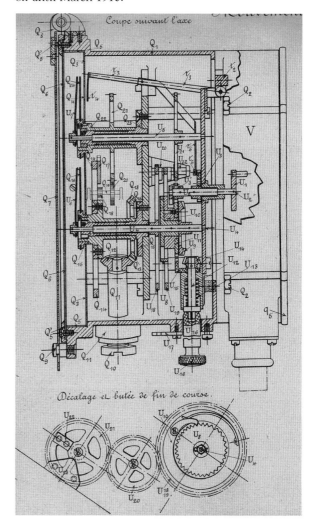

Cross-section of an LA order transmitter showing the increasing complexity of these devices compared with the simple manometer and volt meter-type devices they replaced. (Author's collection)

The debate concerned only the transmission of distances; all other data would still be transmitted via the Germain system. In the end, the French invented their own stepper motor system called *transmetteurs d'ordres Lecomte-Aubry* (*appareils L.A.* for short). These were devised by LV Lecomte and designed by one of the Bourdon Company's engineers, Aubry. Thus the semi-dreadnoughts of the *Danton* class were completed with both the Germain system (orders, bearing and deflection) and the new L.A. transmitters (range).

During this period the torpedo threat, and more importantly the need to engage torpedo boats at greater ranges, led to another series of data transmitter designs. Firstly in 1901, requests were made to replace 37mm guns with 47mm guns. In 1904 the armoured cruiser *Léon Gambetta* carried out tests of various primitive data transmitting systems between makeshift spotting posts and the light guns. Many of these data transmitting systems were akin to what had been seen during the 1890s for main calibre guns. There were systems using lights, and even wooden pulleys and flip boards. Around 1906 it was generally accepted that there should be four spotting positions (bow, stern, port and starboard), each controlling a section of small guns. In the end it was decided that orders would be transmitted using the older and smaller manometers from the Germain system (themselves being replaced by larger units for the main guns).

Telescopic Gun Sights

Telescopic sights had existed ever since rifled guns appeared, but they were not made regulatory in the French Navy until 1905 despite many previous attempts. Before this, the standard was for open gun sights and it was felt that telescopic sights had the following disadvantages:

– Field of vision too small, so difficult to find the target – especially at night.
– Vision affected by fog, smoke and rain.
– Useless on guns with violent shocks.
– More fragile and could lose their clarity quickly.

However, the advantages of telescopic sights were as follows:

– Line of aim perfectly defined.
– While open sights required the lining up of three points (front sight, back sight and target), telescopic sights required the alignment of only two (cross-hairs and target).
– Target appeared bigger and easier to determine when within the cross-hairs.
– Easier to learn to use.
– Eye could move slightly without breaking the line of sight, thereby facilitating continuous aim.
– Cross-hairs in the reticule could be several, to cater for deflection and angle.
– Special lighting could be used for pointing at night.

The first sight to be made regulatory in 1905 was the telescopic sight by Avizard, Petit and Krauss, but from 1907 the principal telescopic sight of the French Navy was designed by CF Petit. The latter sight was first trialled on 28 May of the same year, and was generally successful for medium calibre guns (see table). In 1907, with the battleships of the *Danton* class and the armoured cruisers of the *Edgar Quinet* class on the stocks, it was felt that the 24cm and 30cm weapons would need sights with two types of magnification: one at around 5x for close range and night actions, the other around 15x for long range.[3] For this requirement the telescope produced by Krauss was introduced as standard on 10 March 1910. Unfortunately an instruction from the Navy Minister dated 11 July 1911 forbade the use of the 15x magnification device, as it was found to be difficult to keep the twin lenses and carriers in the middle of the sight perfectly parallel. The French therefore entered the First World War with no gun sight capable of more than 5x magnification, although they did become aware of Britain's Ross sight in January 1914 while designing guns for Japanese destroyers. Unlike the Krauss sight, this used a single lens and carrier in the middle which could be adjusted to any magnification between 5x and 21x.

All telescopic gun sights were of the telescope type; the French did not use prismatic nor periscopic sights at this time. Gun sight telescopes came in various sizes from 150 to 850mm in length. Eye pieces would be between 5 to 8mm in diameter for a field of vision between 9 and 17 degrees. All gun sights were backed up with either a *collimateur de guerre* or a *collimateur Krauss* which acted as a robust open sight. These were solid, rectangular tube-

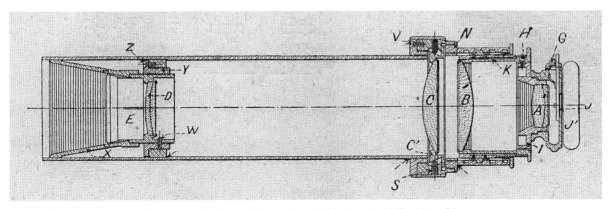

The standard telescopic gun sight by Avizard, Petit and Krauss from 1905. (Jacob, *Artillerie Navale*)

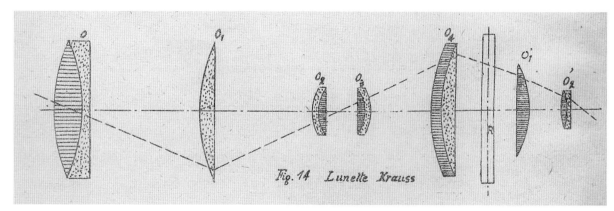

The arrangement of the lenses within the Krauss gun sight from 1910. The two smaller lenses in the middle (O2 and O3) could be moved closer or further apart to adjust magnification from 5x to 15x. In practice it was found hard to keep them parallel in day-to-day service. (Author's collection)

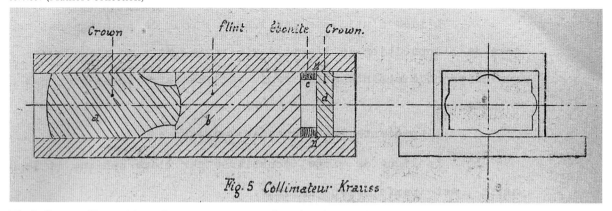

The Collimateur Krauss: *'a' is a glass crown or converging lens, 'b' a diverging flint lens, 'c' an ebonite spacer, and 'd' a glass reticule covered in a dark lacquer with pair of completely transparent cross hairs engraved in them. This* Collimateur Krauss *remained in use throughout the Great War, supplementing the standard* Collimateur de guerre. *(Author's collection)*

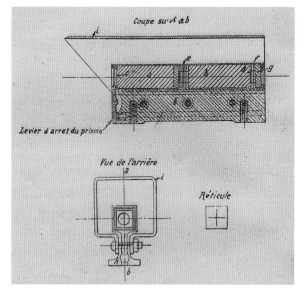

The Collimateur de guerre. *This used two blocks of flint 'b', the forward one having a convex edge on the front and a metal coated rear edge into which the cross hairs were inscribed. The two blocks and the glass reticule were separated by small slithers of tin (which had a hole cut into them). Note the outer protective box 'i' intended to protect the sight from rain. (Author's collection)*

like devices with three elements: a fore lens about 6cm thick with convex front and back edges, a flint cube in the middle, and a plain lens at the back covered in a non-transparent varnish with two clear lines cut into them. When taking aim, the cross-hairs would be lined up with the target's bow at the waterline. Light coming from the device was well aligned like that of a telescope without any magnification. Despite the fact that the image lacked clarity compared to either a telescope or an open sight, aiming via a collimator remained superior to using an open sight.

Rangefinders

Tests carried out aboard the battleship *Iéna* on 30 July 1903 using a Fleuriais stadimeter[4] showed that the time taken to calculate the range using set silhouette charts and a calculating circle took far too long when faced with modern fast-approaching targets such as torpedo boats. In that same year Ponthus et Tharrode produced a new model of stadimeter, followed by enhanced versions in 1908. This was a split-glass model and used an attached drum which turned as the two images of the mast were placed one on top of the other. Markings along an edge corresponded to the mast height, and the operator, when

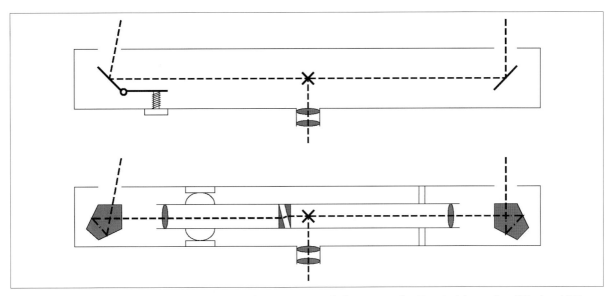

The upper drawing shows the mechanical principles of the Le Cyre rangefinder mentioned in Part 1 of the article in Warship 2010. *The rangefinder used a single tube housing both the outer mirrors and the inner prisms, and demonstrates the theoretical principles of a coincidence device. One outer mirror had a screw which could be adjusted to allow coincidence. While theoretically sound, comparison with the more complex Barr & Stroud mechanical model shown below shows that the Le Cyre model ignored certain realities. Ships are moving, flexing and vibrating platforms working in varying environments and temperatures. The lower rangefinder used pentagonal outer prisms that provided a fair degree of auto-correction to vibration and flexing. On top of this, the inner optics were housed in an inner tube which provided some protection against the elements and high/low temperatures. Finally, the outer prism no longer had any mechanical movement; instead the inner optics were manipulated mechanically to pick light from a different angle from the outer prism.* (Drawing by John Spencer, 2011)

placing the images on top of each other, would read the corresponding range on the drum directly. This was much easier to operate than previous types. There were generally two models: a large version for the spotter in the mast, and a smaller version for use in turrets.

Even this model still required successful identification of the target and knowledge of the target dimensions. However, the conclusion of the tests aboard *Iéna* was that the ideal would be to have a rangefinder which was independent of knowledge of target characteristics.

The French were already aware of Barr & Stroud's rangefinders quite early on, but it was not until 1907 that the French adopted the 9ft FQ2 model. In general, by 1910 recent capital ships were fitted with two such devices in open mounts on each side of the navigating platform. The *Danton* class and the cruiser *Waldeck Rousseau* had 4ft 6in rangefinders built into their turret roofs as designed. Barr & Stroud had succeeded where Le Cyre had failed because of three main features. Firstly the outer arms refracted light to the centre via a pair of pentagonal prisms (see figure). These would provide some correction of errors caused by flexing and vibration to the device. Secondly, while the outer prisms were held fairly solidly by a lightweight external tube, the inner optics were contained within an even more solid inner tube that was protected against various disruptive influences. Thirdly, neither of the outer prisms actually moved (unlike the plain Le Cyre mirrors); instead, part of the inner optics would – in effect – turn[5] to pick light from a different part of the prism in order to create the angle of coincidence.

All these monostatic devices the French had tested were coincidence rangefinders in which the split upper and lower images were matched to form a whole image and thus give the range. Despite having a rangefinder now independent of knowledge of target characteristics, it was still considered that the best rangefinders on the ship were the guns themselves.

Data Analysis: Calculators and Range Clocks

In July 1891, the *Revue Maritime* published an article written by a certain LV Goujon about a device that would enable a commander to change his ship's position in respect to another ship to a new desired position in the shortest possible time. The device was mainly intended for use during tactical manoeuvres in which changes in formation needed to be executed quickly. The device also had uses in gunnery; one could, for example, calculate the quickest route to move the firing ship to the best firing position in the shortest time. Equally, it could be used to a limited extent to track a target and give some rough distances and bearings. Even if the target disappeared, it would still be possible to provide some form of current and future estimates of where the target would be. The *quadrille* disc looked similar to the Royal Navy's Dumaresq – a device which also employed vector principles to calculate the apparent course and speed of one ship against another. However, it did not calculate target rate data; instead it used a methodology of trigonometry to determine ship position – and hence bearing and distance.

In 1894, Serpette's report discusses the arrangement inside a military mast. Four semi-circular discs, each covering one quadrant of the horizon, were fitted to the

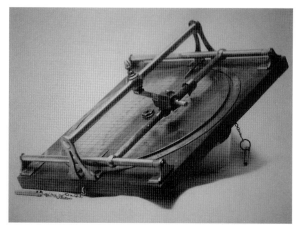

The French Plateau calculateur. *Unlike their Royal Navy counterpart the* Dumaresq, *early French devices were portable.* (Author's collection)

A top view of the Plateau calculateur. *This provided the range rate for the range clock shown in the next figure, and also speed across data (bearing rate) for gun sight setting.* (Author's collection)

mast. They were used to indicate clearly the target. Distance was measured by a Fleuriais rangefinder. Thereafter, it appears that there were many designs and proposals for 'roses' (bearing compasses) and drawing boards for use in help with the calculations. None appeared to be very practical according to the report, and details are sadly lacking. However, it goes on to mention the use of a geometrical calculator by LV Amet that may have been similar to the above. If the purpose was the calculation of the deflection, then the ship's yaw would have made the small changes in bearing impossible to measure and interpret, and the equipment was thus useless as a deflection calculator.

In 1903, LV Lafrogne proposed a range clock complete with two rate calculators. The first was similar to the Royal Navy's Dumaresq in terms of calculation; the second involved taking ranges over a period of time and calculating directly the rate from the difference. Between September 1905 and February 1906, tests were carried out with three new devices. The devices worked together and were intended to facilitate the calculations of the gunnery officer, which were recognised to be his hardest task.

The range clock was similar to Britain's Vickers clock,

France's first range clock, the Pendule Lafrogne. *Note the five keys below the dial. These early range clocks were simple devices that would add or subtract a constant range rate provided by the* Plateau calculateur *from the current range.* (Author's collection)

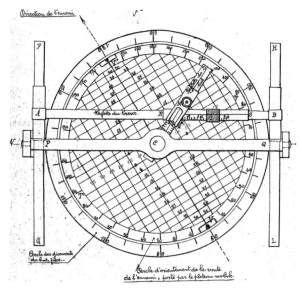

A drawing of the Plateau calculateur. (Author's collection)

in that it kept range by adding or subtracting distance at a set amount from a pre-set distance. However, unlike the Vickers device, which used a variable speed drive, the French device used five differentials. There were five keys, one for each differential and each corresponding to a speed of approach of 1m, 2m, 4m, 8m or 16m per second respectively. The operator would punch in the combination of keys to match the desired speed.[6] By the end of 1906, the *pendule Lafrogne* (range clock) and *plateau calculateur* (Dumaresq) had been made regulatory standard.

In 1909 a modified version of the *plateau calculateur* appeared, designed by LV Lecomte, followed by a version in 1911 giving the total range rate using a separate 'T' bar outside the circular disk – and thus a lot easier to read. This last version would be used in France's first fire control tables (these will be covered in a later article).

Methods of Firing Analysis and Fire Control

The French developed three types of centralised fire control; each may be considered an evolution of the previous method. In 1906 the *Commission d'études pratiques d'artillerie navale* (CEPAN) tested all three methods and, for obvious reasons, the last and most evolved method was proved to be the best method for centralised fire. However, as will be seen in the next section, older methods still had their uses under certain circumstances on the eve of the Great War.

1. Tir sur limite[7]

This was the oldest method developed, and was in use during the 1890s. It called for all guns to fire at will using gunnery data provide by the fire control officer. If the target was approaching, the guns would fire at a marginally

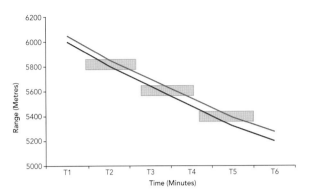

This graph typifies Tir sur limite *method. The two lines show the actual inner and outer ranges as the target approaches. All targets have a danger zone, an area that can be represented as a 2-dimensional target shadow on the surface of the sea. As the range closes, the trajectory of the shell flattens, and the corresponding danger zone therefore increases. From the graph, the reader will therefore observe the lines getting farther apart as the range decreases. The three boxes crossing the lines are distances the guns are firing at. Moving left to right (and therefore with time), it will be observed that the first shells of the beating zone fall short of the target, then, as the target approaches, its danger zone crosses the beating zone, until it passes through and the shells are observed to fall behind the target. Fire then shifts to the next beating zone. It will be observed that the target is left alone for brief periods between zones. (Graph by Stephen Dent and the author)*

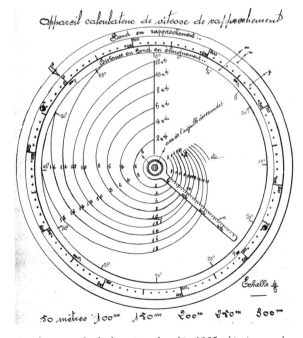

Another type of calculator introduced in 1905, this time used to calculate the range rate directly from two measured ranges and the time interval between them. (Author's collection)

shorter distance, a distance which the target should eventually sail through. Once the fall of shot had started to be observed falling beyond the target, a new shorter range that the target must sail through would be used, and so on.

The method was entirely dependent upon the observation of fall of shot. It had advantages over later methods when a fire solution was needed rapidly at ranges under 5000m. Effective gunnery ranges were raised from 2000m to 5000m and even eventually 9000m, indeed any distance where observation of the fall of shot was possible. It also did not require accurate input from rangefinders, and could be used effectively without plotting. The big disadvantage, which became apparent at longer ranges, was the short periods between switching gunnery ranges when the target would not be under fire. Indeed, given time a target could even manoeuvre away from the 'beaten zone'.

2. Méthode télémétrique (Rangefinder Method)[8]

This method sought to maintain all salvos on the target once the target had been found by constantly measuring (and often plotting) the range. Once found, gunnery range would be constantly adjusted using new range data to try and keep the 'beaten zone' on the target. To employ this method effectively, French gunnery manuals stated that the following conditions must apply:

– The fall of shot was observable.
– Accidental errors by rangefinders were negligible.
– Ranges were measured at short and regular intervals (at most every 30 seconds).

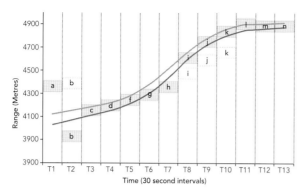

This is reproduced from the 1913 artillery course book (see sources) and is used to highlight the Méthode télémétrique. The letter 'a' shows that the first gun range (and measured range) is incorrect with shells falling over; a new estimate 'b' then falls short, while 'c' clearly lands within the danger zone of the target – at this point the gunnery officer has found the correction value to be applied to the rangefinder range. The officer continues to adjust gun range in line with changes observed in the rangefinder range. However, at 'g' the target begins to open the distance at a faster rate, and we observe at 'h' that the current correction value is no longer sufficient. Values 'i', 'j' and 'k' in dotted boxes show what would happen if the correction is insufficiently adjusted, while those in solid boxes show how more experienced officers quickly adapt to the greatly increased range rates. This method therefore makes it hard to appreciate the change in range rate rapidly. (Graph by Stephen Dent and the author)

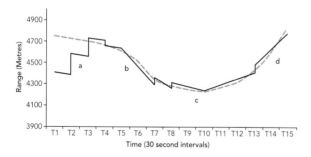

From the same course book: the Méthode chronotélémétrique. The broken curved line shows the actual target range over time. The solid jagged line shows the range on the range clock over time. The letter 'a' shows the range search period, with the ranges being underestimated at first but gradually increased until the range has been found. Despite the first range estimate being short, the range rate from the calculator is correct as the solid lines are – more or less – with the actual range. The letter 'b' shows the range coming down fast; range rate is calculated and adjusted on the clock accordingly. The letter 'c' shows the range rate reducing and then inverting while 'd' shows the range rate increasing once more as the range increases rapidly. The appearance of calculators and clocks made it possible to get a better estimate on the rate at which range was changing, and therefore allow the gunnery officer to keep his guns on target. The next step would be to automate these manual tasks. (Graph by Stephen Dent and the author)

(As will be seen later, this method was often employed under certain circumstances even if the first condition could not be fulfilled.)

Theoretically, the fire control officer would first try to find the range. This would give him a comparison between rangefinder distance and gun distance and that difference would serve as the correction (the corrector value) to be made as new distances were measured. If the target started to approach or move away at a different speed (range rate), the gunnery officer would start to observe that the fall of shot was falling either in front of or beyond the target and would modify the corrector value accordingly.

This method could also be used under conditions when observation of the fall of shot was not possible, such as when several ships were engaging one target, or when the main guns needed to fire under local control. Then the corrector value became the best guess of the gunnery officer concerned (a case of marksmanship).

In practice, however, the rangefinders themselves might not be supplying accurate and consistent data; rangefinders might also not be able to supply data on a regular basis. In both cases the guns would be thrown off target. It was therefore felt that the first method, *tir sur limite* (based entirely on the observation of fall of shot alone), was a far more deliberate and accurate method of directing fire even if there were periods when the target would not be under fire.

3. Méthode chronotélémétrique (Time and Range Method)

In the first method above, fire was directed mainly by fall of shot, and for short periods the target was not under fire. In the second method, fire was directed mainly by the range readings from a rangefinder, and fire would eventually move away from the target due to changes in the range rate and the unreliability of the rangefinder.

The *méthode chronotélémétrique* used both the observation of fall of shot and constant range measurements. However, the key difference lay in the constant use of the *vitesse de rapprochement* (later called *vitesse radiale*), or range rate. To this end, the fire control officer used both a *plateau calculateur* and the *pendule Lafrogne* (range clock), and – more importantly – range plotting by hand.

Initial ranges were again provided by a rangefinder; other observations such as bearing, ship speed, inclination and target ship speed were set on the *plateau calculateur*, which provided the range rate and bearing rate (the latter used as part of the deflection calculation).

The fire control officer estimated the initial gun range, and entered this into the range clock along with the range rate. The clock adjusted the range constantly over time according to the range rate. If the first shots fell short, the gun range was corrected accordingly until the range was found. Equally, the fire control officer might correct the range rate over time or both. This method made constant use of both the observation of fall of shot and ranges sent from the rangefinders, and did not just rely on one of them.

The method was felt to have the following advantages: if the observation of the fall of shot became impossible (several ships shooting at target), then the rangefinders continued to provide data; if the rangefinder failed, fire was still directed by the fall of shot; and if the target disappeared, the clock would continue to provide range data for a short period.

This method was used as the *cas général* (general case) by the French on the eve of the Great War, and also formed the basis for France's first fire control table which will be discussed in a future article.

Firing Methods Employed at Sea

The theoretical *cas général* was for centralised fire using the *méthode chronotélémétrique*. There were three phases:

1. Période préparatoire (preparation phase)
As soon as the target appeared, the fire control officer would identify the target, look up its characteristics in the *carnet de silhouettes* (recognition handbook), and advise all sections to allow them to fire independently in case they became isolated. He would also determine the initial gunnery elements (bearing, range, deflection) so that the guns could be made ready to fire when ordered to do so at the ideal tactical moment. These gunnery elements would be determined constantly by observations, using one of the data analysis methods above.

2. Période de recherche (observation phase)
As soon as the guns opened fire, the second phase of the gunnery duel commenced. Despite all the initial measurements and calculations, the French recognised that the ship's guns still remained the best rangefinder. Even at this time, it was accepted by the French that individual shots had little value in determining a target's range, and the preference was to fire salvos from at least three guns. Observation would be made first for direction and then for range, in part because it was easier to get the guns firing on the correct bearing first, but also because it was harder to determine if the shells were falling short, on-target or over unless the shells were falling in line.

In general, a gunnery officer was expected to have fire corrected for direction by the second salvo. To do this the following method was used: the angle between the centre of the target and the fall of shot was measured by a stadimeter. As the target mast height was often known, the angle between the base and the top of the mast was also measured. The first angle was divided by the second to give a number. The mast height was multiplied by that number and then divided by the range. The resulting number was multiplied by 1000 to give the deflection correction required (in *millèmes* or mils, 1/1000th of a Radian or approx 1/6400th of 360 degrees).

For distance, range would be increased or decreased by

The croiseur cuirassé Pothuau. Manned for trials on 19 September 1896, this small armoured cruiser of 5600 tonnes and her near-sisters were too influenced by the protagonists for a guerre de course. *Compared to their foreign counterparts they were too small and too weak. For a* guerre de course *they were too few; likewise they were too large to be used as scouts for the fleet. On 17 April 1906 Ponthuau became a gunnery cruiser for l'Ecole d'application du tir à la mer (EATM). Her role was not only to train new gunnery personnel but also to trial new gunnery devices. She retained this role until the start of the Great War when she once more served as a cruiser, resuming her gunnery role from 1919 until 1926. She was stricken on 12 June 1926, removed from the fleet list on 3 November 1927 and sold for scrap on 25 September 1929. (Courtesy of Robert Dumas)*

300m until the salvos fell just before or just beyond the target. The range would then be adjusted by 150m. During this time, it was important for an officer to have a good notion of time and how much time had passed between firing and when the shot was due to fall.

3. Période d'efficacité (hitting phase)
Once the target was found, the final phase could begin. The observer's role would be to observe the number of shots from each salvo falling in front and beyond the target, to its left and right, the object being to ensure that equal numbers of shell fell in each direction and to make adjustments accordingly.

In theory, for distance the gunnery officer would make the following adjustments based upon the following observations:

- If most shots were observed falling either in front of or beyond the target, range was modified by ⅙ of the beating zone size (area of dispersion).
- If three consecutive shells fell just short or over, range was modified by ⅓ of the beating zone size.
- If straddling was lost entirely, the range was corrected by one beating zone size.

During the battle, an officer able to determine the target's danger zone, and equally able to establish that the target danger zone was equal to or greater than the beaten zone, would (in theory) expect all shots to become hits once the range and deflection had been correctly adjusted.

Gunnery Officer training also provided for three *cas particuliers* (special cases) which may be summed up as follows:

1. Tir en autonomie (local fire control)
This method was to be used by the main armament once centralised fire control was lost or communications had been ruptured. If the turret had no range clock, the *méthode télémétrique* was employed. As the turret might be one of several firing independently, observation of the fall of shot would be impossible. It was generally accepted that the last known deflection was correct and would not be modified unless the pointer had reason to decide otherwise (target changing course, for example). As a rule of thumb, deflection would not be adjusted below 6 *millèmes*. Ranges would be taken from measured ranges observed by the turret rangefinder (in most cases a stadimeter) and then adjusted to give the gun range. The lack of effective observation would deny the use of the best rangefinder in the turret, meaning the gun itself, and would therefore be far less effective than centralised control. A gun losing contact with the *PC Artillerie* (Central) would probably be better off ceasing fire to avoid confusing the observer for weapons still in contact.

2. Tir contre les bâtiments lance-torpilles (fire against torpedo boats)
Torpedo boats presented a major problem. Their attacks could happen suddenly, involving multiple small units all with fast speeds of approach. A target first observed at medium range could quickly arrive at short range. It was generally accepted that there would not be time to identify and determine its characteristics, nor to determine which of several targets was to be the first to be engaged.

The objective in this situation was clearly to engage the targets rapidly, and to stop the attack in the minimum period of time. As mentioned earlier in the article, the anti-torpedo boat guns were split into four sections, each controlled by a central observation post. Given the constraints on obtaining firing data, the French therefore used the oldest of the firing methods outlined above, *tir sur limite*. Torpedo boats would have to sail through a beaten zone on their way to the target, with the zone being progressively shifted as the targets closed in.

3. Tir de nuit (night firing)
Night action presented many problems. It could happen suddenly, at close range, and the target would have unknown characteristics. Guns would be required to open fire or reply with the shortest possible delay, and it was expected that there simply would not be time for all the fine calculations to be determined and sent by the centralised fire control team.

To deal with this eventuality, each evening, when the commander had sent the command '*Suspendez le feu*' (cease fire), range and deflection data were pre-calibrated on all guns using informed guesses determined by the fire control officer. The maximum range would not exceed that capable of being illuminated by the searchlights, and was therefore never greater than 1500m. A second, closer range would also be pre-calibrated.

Upon engagement, the *chef de section* would get the gun on line for deflection, adjusting it six *millèmes* until the correct deflection was found. For range, engaging the target could be considered a crude form of the *tir sur limite*, except that this time only two ranges were to be used: the initial pre-set range, which would then switch to the second closer range as the target approached (or back again as the target moved away).

[It should be noted however, that night firing exercises include both the above and the *cas général*.]

4. Tactique de Section/Tactique de Division (firing by section of two, or division of three ships)
Firing in pairs would call for the first ship to fire at the target for 15 to 25 seconds in order to regulate its fire, followed by the second ship firing for 15 to 25 seconds. Once regulated, both ships would engage and maintain contact with the target using the *méthode chronotélémétrique* – albeit based mainly on rangefinder readings (so *méthode télémétrique* with calculator and range clock). Exercises of this nature were performed regularly, and in 1910 were carried out at distances between 5000m and 7600m. The two ships would generally be 400m to 500m apart, and the exercise would generally last around six minutes. It is difficult to determine the date when these methods appeared, but they were certainly in force and being practised by 1908.

How Well Did They Perform?

In 1910 the battleship *Démocratie*, shooting at a distance of 7000m, managed to place all eight of her 305mm shots

The French battleship Démocratie, *on which were the latterly famous French Admiral Georges Edmond Just Durand-Viel served as gunnery officer in 1911. Between 1931 and 1937, Durand-Viel served as head of the French Naval Staff (title:* Chef d'état major de la Marine*). (Courtesy of Robert Dumas)*

on the target; *Justice*, during the same practice, scored six out of eight. During a 'firing by section' exercise with *Démocratie* and *Vérité*, the number of shots fired and hits scored was impressive: eleven 305mm shots on the target in 1min 30secs.

On 18 February 1911 on board the *Justice*, the assessor wrote the following: 'Fire undertaken with two passes at distances varying between 8500m and 7000m. Out of 64 shots, fired under unfavourable light conditions, 31 shots hit the *Fulminant*, 10 of them hit the target on the armoured belt at the waterline.[9] The first pass to starboard was particularly impressive; during four minutes of firing, of the 28 19cm and six 30cm shells fired, 20 of the 19cm and three of the 30cm hit the target. The score of 60% attained in that one pass is a record for the French Navy at that distance during firing practice.'[10]

Between 10-13 June 1912, while firing in pairs, the salvos of '*Patrie* and *République*, engaged at 8000m, were well grouped', while those of '*Justice* and *Vérité* at a little more than 8000m caused so much damage to the targets that gunnery practice scheduled for cruisers has had to be postponed.' In a practice aboard the *Justice* on 4 April 2011, using just telephones with gunnery data sent from a secondary post, 30% hits were obtained at 7500m. Of the 164mm aboard the *Patrie* it was said that the ship: '... possessed artillery with very high rates of fire from which high hitting scores can be expected at 5500m to 6500m.

In 1911 Captain Darrieus wrote to express his regret '... that the *République* was not subjected to the same modification which had allowed an increase in the offensive power of the four ships of the *Justice* class ... particularly since at modern combat distances of 8000m to 9000m the 19cm has incontestably far superior ballistics to the 16cm'. During gunnery practice in 1913, out of 198 164mm shells fired by *Patrie*, 72 (36%) hit the target. However, out of the 80 194mm shells fired by *Vérité*, 49 hits were scored (61%). In the same exercise, *Justice* fired 74 194mm shells, scoring 34 hits (46%). The difference was put down to the greater dispersion of the smaller weapon as the range increased, which in the author's mind was probably due to greater time of flight leading to increased pointing errors.

Conclusion

Within the first months of the First World War, the French were shocked to discover the opening salvos between British and German ships at the Falklands were 3000m to 4000m beyond the range at which their similar weapons could hope to reply. This led to many on-board modifications taking place to increase gun elevation; maximum range of the 305mm gun increased from 12,500m to 13,860m, the 194mm from 12,000m to 14,100m, the 164mm from 10,800m to 11,300m. France's own first opening gunnery engagements of the Great War occurred at ranges between 10,000m and 13,000m. During the brief engagement with the Austrian cruiser *Zenta* and torpedo boat *Ulan*, fire was opened at 09.02 by the *Courbet* at 12,000m with a straddle being observed on the opening salvo. Thereafter the entire division opened fire on the cruiser, no doubt causing some confusion, but gunnery from all ships further down the line was brief.[11] The entire action was fought at ranges between 10,900m to 13,000m, which was at the maximum limits the guns could fire.

Pre-war practice was perhaps too focused on a 'decisive' battle range, the objective being to hit fast and hit often, rather than looking to engage the target at maximum range. Unlike the Royal Navy, the French had little experience of the damage caused by the various guns at different ranges, and it seems that it was not until 1910 or 1911 that the advantages of larger calibres at long ranges began to be appreciated.

French aiming and firing relied heavily on gunners in the turrets with their gun sights, using data transmitted from a central position. This might sound inferior to the Royal Navy's director control, but in practice it could be deadly accurate, with just under a third of the hits being scored on the waterline, the point of aim. France probably developed more gunnery officers with a high level of marksmanship, and this was demonstrated during the Dardanelles Campaign, when their individual gunlaying was often praised by British observers. Unfortunately, the greater battle ranges experienced between 1914 and 1918 had taken marksmanship to its limits, although for the First World War these skills and their associated technical aids proved generally adequate, with only marginal disadvantages against the more automated systems then coming into service. Nevertheless, given the limited angles of elevation of their guns, the French would have found themselves unable to reply at battle ranges experienced between the Germans and the British, even if in theory their fire control techniques could have allowed such an engagement.

Acknowledgements:
Fire control is a technical subject bound by the laws of physics. For the present article, there was the additional problem of there being no technical dictionary to translate French terms into English. In certain cases, some French methods and terms have no exact English equivalent and the author has provided literal translations with descriptions were applicable. I am therefore very grateful first and foremost to John Jordan and John Brooks who have painstakingly gone through and challenged minor details to ensure that the concept fits with what we were describing. I would also like to thank Dr Norman Friedman, Anthony Lovell, William Jurens and Nathan Okun who have provided much practical advice and experience over the years. Finally, I would like to thank my wife Sylvie for all her constant support and script reading.

Sources:
Publications:
Colonel L.Jacob: *Artillerie Navale* Tomes 1 & 2 (Paris 1909).
Amiral Henri Darrieus and Capitaine de vaisseau Jean Quéguiner: *Historique de la Marine 1815-1918* (St Malo 1997).
LV Collos: *Artillerie, Deuxième année d'études année scolaire 1912-1913* (Brest Naval School 1912).
Règlement sur le Service de L'artillerie à bord des bâtiments de la flotte – tome premier VI partie.
Ministère de la Marine: *Manual du Gradé du Canonnage* (Paris 1903).
Dayet: Ecole d'Application d'Artillerie Navale *Cours d'Appareils de visée et de conduite du tir* (1919).
M. Moss and I. Russell: *Range and Vision: the first hundred years of Barr & Stroud* (Edinburgh, 1988)
MP Peira: *Historique de la Conduite du Tir dans la Marine 1900-40* (Mémorial de l'Artillerie Française 1955).
La Revue Maritime 1891 and 1963
G Prévoteaux: *Les Cuirassés de 15000 tonnes* (Outreau 2006).

Archives:
Service Historique Marine – Château de Vincennes: 6DD1-357, 6DD1-366, 6DD1-368, 6DD1-369, 6DD1-401, 6DD1-551, 6DD1-571

Footnotes:
1. The observer would send only target data, the commander would send orders. To say order transmitters had returned a ship to an artillery platform requires some justification. In the days of sailing ships, a gunnery commander could direct all guns on both his own and other decks and see fairly well what was going on. Once guns became isolated in turrets, the officer had little idea at what and under which conditions they were shooting at. Order transmitters gave control back to one gunnery officer, making the ship a single artillery unit again.
2. Most inclinations were rounded to the nearest 10 degrees. The 1913 'Règlement sur le Service de L'artillerie à bord des batiments de la flotte – tome premier VIe partie' shows such exercises, and many more were still in place in 1913, the key difference being that ranges were two to three times greater, and the types of practice more diverse. The number of exercises to be performed, the types of exercises, the quantities of ammunition to be used, even the different types of target to be used, the regulations for measuring the results, etc. were very detailed and well developed, and unsurprisingly led to very well-trained and practised gunners.
3. As magnification increases, the amount of light entering the eye diminishes and thus the target appears dimmer.
4. See *Conduite du Tir* part 1, *Warship* 2010.
5. In practice the angle of light selected is decided by a variable gap between two narrow triangular prisms, one of which moves parallel to the axis of the inner tube.
6. According to Peira, later range clocks had two hands, one indicating actual range, the other gun range. Both hands would have the range reduced at the same range rate. The author has not, however, found additional proof for the range clock with two hands, and Peira's sketch looks nothing like the actual clock used.
7. Also called *Tir sur circonstance*. This method may also be considered as Barrage Fire.
8. This method should not be confused with 'Rangefinder Control' introduced by the Royal Navy in 1913. Although there is a similarity between the British and French methods, the British method would, in addition to the above, depend greatly on plotting ranges and reading off the mean range and range rate..
9. French gunners were trained to aim at the waterline.
10. *Fulminant* was an old coast guard battleship. The overall percentage of hits was 66%.
11. The *République* fired only seven 305mm shells, *Patrie* only two 305mm at 09.15, *Vérité* engaged only her 194mm and fired 16 rounds between 09.13 and 09.21.

MODERN AIR-INDEPENDENT PROPULSION EQUIPPED SUBMARINES

In the latest in a series of articles on modern warships, **Conrad Waters** reviews the latest developments in submarine propulsion technology

The last decade has seen a marked shift in the technological capability of submarines available to the vast majority of navies operating underwater forces. The deployment of increasing numbers of a new breed of diesel-electric patrol submarine equipped with air-independent propulsion (AIP) has opened up the prospect of fielding vessels with a submerged endurance – and thus a reduced vulnerability to detection – that was previously open only to the handful of navies that could afford the massive investment required to operate nuclear-powered boats. This short overview aims to provide a historical background to the widespread introduction of AIP and to describe the main technologies and submarines currently in service. It also attempts to describe some of the strengths and weaknesses of the new capability.

Historical Background

The essential prerequisite of successful underwater warfare has always been based around the concept of stealth. During the early years of submarine operations – effec-

Germany's Type 212A AIP-equipped submarine U-34. The widespread introduction of non-nuclear AIP-equipped boats into operational service during recent years has significantly increased the capability of many mid-sized navies. (German Navy)

tively until the closing years of the Second World War – submarines were little more than submersible torpedo boats that submerged to carry out their attacks or to make good their escape after an engagement.[1] The propulsion system required to carry out this mission became standardised around direct-drive diesel propulsion for sustained surface running and battery-powered electric motors that provided a much more limited underwater endurance. The air-breathing diesels were also used to recharge the batteries whilst on the surface. A number of navies made improvements to this basic system. Most notably, the US Navy developed diesel-electric drive under which all propulsion was provided by the boat's electric motors, with diesel generators being used either to drive the motors or charge the batteries. However, submarines still needed to surface frequently so their diesels could be run.

Improvements in anti-submarine countermeasures during the Second World War radically changed previous operating concepts. The increased potency of aircraft in the anti-submarine role significantly limited the scope for surface transits. Similarly, the advent of effective search radar meant that surface attacks – a standard tactic deployed by the German U-Boat arm – became little short of suicidal. The most effective response was initially the introduction of enhancements allowing better use of existing propulsion systems. These included the German adoption of the Dutch-designed 'snorkel' induction mast to supply air for diesel operation at periscope depth, a dramatic increase in battery capacity for speedier, prolonged underwater operation and better submarine hydrodynamics. These changes came together in the German Type XXI and XXIII 'electro-boats' that started to enter service from mid 1944.[2] Whilst too late to have much impact on wartime operations, these boats had a huge influence on both Western and Soviet submarines in the immediate post-war era.

The introduction of the Type XXI and Type XXIII designs took place against a backdrop of German efforts to produce an alternative to the established diesel/electric battery combination. The initial emphasis was on increasing underwater speed rather than reducing the inherent vulnerability in the diesel powered submarine's frequent need for atmospheric oxygen. The AIP technology selected for investment was based on the work of the renowned engineer Dr. Hellmuth Walter.[3] He envisaged a propulsion plant based on the use of concentrated hydrogen peroxide, also known as high-test peroxide or HTP. In simple terms, Walter's system produced hot oxygen and steam by running HTP over a catalyst. Diesel fuel was then injected to combust with the oxygen, producing the energy needed to drive a high speed turbine. Trials of a prototype HTP plant were conducted in the small experimental submarine *V80* during 1940. These achieved sustained underwater speeds in excess of 25 knots compared with the c.8 knot maximum of the contemporary Type VII.

Although an extensive programme of full-scale boats was authorised, operational deployment of the new technology proved beyond the capabilities of Germany's increasingly war-ravaged industrial base. However, several of the Allied powers attempted to bring the Walter turbine to maturity after the conflict. The British Royal Navy was, perhaps, the most persistent. It refurbished the damaged Type XVIIB U-Boat *U-1407* as the experimental *Meteorite* and commissioned two new-build *Explorer* class submarines as fast underwater targets during the 1950s. Ultimately, however, the inherent instability of hydrogen peroxide militated against its safe and reliable use in submarine propulsion.[4] Additionally, a more attractive option became available when the technical feasibility of nuclear-powered propulsion was proved during the initial trials of the US Navy's *Nautilus* (SSN-571) during 1955. The leading navies quickly settled on this alternative to provide sustained, high speed underwater endurance in their submarines.

Whilst Germany's wartime efforts in the area of AIP were largely focused on Dr. Walter's system, the potential of closed cycle diesel (CCD) propulsion also attracted attention. Both Germany and the Soviet Union carried out experimental work on closed cycle diesels. The latter's efforts culminated in the commissioning of as many as thirty Project 615 'Quebec' class coastal submarines during the 1950s. The Project 615 boats used liquid oxygen in combination with recycled exhaust gases to run a CCD that powered a centre-line shaft during submerged operation, this being supplemented by two conventionally-powered outer shafts for surface running. Unfortunately, the propulsion system proved as troublesome as HTP plants. Difficulties in storing liquid oxygen

A German Type VII U-Boat pictured during the Second World War. Despite efforts to develop AIP technology, it is arguable that most submarines were little more than submersible torpedo boats during this period. (Author's collection)

The Soviet Union's thirty Project 615 'Quebec' class coastal submarines, which used closed-cycle diesel propulsion, remain the most numerous class of AIP-equipped boat to enter service to date. The unreliable and potentially dangerous nature of their propulsion plant – they were nicknamed 'cigarette lighters' by their crews – meant they were a dead-end in Soviet submarine development. (Courtesy of John Jordan)

for long periods limited operational endurance, whilst explosions and fires were also relatively common. The design ultimately became a dead-end in Soviet submarine development as attention increasingly turned to nuclear boats. Nevertheless, CCD has remained a viable AIP technology, and trials of improved prototype systems were carried out with apparent success in both the Netherlands and Germany during the 1990s. However, competing AIP technologies have gained more traction in securing the orders needed to secure ongoing investment. As such, it seems unlikely that CCD propulsion will be employed operationally in the foreseeable future.

The adoption of nuclear power by the leading navies significantly slowed examination of alternative AIP systems. The bulk of their investment in submarines was inevitably directed to maturing atomic propulsion. Meanwhile, the second-tier fleets that remained reliant on conventional propulsion systems were less able to fund the substantial research and development budgets required to make AIP a reality. As such, the initial focus was on squeezing the most out of existing diesel-electric propulsion technology, as well as adapting broader design lessons from the late-war German boats. This process was to see the construction of such classic post-war designs as the British *Porpoise* and *Oberon* classes, France's *Daphné* type and the German IKL bureau's Type 209 extended export series. Whilst producing notable improvements in underwater performance, the need for these boats to surface periodically – at least to periscope depth – to charge their batteries remained a key operational constraint. Eventually, the increased proficiency of anti-submarine countermeasures targeted towards surfaced boats resulted in new AIP systems being developed. Driven largely by the main European manufacturers of diesel-electric submarines, these new systems have adopted different approaches. However, all are based on supplementing rather than replacing diesel-electric propulsion as a boat's primary power source. To date, three main AIP technologies have entered operational service:

Stirling AIP System: This system has been developed by Kockums of Sweden, now part of Germany's Thyssen

Krupp Marine Systems. Based on Stirling-cycle engine technology, it has also been licensed for production in Japan.

MESMA AIP System: Manufactured and marketed by an industrial group headed by France's DCNS, MESMA stands for *Module d'Énergie Sous-Marin Autonome* or 'Autonomous Submarine Energy Module'. It is essentially a closed-cycle steam turbine derived from DCNS' experience of France's nuclear-powered submarines.

Fuel Cell AIP System: Currently the most popular technology, operational systems are based on Siemens' Polymer Electrolyte Membrane (PEM) fuel cells which have been developed for submarine use in conjunction with fellow German company HDW. Interestingly, HDW is effectively the domestic submarine arm of Germany's ThyssenKrupp Marine Systems and therefore a sister company to Kockums.

These competing technologies are described in more detail below.

Stirling AIP System

Description and Development:
The Stirling engine-based AIP system is arguably the most mature AIP technology now in service. Its current use in submarine propulsion originates from long-standing research by Kockums of Sweden, which culminated in construction of a prototype system during the early 1980s. This progressed to the installation of two Mk1 V4-275R Stirling engines in the Type A14 submarine *Näcken* during 1987-88 through insertion of an 8-metre long hull plug. As with all other existing AIP systems, the Stirling installation is designed to enhance submerged endurance by providing a low-powered complement to the main diesel-electric propulsion system.

Although their use in submarines is relatively recent, Stirling engines have a relatively long history. First conceived in the early nineteenth century, their operation is based on the cyclic expansion and compression of an enclosed quantity of working fluid by means of the transfer of heat from an outside source. Typically, the heated gas expands to drive a piston and is then drawn into a cooling chamber for subsequent compression, with the mechanical movement of the piston being converted into electricity.[5] In the Kockums Stirling system, the heat source is provided by burning a mixture of diesel fuel and liquid oxygen in a pressurised combustion chamber, whilst helium provides the working fluid. The combustion pressure is designed to be greater than the pressure of the surrounding seawater down to depths of around 300m, thereby allowing exhaust products to be discharged overboard. The electrical energy generated by the Stirling process is primarily used to power the submarine's main motor, although it can also be used to charge the batteries of the main diesel-electric propulsion system. A simplified schematic of the overall process is shown in Figure 1.

Each Stirling engine provides up to 75 kW of electricity. Installations to date have typically comprised two units for a total of 150 kW overall. This compares with an electrical output of at least 1.5MW from a modern diesel-electric submarine propulsion plant. The Stirling plant therefore has a negligible impact on potential speed; what it does have, however, is a significant benefit in terms of submerged endurance. Published information suggests

1. Kockums Stirling AIP System

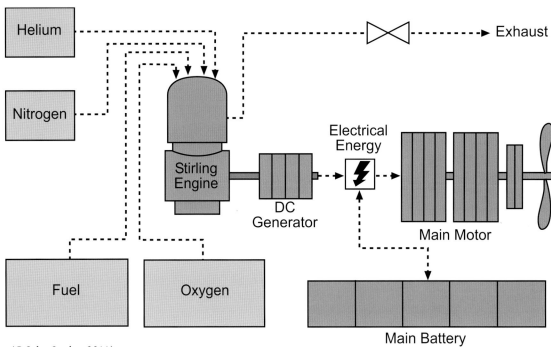

(© John Jordan 2011)

MODERN AIR-INDEPENDENT PROPULSION EQUIPPED SUBMARINES

A cutaway drawing of a Swedish A-19 class submarine. Two Stirling AIP units are located in the compartment aft of the conning tower and main control room. Liquid oxygen is stored on the deck below. (Courtesy of Kockums AB)

that underwater deployments of at least fourteen days at 5 knots are achievable. Overall endurance is effectively determined by the amount of stored liquid oxygen, which is located in cryogenic tanks on a deck below the engines. The Stirling AIP system is also relatively stealthy, being described by Kockums as practically vibration-free, silent and wake-less. Its acoustic signature is further improved through use of resiliently mounted sound-proof modules for each engine. Careful control of exhaust products also ensures that a low infra-red signature is maintained.

Given that Stirling AIP is essentially a modular, add-on system it is as well suited to refitting into existing boats as it is for incorporation into new designs. This is aided by the physical characteristics of the engines, which are relatively small and light-weight in nature. Based on recent conversions, the addition of the relevant AIP module typically adds around 400 tonnes and 12m length to an existing submarine's hull. As maintenance requirements are relatively low, no additions to normal crew size are required. However, the system does have some limitations compared with alternative, fuel-cell based AIP technologies. These include comparatively lower levels of inherent efficiency: liquid oxygen consumption is higher, there is an increased – albeit still modest – acoustic signature, and there are limitations on extreme diving depth resulting from the need to discharge exhaust products. The electrical output available from the current engines is also quite limited, restricting underwater performance on AIP alone. To some extent, these design trade-offs reflect operational requirements in the Baltic, where water depths are shallow and limited transit distances place less of a premium on sustained underwater speed.

Operational Use:
The Kockums Stirling AIP system has been quite successful in attracting orders, currently being in operational service across four classes of submarine in three navies. It has also been specified for the new Swedish A-26 class submarine, which is currently undergoing detailed design development.

Following the success of initial trials in *Näcken*, Stirling AIP was specified for incorporation in the three Swedish A-19 *Gotland* class submarines ordered in March 1990 and delivered to Sweden's FMV – the Defence Materials Administration – between 1996 and 1997. They have been described as the world's first operational submarine class to incorporate an AIP system, although this arguably ignores the claims of Russia's 'Quebecs'. Displacing 1,600 tonnes submerged, the design incorporates two improved Mk2 V4-275R Stirling engines, which supplement a main diesel-electric plant comprising two MTU diesels and a Jeumont Schneider motor. The A-19 class has been very successful in service, undoubtedly facilitating sales of

A close-up view of a Stirling AIP engine unit. The compact nature of the system is readily apparent.
(Courtesy of Kockums AB)

The Republic of Singapore Navy's A-17 class submarine Archer *pictured shortly before re-launch in June 2009. Formerly the Swedish Navy's Hälsingland, she has been refitted with two Stirling engines in a demonstration of the system's flexibility.* (Courtesy of Kockums AB)

Stirling AIP systems. A notable development was the US Navy's lease of *Gotland* herself – complete with crew – for anti-submarine training and trials exercises from June 2005. It has been reported that *Gotland* proved to be extremely difficult to detect during this programme, increasing the US Navy's awareness of the dangers posed by the new generation of patrol submarines. Initially scheduled to last for twelve months, the submarine's deployment to American waters was subsequently extended for a further year.

The three A-19 class boats have been joined in Swedish service by two modernised A-17 *Södermanland* submarines. Originally delivered in the late 1980s as part of the *Västergötland* class, they were equipped with an AIP module during mid-life refits that began in late 2000. Overall capabilities are now similar to the A-19 class, although press reports suggest that a Mk 3 variant of the Stirling engine has been used. The two earlier *Västergötland* class boats have been sold to Singapore under the 'Northern Lights' project announced in 2005. This has

The Japan Maritime Self Defence Force's Soryu *class is also fitted with Stirling AIP engines, built locally under licence by Kawasaki Heavy Industries. These boats are relatively large, and four engines are fitted to provide auxiliary air-independent propulsion.* (JMSDF)

included a similar AIP upgrade to that carried out on the remaining Swedish pair, with the renamed *Archer* arriving in Singapore in August 2011. The relatively shallow waters around Singapore provide quite a similar operating environment to that found in the Baltic, making Stirling AIP a logical choice for a submarine flotilla which is already comprised of older Swedish-built boats.

Kockums' other export customer has also been in Asia, where Japan's Kawasaki Heavy Industries has been licensed to produce Stirling engines for the Japan Maritime Self Defence Force (JMSDF). Following successful installation of a 10-metre long AIP module in the *Harushio* class diesel-electric submarine *Asashio* in 2001, Stirling AIP was specified for the new *Soryu* class which have been entering service at a rate of one per year since March 2009. With a submerged displacement of more than 4,000 tonnes in submerged condition, the Japanese patrol submarines are considerably larger than their Swedish counterparts. This is probably the main reason behind the incorporation of four V4-275R Stirling engines in the design compared with the normal pair in Swedish boats. The precise configuration of the new Swedish A-26 class has yet to be revealed, although it is possible that a further development of the Stirling engine will be incorporated. For example, an increase in combustion pressure would allow effective AIP operation at greater depth than currently allowed.

MESMA AIP System

Description and Development:

The MESMA AIP system has been developed by a consortium headed by DCNS and which includes Air Liquide, Thermodyn, Techniatome and Bertin. Its sole operational application to date has been in Pakistan's 'Agosta 90B' class submarine *Hamza*. Although factory acceptance tests of the system were completed in France as long ago as 2002, it was not until 26 September 2008 that this boat was commissioned into Pakistan Navy service.[6] In a similar fashion to Stirling AIP, MESMA is a supplemental propulsion system installed in a self-contained hull plug that incorporates all the requisite working elements. As such, it can be incorporated into existing submarines without the need to modify the rest of the vessel. A typical installation is just over 8.5m long and displaces around 200 tonnes.

The French MESMA is derived from the country's experience with closed-cycle steam generation in the field of nuclear-propulsion. The principal difference is that a non-nuclear steam generation plant replaces atomic power. In a MESMA system, steam is generated from the combustion of fuel and liquid oxygen.[7] The steam produced powers a turbine connected to an alternator that supplies electricity to the submarine and its electric motors. This can be also be used to recharge the main

Pakistan's 'Agosta 90B' class AIP- equipped submarine Hamza *pictured during launch ceremonies at Karachi Shipyard & Engineering Works in August 2006. She is currently the only submarine in service to be fitted with the DCNS MESMA AIP system.* (DCNS)

2. DCNS MESMA AIP System

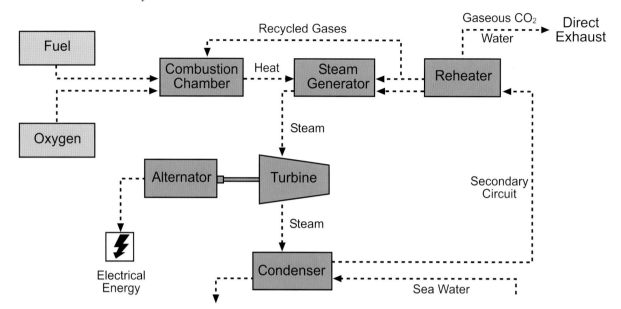

A DCNS MESMA AIP plug seen being prepared for transportation to Pakistan for refit into an existing submarine. The self-contained unit is around 8.5m long and displaces around 200 tonnes. (DCNS)

batteries. Steam is subsequently condensed and re-circulated through the system, with waste carbon dioxide discharged through the hull. As for Stirling AIP, the system is pressurised to allow waste products to be discharged without the noise of an exhaust compressor but MESMA can apparently operate effectively at greater depths – in excess of 350m is claimed. The overall MESMA process is illustrated in Figure 2.

MESMA shares many positive characteristics with Stirling AIP. In addition to the self-contained, modular nature of the system, it is based on established technology, has low ship-board maintenance requirements and uses affordable and readily available fuels. It also provides comparable levels of acoustic discretion, which are assisted by installation in a frame that is insulated from the hull by elastic suspension. Moreover, whilst only a fraction of that available from a nuclear plant, power output is considerably greater than a single Stirling engine at some 200kW. Dependent on alternative plant configurations, this presumably allows greater underwater speed on AIP alone. Against this, published analysis suggests that MESMA has an inherent efficiency that is lower than its competitors, effectively suggesting that greater quantities of liquid oxygen need to be stored for a given endurance. However, DCNS states that underwater operation in excess of three weeks is possible on MESMA propulsion, whilst independent reports suggest that Stirling and MESMA plants have broadly similar submerged capabilities. DCNS also claims that MESMA has the lowest life-cycle cost of any existing AIP system.

Operational Use:
In addition to installing MESMA AIP in *Hamza* during the course of construction, the Pakistan Navy has also ordered additional modules for the two earlier 'Agosta 90B' class boats currently in service with its submarine flotilla. These will be fitted during the course of scheduled

refits. DCNS reported in June 2011 that the second module had completed factory testing at its facility at Indret near Nantes and would soon be ready for dispatch to Pakistan. Trials had also commenced on the third and final module by this time. DCNS is also continuing to market MESMA for a variant of its popular diesel-electric 'Scorpène' type patrol submarine. However, in spite of rumours that India might be interested in the system for at least some of the six boats that are currently under construction at Mazagon Dock in Mumbai, no further orders have been confirmed to date. With Spain's Navantia, DCNS' previous partner in the 'Scorpène' programme, proving cautious, despite having selected fuel cell technology for its new S-80 class submarines and other potential customers, there has to be some uncertainty over MESMA's long-term potential as an AIP technology.

PEM Fuel Cell AIP System

Description and Development:
Although the first widespread use of fuel cells was driven by the US space programme, the successful application of this technology to submarine propulsion has been based on longstanding research work by German companies. This culminated in the installation and subsequent trials of a prototype alkaline-based fuel cell plant in the German Type 205 submarine *U-1* during the late 1980s, the first time fuel cells had been used in a submarine. The promise shown by the system was sufficient to encourage further development of an operational plant based on Siemens' polymer electrolyte membrane technology that was incorporated in the German Navy's New Type 212A design.[8] An initial batch of four of these boats, which were designed by HDW and Thyssen Nordseewerke in conjunction with IKL, was authorised in July 1994. The first of these, *U-31*, was commissioned in October 2005.

The basic principle behind fuel cells is the conversion of chemical energy produced by reactants – a fuel and an oxidant – into electricity. Numerous types of fuel cell have been developed but all essentially comprise three elements: an anode, a cathode and an electrolyte that

3. Siemens PEM Fule Cell: Functional Principle

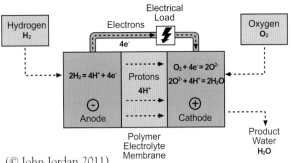

(© John Jordan 2011)

allows charges to move between the two sides of the fuel cell. The Siemens PEM fuel cell uses a proton-conducting polymer electrolyte membrane to separate the anode and cathode. Hydrogen is channelled into the anodic side of the membrane, where it is decomposed into its electrons and protons with the assistance of a platinum catalyst. The polymer electrolyte membrane allows the protons to pass directly to the cathode but blocks the passage of electrons and heavier gases. The electrons have to travel to the cathode via an external circuit, thereby creating an electrical load or current. The electrons combine with oxygen – and the protons – on the cathode catalyst to produce water. This overall conversion process – also known as 'cold combustion' – is shown in Figure 3.

The amount of electrical power produced by an individual fuel cell is relatively modest. As such, individual cells are stacked together in fuel cell modules. These also contain peripheral equipment such as valves and connectors to hydrogen, oxygen and cooling water supplies.

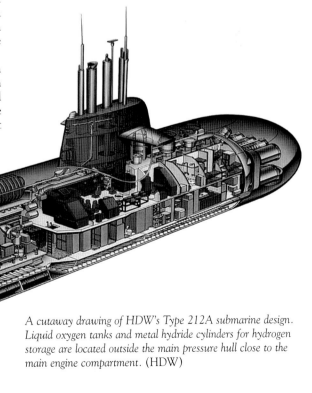

A cutaway drawing of HDW's Type 212A submarine design. Liquid oxygen tanks and metal hydride cylinders for hydrogen storage are located outside the main pressure hull close to the main engine compartment. (HDW)

A Siemens BZM 120 PEM fuel cell module. It produces 120kW of electricity from a stack of 320 individual fuel cells. Two modules are installed in each Type 214 and Type 209 (PN) submarine. (Siemens)

Modules are encapsulated in a pressurised nitrogen-filled container to help early identification and prevention of potential safety issues such as chemical leakage, which result in automatic shutdown. To date Siemens has developed two types of PEM fuel cell module: the BZM 34 and the BZM 120. The former, used in the Type 212A submarine, has a rated power of 34kW from 72 individual cells and weighs 650kg. Each submarine is equipped with nine BZM 34 modules – one of which is a spare that engages automatically in the event of a fault elsewhere – which are connected directly to the boat's main electrical power system. The cost-optimised BZM 120 module – weighing 900kg and with a volume c.40% greater than that of the BZM 34 – produces 120kW of electricity from 320 more compact cells. It has largely been developed for export designs. A typical installation comprises two modules linked to the electrical system by means of a currency converter. This facilitates retrofit into existing boats by allowing adaptation of the fuel cell plant to different battery voltages. In both variants, fuel cells supplement a conventional diesel-electric propulsion system.

The overall configuration of a HDW/Siemens PEM fuel cell-equipped submarine is shown in Figure 4. In common with other AIP designs, oxygen is carried as a liquid in shock-resistant oxygen tanks. The potentially more dangerous hydrogen is stored in metal hydride cylinders, where it is bonded in the lattice structure of the host metal. Waste water generated from the conversion process is fed into water tanks, thereby obviating the need for waste product discharges that are a feature of the two other operational AIP systems. Other advantages include the superior acoustic characteristics of the virtually noiseless cold combustion process and the relatively low temperature (c.80° C) nature of PEM fuel cell operation, minimising infra red signature. PEM fuel cells are also inherently more efficient than competing AIP systems, allowing greater underwater endurance for a given quantity of stored oxygen. Published information suggests that a Type 214 PEM fuel cell AIP-equipped submarine could remain submerged for around one month at very low speeds. Maximum underwater speed on AIP alone is reported as c.8 knots.

4. HDW/Siemens PEM Fuel Cell System

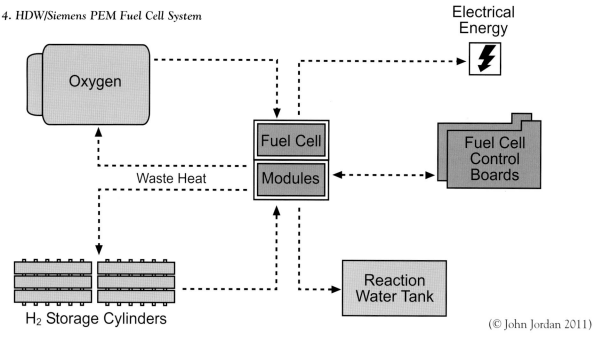

(© John Jordan 2011)

MODERN AIR-INDEPENDENT PROPULSION EQUIPPED SUBMARINES

Operational Use:
As previously mentioned, the Siemens PEM fuel-cell system first saw operational service in the German Type 212A submarines that entered service from October 2005. The second of these, *U-32*, quickly demonstrated the potential of the new technology by completing a submerged transit from the German Bight to the Bay of Cadiz between 11 and 25 April 2006 on AIP propulsion alone. The initial four boats will be supplemented by a further two enhanced units ordered from HDW in September 2006 for delivery by 2013. In addition, Italy's Fincantieri has completed the local assembly of two units of the class that were ordered in 1997; it is also building an additional pair. The class has proved itself well-capable of extended deployment, most notably demonstrated through the despatch of Italy's *Salvatore Todaro* and *Scirè* across the Atlantic for exercises with the US Navy during 2008 and 2009. *Todaro*'s mission was the first time since the Second World War that an Italian submarine had crossed the Atlantic, allowing the US Navy to build on the experience of modern AIP-equipped submarines gained through *Gotland*'s lease.

An image of the Italian Navy's Type 212A submarine Salvatore Todaro *during a deployment to the United States. Her visit during the summer and autumn of 2008 represented the first time since the Second World War that an Italian submarine had operated in American waters. Lengthy deployments such as these have served to demonstrate the enhanced capabilities of AIP-equipped boats to allied navies.* (US Navy)

Portugal's AIP-equipped Type 209(PN) submarine Tridente. *Most commentators regard her as a slightly modified Type 214 boat.* (HDW)

PEM fuel cells – in their BZM 120 guise – are also incorporated in HDW's Type 214 submarine, which has brought significant export success for Thyssen Krupp Marine Systems. With a submerged displacement of more than 1,800 tonnes, the class is comparable in size to the Type 212A design but has a longer, narrower hull and is said to be influenced by the design principles of the earlier Type 209 boats. Type 214 submarines are already in service with the Hellenic and South Korean navies and have also been specified by Turkey under a contract finalised during 2011. The initial Greek boat, *Papanikolis*, was built in Germany by HDW in Kiel but all the other units have been assembled locally, albeit with significant reliance on imported components. In addition, Portugal's Type 209 (PN) AIP-equipped boats are widely considered to be slightly modified Type 214 variants, whilst it is rumoured that Israel's additional batch of Type 800 *Dolphin* class submarines will also feature fuel cell-based AIP propulsion.

To date, only one retrofit of PEM AIP has been attempted in an existing design, with Greece specifying the technology for three of its existing Type 209/1200

The Type 214 submarine Papanikolis, *which was delivered to the Hellenic Navy at the end of 2010 following a lengthy contractual dispute. The class combines the design philosophy behind the earlier successful Type 209 boat with fuel cell AIP equipment.* (Hellenic Navy)

Poseidon class boats as part of the 'Neptune II' modernisation programme agreed in 2002. The project – carried out by the then ThyssenKrupp Marine Systems' subsidiary Hellenic Shipyards with assistance from HDW – involved the insertion of a 6.5-metre hull plug to incorporate the new auxiliary AIP system. Work on the first submarine, *Okeanos*, reportedly commenced in December 2004 for completion by the end of 2007. In the event re-launch was delayed until February 2009. By this time, both the 'Neptune II' and Type 214 'Archimedes' projects had become embroiled in disputes that were to extend to delayed payments, poor performance and allegations of corruption that may well have owed much to the Greek sovereign debt crisis. One consequence was the termination of the 'Neptune II' programme at just one boat. As such, the suitability of PEM AIP for refit into existing submarines has yet to be conclusively demonstrated.

Other Current Developments

Although the fuel cell AIP system developed by HDW and Siemens is currently the only fuel cell based plant currently in operational service, competing systems are already under development. In Europe, Spain's Navantia has allied with local group Abengoa's Hynergreen subsidiary and the United States' UTC Power to manufacture an AIP plant for the new S-80A submarine. Four of these units are currently under construction for the *Armada Española* and launch of the first is scheduled before mid 2012. The new system incorporates so-called reformer technology under which hydrogen is produced on-board from stored ethanol. This is then combined with oxygen in UTC-developed open anode proton exchange membrane cells to generate electricity in broadly similar fashion to the Siemens' system.[9] The S-80A AIP plant has a designed output of 300kW and provides an underwater endurance in excess of fifteen days at 4 knots. In a similar fashion to existing AIP technology, it is therefore intended as a supplement to the principal diesel-electric propulsion, which provides surface and high-speed underwater capabilities. The entire AIP plant is accommodated in a c.8-metre section located in the centre of the submarine.

Elsewhere, Russia's new Project 677 'Lada' class submarines are reportedly capable of being equipped with a supplementary fuel cell-based AIP system, although it seems that this option was not selected for the prototype unit *Saint Petersburg*. In any event, this boat underwent an unusually lengthy series of sea trials prior to commissioning in mid-2010 and there have been suggestions that the new design may have suffered from teething troubles that are not yet entirely resolved. In Asia, the Chinese People's Liberation Army Navy's Type 039A/41 'Yuan' class has also been widely reported to be equipped with AIP technology, possibly a variant of the Stirling AIP system. If these reports are correct, the AIP system will again complement the main diesel-electric plant that constitutes the primary source of propulsion. Although no official details on the class have yet been released, the recent sale of the design to Pakistan may yield more information in due course.

TABLE 1: PRINCIPAL OPERATORS OF AIP EQUIPPED SUBMARINES: LATE 2011

	Stirling AIP			MESMA AIP	PEM Fuel Cell AIP	
	A-17 Type	A-19 Type	*Soryu* Class	Agosta 90B	Type 212A	Type 214
Germany	–	–	–	–	4 (2)[1]	–
Greece	–	–	–	–	–	1 (3)[2]
Italy	–	–	–	–	2 (2)	–
Japan	–	–	3 (4)[3]	–	–	–
Pakistan	–	–	–	1 (2)	–	–
Portugal	–	–	–	–	–	2[4]
Singapore	1 (1)	–	–	–	–	–
South Korea	–	–	–	–	–	3 (6)
Sweden	2	3	–	–	–	–
Turkey	–	–	–	–	–	– (6)
Totals[5]	3 (1)	3	3 (4)	1 (2)	6 (4)	6 (15)

Notes:
[1] Figures in brackets relate to submarines under construction or conversion to AIP, or where construction or conversion is planned.
[2] Greece has also converted the Type 209/1200 submarine *Okeanos* to PEM fuel cell AIP. Orders for two further Type 214 boats have been cancelled for non-payment.
[3] Japan has also converted the *Harushio* class training submarine *Asashio* to Stirling AIP.
[4] Whilst the Portuguese submarines are officially categorised as an AIP version of the Type 209, many commentators consider them as variants of the Type 214 design.
[5] In addition to the countries listed here, Spain has four S-80A class submarines under construction equipped with UTC Power fuel cells, whilst Israel's second batch of Type 800 *Dolphin* class submarines is likely to feature Siemens PEM technology. Additionally, the Chinese Type 039A/41 'Yuan' class is also widely reported as featuring AIP propulsion.

Conclusion

The potential for extended underwater operation provided by the AIP systems that have already been developed has inevitably made it a popular submarine technology. As shown in Table 1, more than twenty AIP-equipped submarines are in service at the time of writing. New construction and refits currently underway or planned will take this to well over fifty within the next decade. Whilst all the different technologies described in this chapter have their proponents, it also seems that PEM fuel cell based-AIP systems have gained most acceptance. This presumably reflects their favourable

TABLE 2: MODERN AIR-INDEPENDENT PROPULSION EQUIPPED SUBMARINES: SPECIMEN DATA

	A-19 Gotland	*Soryu*	Agosta 90B
Design Origin:	Sweden	Japan	France
Operators:	Sweden	Japan	Pakistan
Number:	3	3 (4)	1 (2)
FoC Commission:	1996	2009	2008
Displacement:			
1. Surfaced	1,500 tonnes	2,950 tonnes	1,700 tonnes
2. Submerged	1,600 tonnes	4,200 tonnes	2,100 tonnes
Dimensions:	60.0m x 6.2m x 5.6m	84.0m x 9.1m x 8.4m	76.2m x 6.8m x 5.5m
Complement:	25	65	41
Main Propulsion:	Diesel-electric: 2 x MTU 396 series diesels 2.0MW total output 1 x Jeumont Schneider motor 1.3MW 20/10 knots dived/surfaced	Diesel-electric: 2 x Kawasaki 12V 25/25SB diesels >6 MW total output 1 x electric motor 5.9MW 20/13 knots dived/surfaced	Diesel-electric: 2 x SEMT-Pielstick 16PA4 V185 VG diesels 2.7MW total output 1 x Jeumont Schneider motor 2.2MW 20/12 knots dived/surfaced
AIP System:[2]	Stirling AIP 2 x 75kW V4-275R 5 knots; > 2 weeks endurance	Stirling AIP 4 x 75kW V4-275R > 2 weeks endurance	MESMA AIP 200 kW > 3 weeks endurance
Armament:[3]	4 x 533mm bow torpedo tubes 2 x 400mm bow torpedo tubes Space for c.16 weapons Additional mines in hull girdle	6 x 533mm bow torpedo tubes Space for >20 weapons	4 x 533mm bow torpedo tubes Space for c. 20 weapons

Notes:

[1] Details on submarine specifications remain subject to a considerable degree of secrecy and published information is occasionally contradictory. The above table should be taken only as an indicative guide.

[2] In all cases, AIP forms an auxiliary propulsion system, providing electricity to the main motor. It can also be used to recharge the batteries, which constitute the principle underwater propulsion system.

[3] Armament typically comprises a mixture of torpedoes, anti-surface missiles and mines depending on the inventory and operational requirements of the country concerned.

acoustic stealth and inherent efficiency. However, Stirling AIP is also continuing to achieve success and may well receive a second wind if the new Kockums A-26 submarine currently being designed manages to achieve acceptance with other regional navies looking to renew their submarine fleets.

However, it should be noted that acceptance of AIP is not yet total. A number of navies that have recently acquired new conventionally powered submarines – Brazil, Chile, India and South Africa are notable examples – have chosen not to specify AIP. In addition, there is little sign that the current major operators of nuclear-powered attack submarines such as the United States, the United Kingdom and France will adopt the new technology to replace or supplement their existing boats. To a large extent, this reflects the relative strengths and weaknesses of the current generation of AIP systems. In essence, they work well in increasing the effectiveness of boats operating defensively in relatively confined waters but offer less for submarines operating offensively on an oceanic basis.

Evidence to support this conclusion is provided by the information set out in Table 2, which contains technical data on a range of current AIP-equipped submarine classes. It can be seen that, whilst the typical output of a conventional diesel-electric submarine propulsion plant is around 3MW, current generation AIP installations only produce around one tenth of this. The comparison with a modern nuclear powered attack submarine, which can sustain over 20MW on a virtually indefinite basis, is even more marked. At least in its current form, AIP is therefore only able to act as a low speed adjunct to a more traditional propulsion system and offers little of the prolonged, high speed endurance provided by nuclear-powered boats. It is therefore not surprising that nations with blue water, oceanic naval ambitions such as Brazil and India seem to have prioritised the acquisition of nuclear propulsion technology over investment in AIP.

In spite of this, the emergence of AIP-equipped submarines is a notable development which will inevitably have a significant impact on future naval operations. The addition of an AIP plant provides a traditional diesel-electric submarine with much reduced vulnerability in littoral areas or other confined waters. It can use its AIP capability to loiter in its submerged state for weeks before switching to battery operation for a limited period of high speed activity, for example to conduct an attack or to evade detection. This cycle can be repeated as necessary. In addition, overall underwater operating radius is significantly extended compared with

MODERN AIR-INDEPENDENT PROPULSION EQUIPPED SUBMARINES

Type 212A	Type 214
Germany	Germany
Germany / Italy	Greece / S Korea / Turkey
6 (4)	4 (15)
2005	2007
1,500 tonnes	1,700 tonnes
1,800 tonnes	1,900 tonnes
57.2m x 7.0m x 6.0m	65.3m x 6.3m x 6.6m
23-28	30-35
Diesel-electric:	Diesel-electric:
1 x MTU diesel	2 x MTU 16V 396 diesels
3.1MW total output	4.2MW total output
1 x Siemens Permasyn motor	1 x Siemens Permasyn motor
2.9MW	2.9MW
20/12 knots dived/surfaced	21 knots/11 knots dived/surfaced
Siemens PEM	Siemens PEM
8+1 x 34kW BZM 34 modules	2 x 120kW BZM 120 modules
8 knots; c. 4 weeks endurance	8 knots; c. 4 weeks endurance
6 x 533mm bow torpedo tubes	8 x 533mm bow torpedo tubes
Space for 12 weapons	Space for 16 weapons

existing boats. This substantially increases overall flexibility. It should also be noted that AIP technology also offers useful offensive capabilities where rapid underwater transit is not a prerequisite. For example, AIP-equipped boats are likely to be particularly well-suited to the increasingly important task of covert surveillance, given they enjoy better stealth characteristics than the nuclear-powered boats often used in this role.

All in all, the operational deployment of AIP systems represents a major technological milestone in a process that can be traced back to the height of the Second World War, if not before. On a more practical basis, it offers second tier navies the prospect of acquiring an effective stealth capability at an affordable cost. As such, it goes some way to restoring the balance of power between the fleets of the 'blue water' navies and those of less wealthy, regional naval forces. The operational challenges faced by future commanding officers of the US Navy, People's Liberation Army Navy and other major fleets will certainly become more complicated as a result. Moreover, further investment in AIP systems that is already underway offers the promise of much higher electrical output and greater efficiency in the foreseeable future. As such, the full potential of non-nuclear AIP has yet to be achieved.

Kockums A-19 class submarine Gotland *pictured whilst running on the surface. The first operational AIP-equipped class of submarines when delivered between 1996 and 1997, they now comprise just a small proportion of over fifty AIP-type submarines in service, under construction or planned. (Courtesy of Kockums AB)*

Sources:

This chapter has drawn heavily on contemporary defence industry and government marketing literature, press releases and associated new reports. In addition, the following sources provide a body of more permanent reading material:

John Buckingham, Christopher Hodge & Timothy Hardy, 'Submarine Power and Propulsion – Trends and Opportunities', paper presented at Pacific 2008, Sydney, Australia, BMT Defence Services Ltd, Bath 2008.

Martin Driver, 'Holding breath on AIP', *Jane's Navy International* (June 2005), IHS Jane's, Coulsdon, pp.20-25.

Norman Friedman, 'Submarines', *Conway's History of the Ship, Navies in the Nuclear Age*, Conway Maritime Press, London 1993, pp.70-88.

Peter Hauschildt & Albert Hammerschmidt, 'PEM Fuel Cell Systems – An attractive energy source for submarines', *Naval Forces* (October 2005), Mönch Publishing Group, Bonn, pp.30-33.

David Miller, *U-Boats, History, Development and Equipment 1914-1945*, Conway Maritime Press, London 2000.

Edward C Whitman, 'AIP Technology Creates a New Undersea Threat', *Undersea Warfare – Fall 2001*, Department of the Navy, Washington DC.

Footnotes:

1. This is a simplification, as the evolution of tactical doctrine differed from navy to navy. The German U-Boat campaign in the Atlantic relied heavily on surface night-time attacks during the early years of the war. A similar approach was often used to devastating effect by US submarine forces in the Pacific. Submarine forces operating in coastal or other confined waters inevitably tended to spend less time on the surface.
2. The first Type XXIII coastal submarine, *U-2321*, was commissioned in June 1944. Operational use of the type did not commence until 1945 and only a handful of the more than sixty boats completed carried out a war patrol, accounting for five Allied ships. The first ocean-going Type XXI boat, *U-2501*, was also delivered in June 1944 but only two of some 120 launched before the German surrender made operational deployments.
3. Dr. Hellmuth Walter (1900-1980) was one of the leading German engineers of the Second World War. In additional to his pioneering work on AIP equipped submarines, he was also heavily involved in the development of aircraft rocket engines. This included the Walter HWK 109-509 used in the famous Messerschmitt Me 163 Komet.
4. Safety problems with HTP include its highly corrosive nature, the likelihood of a catalytic reaction with many common metals and an associated danger of spontaneous combustion. The Soviet Union and the United States both experienced major explosions on the sole Walter type boats they commissioned. HTP's use to fuel torpedoes has also had a chequered history. HTP-powered torpedoes were responsible for the loss of the British *Sidon* in June 1955 and the Russian *Kursk* disaster in August 2000.
5. A detailed description of the scientific principles governing the various AIP systems discussed is beyond the scope of this chapter. Readers are directed towards alternative sources – including many available on the Internet – if further explanation is sought.
6. Although constructed to a French design and comprising many French-built components, *Hamza* was assembled by Karachi Shipyard & Engineering Works in Pakistan. Only the second submarine to be completed in Pakistan following her non AIP-equipped sister *Saad*, her lengthy construction span is probably explained by the challenges inherent in the inward transfer of new technology. Additionally, a bomb attack in Karachi in May 2002 that killed eleven French engineers working on the submarine project may well have resulted in further delay.
7. Initial descriptions of MESMA suggest that a combination of ethanol and oxygen are burnt in the combustion chamber. However, more recent reports suggest that normal diesel might be substituted for the ethanol, simplifying fuel storage arrangements.
8. PEM technology was first developed by General Electric of the United States in the 1960s and was used in the National Aeronautics and Space Administration's (NASA's) Project Gemini manned space programme with mixed results. Siemens licensed this technology from General Electric.
9. Siemens' polymer electrolyte membrane cells are an example of proton exchange membrane technology. The PEM acronym is used interchangeably.

YAHAGI:
One Light Cruiser at Leyte Gulf

Massed torpedo attacks by flotillas of destroyers led by light cruisers were a key element in the fleet battles the IJN prepared for during the 1930s. **Mike Williams** recounts the last of these attacks, which took place during the battle of Leyte Gulf, from the perspective of the *Yahagi*, flagship of the 10th Destroyer Squadron.

The late Captain Hara Tameichi left one of the most memorable accounts of the Pacific War at sea in his notable work '*Japanese Destroyer Captain*'. From his unique perspective he related his experiences during Operation '*Ten-ichi-go*' ('Heaven One'), the forlorn *Yamato* sortie in April 1945, when he commanded the light cruiser *Yahagi*. This fated Okinawa foray is covered in a number of other authoritative works portraying every aspect of this operation in forensic depth and detail. The extensive coverage of *Yahagi*'s participation in this final sortie of the Imperial Japanese Navy (IJN) has, however, been at the expense of any corresponding attention paid towards her very active role in her one other major operation, when she sailed with Vice-Admiral Suzuki Yoshio's Second Section of the Mobile Fleet's First Striking Force, *Daiichi Yugeki Butai* (also known to posterity as 'Force A', or Centre Force), to

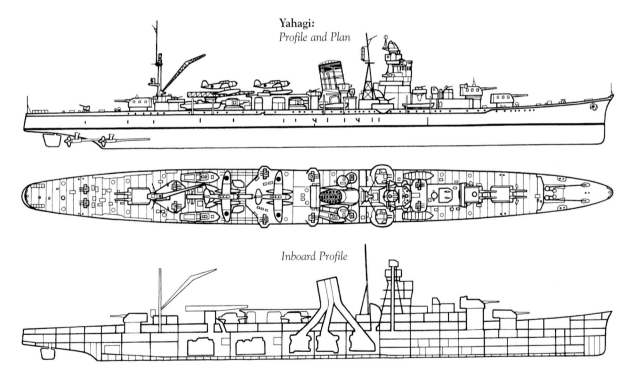

Yahagi:
Profile and Plan

Inboard Profile

Designed as a flagship for the IJN destroyer flotillas (Design No.C-41), Yahagi cost some 26,400,000 Yen to build. With a 2/3 trial displacement of 7,890t, length was 174.5m overall, beam 15.2m, and (mean) draught 5.69m. Six Kampon boilers provided steam for four Gihon geared turbines, producing 100,000shp, capable of driving her slim hull form through the water at 35kts, while a fuel oil capacity of 1,406t gave her a range of 11,670km at an economical 18kts. Protection comprised a 60mm CNC waterline belt with a 20mm deck, also of CNC steel, over the machinery spaces; there were armoured boxes with 55mm sides and 20mm crowns over the magazines, and the gunhouses had 19mm plating. The total weight of protection was 657t (541t armour + 116t protective plate). The main armament of six 15cm/50 Type 41 guns (165rpg) in twin pivot mountings was supplemented by four 8cm/60 Type 98 high-angle guns (255rpg) also in twin mounts, and as completed Yahagi carried fourteen 25mm Type 96 cannon (2,500rpg) in two triple and four twin mountings. The torpedo outfit was eight 61cm tubes in two Type 92 quad mounts, and sixteen oxygen-propelled Type 93 Mod.1 torpedoes – there was provision for forty-eight mines to be carried in lieu; eighteen Type 95 depth charges were normally carried. There was a catapult for two scouting floatplanes amidships. (Drawing by the author).

A well-known view of Yahagi *which remains the best overall image of the ship. She is shown leaving Sasebo 19 December 1943 just prior to her commissioning. (IJN Department of Naval Aeronautics).*

be abbreviated to 1YB throughout this study, under the overall command of Vice-Admiral Kurita Takeo, at the epic Battle of Leyte Gulf, fought during late October 1944 in the contested waters off the Philippine Islands.

Given the scale of this battle, the lack of coverage given to this relatively small vessel is understandable. If she is mentioned at all, her supporting role in the diverse phases of this protracted battle are not deemed worthy of detailed comment. However, when considering *Yahagi*'s part in the crucial final chase off Samar, one pivotal question comes to the fore: how did she and her destroyers, all veteran units with highly proficient crews, wielding the most potent torpedo seen during the war, fail to achieve a single hit upon a beleaguered enemy formation at their mercy? What or who was responsible for this failure at this critical time?

In this attempt to provide an accurate description of *Yahagi*'s part at Leyte, the personal account of 2nd Lieutenant (Junior Grade) Ikeda Kunitake, stationed throughout the battle on *Yahagi*'s bridge, has been of inestimable value.

The Path to Leyte Gulf 1944

Yahagi was ordered as the third of four *Agano* class light cruisers. Authorised under the 1939 naval estimates, designed by Naval Constructor Fukuda, she was laid down on 11 November 1941 as Cruiser 'B' No.134 at Sasebo, subsequently launched on 25 September 1942, and commissioned on 29 December 1943 under Captain Yoshimura Matake, being assigned to Vice-Admiral Ozawa Jisaburo's 3rd Fleet as flagship of Rear-Admiral Kimura Susumu's 10th Destroyer Squadron (10DS) to replace its former flagship, the damaged *Agano*.

Yahagi set out from Kure for a short transit to Iwakuni on 4 February 1944, before proceeding to Sumoto the following day. Two days later she sailed for the South China Sea accompanying the carrier *Shokaku*, together

A rare onboard photo of Yahagi's *forecastle looking towards her bridge. The main armament of six 15cm/50 guns was 'recycled' from older, discarded ships. The guns were mounted in three Type 'C' enclosed gun-houses with light 19mm plating. Each twin mounting weighed 72t, had a traversing speed of 6° per second, a rate of elevation of 10° per second, and a fixed loading angle of 7°. Rate of fire was one 45.36kg round every 10 seconds; the separate bagged charge weighed 12.76kg. A muzzle velocity of 850m/s gave these guns a maximum range of 21,000m and a ceiling of 8,000m, but a maximum elevation of just 55 degrees, allied to their low training speed, made them mediocre anti-aircraft weapons. Note the Type 94 main gunnery director located atop the bridge structure. (IJN Department of Naval Aeronautics).*

The destroyer Yukikaze, *one of the Kagero class units which made up the 10th Destroyer Squadron (or Flotilla, known as Suiraisentai) These were powerfully armed units displacing some 2,450t, capable of 35kts, possessing eight 61cm torpedo tubes. By the time of Leyte the superimposed twin 12.7cm/50 mounting aft had been sacrificed to enhance the 25mm anti-aircraft armament, which now totalled between 18 and 24 guns. (IJN Department of Naval Aeronautics).*

Yahagi, at Lingga Roads off the east coast of Sumatra just to the south of Singapore, a vital forward base astride the strategic Malacca Strait. This evocative image was taken in October 1944. (IJN Department of Naval Aeronautics)

with the heavy cruiser *Chikuma* and four destroyers, arriving at Seletar Naval Base (Singapore) 13 February, before moving on to Lingga Roads on 18 February for a work-up and training period. On 11 May she left for Tawi Tawi with Ozawa's 1st Carrier Striking Force, arriving at her new forward base on 15 May.

When Admiral Toyoda Soemu sent out a signal activating Operation 'A-Go', the planned defence of the Marianas, on 13 June, the first moves in what would become the debacle of the Philippine Sea commenced, as *Yahagi* left for Guimaras with Ozawa's Force to oppose the American 5th Fleet in the decisive battle for Saipan. The rescue of survivors from *Shokaku* was her single most important contribution, before the battered Mobile Fleet retired to Nakagusuku Bay (Okinawa) for refuelling on 20 June. *Yahagi* arrived at Hashirajima anchorage four days later. From late June to early July she was dry-docked and refitted at Kure, then on 8 July she departed Kure, assisting in carrying troops and material south in company with other units. On 10 July they arrived at Nakagusuku Bay, departing two days later for Manila, where *Yahagi* arrived on 14 July, leaving three days later bound for Singapore. She then sailed for the Lingga Roads to commence a period of intensive training with the 2nd Fleet under Kurita.

Upon definitive confirmation of the initial American moves against Suluan Island at the mouth of Leyte Gulf on 17 October 1944, Operation 'Sho-Go 1' ('Victory, Option 1') was initiated. *Yahagi* set out on the 18th with the rest of Kurita's 1YB. She entered Brunei Bay on the 20th, and during her two days here awaiting refuelling, the extensive stripping of all combustible materials begun while at Lingga was completed, rendering the quarters and between-decks gaunt and bare. Canvas-encased sisal rope bags were used for splinter and bullet-proofing to exposed gun tubs, bridge decks, directors, and ammunition hoists, while the open positions were further protected with steel cables and manila ropes hung as improvised splinter protection.

At 08.20 on the 22nd the First Section of 1YB set out, followed by the Second Section including the 10DS, to transit the San Bernardino Strait. At 15.30 Vice-Admiral Nishimura Shoji's 2YB (Southern Force Vanguard) departed to rendez-vous with the 2YB Rearguard Force from Manila under Vice-Admiral Shima Kiyohide, for passage through the Surigao Strait. These formations were choreographed in a giant naval pincer movement to enter Leyte Gulf in the early hours of the 25th from the north and south respectively.

However, these opening moves by the Japanese Fleet did not go unopposed. The opening engagement of this protracted battle was to take place at 05.24 on the 23rd in the Palawan Passage, when stalking American submarines attacked Kurita's First Section, devastating the 4th Cruiser Squadron (4CS). Flagship *Atago* was torpedoed, her survivors being rescued by the destroyers *Kishinami* and *Asashimo*. Then at 05.56 *Maya* was hit, *Akishimo* rescuing her survivors. Finally, at 06.34 *Takao* was struck and crippled, having to turn back to Brunei shepherded by *Asashimo* and *Naganami*. The destroyers of the 2DS were much employed this night. However, *Yahagi*'s own 10DS was not a direct participant in these events, as it was stationed some 12,000m astern with the Second Section; the ships began their own depth-charge preparations in case they were attacked. However, the rest of the day proved uneventful, and at 18.00 the remnants of Kurita's depleted 1YB entered the waters off Mindoro leading to the Tablas Straits and Sibuyan Sea.

24 October: The Battle of the Sibuyan Sea

At 06.00 all ships went to General Quarters, closed up, and proceeded at 20 knots, in the expectation of heavy air

Battle of the Sibuyan Sea:
The Japanese Defensive Formation

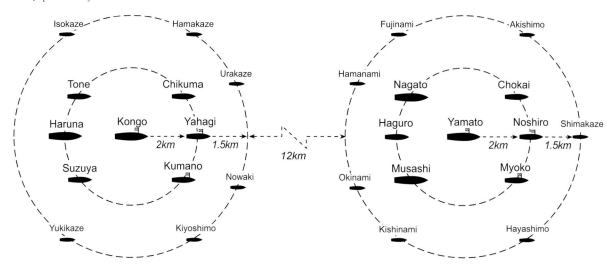

(Redrawn by John Jordan from material supplied by the author)

attacks that day. An hour later *Yahagi's* two Aichi E13A1 Type 0 'Jake' reconnaissance floatplanes were prepared for launch, to scout ahead of 1YB. Ikeda noted how Captain Yoshimura had specific instructions for the pilots, Flight Lieutenant Sasaki and Flight Petty Officer Kawakami. San José airfield on Mindoro was to be their return destination, to minimise the danger of fire on board ship in the action to follow. At 07.30, training her single midships catapult to clear her structure, *Yahagi* left her station and stood into the wind to allow Sasaki's floatplane to be launched. At 08.00 Kawakami was dispatched, and the vital communications check from both aircraft back to *Yahagi* was satisfactory. Ikeda was later to note that around noon he heard Sasaki radio that three enemy fighters were following him, and that silence then followed. From this it is concluded that his prolonged sweeps over the waters to be transited had cost him and his two-man crew their lives; there was no mention of Kawakami's floatplane.

A superb bow quarter view of the lead-ship of the class, Agano, taken during work-up off Truk on 7 December 1942. Note the Aichi E13A1 Type 0 'Jake' reconnaissance aircraft on the single centreline 25.6m Type 1 No.2 Model 11 catapult. Forward of this, on the raised platform abaft the funnel, with its distinctive Hiro Type 91 pusher engine, is an Aichi E11A1 Type 98 'Laura' three-man night reconnaissance flying-boat. Yahagi had the shorter 19.4m Type No.2 Model 5 catapult, and generally operated two 'Jakes'.
(IJN Department of Naval Aeronautics).

Just after 08.10 Kurita's 1YB was spotted by enemy aerial scouts, but the underwater threat was also omnipresent. By 09.00 the force had reached the narrow and confined waters of the Tablas Strait, where a submarine ambush was possible. With the disaster that befell the 4CS the previous day still fresh in Japanese minds, a suspected periscope sighting from *Noshiro* at 09.52 instigated an emergency turn together. This disruption was compounded when aerial contacts, closing rapidly, materialised on various ships' radars at 10.10. Speed was increased to 22 knots. The first air attack commenced at 10.30 and lasted around five minutes, demanding extreme manoeuvres, ably carried-out on board by Quartermaster Nakagawa, *Yahagi*'s helmsman. The main ordnance of battleships opened up, followed by the main guns of the heavy cruisers, then by the massed medium-calibre batteries of all ships, which unleashed their multi-coloured Type 3 *Sanshikidan* shell, and finally by the multiple 25mm machine guns. The premier units of the First Section were seemingly singled out for attack; *Yahagi*'s following Second Section remained temporarily unscathed.

Another potential submarine sighting from *Noshiro* in the vanguard at 11.24 called for another series of emergency turns, the destroyer *Akishimo* carrying out a depth-charge attack, as the 1YB manoeuvred away from the scene. For those on the trailing *Yahagi*'s bridge, the waters now being negotiated called for the current circular air-alert cruising order to be revised to an anti-submarine one, before another aerial assault at 11.40 revised these considerations, in what was to be another testing five minutes of intense anti-aircraft action.

Yahagi's radar had located the enemy aircraft at 50km and she instantly closed up, crew-members stopping their rushed early midday meal at their action stations. With speed set at 24 knots, the defensive barrage resumed with the 25mm battery just forward of the bridge eventually challenging the closing enemy with a hail of fire which caused the bridge to shudder violently. No direct hits were received, but *Yahagi* suffered a near-miss to port some 10m abreast the bridge which raised a towering water column alongside. It was reported that No.4 port-side 25mm triple mount had been damaged, and that splinters had penetrated the hull; two men had been killed and five wounded. An enemy torpedo bomber now closed from the port side. Ikeda thought evasion was a little late, but hard left rudder and full ahead, combined with her fierce fire, forced the enemy plane to drop too far ahead; the torpedo missed, leaving a white trail very close to the ship. Around noon the air alert ended and speed was reduced to 16 knots to conserve fuel; an easterly course was maintained.

No sooner had the last enemy plane retired than another enemy submarine report swept through 1YB. Both *Yahagi* and *Noshiro*, leading their respective Sections, reported returns from their bow-mounted Type 93 Model 2 hydrophones just after noon. Eyes that had been preoccupied with the sky now suddenly sighted suspicious objects breaking the surface of the water. 1YB again took avoiding action and increased speed, but soon the underwater alert was down-graded, as all ships prepared for the expected third aerial attack. It duly commenced at 12.15, again lasting four to five minutes. Speed was now limited to enable the damaged *Musashi* to

The Battle of the Sibuyan Sea

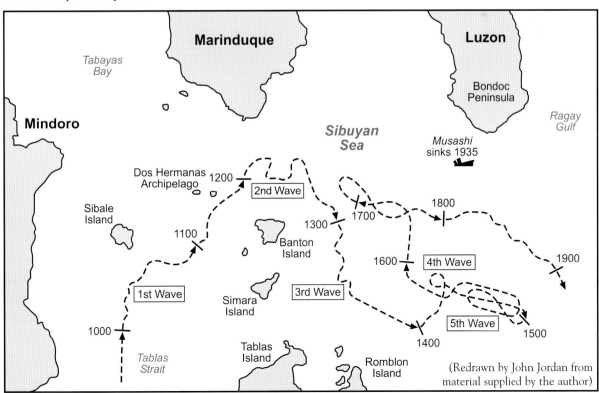

(Redrawn by John Jordan from material supplied by the author)

keep up. During this phase Ikeda had the impression that 1YB struggled to fight against being struck simultaneously from above and below, as the two previously tight circles became disorganised to counter an apparent underwater attack while pouring anti-aircraft fire skywards. There now appears to have been a merging of the previously separate Sections into a single formation.

Early in the third attack, in order to view the overall scene, Ikeda went to the port side of the signal bridge and leaned out. A tremendous concussion almost made him fall, and upon recovering his equilibrium he had the overpowering feeling of the deck bouncing, causing an upheaval exactly like an earthquake. The ship had been hit aft, close to the vital rudder and screws. Damage reports soon confirmed the hull was intact, but three crew spaces were destroyed. Before Ikeda and the bridge crew fully recovered, he felt as if he was being beaten again, as a second upheaval shook *Yahagi*. A bomb fell on the foredeck, destroying the starboard chain locker, breaching the hull, simultaneously with a towering water column from a near-miss abreast the bridge to port – a double blow from which the entire ship again shook and trembled. Running at high speed, the damaged bow would be greatly affected by any wave action, a very severe blow. The hole in her starboard hull forward was said to be 4m in diameter, thankfully above the waterline, but with countless holes in her 16mm to 22mm thick side plating; bulkheads had also been penetrated, and flooding occurred in adjacent compartments before a containment boundary was established. All knew that a crippled ship was a vulnerable one. Damage control on board IJN ships was not as extensive or as proficient as on board Allied vessels; on *Yahagi*, there were only sixty-three emergency lights distributed throughout her entire ship, supported by fewer than sixty 6V hand-held battle lanterns, offering the barest minimum of illumination. In difficult conditions her crew fought to contain the damage forward.

There is no incontrovertible evidence to fully establish what actually occurred, but it is thought that *Yahagi* was attacked by two F6F Hellcats, each delivering two 500lb (226kg) general-purpose bombs with instantaneous fuze. The first obtained a hit and a distant miss (dud) aft, the second the hit forward and a near-miss off to port. A direct comparison with the bomb damage received by her close cousin *Oyodo* off Etajima on the 24 July 1945 is enlightening. Two 500lb GP bombs struck her upper deck aft, in the vicinity of her catapult, which detonated on impact and produced holes some 3m to 4m in diameter, with attendant splinter damage similar to *Yahagi*'s. The series of near-misses *Oyodo* received in this attack are also worthy of comment, as they inflicted numerous splinter holes above the waterline, with concussion indentations to her hull plates mentioned, but no ruptures or sprung plates. While the damage forward was the subject of repeated comment from Ikeda over the following days, the hit aft is ignored, indicating that it was superficial.

The general speed of 1YB was now 18 knots, as the fourth aerial attack broke over Kurita at around 12.50, this time seemingly concentrating upon other units, and rendering some respite to the trailing *Musashi*. The captain of the cruiser *Tone* suggested that the entire Second Section, including *Yahagi*, provide direct support for *Musashi* to defend her against further aerial attacks, but a fifth wave, which began at 13.15, followed by a sixth wave from 15.20, crippled the battleship. Her speed dropped to 6 knots, and a number of other ships were now also damaged. Under this intense and constant aerial onslaught, at 15.30 Kurita reversed course westwards.

During a respite, Ikeda's close friend Lieutenant Ito (Itou) came to the bridge, eyes alight with excitement, claiming (optimistically) that at least ten enemy aircraft had been destroyed. Ito showed Ikeda his binoculars which had hung around his neck; a hit had scooped out the central part saving him. He had been in a truly dangerous place at his post at the lightly protected starboard twin 8cm high-angle gun below the bridge.

Noshiro undergoing her trials off Tokyo Bay in late June 1943 without her aircraft – an equal mass weighted replacement being used atop her catapult as a substitute. Note the location of her Type 94 high-angle director and rangefinder abaft the funnel; Yahagi's was forward, while the configuration of the Type 94 main armament director atop the bridge also differs from Yahagi's. In this view Noshiro carries a Type 21 air-search radar A4 mattress antenna at the base of the director tower; Yahagi had a similar set and by October 1944 had also been fitted with Type 22 'horn' surface and Type 13 'ladder' air search radars (both fitted July 1944); radar intercept receivers had been installed February/March 1944. It is reported that constant adjustments needed to be made to this equipment, and that half the vacuum tubes sent from Japan were useless while the rest could be used only with difficulty. The topography of the Sibuyan Sea, which was studded with islands, some with high terrain, made the early detection of enemy air strikes difficult for the operators. (IJN Department of Naval Aeronautics).

A postwar image of Oyodo under the breaker's torch, with her machinery spaces exposed. The two large box structures forward are her forward fuel tanks, located in the same area as the ones in Yahagi which suffered splinter damage on 24 October 1944. Note the centreline bulkhead dividing Oyodo's principal boiler and engine spaces; the Agano class had only a partial centreline bulkhead, but it remained an Achilles heel in the event of flooding of the after boiler rooms and the engine rooms for the wing turbines; off-centre flooding risked rapid capsizing in such a moderately-sized vessel. (Harima Shipyard, Kure).

In appraising *Yahagi*'s ability to defend herself against aerial attack, it is apposite to quote the report of the postwar USN Technical Mission to Japan. It claimed that for 25mm fire, some 1,500 rounds were deemed necessary to down an aircraft at less than 2,000m range and 1,000m

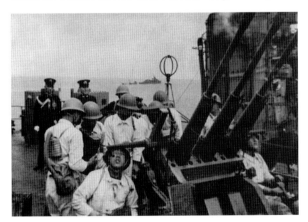

A triple 25mm/60 Type 96 mount aboard the light cruiser Oyodo during an exercise; the triple mounting had a nine-man crew, which was generally exposed to strafing by enemy aircraft. By October 1944 Yahagi carried 48 barrels in ten triple and eighteen single mounts. These manually controlled guns were capable of a practical 150rpm (260rpm theoretical), had an elevation of 85°, and fired a 250gm round to a ceiling of 5,250m; maximum range was 7,500m. (IJN Department of Naval Aeronautics).

height; beyond these limits 25mm fire was deemed completely ineffective. As for heavier ordnance (10cm to 12.7cm – no estimate for 8cm), success at more than 8,000m was considered doubtful, with the best results stated to be under 4,000m. The absence of radar control was felt to be crucial to the inadequacies of the Japanese anti-aircraft system.

At 17.15 Kurita again reversed his course to head eastwards at 24 knots. Ikeda summed up the overall situation: they were now resolved to transit the Visayan Sea and breakout through San Bernardino Strait and into Leyte Gulf, but under cover of night, their only counter to crippling enemy air strikes. Judging from that day's attacks, they conjectured that massed formations of enemy aircraft carriers awaited them off Samar. There was no news of Japanese aerial successes, and no indication that the enemy's main force had been diverted by decoy tactics. The Japanese force changed formation into line ahead for the narrow passage, with a 1,000m interval between ships, speed 22 knots. There was an expectation of attacks both by enemy motor torpedo-boats lurking in the shadow of the islands and also by submarines.

Musashi had finally capsized and sunk at 19.35. *Hamakaze* and *Kiyoshimo* rescued survivors. The heavily-laden destroyers then proceeded to Manila, severely depleting the already limited destroyer screen. It had been a devastating day; the powerful aerial elements of 3rd Fleet's Task Force 38 (TF 38) had flown 259 sorties, mostly by Hellcats. However, even this weight of attack proved insufficient to neutralize the threat from Kurita's force, in marked contrast with the 527 sorties to be flown against Ozawa's much weaker 'Decoy' Northern Force the following day.

25 October – The Battle off Samar

Unknown to all on board 1YB, their passage to Leyte was not to be contested. Admiral Halsey's decision to take the entire 3rd Fleet northwards to attack Ozawa's carriers, acting as a diversionary force, left San Bernardino Strait completely unguarded. 1YB therefore emerged unopposed at 00.35, a still formidable force consisting of four battleships, six heavy cruisers, two light cruisers and eleven destroyers. Kurita's night scouting formation adopted after the passage of the Strait placed *Yahagi's* 10DS in line ahead, to the extreme left (east) flank of his advance, with the 7CS then 5CS, and 2DS respectively, 5km apart to the west, followed by the capital ships of the 1st and 3rd Battleship Divisions (see graphic).

On *Yahagi's* bridge, Ikeda noted at 03.00 that course was 180 degrees, speed 18 knots. Only later would he discover that around this time 2YB was being utterly destroyed in the Surigao Strait by the battle line of the US 7th Fleet. Kurita would be unsupported off Tacloban. 1YB should by now also have been engaged but for being several hours late, the schedule thrown off due to fighting off the heavy enemy air attacks the previous day. At around 04.00 the emergency repairs forward were completed. Captain Yoshimura appreciated the tremendous efforts of the damage control team under Executive Officer Commander Shinichi Uchino. *Yahagi* was now capable of steaming at 28 knots; however, 30 knots or more was deemed unreasonable. As squadron flagship speed was essential, but it was now constrained by the need to avoid further damage. A further constraint on *Yahagi's* ability to steam at high speed for prolonged periods was that it was unclear how much of the fuel remaining in her forward tanks had been lost or contaminated by sea-water.

At 05.00 everyone went to action stations. At around 06.45, through the speaking tube from the air defence command post atop the bridge, Ikeda heard: 'Enemy sighted'. The eyes of the Captain and Commander then swept the horizon through binoculars, reporting to *Yamato*: 'Enemy bearing 110 degrees, distance 26,000m'. At the same time *Yamato's* high-mounted radar picked up what was presumably dawn anti-submarine aerial patrol activity from carriers to the south. *Yahagi* was lead ship of the left-most wing in the search formation of 1YB, closest to the enemy, hence her early visual detection. As her speed was increased to 24 knots, masts were visible; however precise enemy ship classification was difficult from her low bridge. On *Yamato's* gunnery platform high atop her tower structure, Kurita's Operations Officer, Commander Tonosuke Otani, could make out the flat-topped silhouettes of large aircraft-carriers on the obscured horizon through an optical range-finder. Within minutes various lookouts throughout 1YB reported the enemy formation, which appeared to be composed of at least six *Essex* class fleet carriers, together with two battleships, along with ten or more heavy cruisers of the *Baltimore* class; critically, aircraft were being launched. The imagination of Kurita's Chief-of-Staff, Admiral Koyanagi, reinforced the growing belief that they had indeed stumbled upon fleet carriers with heavy protection, a belief that was to grow into a fatal conviction which was to govern all Japanese actions.

Kurita had apparently succeeded beyond his wildest expectation. All assumed they had found a detached carrier Task Group (TG), one of four such powerful formations from Vice-Admiral Mitscher's TF 38, each possessing at its core at least two *Essex* class carriers, each capable of launching up to 100 strike aircraft, and two *Independence* class light carriers each with up to 45 aircraft. However the situation was critical; any delay in changing into a formal battle formation could lose them the decisive moment. 1YB had no hope of defending itself against another massed aerial assault; it had to destroy or incapacitate the carriers' ability to launch aircraft without delay, employing gunnery to wreck their flight decks.

The true composition of the exposed units of Vice-Admiral Kincaid's 7th Fleet, Rear-Admiral Clifton Sprague's Task Unit 77.4.3 (call sign: 'Taffy 3'), six escort carriers, three destroyers, and four destroyer escorts, was unknown to those on *Yamato's* bridge, as was the presence of Taffys 1 and 2, likewise supporting the landings off Leyte to the south-east. In all there were eighteen escort carriers operating some 450 aircraft, mostly FM-2 Wildcat and TBM Avenger torpedo bombers – all that now stood between 1YB and the Allied landings off Tacloban.

Kurita had intended to adopt a balanced circular anti-aircraft defensive formation, with the two destroyer squadrons deployed on the outer ring, with the heavy cruisers and capital ships within this mutually supporting layered circular deployment. This deployment was precluded by events; a 'General Attack' was ordered, with each of the major units deploying as they saw fit in their

Night Cruising Formation:
Exit from San Bernadino Strait

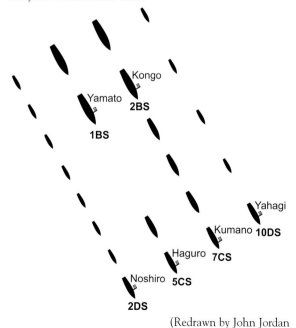

(Redrawn by John Jordan from material supplied by the author)

pursuit of the enemy, and with the destroyers ordered to the rear – an order possibly influenced by *Yahagi*'s restricted speed. An already confused situation was greatly exacerbated by the deteriorating weather conditions, with heavy rainsqualls, and the units of Taffy 3 now also laid a very effective intense smoke screen, making long-range gunnery using optical rangefinders problematic.

Yamato, which had opened fire with her main 46cm guns at 06.58 at the carriers 32,000m distant, now fired her 15.5cm/60 secondary armament at their 27,400m maximum range at 07.06 (against the destroyer *Johnston*). Although nominally close to the calibre of the main guns carried by *Yahagi*, the latter's six veteran 15cm pieces (max. range: 21,000m) remained silent. Taffy 3 soon fought back, its Avengers and Wildcats taking off with whatever ordnance was available to harass the closing enemy; a few were armed with torpedoes, but most with anti-personnel bombs, rockets, depth-charges, and 0.5in machine-guns, or in some cases nothing at all. The American destroyers simultaneously closed to launch their torpedoes, and to fling 5in/38 (12.7cm) shells at the Japanese battleships and cruisers.

The utter confusion of the general attack is a contributory factor to one ambiguous aspect of *Yahagi*'s story: her track throughout this action. If the movements of *Yahagi* and the 10DS are even mentioned in one particular account, this is invariably contradicted by another. All that can be established beyond doubt from the sources consulted is that *Yahagi*'s general movements conformed to the general flow of the chase, initially eastwards until 08.00, then southwards until 09.00, by which time she had found herself in an unexpectedly favourable position to the west of 1YB, forming the northern pincer to a heavy cruiser envelopment from the east, closing in upon

OPPOSING FORCES
Actual and Perceived

Essex Class

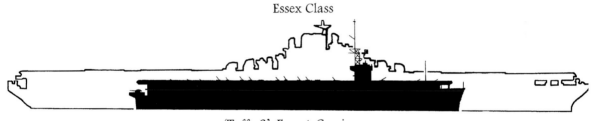

'Taffy 3', Escort-Carriers:
St. Lo (CVE-63), White Plains (CVE-66), Kalinin Bay (CVE-68)
Fanshaw Bay (CVE-70), Kitkun Bay (CVE-71), and Gambier Bay (CVE-73)

Destroyers:
Hoel (DD-533)
Johnston (DD-557)
Heermann (DD-532)

Destroyer-Escorts:
Samuel B. Roberts (DE-413)
Dennis (DE-405)
Raymond (DE-341)
John C. Butler (DE-339)

Yamato Class

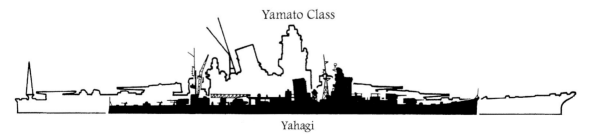

Yahagi

17th Destroyer Division:
Urakaze, Isokaze, Hamakaze, and Yukikaze

(Drawn by the author)

The destroyer Hayanami, *of the* Yugumo *class. Most of the units of Rear-Admiral Hayakawa's 2nd Destroyer Squadron led by* Noshiro *(Captain Kajiwara) comprised ships of this type. The Yugumos were similar in size and capability to the Kageros, and like the latter had lost their after superimposed 12.7cm mounting by late 1944; light AA armaments by this time ranged from 15 to 28 25mm. (IJN Department of Naval Aeronautics).*

The midships section of Oyodo *after hits received on the 19 March 1945 during Task Force 58's initial aerial assault upon Kure, when she received three 500lb bomb hits. This image shows her after dry-docking at Kure (23 March to 1 4 April 1945), and illustrates the insubstantial nature of a light cruiser's superstructure. The funnel, with its light 10-12mm plating, was vital for uptake, draft and vent functions, and if damaged significantly affected boiler performance. (IJN Department of Naval Aeronautics).*

Taffy 3, just before Kurita purportedly 'lost his nerve' and ordered the general retirement north, to which all ships had complied by 09.30.

With *Yahagi's* track impossible to accurately determine, one has only to conceive of her following the general 'flow' of the developing action, initially virtually as a spectator, finally becoming a direct participant as a growing number of Japanese ships began to be hit and fall out. An enemy plane was splashed off her port side as desperate ship handling repeatedly saved her, but at 07.25 three aircraft closed. The ship was turned hard to port, with all fully expecting a repeat of the bombing experienced the previous day, but they were instead severely strafed from stem to stern. Chief Warrant Officer Kajiki, standing next to Ikeda, was killed, along with one petty officer and two seamen on the bridge, while return anti-aircraft fire shook the ship. Lieutenant Ito, whose action station was only 10m from Ikeda, was mortally wounded; his assistant on the 8cm mount, Mate Takahashi, took over, as the 25mm guns directed an intense barrage at a flight of perceived enemy 'torpedo' planes off to starboard, breaking up the low altitude attack. Despite the hole in her side forward *Yahagi* increased speed to 30 knots as the air attacks increased in intensity, with reinforcements from Taffys 1 and 2 now entering the fray. *Yahagi's* 25mm guns literally glowed, and those on deck without a steel helmet or protection suffered grievously as shell fragments and bullets took their toll.

The increased strain on *Yahagi's* bow gradually aggravated the flooding forward, but battle speed had to be increased to 32 knots. Captain Yoshimura glared motionlessly in the direction of the enemy as *Yahagi* followed them south, with an enemy destroyer (presumably *Hoel*, but possibly *Johnston*) sighted to port at 15,000m through a break in the smoke screen. *Noshiro* and the 2DS, almost parallel to *Yahagi* and the 10DS in their joint advance southward, came under fire, water columns rising around them in the gunnery duel. *Noshiro* was hit on her starboard side by a 5in shell and other Japanese ships were also severely damaged: *Kumano* had already lost her bow, while the cruisers *Suzuya*, *Chokai*, and *Chikuma* were all destined to be sunk in this precipitate action off Samar.

Throughout everything *Yahagi's* primary goal was the aircraft carriers, despite the enemy destroyers' extremely accurate radar-controlled fire. The 10DS alone had four destroyers to the immediate enemy's apparent three, without taking into account the advantage of a light cruiser leader. However, Ikeda notes that Japanese shooting was inferior, with the battle damage of the previous day causing failures in their radar ranging equipment, compelling them to rely on optical sights only. However, composed correction shooting by Commander Nagai, along with that of her destroyers, enabled the ships to find the range; their third salvo hit *Hoel*, which took on a list to starboard and hauled out of action, sinking at 08.55.

Lookouts on the hard pressed *Kalinin Bay*, firing her single 5in gun through an effective smokescreen as a line of 203mm-gunned Japanese heavy cruisers closed down to 14,600m from the north-east, now observed what at first appeared to be five destroyers approaching from the north-west. *Yahagi* and her four consorts entered the gunnery duel against the escort carriers, and closed to within 9,600m, but from 08.30 there was a concerted aerial assault upon 10DS by all available aircraft. *Fanshaw Bay* recorded a 6in (15cm) shell hit received at approximately 08.50 (specifically not a 203mm) from a six shell salvo, presumably from an *Agano* class unit, although it is unclear whether this was from *Yahagi* or *Noshiro*.

At 08.40, Lieutenant-Commander Evans on board *Johnson* (which had been crippled by *Kongo* at 07.30) had attempted to interpose his single destroyer between the 10DS and his charges, closing to within 6,900m of the Japanese force. *Yahagi* shifted target to *Johnston*, the damaged American destroyer displaying immense courage in engaging the superior Japanese force. Around 09.00 *Yahagi* was hit by a 5in shell on her port side, damaging her upper wardroom, then being used to treat the wounded. The shell caused the death of two petty officers and three seamen and a fire was started. Smoke shrouded the bridge and emerged from the speaking tubes, which had no sealing valve or gas-tight diaphragm, from below. The damage control party was immediately mustered. The fire was thought to be in the vicinity of No.2 magazine, but

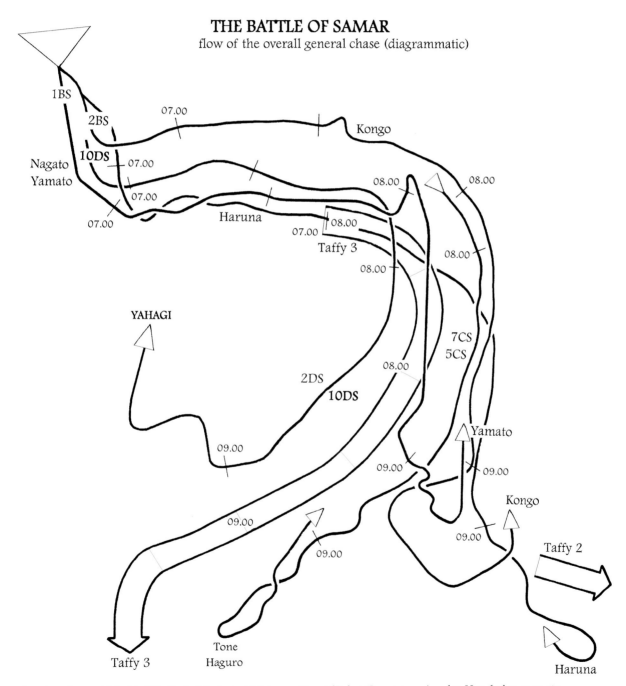

Based on plans published in 'The End of the Imperial Japanese Navy' (Robert Cox: internet) and in Hornfischer, opus cit. (Drawn by the author)

The Type 92 quad torpedo tubes with their reload lockers carried by Yahagi *and the destroyers of 10DS. They are seen here aboard the Kagero class destroyer* Shiranuhi *while docked at Maizuru in late 1942. The mounting was unarmoured; the fully enclosed spray shield was of 3mm plate and the tubes themselves were of mild steel 5mm thicksheet, while the outer shell of a torpedo was 3.2mm-1.8mm thick, offering limited protection against splinters. At the outbreak of war, the IJN possessed the world's finest torpedo, the Type 93 Model 1, the fabled 610mm (24in) 'Long Lance'; 9 metres long and with an all-up weight of 2,700kg, it had a potent 490kg warhead. The torpedo was propelled by a two-cylinder horizontal reciprocating engine driven by 128 litres of kerosene and 980 litres of pure (98%) oxygen, compressed to 230 atmospheres (225kg/sqcm) in a one-piece forged chamber, which gave superlative performance and efficiency. In theory there were various speed and depth settings. However, in practice the Japanese seldom changed the speed setting once a torpedo was in its tube, and most attacks were undertaken at the standard high-speed setting of 48-50 knots, which gave a maximum range of 20,000m. (IJN Department of Naval Aeronautics).*

there is no record of the magazine temperature regulating or alarm systems being activated at any time, so the fire must have been less serious than initially feared. The valiant crew of *Johnston* claimed a dozen hits upon their light cruiser opponent and her following destroyers, but this one direct hit is all that Ikeda notes. Such confusion on board the battered and beleaguered American vessel, then under concentrated fire from *Yahagi* and her consorts, can be readily appreciated.

In the Type 92 torpedo fire-command post located on the forward anti-aircraft platform together with its 12cm sight, Commander Hiroshi, the Torpedo Officer, had finally sighted the elusive enemy inside the smoke screen, and reported this directly to Captain Yoshimura on the compass platform below. An aircraft carrier (possibly *Kalinin Bay*) could be seen off *Yahagi*'s port bow, and a squadron torpedo attack was immediately ordered. The bridge wings each mounted an 18cm binocular Type 1 Model 1 torpedo sight, positioned in front of a Type 97 Model 2 torpedo director (*Hoiban*) The *Hoiban* was a sophisticated sighting mechanism, a column supporting several annular rings for inputting every conceivable constant and variable pertaining to an accurate firing solution: known and estimated bearing, range, angle, and speed, etc. A marker was used to indicate a firing bearing for line of sight, thus when an elusive target once again came into view an immediate launch could be ordered. Supporting this was a Type 93 target course and speed instrument (*Sokutekiban*), for data input into the Type 93 computer (*Shahoban*) installed below the bridge, used to confirm all crucial known, observed and estimated parameters. With such a system it was deemed possible to conduct a blind firing should a target enter a smoke screen or be similarly obscured. Given the importance of the decision to launch a massed torpedo strike, to be triggered by Hiroshi in the central Type 92 post, it could be executed only on the express order of the 10DS commander, Rear-Admiral Kimura.

A considerable part of the intense training undertaken at Lingga in the weeks before this sortie had been specifically committed to such a decisive surface action. With no integral carriers, and minimal or non-existent air cover expected, Kurita had trained his crews in the art of swift surface interception, gunnery, and long-range torpedo strike, with the preferred option of a night action prominent. A night attack had been denied due to the protracted aerial battles of the 24th, but Japanese ships were by now skilled in the art of daylight torpedo strikes at close range.

Because Kimura believed that his division was pursuing a powerful task group comprising fleet carriers and their screening ships, all of which would be capable of 30 knots plus, and with *Yahagi* now straining to achieve anything above 28 knots, he felt that it could never overhaul the enemy or achieve a more favourable launch position. He determined that his force had to strike now, despite the gunnery dual with *Johnston*, now down to 6,800m, by which Ikeda confessed they were still distracted. With enemy planes approaching, evasive manoeuvres would be difficult now that the ships were embarked on their torpedo run. No bombs followed, but fierce machine-gun strafing continually swept the decks; Petty Officer Abe was killed instantly by a bullet to the throat, while ordinary seaman Maeda had his helmet pierced and died instantly. Commander Hiroshi, now himself nursing a wounded hand, still tracked the enemy carriers, while his subordinates, Lieutenants Kawahara and Nakamoto, stayed close by in case he fell.

Yoshimura and Hiroshi knew the range was well within the capabilities of their torpedo armament; even allowing for the poor visibility, a spread of torpedoes could succeed at this decisive moment. For Yoshimura it was the chance of a lifetime. Here at last was a sight of the elusive fleeing enemy within torpedo range; if he delayed for another instant the enemy could escape into the blanketing smoke screen again. Hiroshi unwaveringly concurred. The preparation flag was raised and repeated in turn by the four trailing destroyers, each of which trained both pairs of quadruple torpedo tubes to port.

Commander Hiroshi's dedicated team saw the enemy aircraft carrier briefly in their sights, and input the target data, including enemy speed (which determined deflection) ready to launch. Hiroshi depressed the central firing trigger at around 09.10. There was to be a single coordinated torpedo salvo; there is no mention in Japanese accounts of any planned follow-up, even though a full manual reload could be accomplished in five minutes by a skilled crew. Torpedo discharge reports came from the launching tubes; *Yahagi* launched all seven available torpedoes, the eighth having been damaged by enemy strafing; her following four destroyers followed suit with their thirty-two torpedoes. The time to arrival was nine minutes, equating to a range of 13,500m. Immediately after launch *Yahagi* and her destroyers were again free to manoeuvre to evade *Johnston's* harassment and some distracting aerial attacks. Miraculously, they had escaped serious interference during the launch phase.

It should be noted here that such massed torpedo launches in the past had achieved mixed results. At the (Second) Naval Battle of Guadalcanal on 15 November 1942, the 10DS under Kimura in his then-flagship *Nagara* had launched between thirty and forty 'Long Lance' torpedoes in the direction of the battleship *South Dakota* (BB-57); they missed their target but struck the destroyers *Preston* (DD-379), *Walke* (DD-416) and *Benham* (DD-397), which were either sunk or had to be scuttled. At the Battle of the Java Sea fought on 27 February 1942, the Japanese purportedly fired 92 torpedoes, in a series of mass launches, scoring only a single hit upon the Dutch destroyer *Kortenaer*. In a subsequent phase of the battle, however, the Dutch cruisers *De Ruyter* and *Java* were sunk by a single Long Lance salvo. Thus, the results thus far of these mass torpedo strikes had been variable.

In order to verify the results on the aircraft carrier(s), an experienced lookout was specifically allocated. The torpedoes evidently arrived twenty seconds earlier than estimated, the lookout's report rang out; a tall water column was already collapsing, and an enemy aircraft carrier was hidden by its shadow. Despite the distance and the poor visibility, all thought it an unambiguous sinking. But as all students of the battle know, the torpedo attack of the 10DS failed, probably due to a gross miscalculation in all computations. Throughout the pursuit Japanese observers had mistaken the carriers for main Fleet units, vessels capable of well over 30 knots, whereas the escort carriers had a maximum speed of 19 knots. If all of Commander Hiroshi's calculations were based upon the former's assumed speed, then the subsequent launch, however broad the spread, was doomed to fail.

The fixation upon fleet carriers was compelling. Overwhelmed by a heady mixture of battle fatigue, blind excitement and a desire to believe that their action could be a decisive moment in the war, the Japanese refused to consider other alternatives. This was despite incontrovertible visual evidence which revealed the true nature of their adversary. When *Kumano* closed with Taffy 3's defences, ignoring the destroyers as she concentrated upon the fleeing carriers beyond, Vice-Admiral Shiraishi Kazutaka, Captain Hitomi Soichiro and the entire cruiser's bridge personnel had all seen small carriers as

The crew of the Agano assembled on the forecastle and forward superstructure soon after her completion. Designed for a crew of 700 officers and men, the wartime complement of these ships totalled 850. (IJN Department of Naval Aeronautics).

early as 07.16, and this was noted officially in the ships log. But this revelation was never communicated to Kurita, perhaps due to the raking 5in fire and devastating torpedo hit *Kumano* received from *Johnston*, which crippled her, compelling Shiraishi to transfer to the also-damaged *Suzuya*.

A further possible factor in the failure of the torpedo strike is that the depth setting, which was made prior to firing with the torpedo already in the tube, was calibrated for the deeper draught of a fleet carrier (8.38m), and that some torpedoes may have passed under both the destroyers (4.2m draught) and the escort carriers (6.32m) without exploding. The Type 02 warhead on the Long Lance was fitted with a non-influence (ie contact) pistol, and the lack of any visible track would have made the American ships unaware of near-misses. The single explosion witnessed from *Yahagi*, perhaps from a premature detonation of a faulty torpedo, was in line with Taffy 3, thereby giving added weight to this theory.

There remains some doubt as to who made the decision to launch this final effort of 1YB – and indeed the IJN – in this ultimate surface fleet battle of the Pacific War. Ikeda's detailed personal account of the action from his unique perspective on *Yahagi*'s compact compass platform makes no mention of Captain Yoshimura or Commander Hiroshi consulting, communicating, or conferring with Rear-Admiral Kimura at any stage; indeed there is no mention of the latter's involvement in the decision to commit the 10DS to the torpedo attack. Kimura has been much maligned and held personally responsible for this failure at this decisive moment in the battle, certainly by Hara, but it is not clear that he was actually responsible. There is no evidence that the admiral had been incapacitated earlier in the action, leaving the execution of this strike to Yoshimura. The absence of Kimura's name from Ikeda's account of the decision-making which led to the torpedo attack is therefore puzzling, although Kimura's continued active service and promotion to Vice-Admiral five months later suggest that no official blame was levelled at him in any subsequent enquiry.

After this abortive torpedo attack, Kurita abandoned his attempt to battle on to Leyte Gulf and the Allied landings off Tacloban. However, Ikeda's account suggests that Yoshimura, again without apparent reference to Kimura, did not immediately respond to Kurita's 19.11 order to retire. Instead *Johnston* now received the combined attention of 10DS's guns for about ten minutes. She was blanketed by an avalanche of shells – she would sink at 10.10 – but by 09.30 all Japanese ships had reluctantly broken-off the action. Kurita had designated enemy aircraft carriers reported to be north-east of Samar for destruction, and ordered 20 knots, which was the maximum speed

A group portrait of the Agano's *officers, taken at Sasebo on 30 October 1942; she was commissioned the following day under Captain Nakagawa Ko.* Yahagi *replaced her sister as flagship of the 10th Destroyer Squadron after* Agano *sustained torpedo damage in November 1943 (IJN Department of Naval Aeronautics).*

possible given the many damaged vessels in his force. This reversal of the primary goal was a puzzle on board *Yahagi*, but Ikeda assumed that the decision was well-founded. It was probable that all transports in the Gulf would have been dispersed, the enemy had overwhelming air power, and there was a perceived inability to pursue the enemy TG, which appeared to have a speed advantage, even though the same considerations would apply to any new alleged TG to the north.

The battered remnants of 1YB were still certainly not safe; at around 11.00, black specks were seen on the horizon. Kurita's forces were widely dispersed but strove to adopt a defensive combat formation, as aircraft started circling outside normal firing range. With anti-aircraft fire opening up from *Yamato*'s main guns, the planes scattered to attack simultaneously from all sides. Each warship maintained its place within the defensive ring formation, but because the number of ships had decreased, the ratio of aircraft to ships had increased. These were not lightly armed aircraft from Taffy 3, but fully-armed strike aircraft from the fleet carriers of TG 38, which had belatedly been sent to neutralise Kurita.

It seemed to the Japanese crews as if when one air raid ended, another appeared on the horizon; only good ship handling enabled *Yahagi* to evade several dozen bombs and torpedoes. But late in the day, at approximately 16.00, in what Ikeda believed to be the tenth attack, *Yahagi*'s good fortune and ship handling failed when the ship was badly shaken by a near-miss alongside to starboard, which sent bomb fragments scything through the thin hull plating. Splinters struck the first discharge tube of the after Type 92 quad torpedo mount, penetrating either the 12mm thick oxygen cell of the torpedo or exposed piping and instantly igniting its high-pressure liquid oxygen. It was estimated that the temperature within the mounting rose to 2,000 degrees Celsius; the nine men under Senior Chief Petty Officer Yamada died instantly. The implications of a hit in this crucial area were recognised by all on board *Yahagi*; just hours before, the heavy cruisers *Chokai* and *Suzuya* had been lost when damage to their torpedo tubes had initiated devastating explosive chain reactions within their superstructures. If the damage control party, aided by the surviving 25mm crews nearby, had not rapidly extinguished the fire which gutted the after torpedo mounting before it detonated a warhead, the implications for *Yahagi* were manifest.

The detonation of a single 490kg (Type 97 explosive, 60% TNT, 40% exanitrodiphenylamine) warhead on board was enough to sink a destroyer or fatally damage a cruiser. As American air strikes against Japanese ships became more common and intense, captains under air attack had to decide whether to jettison their torpedoes to prevent them from being detonated, or retain them for later use. At Okinawa Captain Hara, then-commander of *Yahagi*, had to agree with his torpedo officer, Lt.-Cdr. Takeshi Kameyama, to the disposal of all torpedoes at the commencement of the air attacks, effectively discarding the cruiser's most potent and effective ship killer and rendering *Yahagi* virtually impotent in any assault upon the American Fleet off Okinawa.

At around 18.30, what was calculated to be the eighteenth air raid ended; only the fast-approaching night

Battle of Leyte Gulf
Kurita's Much-Depleted Force Retires on the San Bernadino Strait

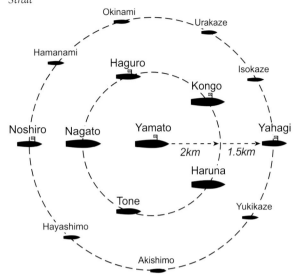

(Redrawn by John Jordan from material supplied by the author)

saved the remnants of 1YB from further loss, and it now faced the prospects of another aerial trial the following day. *Yahagi*'s decks were scattered with combat debris, her plating was riddled with splinter holes, and there were approximately 200 wounded for the chief surgeon and medical staff to take care off. 1YB entered the San Bernardino Strait around 21.00 in line astern for its three-hour passage. Despite the numerical advantage held in every category of ship by the American 3rd and 7th Fleets and their total dominance of the air, Kurita's surviving ships succeeded in escaping Halsey's distant aerial strikes and the fast-approaching force of fast battleships under Vice-Admiral Lee detached from Halsey's main force, which arrived too late to cut him off. Only the straggling destroyer *Nowake* (10DS) was caught; she was sunk by the advance cruisers and destroyers of TG 34.5 off Legaspi with all hands, including all survivors from *Chikuma*.

26 October: Conclusion

At dawn on the 26th, everyone aboard the Japanese ships knew they had to get away from under the aerial threat of the enemy as soon as possible. They had transited the Sibuyan Sea that night, but they were still in range of enemy air attack. As the eastern sky became lighter, with a fine day in prospect and their own defences reduced by half, escape was not going to be easy. Commencing at 08.00 1YB was attacked by TG 38's carrier aircraft in the Tablas Strait west of Panay, the first of many air attacks that day. One bomb hit *Noshiro*; the damage was quickly repaired, but the ship appeared to be singled out for a fatal attack at 08.52, when a torpedo struck her amidships, wrecking her boiler rooms, and she came to a halt. *Hamanami* went alongside to take off her crew and she

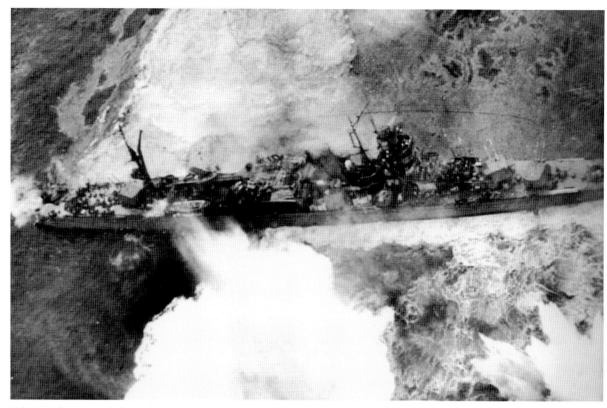

Yahagi under air attack during her last sortie with Yamato and the Surface Special Attack Force. She was hit by an aerial torpedo at 12.46 and went dead in the water; she was subsequently hit by twelve bombs and six more torpedoes, and at 14.05 capsized, taking 446 members of her crew with her. (USN).

sank at 11.13. *Yahagi* was unable to help her stricken sister-ship.

Around 13.00, a formation of thirty-two B-24's at high altitude was detected. Their first pass was to observe the course and speed of the warships, the second approach a level bombing run at a much lower altitude. The Japanese counter-fire was fierce, the target being very easy to track, and it succeeded in breaking up the formation, no damage being inflicted; one bomber was downed, and several departed with smoke trailing from them. Given room to manoeuvre and an attack by aircraft in formation, maintaining a steady course, the Japanese were confident that they could fight back effectively. This was destined to be the final action, but the air alert was strictly maintained along with an anti-submarine guard.

On board *Yahagi*, after the fierce battles of the past three traumatic days, 52 men had died, and arrangements were prepared for burial at sea to take place at 17.00 on the

The surrendered Sakawa stripped of her armament and moored at Yokosuka on 20 February 1946. She was destined to succumb to the 'Able' atomic bomb test off Bikini Atoll on 1 July 1946, sinking the following day after suffering extensive structural damage aft from the massive air-burst detonation just 500m away. Sakawa was similar in most respects to Yahagi. In this view the degaussing coil around the upper hull is particularly prominent; many of the scuttles on the lower deck had been plated over during 1944 to improve watertight integrity. (Yokosuka – USN)

26th. A quarter of her crew had been casualties. At dawn on the 27th, the remaining ships emerged into 'safe' waters, well beyond the range of carrier aircraft. They had avoided the direct route down the west coast of Palawan Island in light of the damage inflicted upon 1YB on the 23rd, and had taken a more westerly route through the Spratly archipelago which, with its many reefs, was a danger area for navigation but recognised as a submarine safety zone marked according to a secret chart.

The close of the *Sho* venture found *Yahagi* at Brunei on the 28th with the broken remnants of the IJN, and the principal objective of this article draws to a close with her survival of the Leyte debacle. Even at Brunei *Yahagi* was not safe. On 16 November that base was attacked by a powerful force of land-based bombers and fighters. That same day the 10DS was officially deactivated, and *Yahagi* was assigned as flagship of the newly reconstituted 2DS under Rear-Admiral Komura Keizo, which departed from this now exposed anchorage that evening bound for Japan. Between 24 November and 18 December *Yahagi* was at Sasebo under repair and refit. On 20 December Captain Yoshimura assumed command of the fast battleship *Haruna*, while Captain Hara took over *Yahagi* for the final phase of her career. Between 21 December 1944 and 29 March 1945 she was stationed at Hashirajima along with the battleship *Yamato*, and on 6 April she sortied in company with the latter in Operation '*Ten-Ichi-Go*', to attack the massed American Invasion Forces off Okinawa. On 7 April, the remnants of the once mighty 2nd Fleet was attacked by massed waves of some 400 American carrier aircraft and overwhelmingly routed, leaving the destroyers *Fuyuzuki*, *Yukikaze*, and *Hatsushimo* to rescue 280 survivors from *Yamato*, 555 from *Yahagi*, and just over 800 from *Isokaze*, *Hamakaze*, and *Kasumi* (*Asashimo* was lost with all hands). Some 4,250 Japanese naval personnel perished in this final sortie of the IJN, including 446 men from the *Yahagi*.

Sources:
Green, William, *Warplanes of the Second World War Vol.5 – Flying Boats*, Macdonald & Co. (London 1962).
—— *Warplanes of the Second World War Vol.6) – Floatplanes* (Macdonald & Co., London 1962).
Hastings, Max, *Nemesis – The Battle for Japan, 1944-45*, Harper Collins (London 2007).
Hornfischer, James, *Last Stand of the Tin Can Sailors*, Bantam Books (New York 2005).
Hoyt, Edwin, *The Battle of Leyte Gulf*, Jove Books (New York 1983).
Ito, Masanori, *The End of the Imperial Japanese Navy*, Weidenfeld and Nicolson (London 1962).
Japanese Naval Vessels – Maru Special 5: Agano and Oyodo classes (Japan 1976).
Lacroix, Eric and Wells, Linton, *Japanese Cruisers of the Pacific War*, Chatham Publishing (London 1997).
Millot, Bernard, *Divine Thunder*, Mayflower Books (St Albans 1974).
Mitsuru, Yoshida, *Requiem for Battleship Yamato*, Constable (London 1999).
Tameichi, Captain Hara, *Japanese Destroyer Captain*, Naval Institute Press (Annapolis 1967).
Patton, Wayne, *Japanese Light-cruisers of World War II*, Squadron Signal Publications (Texas 2005).
Skulski, Janusz, *The Heavy Cruiser Takao*, Conway Maritime Press (London 1994).
Spurr, Russell, *A Glorious Way to Die* Sedgwick & Jackson (London 1982).
Yoshimura, Akira, *Battleship Musashi*, Kodansha Europe Ltd. (London 1999).

Internet
Lieutenant Ikeda's personal account – http://www5f.biglobe.ne.jp/~ma480/senki-ikeda-hitouoki1.html.
Imperial Japanese Navy Page (Parshall & Tully) – www.combinedfleet.com.

RUSSIA'S 'AMERICAN' MONITORS:

The *Uragan* Class[1]

In response to an international crisis that arose in 1863 over Russia's suppression of the Polish revolt, the Russian Imperial Navy embarked on an emergency programme of building American-style monitors. **Stephen McLaughlin** *describes the origins, construction and careers of these vessels.*

The Polish Crisis 1863-1864

During the latter part of the eighteenth century Poland, weakened by internal disorders, had gradually been devoured by her neighbours, with the last independent provinces being absorbed by the Russian empire in 1795. At the Congress of Vienna in 1815 the Kingdom of Poland was created, but it was under the rule of the Russian emperor. In 1830-1831 a large-scale Polish rebellion was brutally suppressed by the Russian army, after which an uneasy peace was maintained for three decades. But in February 1861 Russian soldiers opened fire on a demonstration in Warsaw, killing many. Emperor Aleksandr II, hoping to avoid another open rebellion, appointed his younger brother, the Grand Duke Konstantin Aleksandrovich, as Viceroy of Poland. Konstantin, the General-Admiral of the Navy, hoped to create a semi-autonomous Poland with a liberal form of government. But on his second day in Warsaw he was slightly wounded by a Polish nationalist named de Jonza, and this set the tone for the coming months. By early 1863 Russia's Polish and Lithuanian provinces were again in open revolt.

Polish emigrés abroad hoped to convert western sympathy for the uprising into concrete support, and the governments of both Britain and France expressed strong disapproval of Russia's harsh suppression of the revolt. These same two powers had fought against Russia during the Crimean War, which had ended only seven years earlier, and Russia feared that she might soon find herself again at war with them and their ironclad navies. Defence preparations were therefore hastily mounted, including an emergency shipbuilding programme that included ten monitors patterned after the American *Passaic* class – the ships that form the subject of this article.

Design and Construction

While Konstantin was in Warsaw, the management of naval affairs was left to the Director of the Naval Ministry, Admiral N.K. Krabbe. Although he had spent much of his career in shore assignments and was regarded as a 'landlubber' by many officers, he was an intelligent man and an able administrator.

As the diplomatic situation deteriorated in the spring of 1863, the Naval Ministry sought ways to bolster the maritime defences of St. Petersburg. Two ironclads, the floating batteries *Pervenets* and *Ne tron menia*, were already under construction, although the latter had only recently been laid down, while the contract for a third ship of similar type, *Kreml*, was still under negotiation.[2] It was clear that none of these ships would be ready soon, although in the summer and autumn of 1863 additional money was allocated to accelerate their progress. By this time, however, construction of a completely different type of ironclad – single-turret monitors built to the design of the Swedish-American engineer John Ericsson – had already begun.

Russian interest had been caught by the battle at Hampton Roads between the ironclads USS *Monitor* and CSS *Virginia* in March 1862. Ericsson's *Monitor* was a break from previous warships – as Donald L. Canney has pointed out, *Monitor* 'was the first naval vessel that was designed as a naval fighting "machine", rather than as a ship adapted to warfare'.[3] The monitors were in fact 'weapons systems' in the modern sense, the entire vessel designed to get the two heavy guns into battle; anything that did not contribute to that purpose was eliminated from the design. The result was a vessel that was both simple and powerful.

These were characteristics that appealed to Russia's naval leadership, faced as it was with the daunting prospect of having to defend St. Petersburg against a maritime attack by one, if not both, of the world's greatest navies. No time was lost in sending a mission to the United States to study the new type of ironclad, and by the summer of 1862 three officers, led by Captain 1st Rank S.S. Lesovskii – a member of Konstantin's trusted inner circle – had arrived in America.[4] The other members of the group were naval constructor Captain N.A. Artseulov and artillery specialist F.N. Pestich.[5] As representatives of the Union's only friend amongst the great powers of Europe, few limits seem to have been placed on where the Russian officers could go and what they could see.

It seems likely, for example, that Lesovskii either visited or was shown plans for the USS *Roanoke*, a wooden frigate undergoing conversion to a three-turreted ironclad at the Novelty Iron Works in New York, for on 24 July/5 August 1862 he wrote to Admiral Krabbe suggesting a similar conversion of the incomplete frigates *Petropavlovsk* and *Sevastopol*. (Note that in the nineteenth century Russia still used the Julian calendar, which was twelve days behind the Gregorian calendar used in the west; hence, dates are given in the format Julian/Gregorian.) At about the same time he set off for Vicksburg to look in on the operations of the Flotilla on Western Waters, and in December he attended the trials of the *Passaic*-class monitor USS *Montauk*, whose captain was Commander John L. Worden, who had commanded the *Monitor* during her action with the *Virginia*.[6] Lesovskii was apparently impressed by what he saw, and was soon a confirmed monitor enthusiast; after his return to Russia he extolled the type in an article in the professional naval journal *Morskoi sbornik*, labelling high-freeboard ironclads like the USS *New Ironsides*, HMS *Warrior* and the French *Gloire* as mistakes that were unlikely to be repeated.[7] Nor was Lesovskii the only convert; his travelling companion, naval constructor Artseulov, also became an advocate for the type.

The Russians had not simply been caught up in the 'monitor craze'; the monitor must have seemed ideally suited their country's needs. The maritime defences of St. Petersburg needed to be bolstered as quickly as possible, and here was a new type of ship that was structurally simple and could therefore be built quickly (the original *Monitor* had been contracted on 4 October 1861 and was commissioned on 25 February 1862). It could carry a powerful armament, and its shallow draught made it well-suited to the waters around Kronshtadt and the eastern Baltic. And perhaps most importantly, it was armoured with layers of 1in plate – the greatest thickness that Russia's nascent industry could produce.

Lesovskii and his companions must therefore have been gratified when American officials proved willing to provide the complete plans and specifications of the new *Passaic* class monitors. But although the design was Ericsson's, the plans didn't come directly from him; they 'were furnished to Russia from Washington' – not from Ericsson's Ironclad Office in New York.[8] Ericsson was Swedish by birth, and therefore held no love for Russia – the two countries had fought several bitter wars during the eighteenth and early nineteenth centuries, ending only in 1809 when Russia had wrested all of Finland from Sweden. Nevertheless, Ericsson reconciled himself to the gift of the *Passaic* plans, his conscience perhaps eased by the fact that he was at that very time providing technical assistance to Sweden in the design of its own monitors.[9]

Meanwhile, in Russia, events were moving with unaccustomed speed. Since 1862 a committee, chaired by Vice-Admiral P.A. Rumiantsev, had been laying the groundwork for a new shipbuilding programme, and in early 1863, presumably having heard that the American plans had been obtained, it recommended the immediate construction of no fewer than ten monitors.[10] On 11/23

Veshchun early in her career and riding (relatively) high in the water – note how at the stern the lower edge of the raft's overhang rises above the water. Although no boats are slung on the davits abaft the turret, it is easy to see how the boats blocked the arc of fire on after bearings. As yet there is no bulwark atop the turret, just a palisade of rolled hammocks. The pillar-like object atop her pilot-house is probably her binnacle; this position was meant to isolate the compass as much as possible from the ship's iron hull. (U.S. Naval History and Heritage Command Photograph NH 84753)

March 1863 Admiral Krabbe approved the programme, which also included the two-turreted *Smerch*, a vessel with Coles turrets. The fact that such an extensive programme was adopted before anyone in St. Petersburg had even seen the American plans – Artseulov arrived in St. Petersburg with them five days *after* the programme was approved – is a sign of just how desperate the Russians believed their situation to be.

Since time was critical, the Shipbuilding Technical Committee decided to use the American drawings without alterations – although, inevitably, small changes crept in during construction. It was decided to build the ships not only in the usual state shipyards, but in private yards as well – and two were contracted to the Belgian Cockerill firm, which built the ships and then sent them, disassembled, to St. Petersburg for re-assembly.

The programme received a setback when Artseulov, who had done so much to promote the monitors and had drawn up their specifications for Russian manufacturers, died unexpectedly on 27 November/9 December 1863. The overall supervision of the project passed to Colonel A.Ia. Gezekhus of the construction corps. He faced a difficult task; the simultaneous construction of eight monitors in St. Petersburg made great demands on the shipyards, and skilled workers were scarce. Before long the building of the batteries *Ne tron menia* and *Kreml* practically ceased as workers were transferred to the higher-priority monitors; other emergency measures included the Naval Ministry's request that the nearby provinces send craftsmen to St. Petersburg and the use of naval ratings in the construction work. Rudimentary efforts were made at 'series' production of some items, with one officer placed in charge of the manufacture of a single component for all ships; thus the general supervision of construction was placed under the authority of Captain-Lieutenant I.F. Likhachev; Staff-Captain A.D. Pribbe, an engineer, supervised the building of the engines; the prospective commander of *Uragan*, Captain-Lieutenant N.A. Fesun,

TABLE 1: BUILDING DATES

	Bronenosets	*Edinorog*	*Koldun*
Ordered:	—	—	—
Added to List:	26 Aug/7 Sep 1863	26 Aug/7 Sep 1863	26 Aug/7 Sep 1863
Construction begun:	5/17 Jun 1863	1/13 Jun 1863	28 Oct/9 Nov 1863
Laid down:	12/24 Dec 1863	19 Nov/1 Dec 1863	27 Nov/9 Dec 1863
Launched:	12/24 Mar 1864	21 May/2 Jun 1864	26 Apr/8 May 1864
Entered service:	25 May/6 Jun 1865	15/27 Jul 1865	1865
Builder:	Carr & MacPherson, St. Petersburg	S.G. Kudriavtsev, Galernyi Island	Cockerill, Belgium; assembled at Gutuevskii Is.
Constructors:	N.G. Korshinov	A.A. Svistovskii	K.V. Prokhorov
Cost (hull and machinery):	1,148,000 rubles	1,141,800 rubles	1,237,000 rubles

	Latnik	*Lava*	*Perun*	*Strelets*
Ordered:	—	—	—	—
Added to List:	26 Aug/7 Sep 1863	26 Aug/7 Sep 1863	26 Aug/7 Sep 1863	26 Aug/7 Sep 1863
Construction begun:	5/17 Jun 1863	15/22 Jun 1863	15/22 Jun 1863	1/13 Jun 1863
Laid down:	12/24 Dec 1863	3/15 Dec 1863	3/15 Dec 1863	19 Nov/1 Dec 1863
Launched:	10/22 Mar 1864	27 May/8 Jun 1864	18/30 Jun 1864	21 May/2 Jun 1864
Entered service:	2/14 Jul 1865	20 Aug/1 Sep 1865	20 Aug/1 Sep 1865	15/27 Jul 1865
Builder:	Carr & MacPherson, St. Petersburg	Semiannikov & Poletika, St. Petersburg	Semiannikov & Poletika, St. Petersburg	S.G. Kudriavtsev, Galernyi Island
Constructors:	N.G. Korshinov	Aleksandrov	Aleksandrov	A.A. Svistovskii
Cost (hull and machinery):	1,148,000 rubles	1,142,7,000 rubles	1,142,700 rubles	1,141,800 rubles

	Tifon	*Uragan*	*Veshchun*
Ordered:	—	—	—
Added to List:	26 Aug/7 Sep 1863	26 Aug/7 Sep 1863	26 Aug/7 Sep 1863
Construction begun:	26 Jun/8 Jul 1863	26 Jun/8 Jul 1863	28 Oct/9 Nov 1863
Laid down:	19 Nov/1 Dec 1863	19 Nov/1 Dec 1863	27 Nov/9 Dec 1863
Launched:	14/27 Jun 1864	15/27 May 1864	26 Apr/8 May 1864
Entered service:	1865	1865	1865
Builder:	New Admiralty, St. Petersburg	New Admiralty, St. Petersburg	Cockerill, Belgium; assembled at Gutuevskii Is.
Constructors:	A.Ia. Gezekhus	A.Ia. Gezekhus	Kh.V. Prokhorov
Cost (hull and machinery):	1,105,800 rubles	1,105,800 rubles	1,237,000 rubles

Notes:

Added to List: the date a ship was officially added to the List of the Fleet and given a name.

Construction Begun: the date when the first iron was laid on the slipway.

Laid Down: the date of the ceremonial keel-laying, not necessarily corresponding to an important stage in the ship's construction.

oversaw the equipment of the vessels, and Captain-Lieutenant I.P. Belavenets looked after the compasses. The construction of the Cockerill-built ships was monitored by Captain-Lieutenant A.I. Fëdorov, and their assembly in St. Petersburg was supervised by Second Lieutenant Kh.V. Prokhorov of the construction corps, who had earlier supervised the construction of the iron-hulled gunboat *Opyt*.

In the end, the crisis that had inspired all this frenetic activity passed as quickly as it had arisen; by May 1864 the Polish rebellion had been effectively crushed, and relations with Britain and France soon returned to their normal level of diplomatically correct mutual suspicion. As a result, the pace of work on the monitors slowed; the *Uragan* class ships didn't enter service until 1865, about two years after the start of construction. (See Table 1 for construction dates.)

General Features

The basic idea of the *Monitor* was simple – a single rotating turret with the widest possible field of fire, mounted on a low-freeboard 'raft'. This raft – the visible 'hull' of the monitor – was actually not the hull proper; this was the 'lower vessel', containing living quarters, engine, stores, etc., which was attached to the bottom of the raft and was of considerably smaller dimensions. This created another of the defining features of the Ericsson ironclad – the overhang of the raft. This served to protect the lower hull, propeller and rudder from shot and shell, and provided a degree of protection against ramming, since the stem of an attacking ship would (hopefully) be stopped by the raft overhang before the ram reached the hull proper.

The raft was so low in the water – freeboard was about 18in – that the deck was constantly awash in anything other than a dead calm. Modern tests have shown that this greatly reduced the motions of the ship in a seaway – the weight of water on deck actually dampened the quick roll to which a ship with such a high metacentric height (circa 14-15ft) would otherwise have been subject. However, the disadvantages of the low freeboard in rough weather later became tragically clear when *Monitor* herself was lost in a storm off Cape Hatteras in December 1862. The *Passaic*-class monitor *Weehawken* was another victim of low freeboard; she foundered on 6 December 1863 when a 'mild gale' hit her suddenly when she was lying at anchor with hatches open.

The *Passaic* class – and consequently the *Uragan* class – shared all these features with the original *Monitor*, and were very similar in outward appearance to the prototype. In fact, however, they were built to an entirely new design with many improvements resulting from experience gained at the Battle of Hampton Roads. To begin with, they were one-third again as large as the *Monitor*: 1,335 tons vs. 987 tons.[11] This was largely a consequence of the decision to mount two 15in Dahlgren guns instead of the *Monitor*'s 11in guns. The latter guns had been unable to penetrate *Virginia*'s 4in armour, although in fact this was not the fault of the guns themselves; during the battle only half-charges had been used due to fears – unfounded, as was later shown – that the Ericsson-designed gun carriages would not withstand full charges. Nevertheless, the 11in gun was regarded as inadequate for fighting armoured ships.

Another important change in the *Passaic* class was in the hull form. The underwater hull of the original *Monitor* had been designed for ease of construction, not for hydrodynamic performance. The raft and hull had a parallel midbody for much of their length, and followed simple curves to the stem and stern; the sides of the lower hull were angled sharply outwards from the flat, keel-less floor. The *Passaics* not only had a proper keel, but a more ship-shaped raft and hull as well, which made them better sea boats. The overhang of the raft amounted to about 3ft 8in along the sides, but was far greater at the bow and stern – the length of the hull proper was 159ft, stem to sternpost, while length overall was 201ft.[12] The overhang forward had a well for the four-fluked anchor, while aft the overhang protected the propeller and rudder. The bottom of the after end of the raft's overhang swept upwards, a feature intended to reduce drag; the raft also featured a slight sheer fore and aft.

The hull was constructed of 0.5in (12.7mm) iron, with a box-shaped keel made from 0.75in (18.9mm) iron. Internally the hull was divided into six compartments by transverse bulkheads at frames 1, 9, 51, 61, 69 and 100. Apparently only the bulkheads at frames 51 and 61 – that is, the forward and after ends of the turret compartment – were watertight; these were also made from 0.5in (12.7mm) iron. From fore to aft, the compartments were: the anchor windlass compartment; the officers' and crew's quarters and wardroom; the compartment under the turret, which in addition to the turret machinery contained the galley and sick-bay; the central coal bunker; the machinery compartment; and finally an engineering storeroom. There were two longitudinal bulkheads running from frame 53 to frame 93; these formed, with the transverse bulkheads at frames 51 and 61, a sturdy box supporting the turret. The longitudinal bulkheads also served as supports for the deck beams; forward of frame 51, where there were no longitudinal bulkheads, support was provided by three rows of pillars. The deck itself was made of two layers of pine, supported by heavy wooden beams.

The most visible change in the *Passaics* was the transfer of the pilothouse from the forecastle to the top of the turret, where it was fixed so that it did not rotate with the turret. This solved a problem all too evident in the *Monitor*, where the guns could not be fired within 30° of the keel-line on forward bearings without deafening and dazing the men in the pilothouse. It also made communication between the ship's commander and the gunners much easier – in the *Monitor* orders had to be passed from the pilothouse to the turret by messenger. Another change was the partially armoured funnel, replacing the short, removable funnels of the *Monitor*, at the cost of a reduction in the field of fire on after bearings.

Eight of the ten *Uragan* class were built to the American drawings with as few changes as possible, but on 15/27 June 1863 – two months after the ironclad attack on Charleston had revealed weaknesses in the *Passaic* class monitors – changes were approved for the

WARSHIP 2012

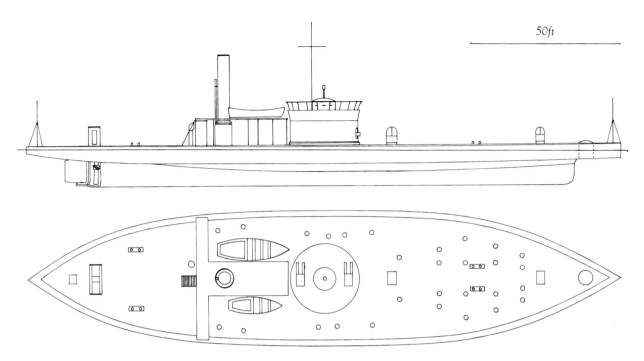

Uragan – *elevation and upper deck plan* (Drawings by Ian Sturton)

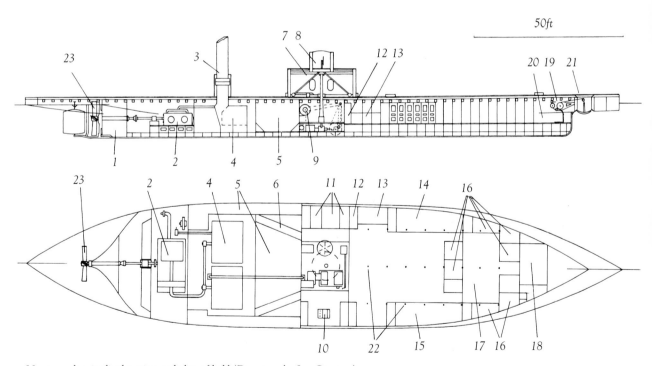

Uragan – *longitudinal section and plan of hold* (Drawings by Ian Sturton)

Key:
1. After Peak
2. Steam engine
3. Funnel
4. Boiler
5. Coal bunkers
6. Passgeway
7. Gun turret
8. Conning tower
9. Ventilator
10. Galley
11. Water closets
12. Storeroom
13. Locker
14. Shot/shell magazine
15. Powder room
16. Officers' cabins
17. Wardroom
18. Crew's quarters
19. Capstan
20. Chain locker
21. Anchor hawse-hole
22. Pillars
23. Propeller

RUSSIA'S 'AMERICAN' MONITORS: THE *URAGAN* CLASS

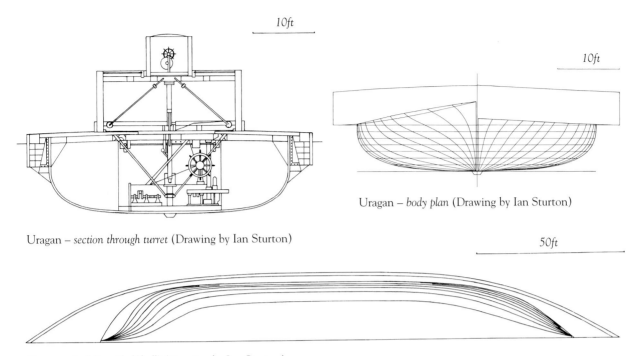

Uragan – *section through turret* (Drawing by Ian Sturton)

Uragan – *body plan* (Drawing by Ian Sturton)

Uragan – *hull lines (half hull)* (Drawing by Ian Sturton)

two Belgian-built vessels. Iron deck beams were specified near the funnel instead of wood beams, the conning tower armour was increased from 8in to 11in, and the turret was moved 3ft (0.9m) forward to correct the trim. It is not clear why similar changes were not made in the Russian-built ships. (See Table 2 for the characteristics of the ships as designed and completed.)

The American ships had a design displacement of 1,335 tons and a draught of 10ft 6in, but these figures were apparently exceeded in the ships as built – in December 1862, as the first of the class were completing, Ericsson complained that '[m]uch useless weight was put into the Passaic against my remonstrances to please her Commander'.[13] Worden, captain of the *Montauk*, reported that in fighting trim his ship would have a draught of about 11ft 5in – almost a foot deeper than designed, suggesting a displacement of about 1,500 tons.[14] Some of the Russian ships were even worse, although why this was so is not clear. Their dimensions were apparently slightly greater than those of the American (length 201ft instead of 200ft, beam 46ft instead of 45ft), and displacement 'according to the drawing' is given as 1,566 tons, while actual displacements reportedly ranged from 1,382 to 1,666 tons, although no individual vessels or conditions of loading are specified.[15] It is possible that, knowing the American ships had turned out overweight, the Russians altered the lines of the ships to add some needed buoyancy. Another factor that may have led to displacement increases was that Russian captains had a long history of demanding changes (usually requiring added weights) during construction – the same problem that had so vexed Ericsson. The rush to build the ships, and lax weight controls in the shipyards, may also have played a part. Whatever its causes, a drastic weight-reduction measure was apparently called for: it was decided not to install the 1in deck plating of the *Passaic* class monitors, leaving their Russian counterparts without any deck protection at all. Although this saved about 100 tons, it came at a time when the Naval Ministry was ordering the deck protection of other ironclads *increased* because of damage

TABLE 2: CHARACTERISTICS AS DESIGNED AND COMPLETED

Displacement:	1,500 - 1,600 tons
Dimensions:	201ft oa x 46ft x 10ft 2in – 10ft 10in
	61.3m oa x 14m x 3.1 – 3.3m
Armament:	Two 9in (229mm) smoothbores as completed
Protection:	Wrought iron armour, all thicknesses made from 1in layers
	hull sides: 5in (127mm)
	turret: 11in (279mm)
	conning tower: 8in (203mm)
	funnel base: 6in (152mm)
Machinery:	Two boilers, one horizontal direct-acting engine, 340-500ihp
Speed:	5 – 7.75 knots
Endurance:	190 tons coal; 1,440nm at 6 knots
Complement:	1865: 8 officers, 88 enlisted; 1877: 10 officers and 100 enlisted.

TABLE 3: ARMAMENT

Guns:			
Calibre and Length:	**9in** (a)	**10.75in** (b)	**15in (old drawing)** (c)
	229mm	273mm	381mm
Model:	?	?	?
Dates:	1863	1865	1864
Weight:	12,449kg	11,908kg	~19,900kg
Barrel length:	4,521mm/19.8 cal	4,521mm/16.56 cal	?
Bore length:	4,013mm/17.5 cal	4,013mm/14.7 cal	9 cal
Rate of fire:	?	?	?
Projectiles & Performance:	Cast-Iron Shot	Cast-Iron Shot	Cast-Iron Shot
Weight:	41.4kg	72 – 73.7kg	199.8kg
Charge (black powder):	15.25kg	16.38kg	?
MV:	?	477m/sec	360m/sec
Range:	2,652m @ 8°	3,658m @ 14°	?

(a) Originally purchased from Krupp with the intention of rifling the tubes in Russia; however, problems with rifling systems led to some tubes being used as smoothbores, with cast-iron jackets added to the breeches. Many tubes were subsequently converted to rifles, with reinforcing added. The charge used in the monitors was apparently 12.3 kg, but performance figures for this charge are not available. These guns were replaced aboard the monitors by 15-inch Rodman-type smoothbores in 1866-1867, which were in turn replaced by rifles.

(b) These guns were originally Krupp-made 9-inch steel smoothbores. The unusual calibre was the result of a failed attempt by the Izhorskii Works to rifle two of these barrels. In order to make some use of the damaged tubes, they were bored-out to 10.75-inch and mounted in *Edinorog*. These were the only two guns of this calibre in Russian service. By 1878 they had been replaced with 9-inch rifles. Armour penetration at 400 sazhen (854m) is given as 114mm armour plus 864mm wood backing. Accuracy is described as a 'very mediocre'.

(c) Cast at the Olonets Works. Adapted from the American Rodman gun, with the bore cast with the gun, not drilled, and the bore was water-cooled after casting. Trials were started on 27 June/9 July 1865. The gun successfully passed trials, surviving over 500 shots. Proving ground trials indicated that these guns, when firing steel shot, could 'demolish' 6-inch armour at ranges up to 740m. By 1873 all guns aboard the monitors had been replaced by rifles.

sustained by the Danish ironclad *Rolf Krake* in action with Prussian shore batteries in April 1864.

Despite their relatively simple design, the ships proved to be expensive, with an average final cost of 1,155,060 rubles each, handsomely exceeding their contract cost of 600,000 rubles. The explanation for this probably lies in the extraordinary efforts that were taken to complete the ships as quickly as possible during the Polish crisis.

Armament

The defining characteristic of the monitor was its single turret, and those of the *Uragan* class ships followed their American model almost exactly. The turret had an internal diameter of 21ft (6.4m)[16] and was 9ft (2.74m) high; it rotated on a massive iron column 12in (305mm) in diameter. Normally the turret rested, immobile, on a brass ring set in the deck; to rotate, it had to be raised slightly off the deck with a manual screw-type mechanism, at which point its entire weight was supported by the central column.

This system was simple and robust but it had several drawbacks. First, it took time to raise the turret for rotation; even more serious was the relative ease with which it could be jammed by hits near its base – splinters could wedge themselves into the gap between turret and deck. And of course that gap could allow water to leak into the ship in rough seas. Over and above the obvious disadvantages in terms of keeping the ship afloat, the incoming water fell on the hot ventilation and rotating machinery in the compartment below, where it was turned into vapour, which rose up through the turret and annoyed the gunners.

While the *Passaics* were designed to carry 15in Dahlgren smoothbores, the Russians hoped to arm the *Uragans* with 9in (229mm) rifled guns. However these guns were not available when the ships entered service, so 9in smoothbores were mounted instead. These were not really powerful enough to fight ironclads, and since there were continuing problems with the development of the 9in rifles it was eventually decided to follow the American example and mount cast-iron 15in smoothbore guns. The guns in the Russian monitors, however, were of the Rodman, not the Dahlgren, type. Although no reason is given for the change, it is know that Dahlgren was jealous of his methods and had been greatly angered a few years earlier when guns of his pattern were used to arm the Russian screw frigate *General-admiral*, built at the Webb shipyard in New York.[17] So perhaps the U.S. Navy Department decided to provide the Russians with the specifications for the Rodman guns in order to keep everyone – Dahlgren and the Russians – happy. The Russian 15in guns were cast at Petrozavodsk and mounted in the ships in 1867-1868. These were replaced starting in 1876 with 9in rifles when these guns finally became available. The exception to this was the *Edinorog*, which

Guns:

Calibre and Length:	9in/17.3 (Old Drawing) (d)	9in/20 (New Drawing) (e)	9in/22 (f)
	229mm	229mm	229mm
Model:	1867	1867	1877
Dates:	Entered service 1869	?	1881
Weight, inc. Breech:	12,711kg	15,070kg (new Krupp guns)	15,348kg
		15,225kg (new Obukhovskii guns)	
Weight of Breech:	?	524kg	491kg (or 573kg)
Type of Breech:	Cylindro-prismatic wedge	Cylindro-prismatic wedge	Cylindro-prismatic wedge
Barrel length:	3,962mm/17.33 cal	4,572mm/20 cal	5,016mm
Bore length:	3,353mm/14.66 cal	3,873mm/16.9 cal	4,318mm/18.89 cal
Rifled length:	?	?	3,174mm
Number of grooves:	32	32	52
Depth rifling:	2.79mm	2.79mm	1.52mm
Rifling Twist:	60 calibers	61.45 calibers	66.9 cal., increasing to 45 at muzzle
Rate of fire:	?		? ?
Projectiles & Performance:	Common Cast Iron	Common Cast Iron	Steel
Weight:	122-124kg	122-124kg	126.2kg
Length:	2-2.5 cal	2-2.5 cal	2.7 cal
Burster:	3.5-4.5kg black	3.5-4.5kg black	?
Charge (black powder):	19.45kg	30.7 kg 'battle' (wartime only)	33.6-35.3kg
MV:	386m/sec	447m/sec	471m/sec
Range:	?	?	3,660m @ 8.7°

(d) Conversions from the steel-barreled, cast-iron-reinforced 9-inch smoothbores ordered by the Naval Ministry from Krupp in 1863. In March 1865 Krupp offered to convert these barrels to rifles, and nineteen guns were sent back to Germany for this work; in addition to being rifled, the original cast-iron jackets were removed and replaced with two layers of steel bands. The 'old' and 'new' drawing 9in guns were apparently used interchangeably.

(e) The Naval Ministry ordered twenty-two 9-inch rifles of a new design from Krupp, and soon afterwards the Obukhovskii Works began manufacturing guns to the Krupp design. Many of these barrels were subsequently converted to 9-inch model 1877 guns. (See also the notes for the 'old drawing' 9-inch gun.)

(f) All guns were re-worked 9in 1867 guns and were used to re-arm the old ironclads. The guns were lengthened by adding an extension and inserting a new inner tube; in essence, the gun was completely remade, with the breech block and reinforcing hoops retained. By 1890 there were twelve guns still in service. The performance figures are uncertain.

apparently never carried the 15in Rodman guns. Instead, she had two 10.75in (273mm) steel smoothbores; these had started out as an early attempt at 9in steel rifles, but the rifling was unsuccessful and the tubes were rebored to remove it. By 1878 these unique guns had been replaced by 9in rifles.

Ammunition outfit for the 9in smoothbores was 150 rounds, reduced to 50 rounds for the 15in guns. Explosive shells, solid shot and canister were carried.

Protection

The armour protection of the *Uragan* class for the most part followed the pattern set by their American cousins, using layers of 1in (25.4mm) armour to build up impressive thicknesses. It was known that laminated armour was far less effective than solid plate, and there had initially been some interest in ordering thicker plates from the British firm of John Brown & Co., but the company's quoted delivery time was too long. Despite the decision to use 1in plate, most of the iron used in the eight monitors built in St. Petersburg still had to be ordered in Britain, probably because delivery times were shorter than for Russian factories, whose limited capacities may have been taken up in producing plate for the iron-hulled batteries already under construction.

Despite its reduced effectiveness, the great thickness of the laminated armour, combined with the curved surfaces and the small areas of the exposed above-water structures, provided these vessels with a substantial degree of protection. The sides of the raft were protected by five layers of 1in armour plate; the three outer layers were 60in (1.5m) high, the fourth layer 48in (1.2m) high, and the innermost layer 30in (0.75m) high. Thus the side armour in effect 'tapered' from 5in (127mm) to 3in (76mm) at the lower edge some 42in (1.1m) below the waterline. The side armour was backed by thick wooden beams, amounting to about 36in (0.9m) at maximum.

The turret was the area most likely to be hit, and so had the heaviest protection – eleven layers (11in/279mm). There was no wood backing, which may have inspired Colonel Gezekhus to propose that a final layer of thick sheep-felt be fitted as sound insulation, to deaden the

A rather blurry but still interesting photograph of Lava, *probably at Kronshtadt – one of the fortress' old batteries is visible beyond her bow. Although taken early in her career, several changes may be noted from the photo of* Veshchun *perhaps most importantly, she is clearly riding deeper in the water and trimming slightly by the stern. Other changes include the solid bulwark ('rifle screen') around the top of the turret, a taller signal mast with a yard, and the protective ring around the base of the turret. The narrow barrels of her 9in smoothbores project from the gunports; when the 15in guns were mounted in the late 1860s, their muzzles were too wide to fit through these gunports. Note also the canopy rigged above the turret, visible mostly by its shadowed underside. (U.S. NHHC Photograph NH 84754)*

noise of striking projectiles. The gunport stoppers were changed from the pendulum type used on the original *Monitor*; the *Passaic* class – and so also presumably the *Uragan* class – used crank-shaped cast-iron stoppers, pivoting from the floor and roof of the turret. In the closed position, the stopper covered the gunport; for firing it swung aside.

The pilot house was protected by eight layers (8in/203mm) of armour, except in the Cockerill-built *Koldun* and *Veshchun*, where it was increased to 11in – probably in response to the weakness of the *Passaics'* pilot-houses revealed during the attack on Charleston on 7 April 1863. The funnel was jacketed to a height of 7ft (2.1m) by six layers (6in/152mm) of plate. The deck protection has already been mentioned; while the *Passaics* had 1in deck armour (made up of two layers of 0.5in iron), the Russian ships when completed did not have any deck protection beyond that provided by two layers of pine beams and their supporting structure. Sometime after their completion *Bronenosets*, *Koldun*, *Latnik*, *Lava* and *Perun* received 0.5in (12.7mm) iron deck plating, and similar plating was prepared for *Edinorog*, *Strelets*, *Tifon*, *Uragan* and *Veshchun*; the plates were fitted to the deck, drilled for the bolts, numbered, and then placed in storage in the event of future need. Perhaps the ships that received the deck plating had smaller displacement and could bear the weight without reducing their freeboard unduly.

Machinery and Trials

The machinery seems to have been the one feature in which the Russians departed substantially from the American prototypes, although the sketchiness of the available information makes categorical statements impossible. The *Passaics* had two Martin patent vertical water-tube boilers with a heating surface of 3,600ft^2 (334.4m^2), while the engine was of the relatively complex vibrating lever type. This engine, designed by Ericsson, was widely used in the ships of his design, but was unknown in the Russian service. Instead, a more familiar two-cylinder horizontal direct-acting engine of the Humphrys & Tennant type was fitted, while the boilers are described as Morton rectangular boilers with a working pressure of 20lbs/in^2 (1.4kg/cm^2), and a heating surface of 3,130ft^2 (290.7m^2).[18]

There was a single four-bladed propeller, 12ft (3.6m) in diameter. Due to the shallow draught of the ships, the top of the propeller revolved in a well in the bottom of the raft. The total output of the plants varied widely from ship to ship, ranging from 340 to 500ihp, producing speeds of 5 to 7.75 knots. The machinery was manufactured by a variety of firms (see Table 4). It is interesting to note that *Bronenosets* and *Latnik* – both engined by Carr & MacPherson (a Russian firm founded by a pair of Scots) – were, respectively, the fastest and slowest ships of the class. Clearly there were serious inconsistencies either in the

Bronenosets, *anchored among a wide variety of ships, probably off Kronshtadt in the 1870s. The turret is trained to starboard, so we are looking at its port side and rear; the bulwark atop it has been modified, with squarish sponsons added for light guns. The davits and boats have been raised, clearing the turret's arc of fire on after bearings, but it is unclear whether the hurricane deck between turret and funnel has been added yet. (Courtesy Boris Lemachko)*

manufacture of the engines or in the skill of the engine-room staff. It should also be noted that the two ships engined by the Belgian Cockerill firm were not noticeably superior to the ships with Russian-built machinery.

The fuel supply amounted to 190 tons of coal, carried in one central and two side bunkers next to the machinery spaces. This was in theory sufficient fuel for ten days at 6 knots, or 1,440nm.

Auxiliary machinery included two small engines, one for driving the ventilation system (20hp) and the other for rotating the turret (15hp). There were also two pumps of the Gwynne type for clearing water out of the engine room and the compartment under the turret; their capacities were 2.8 tons/min and 5.5 tons/min respectively.

The trials of the ships were judged satisfactory, on the whole; steering was adequate and the ships had an easy motion. The acceptance commission noted that *Koldun* had the best sea-going qualities, *Latnik* the worst. Later experience showed that in rough weather the deck was covered with water – so much so, in fact, that the turret formed its own bow wave, which made it impossible to use the guns.

TABLE 4: MACHINERY AND TRIAL SPEEDS

Name	Engined by	Date of Trials (Old Style)	Speed (knots)
Bronenosets	Carr & MacPherson	9 Oct 1864	7.75
Edinorog	Baird	19 Jun 1865	5.75
Koldun	Cockerill	21 Jul 1864	6
Latnik	Carr & MacPherson	31 May 1865	5
Lava	Izhorskii	12 Jul 1865	6.5
Perun	Izhorskii	16 Aug 1865	6.75
Strelets	Baird	6 Jul 1865	6
Tifon	Baird	19 Jun 1865	6.7
Uragan	Baird	31 May 1865	6.5
Veshchun	Cockerill	21 Jul 1864	6.75

Note: Speeds were recorded by log, not on a measured mile, and so are subject to considerable inaccuracy.

Modifications

The reserve of buoyancy in monitor-type ships was very small, so any modification involving additional weight could be made only with great care. In the American ships it was eventually found necessary to increase the buoyancy by deepening the raft by 15in. No such change was made in the Russian ships, so their modifications were more limited in scope; nevertheless the *Uragans* underwent considerable changes during their long careers, some of which greatly altered their outward appearances.

Initially most modifications were minor and addressed some of the faults of the American prototypes. One such 'fix' was the ring fitted around the base of the turret; during the attack on Charleston in April 1863, splinters from nearby hits had jammed monitor turrets by lodging between the base of the turret and the deck. The solution was to fit an iron ring around the base of the turret, and this was done on the American *Passaics* during the Civil War. A similar addition was made on their Russian counterparts, probably some time later. These rings were 5in (127mm) thick and 15in (381mm) high, and can be seen in some photographs of the ships.

Another alteration that can be characterised as a fix was the partial fairing in of the overhang of the raft with wooden beams. One of the greatest criticisms of Ericsson's monitors was this discontinuity between raft and hull proper; many thought it would lead to a severe slamming effect as a monitor pitched in heavy seas, and the loss of the original *Monitor* in December 1862 was sometimes ascribed to the raft and hull separating. (This was not in fact the case – the discovery of her wreck showed that the raft-hull system was intact. The major causes of her loss seems to have been water working its way in under the turret and through the anchor well and windlass arrangements forward.) As a result, there were concerns about the effects of the overhang on the ships' behaviour in rough seas, and the Shipbuilding Technical Committee decided to add a triangular 'filler' between raft and hull made of wooden beams. The fairing on the Russian ships increased their buoyancy and also provided a small degree of extra protection against ramming.

Another modification was an attempt to resolve the problem of a drop in boiler pressure noted when all the auxiliary machinery was in operation. On *Veshchun* an auxiliary boiler was installed (date unknown, but probably around 1870) in the central coal bunker. This, however, led to a serious reduction in steaming range, and the modification was not repeated in any of her sister ships.

The re-arming of the ships with Russian-made 15in Rodman guns in 1867-1868 has already been noted; this inevitably led to an increase in weights, which was compensated for by removing some ballast. In 1873 a hydraulic mechanism of American design for raising the turret was installed on *Koldun* and went through a lengthy trials period, but was finally rejected in 1876 because it required 3-7 minutes to raise the turret, which was considered too long. In 1878 the long-expected 9in (229mm) rifled guns finally began to be installed.

The most visible change to the outward appearance of the monitors was the erection of a hurricane deck from the turret to the funnel, with a small elevated platform for a single light gun immediately abaft the funnel; this was probably done in the 1870s. This allowed the engine room skylight to be raised to the hurricane deck, which meant that it could be kept open in rough weather. The boats and davits, located abaft the turret, were also raised to the level of the hurricane deck, which had the effect of allowing the turret to train farther on after bearings, giving a total arc of fire of 310°.

Early in the careers of the monitors rolled hammocks seem to have been used to offer some protection to men atop the turret; subsequently, more substantial protection in the form of outward-curving armoured bulwarks (similar to the 'rifle screens' on American monitors) were installed around the turret's top. Some time later – probably in the mid- or late 1870s – three squarish sponsons were added to these bulwarks, one on each side of the turret, and one on the forward face above the gunports, each supporting a rapid-firing anti-torpedo boat gun. Another light gun was carried immediately abaft the funnel on a small platform above the hurricane deck, giving all-round coverage. These appear to have been

The name ship of the class, Uragan, probably photographed in the late 1870s or early 1880s. This broadside view makes her sheer aft particularly evident. The sponsons for anti-torpedo boat guns projecting from the turret's bulwark can be seen, as well as the hurricane deck linking the turret to the funnel, immediately abaft of which is a small elevated platform for another light gun. (Courtesy Boris Lemachko)

RUSSIA'S 'AMERICAN' MONITORS: THE URAGAN CLASS

A view of Koldun, *probably taken at about the same time as the preceding photograph of* Uragan, *and showing the same modifications. Note that the funnel is painted in a light colour with a dark top, whereas* Bronenosets *showed an all-light funnel and* Uragan *an all-dark one; in the American monitors the funnels were painted differently to distinguish the nearly identical ships from each other, and it is possible that the Russians adopted this practice.* (Courtesy Boris Lemachko)

1.75in/44.5mm Engstrem guns, an early type of quick-firer of Swedish design introduced into the Russian navy in the mid-1870s. The guns were equipped with shields.

Careers

Ironically, less information is available regarding the active service of these ships than about their careers as hulks after being stricken. The monitors were usually part of the Armourclad Squadron, and after 1869 some of the *Uragan* class were to be found in the annual summer cruises of the Artillery Training Detachment, which trained gunnery officers and seamen gunners. They spent their years entirely in the Baltic, cruising from one training ground to another during the navigation season, which generally lasted from April to September. Over the long winters they would be laid up at Kronshtadt; this was the time when most modifications were made. Aside from occasional groundings or collisions – none of them fatal – these ships seem to have led rather uneventful lives, and after about 1890 they rarely put to sea. The few details known about their careers are noted below.

To prevent repetition, several events in the lives of the *Uragan* class ships may be mentioned. First, in July-August 1865 nine of the monitors – *Latnik* was apparently the exception – cruised to Stockholm under the command of the General-Admiral of the Navy, the Grand Duke Konstantin Nikolaevich; *Strelets* served as his flag-

ship. Second, on 1/13 February 1892 all of the monitors were reclassified from 'monitors' to 'coast defence armourclads'. Third, all of the ships were turned over to the Port of Kronshtadt authorities on 24 June/6 July 1900 for disposal, and all were stricken from the fleet on 5/17 August of the same year.

As a final note, the accent marks in the names of ships indicate the stressed syllable.

Bronenósets (an armour-clad warrior or warship): Trials in October 1864; maximum speed was 7.75 knots, making her the fastest ship of the class. She then joined the Armourclad Squadron. After being stricken she was converted to a coal barge in 1903 – the side armour and wood backing were removed and the hull was divided into three holds – and redesignated *Barzha* (barge) No.34, then *Barzha* No.51, and from 1914 *Barzha* No.324. She sank in the Gulf of Finland in a storm during the First World War.

Edinoróg ('unicorn' or 'narwhal'; also a type of Russian muzzle-loading cannon): Trials in June/July 1865. After being stricken she was converted into a storeship for mines in 1912 and redesignated *Blokshiv* (hulk) No.4 on 27 June/10 July 1912. Left behind at Helsingfors (modern Helsinki) by Soviet forces in April 1918; subsequently returned to the Soviets under the terms of the Treaty of Brest-Litovsk. Redesignated *Blokshiv* No.2 on 1 January 1932; survived the Second World War and was redesignated *BSh-2* on 16 May 1949. Stricken on 27 June 1957 and turned over to the Kronshtadt Yacht Club. Her subsequent fate is unknown.

Koldún ('wizard'): Trials in July/August 1864. After being stricken she was converted to a coal barge in 1903 (side armour and wood backing removed, hull divided into three holds) and redesignated *Barzha No.31*, later *Barzha No.50*, and from 1914 she was designated *Barzha No.323*. She was left behind in Finland when it was evacuated by the Bolsheviks in April 1918, and was subsequently broken up in Finland.

Látnik (an armour-clad warrior): Trials in May/June 1865. She apparently suffered some (unspecified) hull damage in September 1865. After being stricken she was converted to a coal barge in 1903, the side armour and wood backing removed, the hull divided into three holds; redesignated *Barzha No.38*, from 1914 *Barzha No.326*. She was abandoned in Finland by evacuating Red forces in April 1918, and was subsequently broken up there.

Láva ('cavalry charge' or 'avalanche'): Trials in July 1865. In March 1870 she was assigned to the new Artillery Training Detachment. After being stricken she was used as a floating barracks from 1902 to 1908 for the Third Destroyer Flotilla, then used as a 'ranging-shot station' (*pristrelochnaia stantsiia*) – presumably involved in gunnery practices, perhaps for parties observing the fall of shot around a target. She was redesignated *Blokshiv No.1* on 1/14 April 1911 and used as a mine storeship during the First World War until 1916, when she was converted to a floating hospital (reportedly receiving her old name). She was abandoned at Helsingfors by retreating Red forces in April 1918 and interned under the terms of the Treaty of Brest-Litovsk; she was retroceded to Soviet Russia in 1922 but was subsequently broken up in Finland. (Some reports indicate that she was still in existence in 1941.)

Perún ('thunderbolt'; also the old Slavic god of thunder): Trials in August 1865. Accidentally rammed by the turret-frigate *Admiral Chichagov* during manoeuvres on 6/18 July 1875; the monitor sustained only minor damage. After being stricken she was used as *blokshiv* by the pilot service and renamed *Lotsiia* ('Pilot') in 1915. She was hit by artillery and damaged by the resulting fire during the Kronshtadt uprising of 1921; laid up as a result. On 23 September 1924 she was run aground close to the shore by flood waters and subsequently broken up.

Streléts (a member of the *Streltsy*, a military caste of 16th and 17th century Muscovy; the word means 'shooter' and is analogous to 'musketeer'): Trials in July 1865. In July 1875 she was one of several ships that assisted the turret-frigate *Admiral Chichagov*, which had run aground near Transund (near Vyborg); two men were seriously injured when a towing hawser parted; one later died of his injuries. After being stricken she was converted into a floating workshop in 1901, redesignated *Plavmasterskaia No.1* ('Floating Workshop No.1') on 22 February/7 March 1901. She continued in service until the end of 1955; her subsequent fate is unknown; one report indicates that her hull is still in existence.[19]

Tifón ('typhoon'): Trials held in June/July 1865. On 14/27 October 1909 she was redesignated *Blokshiv No.3* and converted to a mine storage hulk. She was at Helsingfors in early 1918 and seized by the Finnish government after the Red forces evacuated. She was retroceded to the Soviet government in 1922, but subsequently broken up in Finland.

Edinorog *probably in the 1880s. Visible here are the three sponsons for anti-torpedo-boat guns around the top of the turret, one on each side and one on the forward face. Note how the ship seems now to trim by the stern, in contrast to the first photograph, of* Veshchun *soon after her completion.* (Courtesy Boris Lemachko)

A stern view of Koldun, *giving a good idea of the bridgework added to these ships. The shielded anti-torpedo-boat gun on the uppermost platform abaft the funnel is particularly evident in this shot, as is the light gun in the starboard sponson on the turret – probably an Engstrem 1.75in gun.* (Courtesy Boris Lemachko)

Uragán ('hurricane'): Trials in May/June 1865. After being stricken she was converted to a coal barge and redesignated *Barzha* No.39 in 1903; later *Barzha* No.52, and finally *Barzha* 325 from 1914. She was also used at Sveaborg (near Helsingfors). She was left behind in Finland in April 1918 when the Soviet forces evacuated and subsequently broken up there.

Veshchún ('soothsayer'): Trials in July/August 1864. In 1903 she was converted into a coal barge and redesignated *Barzha* No.44, then in 1914 renamed *Barzha* No.327; she was used at Kronshtadt and Sveaborg. Left behind in Finland when the Soviet Navy evacuated in 1918; subsequently broken up in Finland.

Acknowledgements:
I would like to express my gratitude to Ian Sturton for providing the drawings and to the late Boris Lemachko for providing photographs. Keith Allen, Brooks A. Rowlett and Bill Jurens provided valuable help in sorting out the displacement of the *Passaic* class. And as always Jan Torbet ran a critical eye over each version of the article.

Sources:
The major source for these ships is V.I. Lysenok, 'Bronenosnye bashennye lodki tipa "Uragan"' (*Sudostroenie*, No.3, 1985, pp.69-72). V.Iu. Gribovskii, and I.I. Chernikov, *Bronenosets 'Admiral Ushakov'* (St. Petersburg: Sudostroenie, 1996), pp.25-30, provides additional information. Background information on the American prototypes of these ships, the *Monitor* and the *Passaic* class, is taken from Donald L. Canney, *The Old Steam Navy*, vol. 2: *The Ironclads, 1842-1885* (Annapolis: Naval Institute Press, 1993), vol. 2, pp.25-34, 75-84, and Edward M. Miller, *U.S.S. Monitor: The Ship That Launched a Modern Navy* (Annapolis: Leeward Publications, Inc., 1978). Most of the few details about the careers of the *Uragan* class ships comes from S.S. Berezhnoi, *Lineinye i bronenosnye korabli – kanonerskie lodki: spravochnik* (Moscow: Voennoe izdatel'stvo, 1997), pp.75-80. The visit of nine of the monitors to Stockholm in 1865 was reported in the *London Times*, 5 September 1865, p.7; a few highlights in the careers of these ships are incidentally noted in R.M. Mel'nikov, *Bashennye bronenosnye fregaty* (St. Petersburg: Boevye korabli mira, 2002), pp.36, 45-48.

For details of the main armament I have relied on L.I. Amirkhanov, *Artilleriia rossiiskikh monitorov* (St. Petersburg: Gangut, 1998), especially pp.28-32, where there is a detailed table showing what guns were carried by which ships, based on the reports of the ships' captains.

Notes:
1. These ships are usually referred to as the *Bronenosets* class in western publications, but they are called the *Uragan* class in Russia.
2. See Stephen McLaughlin, 'Russia's First Ironclads: *Pervenets, Ne tron menia* and *Kreml'* (*Warship* 2011, pp.112-129).
3. Canney, *The Old Steam Navy*, vol. 2, p.34.
4. Letter from the Secretary of the Navy to Flag-Officer Charles H. Davis introducing 'Captain Lessovsky', 12 July 1862; *Official Records of the Union and Confederate Navies in the War of the Rebellion* (31 vols., Washington: Government Printing Office, 1894-1927), series I, vol. 23, p.256.
5. Although it is not mentioned explicitly in Lysenok's article cited in the sources, the fact that Lesovskii's group was sent to the United States specifically to study the *Monitor* type is

indicated in the brief biography of Artseulov in *Russki biograficheskii slovar'* (St. Petersburg: Izdanie Imperatorskago Russkago istoricheskago obshchestva, 1896-1918), vol. 2, p.336. Pestich is not mentioned in Lysenok's article, but is named in Kipp, 'The Russian Navy and the Problem of Technological Transfer: Technological Backwardness and Military-Industrial Development, 1853-1876' (in *Russia's Great Reforms, 1855-1881*, edited by Ben Eklof, John Bushnell and Larissa Zakharova; Bloomington: Indiana University Press, 1994, pp.115-138), p.128.

6. Richard E. Waldman, 'Question 42/84' [U.S.S. Montauk]. (*Warship International*, vol. XXI, No.4 [1984]), p.435; *Dictionary of American Naval Fighting Ships* (Washington: Naval History Division, 1960-1981), vol. 4, p.424.

7. S.S. Lesovskii, 'Zamechaniia kontr-admirala Lesovskogo na stat'iu United Service Gazette o Rezul'atakh ispytaniia bronenostsev' (*Morskoi sbornik*, 1863, No.8, pp.445-451), pp.446, 450.

8. William Conant Church, *The Life of John Ericsson*, 2 vols. (New York: Charles Scribner's Sons, 1907), vol. 2, p.76; letter, Donald L. Canney to the author, 8 August 1995.

9. Howard J. Fuller, *Clad in Iron: The American Civil War and the Challenge of British Naval Power* (Annapolis: Naval Institute Press, 2008), p.110; Daniel G. Harris, 'The Swedish Monitors', *Warship 1994* (London: Conway Maritime Press, 1994, pp.22-34), pp.22-24.

10. L.G. Beskrovny [Beskrovnyi], *The Russian Army and Fleet in the Nineteenth Century: Handbook of Armaments, Personnel and Policy* (Gulf Breeze, FL: Academic International Press, 1996), pp.303, 305.

11. There is some confusion over the displacement of the *Passaic* class; many publications, including the authoritative *Dictionary of American Naval Fighting Ships* (vol. 3, p.758) list a figure of 1,875 tons, but the increase over the *Monitor's* dimensions is too small to account for such an increase. The figure of 1,335 tons come from Church, *Life of John Ericsson*, vol. 2, p.8n; it is supported by Donald L. Canney, 'The Union Navy During the Civil War, 1861-65' (*Warship 1995*), p.18, and Paul H. Silverstone, *Civil War Navies, 1855-1883* (Annapolis: Naval Institute Press, 2001), p.5. A rough calculation of displacement, based on the lines of the *Passaic* class shown in Canney, *The Old Steam Navy*, vol. 2, p.81, confirms the 1,335-ton figure. The origins of the 1,875-ton figure remain obscure.

12. The figure of 159ft comes from Canney, *The Old Steam Navy*, vol. 2, p.76; Lysenok gives the length of the lower hull as 173ft 11in, but evidently includes the rudder.

13. Ericsson letter, quoted in William H. Roberts, *Civil War Ironclads: The U.S. Navy and Industrial Mobilization* (Baltimore: The Johns Hopkins University Press, 2002), p.44.

14. *Armored Vessels in the Attack on Charleston*, U.S. Congress, House of Representatives, 38th Congress, 1st Session, Executive Document No.69, (Washington: Government Printing Office, 1864), p.43. This document is included in the Congressional Serial Set, vol. 1193. The displacement of 1,500 tons is based on my estimate of 16 tons per inch immersion for the class.

15. Gribovskii and Chernikov, *Bronenosets 'Admiral Ushakov'*, p.28. The one-foot difference is length and beam seem to be real, and not artifacts of conversion to and from metric measurements – but conversion errors cannot be ruled out entirely.

16. The *Passaics* had a turret diameter of 21ft (Canney, *The Old Steam Navy*, vol. 2, p.77); Lysenok, p.69, gives the same dimension for the *Uragans* as 6.28m = 20ft 7in. I have used the 21ft diameter here on the assumption that the dimensions slipped somewhere in the conversion to the metric system. It is possible, however, that the internal diameter of the Russian turrets was indeed slightly smaller than that of the American ships – perhaps due to the sound-absorbing layer of sheep-felt proposed by Colonel Gezekhus (see the section on protection).

17. Robert J. Schneller Jr. *A Quest for Glory: A Biography of Rear Admiral John A. Dahlgren* (Annapolis: Naval Institute, 1996), pp.163-164.

18. Lysenok, p.69, refers to these 'Morton' boilers, but I have so far been unable to find any other references to a boiler by this name. It is possible that this is a transliteration error for 'Martin', although I would not expect the vowel sounds to be altered in this way.

19. So says Wikipedia (http://en.wikipedia.org/wiki/Uragan_class_monitor), accessed on 4 May 2011. Unfortunately, no source for this statement is provided.

THE BATTLESHIP *GAULOIS*

To follow his articles on the French pre-dreadnoughts *Iéna* and *Suffren*, **Philippe Caresse** traces the eventful career of the earlier *Gaulois*, one of three battleships of the *Charlemagne* class.

On 25 June 1892, the vice-admiral President of the *Conseil de travaux* (Council of Works) received a message from the Navy Minister which began:

> Monsieur le président, I have decided that studies should be undertaken with a view to the construction of new battleships. In order to secure the maximum reduction in displacement compatible with an armament slightly greater than that of the *Lazare Carnot* and the *Charles Martel*, I have decided that the main guns will be as follows: two twin 30cm guns in a single turret forward and two twin 27cm in a single after turret (turret or barbette-type mounting). The secondary battery is to comprise ten 14cm guns and six 10cm guns. Speed is to be not less than 18 knots

It quickly became apparent that the calibre of the after guns was insufficient to prevail in a gunnery duel with the British battleships of the period, and would, moreover, lack the necessary power for the bombardment of fixed defences ashore. Protection would need to extend over the entire length of the hull with a thickness of 45cm.

In a meeting which took place on 20 June 1893 the *Directeur du matériel* (equivalent to the British DNC) submitted to the Council for discussion six sketch plans for a *cuirassé d'escadre* (fleet battleship) drawn up by the constructors Thibaudier, de Monchoisy, Dupré, Bayssellance, Lhomme and by the Société de la Loire. The 1892 Programme envisaged the laying down of battleships of a modified *Bouvet* type. The designed characteristics were as follows: four 305mm guns in twin enclosed and balanced turrets fore and aft; ten 140mm guns, six 100mm, sixteeen 47mm, ten 37mm and four torpedo tubes. The armoured belt was to have a thickness of 400mm from its upper edge to 0.20m beneath the

The Gaulois *at sea*. (DR)

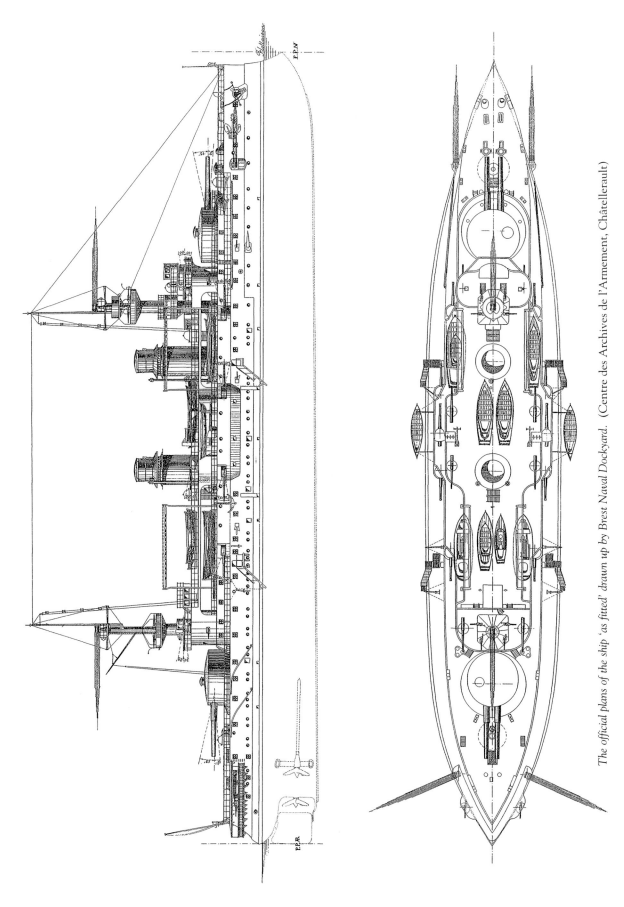

The official plans of the ship 'as fitted' drawn up by Brest Naval Dockyard. (Centre des Archives de l'Armement, Châtellerault)

THE BATTLESHIP *GAULOIS*

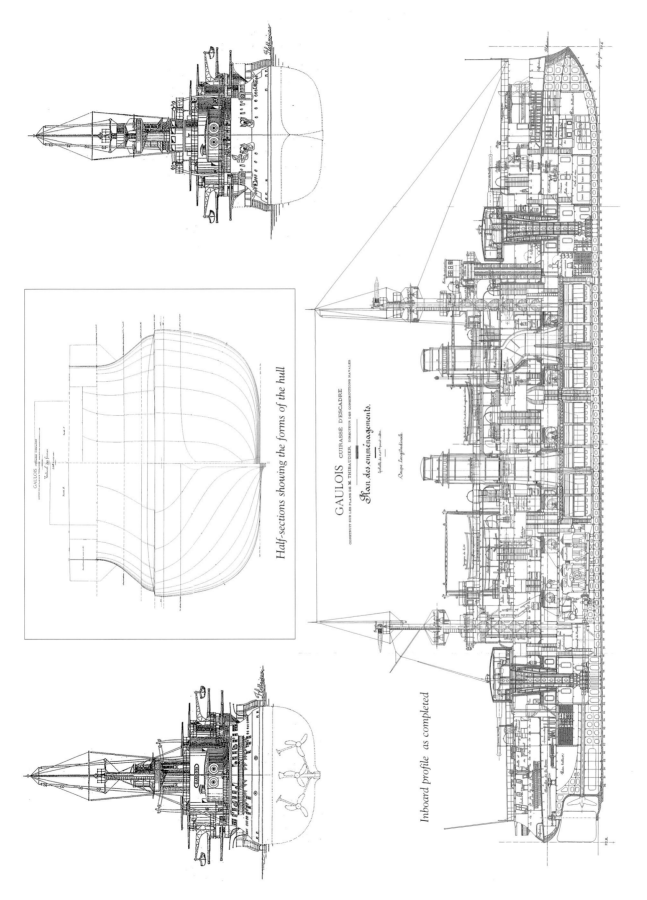

Half-sections showing the forms of the hull

Inboard profile as completed

waterline. The main deck would be 90mm thick including armour plating (on the inclines). Speed would be 18 knots in service, and endurance 4,000nm at 10 knots. Finally, displacement was not to exceed 11,000 tonnes.

The study by Thibaudier satisfied these criteria, and required only minor modifications requested by the *Conseil de travaux*. De Monchoisy had proposed ten 140mm guns in enclosed turrets and a complex distribution of armour; the plan was rejected. Dupré had presented a proposal for a ship with a machinery installation which was too heavy, the compartmentation of the *tranche cellulaire* (the cellular subdivision between the main deck and the lower deck) was regarded as unsatisfactory; it was also feared that the wing turrets would result in a pronounced roll. Bayssellance's design was equally disliked, having a speed of only 17 knots, and a protection system and turret layout which were both regarded as unsatisfactory. The distribution of armour was also regarded as an unsatisfactory feature of the design proposed by Lhomme, while that proposed by the Société de la Loire was rejected on the grounds of insufficient speed and inadequate protection of the hull.

At the meeting of 25 July 1893 a further project from the Société des Forges et Chantiers de la Méditerranée was considered, but a displacement of 11,954 tonnes and a controversial arrangement of the machinery led the Council to request that the plans be modified.

The three battleships of the *Charlemagne* class would therefore be built according to the plans of Thibaudier. They were to be named *Charlemagne*, *Saint Louis* and *Gaulois*. The *Gaulois*[1] was laid down at Brest under the supervision of *Ingénieur de la Marine* Richard. The order was placed on 22 January 1895, but the laying down of the keel had to await the launch of *Charlemagne*, finally taking place on 6 January 1896.

The Battleship Gaulois

Protection
The hull was of mild steel with overlapping plates, and was divided into fourteen watertight compartments which corresponded with the frames.

The armoured belt had a maximum thickness of 400mm, declining to 110mm at its bottom edge, and was 3.26m high; it was manufactured by Schneider and the Société de Chatillon. The main deck was 55mm thick with 35mm plates as reinforcement on the outboard inclines, the latter being manufactured by Guérigny and the Société de St Etienne. The conning tower had walls of 326mm, a 50mm roof, a 30mm floor, and a 200mm communications tube; it was built by Schneider.

On 27 November 1895, the company Hauts Fourneaux, Forges et Aciéries de la Marine et des Chemins de Fer secured the contract for the 305mm turrets. Protection for the latter comprised: 320mm plating for the walls of the turret, 50mm for the roof and the armoured hood, and 270mm for the barbettes. The armoured 'redoubt' for the casemate guns had 150mm plating on the transverse bulkheads and 55mm outer walls with 30mm floors. The total weight of armour was 820.70 tonnes.

Armament
The 305mm turrets were the first twin heavy-calibre mountings in the Marine Nationale. The Mle 1893 gun fired a shell weighing 338.69kg at a theoretical rate of one round every 1.3 minutes. Eight of the ten 138.6mm guns of the secondary battery were in casemates on the Upper Deck; the remaining two were in open shielded mountings on the Forecastle Deck amidships. They fired a shell weighing 36.50kg at a rate of 4rpm. The 100mm guns were located in the lower part of the superstructures; they fired a 25.50kg shell at a rate of 5rpm. The 47mm 'anti-torpedo-boat' guns were distributed between the military masts, the open superstructures and the sternwalk; they fired a 2.46kg shell at a rate of 12rpm.

The 450mm torpedoes each weighed 501kg; there was a modern self-propelled type, the Mle 1892, which was fired from the torpedo tubes, and an older *torpille portée* Mle 1887 which was embarked on the ship's boats. The underwater tubes for the self-propelled torpedoes were located on the lower platform deck to port and starboard, 3.165m beneath the waterline, and were angled at 20° from the ship's axis. The two above-water tubes were installed on the Main Deck just abaft the pivot of the forward 305mm turret, 2.19m above the waterline.

Machinery
The triple-expansion piston engines, which had an operating pressure of 13-14kg/cm^2, were built by the Société de la Loire. The boilers were designed and manufactured by Delaunay Belleville et Cie, and had an operating pressure of 17kg/cm^2. The number of boilers in each group varied from four to six; there was one burner per boiler and per system. Mixed firing gave very satisfactory results during trials. The height of the funnels above their armoured gratings was 24.70 metres.

The centre-line and port propellers turned to the right, and the starboard propeller to the left. The rudder was built by Guérigny. *Gaulois* had a turning circle of 900m at 16 knots.

For damage control there were four Thirion steam pumps each with a capacity of 600m^3 of water per hour. There were also three circulation turbines rated at 500m^3/h, three Thirion pumps for the machinery rated at 30m^3/h, and a single Thirion pump rated at 9m^3/h. The six ventilators for the engine rooms each had a capacity of 40,000m^3/h. Four Sautter Harlé turbo-dynamos each of 600A provided an 83V electricity supply.

Equipment
On completion there were two large-model plotting tables in the conning tower. In 1910 Barr & Stroud FQ-type rangefinders were installed on either side of the foremast. In 1915 a new B&S rangefinder would be embarked.

The searchlight projectors were equipped with a Mangin mirror and combined lamps from Sautter, Harlé & Cie. Two were located forward between decks, and mounted on trolleys with electrical controls. Two more, similarly mounted, were located aft on the sternwalk. The remaining two searchlights were on fixed bases and were located on the foremast and mainmast platforms respectively.

The two 10-metre steam pinnaces could be armed with

TABLE 1: GENERAL CHARACTERISTICS

Length oa	117.70m
Length wl	116.20m
Beam wl	20.26m
Draught at deep load	
forward	7.40m
aft	8.40m
Freeboard at forecastle	6.00m
Displacement, normal	10,361 tonnes
Displacement, deep load	11,325 tonnes

Armament

1899	1915
4 – 305/40 Mle 1893 (2 x II)	4 – 305/40 Mle 1893 (2 x II)
10 – 138.6/45 Mle 1893 (10 x I)	10 – 138.6/45 Mle 1893 (10 x I)
8 – 100/45 Mle 1893 (8 x I)	6 – 100/45 Mle 1893 (6 x I)
20 – 47/50 Mle 1885 (20 x I)	4 – 47/50 Mle 1885 (4 x I)
4 – 450mm TT	2 – 450mm TT
portable – for boats	
2 – 65mm Mle 1881	
2 – 37mm Mle 1885	

Gun	Elevation	Range
305mm	+15°/ -5°	12,900m
138.6mm	+19°30/-5°30	11,000m
100mm	+20°/-10°	10,000m
47mm	+24°/-21°	4,000m

Ammunition Stowage

305mm	180 rounds
138.6mm	2,316 rounds
100mm	2,288 rounds
47mm	10,500 rounds
self-propelled torpedoes	twelve
65mm	251 rounds
37mm	1,050 rounds
portable torpedoes	six

Machinery

Boilers	20 Belleville
Engines	3/4-cylinder triple expansion
Propellers	three 3-bladed 4.30m
Rudder	one of 24.20m^2
Horsepower (trials)	14,220ihp
Speed	18.024 knots
Coal (deep load)	1,101 tonnes
Oil	50 tonnes
Endurance	3,776nm at 10 knots
	1,735nm at 17 knots

Equipment

Searchlight projectors	six 600mm S/L
Boats	two 10m steam pinnaces
	one 7.65m White launch
	one 11m pulling pinnace
	one 10.5m admiral's launch
	two 10m cutters
	one 9m cutter
	three 8.5m, one 8m, one 7m whalers
	two 5m dinghies
	two 3.5m flat bottom boats
	two 5.6m canvas launches
Anchors	three 7.50-tonne Marrel
	two 1.75-tonne kedge anchors
Complement (1905)	26 officers, 642 men.
(as flagship)	58 flag staff

The launch of the battleship Gaulois *on 6 October 1896.* (DR)

The Gaulois *and the* Charlemagne *fitting out in Brest Naval Dockyard.* (DR)

a 47mm gun, a searchlight projector and a Flèche torpedo-carrying apparatus. The 11-metre pulling pinnace could also be armed with a 47mm gun and the two 10-metre cutters could each receive a 37mm gun.

The two bower anchors were in hawsepipes with a third (sheet) anchor stowed on the starboard side of the bow. The anchor chains were 62mm wide and had a length of 26 links.

Completion and Entry into Service

The naval dockyard of Brest did not spare its efforts in building the *Gaulois*, and the latter would be launched only nine months after the laying of the keel. The launch ceremony took place on 6 October 1896 under the direction of the Major General commanding the port, Rear-Admiral de Kerambosquer.

The Gaulois *on speed trials July 1898. Her guns have yet to be embarked.* (DR)

Embarkation of one of the four 305mm guns in October 1898. (DR)

On 12 May 1897, Chief Engineer Sineux of the Société de la Loire arrived to supervise the installation of the propulsion machinery. The boilers would be complete before the end of the year. The first machinery trials with the ship alongside took place on 9 March 1898. In July the newly-appointed CO of the *Gaulois* announced that the first trials had been successful, despite delays in the installation of the main guns. Tests of fuel consumption took place on 19 July, and full power trials on 20 August. From October the battleship would be immobilised at Brest for installation of the 305mm turrets. The official gunnery trials were conducted on 20 and 21 October 1899, and the ship was commissioned two days later and provisionally assigned to the Northern Squadron.

On 18 January 1900, the *Gaulois*, with Ingénieur Rougé embarked, and her sister *Charlemagne* left for Toulon to join the 1st Battleship Division of the Mediterranean Squadron. The passage was conducted at an average speed of 15 knots, and on their arrival in Marseille the ships still had 350 tonnes of coal in their bunkers. However, foul weather in the Bay of Biscay had plagued the ships from the moment they left Brest, and off San Sebastián several

The roof of one of the massive twin 305mm turrets is lifted into place. (DR)

Gaulois and Charlemagne during their transit from Brest to Toulon. (Painting by G Hallo, Armée et Marine)

scuttles were pushed in. The CO also reported that the ship's compass, which was located close to the steering gear, was completely unusable in these conditions.

Captain Le Bris, in his report on the seakeeping and military qualities of his ship, stated:

> In bad weather, with a head sea and at moderate speed, the *Gaulois* behaves in a less than satisfactory fashion: she quickly begins to take seas over the bow and the forward turret and casemates are washed out; this has an adverse effect on fire, and considerable quantities of water penetrate the gun mountings. The bower anchors, which project from the sides of the ship, and the platforms for the searchlight projectors contribute to the enormous amount of spray. Rolling and pitching is less of a problem; the ship is generally a steady gunnery platform. The ship manœuvres well even in confined spaces.

From the military point of view the four 305mm guns are powerful weapons, and the mountings and their associated installations are excellent. The 138.6mm guns, on the other hand, are too light in calibre for a battleship of this size, and the light artillery is poorly distributed and difficult to control. Fire control for the main and secondary guns is good.

The armoured belt, which is perhaps of excessive thickness, has insufficient height above the waterline. Protection for the 138.6mm guns is therefore illusory, as they can be disabled by a shell exploding beneath them.

In February, during exercises in the anchorage at Hyères (east of Toulon), the destroyer *Hallebarde* was ordered to change station and found herself in the path of the *Gaulois*. The collision was unavoidable, and the *Hallebarde* was struck by the battleship on her starboard quarter in the area of the POs' mess. A breach measuring 4m by 1.5m did not prevent the ship from making Toulon in company with the escorting *Dunois*. As for the *Gaulois*, the latter barely sustained any damage in the collision.

On 11 July, following combined manœuvres of the Northern and Mediterranean Squadrons under the command of Admiral Gervais, the fleet anchored in the Cherbourg roads. President Loubet arrived on 18 July, and embarked the following day on the sloop *Elan* to inspect a full naval review. Forty-three major vessels of all types were assembled in seven rows parallel to the outer jetty. The *Gaulois* was part of the 4th line in the company of the battleships *Jauréguiberry*, *Charlemagne*, *Charles-Martel* and *Jemmapes*.[2]

The Mediterranean Squadron then sailed for Brest, where the crew was granted leave on the 23 July, before returning to the coast of Provence. On 22 August the fleet

The Gaulois at her moorings in early 1900. To the left of her is the battleship Neptune. (DR)

The damaged destroyer Hallebarde, *following her collision with the* Gaulois. *(Armée et Marine)*

sailed for gunnery practice and underwent a general inspection in Golfe Juan; it reentered Toulon on 1st September. On the 19th the *Gaulois* conducted torpedo launches, finishing the year without any significant events. From 10 April 1901 President Loubet joined the fleet in the anchorage at Villefranche. Ships present were the *Saint Louis* (VA de Maigret), *Gaulois*, *Charlemagne*, *Charles Martel* (CA Aubry de la Noë), *Jauréguiberry*, *Bouvet*, *Galilée*, *Linois*, *Lavoisier*, *Hallebarde*, *Dunois*, *Flibustier*, *Forbin* and *Cyclone*. The previous evening the Russian Battleship *Alexander II* (Rear-Ad. Birileff) and a gunboat made a spectacular entrance into the anchorage in order to honour the French president. The two squadrons shortly headed for Toulon, where a number of Italian ships were already at anchor, the major unit being the battleship *Lepanto*, flying the flag of Prince Thomas, Duke of Genoa. The Spanish battleship *Pelayo* was also present.

On 3 July the Northern and Mediterranean Squadrons joined up for new naval exercises which extended from the Straits of Gibraltar to Malta, with numerous calls at the ports of North Africa.

On the second to last day of October, the French Government ordered Admiral Maigret, then at sea with the Fleet, to detach the 1st Division to Mytilene on the Island of Lesbos. Rear-Admiral Caillard was in command of this formation and flew his flag in the armoured cruiser *Pothuau*. Caillard headed for the Aegean accompanied by the battleships *Gaulois* and *Charlemagne*, the armoured cruiser *Chanzy*, the 3rd class cruiser *Linois* and the destroyers *Epée* and *Espingole*.

At that time Turkey had promised a French company that it would build quays on the two banks of the Corne d'Or (Tipaza, Algeria). None of these contracts had been honoured and, moreover, two French financiers had been refused the repayment of loans made to Turkey in 1875. After a difficult crossing, two companies of marines were landed in the three ports of Mytilene on 7 November. Faced with this display of force, Sultan Abdul-Hamid gave in to all French demands, and Caillard departed during early December. Following this episode, the *Gaulois* resumed her customary routines, except for exercises with torpedo-boats on 19 February 1902 in the Bay

The Gaulois *on a visit to Marseille. (Author's collection)*

of Ajaccio (Corsica), and the installation of a Gaillard telephone network to link the conning tower to the different gunnery positions.

In May the *Gaulois* was designated to lead the 'Rochambeau Mission' to the United States.[3] The battleship departed Toulon at 1900 on 5 May and headed for Chesapeake Bay with Vice-Admiral Fournier and Generals Brugère and de Chalendar on board. The crossing was made at an average speed of 13.5 knots, and following a brief visit to Fayal Island (Azores), *Gaulois*

The squadron of Rear-Admiral Caillard en route to the Aegean. In the foreground the destroyer Epée, *the* Espingole, *the armoured cruiser* Pothuau, *the battleships* Charlemagne *and* Gaulois, *and the cruisers* Chanzy *and* Linois. *(Armée et Marine).*

The sternwalk of the admiral commanding Gaulois *during the reception accorded to the President of the United States.* (Armée et Marine)

Vice-Admiral Fournier embarks on the Gaulois *in May 1902 to command the 'Rochambeau Mission'.* (Armée et Marine)

dropped anchor at Annapolis at 1600 on the 21st.[4] Two days later, President Roosevelt was received on board with due ceremony. After the inauguration of the statue raised to Marshal Rochambeau in Washington the battleship headed first for New York then Boston. There were further celebrations, and Admiral Fournier finally left US waters on 1st June, calling in at Lisbon on the 11th before returning to Toulon on 14 June. Further major exercises took place from 7 July to 8 August, with port calls in North Africa and Corsica.

In January 1903, Admiral Potier was off Golfe Juan in order to take part in exercises which included the battleships *Saint Louis*, *Charlemagne*, *Bouvet* and *Gaulois*. During the day of the 31st, the squadron was steaming in line ahead when the order was given to form in columns by division. The 1st Division (*Saint Louis* and *Charlemagne*) took station to port with the 2nd Division to starboard, the two columns being abreast. Shortly afterwards the order to again form line ahead was given and the *Bouvet* turned to port, apparently with an excess of rudder. Despite a speed of only 8 knots collision with the *Gaulois*, which was following close behind, was inevitable. The latter reversed engines while the *Bouvet* increased her own speed. This manœuvre avoided the worst, and the two battleships only brushed one another lightly. The *Gaulois* lost two armour plates from her starboard bow and the *Bouvet* had one of her accommodation ladders torn away. The incident did not prevent the *Gaulois* from participating in the naval festivities of Villefranche in February, and in April subsequently sailed for Algiers for

The Collision between the Gaulois and the Bouvet, 31 January 1903.

1. The four battleships are steaming in column by division.

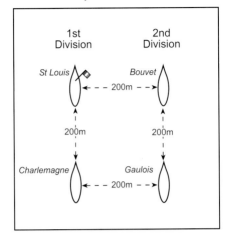

2. The formation is changed to line ahead.

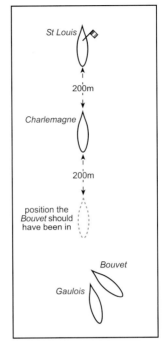

3. The *Gaulois* collides with the *Bouvet*.

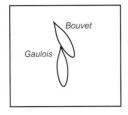

(Drawn by John Jordan using material supplied by the author)

the presidential tour. However, from 11 May she entered Missiessy Dock no.1 for repairs which would immobilise her until 21 September.

On 20 October the *Gaulois*, *Charlemagne*, *Saint Louis*, *Jauréguiberry*, *Bouvet* and *Iéna* (1st and 2nd Divisions) left Toulon for Palma where they spent four days. They then made their way to Port Mahon for a 62-hour visit, leaving for Toulon on the 30th. Out at sea they met with a violent storm, which made headway difficult; the *Jauréguiberry* even lost touch with the squadron for several hours.

On 24 April 1904, President Loubet made an official visit to King Victor Emmanuel in Naples. The French

The damage to the bow of Gaulois *following the collision with the* Bouvet. (DR)

The ships of the 1st and 2nd Divisions during the storm, on their return to Port Mahon. (DR)

fleet was moored in five columns in front of the San Vincenzo and Santa Lucia jetties. Taking part on this occasion were the battleships *Suffren*, flying the flag of Vice-Admiral Gourdon, *Gaulois*, *Saint Louis* (1st Division), *Iéna*, flagship of Rear-Admiral Barnaud, *Bouvet*, *Charlemagne* (2nd Division), the armoured cruisers *Pothuau* (CA Antoine), *Latouche-Tréville*, *Chanzy* and *Marseillaise*, the protected cruisers *Linois* and *Galilée*, and the destroyers *Sarbacane*, *Epieu*, *Carabine* and *Arbalète*.

On 3 May the *Gaulois* was docked for maintenance and reentered service only on the 30th. On 1st June she would rejoin the squadron, which was currently on a visit to Smyrna. The fleet returned to Toulon 3 July following port visits in Greece (Salonika and Athens). Following this there were sorties along the coast of Provence (Southern France) and Corsica. From 3 February 1905, the *Gaulois* was again docked before rejoining the squadron in Golfe Juan on the 22nd.

In March, while in the anchorage off Toulon, the *Gaulois* almost collided with the *Saint Louis*, which was out of control. The presence of mind of the Navigation Officer enabled her to avoid the worst, and the battleship responded quickly to the helm. On 6 October the *Gaulois* would enter the dockyard for modifications to the ammunition hoists for the main turrets. In December a W/T office was installed on board.

At the beginning of 1906 the battleship was transferred to the 2nd Division. From 12-17 April, she would be in Naples with the *Iéna* and *Bouvet* on an aid mission following the eruption of Vesuvius. There was leave for the crew in Palma and North Africa in the Spring. In July a major naval exercise took place and on the 21st *Gaulois* lost an anchor off Cape Blanc; the latter could not be recovered.

In September the *Gaulois* was present at Marseille on the occasion of the laying of the first stone of the Rove Canal. In December sighting binoculars were installed in the 305mm turrets, and during the same year the 305mm magazine arrangements were revised. From 25 February 1907, the ship would be at Villefranche, then in Golfe Juan in company with the battleship *Iéna* and the cruisers *Lalande* and *Du Chayla*. During the summer she would again take part in major exercises with the fleet.

From 28 April 1908, exercises to test divisional tactics were successfully conducted by the 1st and 2nd Divisions. Little else of note took place during the remainder of the year.

On 25 January 1909, the *Gaulois* departed Toulon with the 1st and 2nd Battle Squadrons and the 1st Light Squadron for exercises at sea. There were port calls in Brégançon, Villefranche, and Saint-Tropez. In October

The Gaulois *moored in the anchorage at Toulon. (Photo B.G.)*

A fine view of the Gaulois *taken prior to 1908.* (Cliché Bougault)

the battleship was assigned to the 1st Division of the 2nd Squadron. In December she was due to transfer to Brest, but during the voyage *Gaulois* had a rudder failure which required emergency repairs in Gibraltar.

At the beginning of 1910, there were visits to various North African and Spanish ports. In May major naval exercises took place following which *Gaulois* was in Brest during August, with visits to Quiberon, les Glénans, Houat and Saint Nazaire between September and February 1911. Apart from the customary sorties, the event which stood out was the naval review of 4 September by President Fallières. Parading off Cape Brun were: the battleships *Voltaire* (VA Boué de Lapeyrère), *Condorcet, Danton, Mirabeau, Diderot, Suffren, Patrie, République, Démocratie, Justice, Liberté, Vérité, Saint Louis, Gaulois, Charlemagne, Charles Martel, Jauréguiberry, Carnot, Bouvet, Masséna*; the armoured cruisers *Léon Gambetta, Edgar Quinet, Ernest Renan, Jules Michelet, Waldeck Rousseau, Gloire, Marseillaise, Amiral Aube* and *Jules Ferry*; and the 1st, 2nd, 3rd and 4th Destroyer Flotillas.

TABLE 2: COMMANDING OFFICERS

CV Gadaud	15 January 1898	15 January 1900
CV Salaun de Kertanguy	15 January 1900	15 January 1902
CV De Surgy	15 January 1902	20 March 1903
CV Le Bris	20 March 1903	10 August 1905
CV De la Croix de Castries	10 August 1905	10 August 1907
CV Sourrieu	10 August 1907	1st September 1909
CV Morin	1st September 1909	1st March 1911
CV Aubry	1st March 1911	1st September 1912
CV Briard	1st September 1912	8 June 1915
CV Mourache	8 June 1915	27 December 1916
Flag Officers.		
VA Fournier	5 May 1902	14 June 1902
CA Guepratte	16 November 1914	10 January 1915

Key:

CV = *Capitaine de vaisseau* (Captain)
VA = *Vice-amiral* (Vice-Admiral)
CA = *Contre-amiral* (Rear-Admiral)

The Gaulois preparing to set sail. (Coll Ph. Caresse)

From 27 November the *Gaulois* was in Cherbourg to undergo a refit during which hoods were fitted to the forward and after casemates, Le Las telephones were incorporated into the transmitting system, a firing station was fitted in the after 305mm turret, and Harlé mines embarked, together with other minor works. The battleship again took her place in the 1st Division on 29 February 1912.

From March to August of that year the ship visited Le Fret, Morgat, Quiberon, St Brieuc, Morlaix, Le Havre, Boulogne, Calais and Dunkerque. In October *Gaulois* rejoined the Mediterranean Squadron; the fleet was

Never a pleasant task: coaling ship. (DR)

The anchorage of Villefranche on 2 December 1912. From left to right: the battleships Saint Louis, Jauréguiberry, Bouvet, Gaulois *and* Carnot. *(Le Masson collection)*

involved in routine activities for the remainder of the year.

On 27 May 1913, the battleship again lost one of her anchors, this time in the anchorage at Bizerte. On 10 June a major naval review took place in the presence of *Président du Conseil* Raymond Poincaré. The remainder of the year was spent in routine exercises and maintenance.

In June 1914 it had been planned to assign the *Gaulois* to the Training Division of the Mediterranean, with effect from 1st October. In the event the ship would be integrated into the Complementary Division (*Division de complément*) which was attached to the 2nd Squadron. In the course of major exercises the *Suffren* (CA Guépratte), *Bouvet, Saint*

The Gaulois *in dock.* (DR)

A moment of relaxation for the crew of the Gaulois *in the waters of the Aegean.* (Author's collection)

Louis and *Gaulois* would undertake port visits to Ajaccio, Bizerte and Port-la-Nouvelle. During the following weeks the international situation continued to deteriorate, and the *Armée Navale* prepared itself for future conflict.

The Great War

The first war mission of the older French battleships was the escort of convoys of troops from the Army of Africa.

In September 1914, the dockyard of Sidi Abdallah (Bizerte) had to carry out repairs on the forward turret, which could be trained only with difficulty. The turret was raised and the condition of the Belleville rings supporting the horizontal roller path were found to be in poor condition. The opportunity was taken to effect similar repairs on the after turret as a precautionary measure.

With the events in Turkey the *Gaulois*, commanded by *Capitaine de vaisseau* (CV) Briard, was despatched to Tenedos, arriving 16 November, as a replacement for the *Suffren*, which was due to leave for a refit in Toulon. Admiral Guépratte raised his flag on board in order to supervise naval operations in the Dardanelles. The ships were placed on constant alert, with steam for 20 minutes and with the 100mm guns permanently manned.

On 1st January 1915 the *Gaulois* was at Skyros for coaling. On the 11th there was a small fire in a magazine which was quickly put out. On the 24th, the ship was at Trebuki, again for coaling. On the 31st, a steamer was stopped and boarded. After the boarding party had checked her cargo she was allowed to continue her passage. On 1st February *Gaulois* was at Sigri in company with the *Bouvet* and the *Suffren*, to which Admiral Guépratte had transferred his flag on 10 January. On the 19th, the British battleships *Cornwallis*, *Triumph* and *Vengeance*, the battlecruiser *Inflexible*, and the cruisers *Amethyst* and *Dublin* joined with the *Gaulois*, *Bouvet* and *Suffren* in a bombardment of the forts at the entrance to the straits. The target allocated to *Gaulois* was the field guns located on the coast of Anatolia, on the far side of

The Gaulois *in action off the Dardanelles.* (Photo Marius Bar)

Gunners in their 305mm turret. (DR)

The battleship Bouvet, lost in the attempt to force the Dardanelles on 18 March 1915. (Photo N.D.)

the Dardanelles. Her 305mm guns swept the area of the Orhanie Battery from 16.40 until 17.50. Unfavourable weather then immobilised the ships at Tenedos until the 24th. On 25 January the *Gaulois*, *Queen Elizabeth*, *Irresistible* and *Agamemnon* were given the task of supporting the 'attacking' battleships, with *Vengeance* and *Cornwallis* in the lead followed by *Suffren* and *Charlemagne*, then *Albion* and *Triumph*. The targets were once again the forts of the Gallipoli Peninsula and of Anatolia.

The *Gaulois* anchored 6000 metres off Koum Kaleh and began firing at 10.10. During this gunnery duel the Helles Battery unmasked itself, and the accuracy of its fire compelled the *Gaulois* and the nearby *Agamemnon* to up anchor. Despite everything the *Gaulois* managed to silence the guns at Helles with some well-placed shells. Her work was completed by the 15in guns of the *Queen Elizabeth*. From the *Suffren* came a message of congratulations from the admiral: 'Your fire was very good'. The ship was now 3000m from the coast, and continued the destructive work with her 138.6mm guns. Around 17.00 the fleet ceased fire and retired to the south of Tenedos. Despite her relative success, the *Gaulois* had been hit by two shells. The first, a large-calibre shell, had struck the after part of the armoured belt to starboard, and splinters had penetrated the quarterdeck. The second shell caused only minor damage on the 4th Deck.

On 1st March a reconnaissance was undertaken into the Gulf of Saros. Twenty-four hours later *Suffren* bombarded the Sultan Fort and *Gaulois* the Napoleon Fort. On the 7th, at 10.34, the fortifications inside the strait were bombarded. *Gaulois* was fired upon by a number of field batteries. At 13.27 she was struck by some shell splinters which however caused little damage. Shortly after this, sailors armed with rifles were sent on deck to destroy suspected mines. The action ended at about 14.30, the *Gaulois* having been struck by a 150mm shell to port between the Main Deck and the 1st Deck. There was some deformation of the latter deck, and there was a large hole in the small arms room, some of the rifles having been wrenched from their racks. The body of the shell was found, unexploded, on the armoured access hatch above the machinery; it would subsequently be displayed in the small arms room. On the 11th the *Suffren* and *Gaulois* joined up with the *Irresistible*, *Dartmouth* and *Ark Royal* in the Gulf of Saros. This time the Bulaïr Fort was the target, and was subjected to several salvoes.

At 09.00 on 18 March began a major assault on the enemy fortifications. Two French formations left Tenedos: *Suffre-Bouvet*, and *Gaulois-Charlemagne*. From 11.00 the British ships opened fire on the Chanak forts.[5] At 11.53 *Suffren* and *Bouvet* headed for the Asian shore, then the *Gaulois*, followed at 1000m by the *Charlemagne*, steamed along the European side. The operational plan was as follows: the first of each pair of battleships was to heave to as close as possible to its target, conduct a heavy bombardment, then slip away leaving its place to the second ship.

At 12.38 the *Gaulois* commenced firing against the Dardanus area at a range of 8400 metres. The action between Guépratte's fleet and the forts was extremely lively from the outset. In fourteen minutes *Suffren* was struck by no fewer than 14 shells of all calibres and was lucky not to be racked by an internal explosion. At 14.00 the *Bouvet* struck a mine and disappeared in less than a minute.

For her own part, the *Gaulois* gave way to the *Charlemagne* after her light guns failed to detonate two floating mines. After several passes, Admiral de Robeck, the British commander of the allied force, ordered the French ships to retire. The *Gaulois* was executing her turn when, shortly before 13.50, she was struck by a large-calibre shell which exploded on her quarterdeck,

The crew of the Gaulois *preparing to abandon ship on 18 March 1915.* (ECPA)

causing deformations in the latter deck and the deck below. A few minutes later, a shell struck the ship low on the starboard bow. At the time it was thought that no serious damage had been sustained, but at 14.03 the gun crew in the forward turret reported that the pivot was surrounded by water. It was found that in compartment D (water tank) the first strake of plating had been pushed in between frames 19 and 15. A breach 7 metres by 22 centimetres was admitting tons of water into the ship's bottom and within a short time the engine rooms were flooded up to the walkways. At the same time lifeboats with survivors of the *Bouvet* were closing the *Gaulois*, but when they arrived within hailing distance an officer called to them: 'The Captain requests you not to come alongside, as we too are sinking'. Only the watertight bulkheads could secure the survival of the battleship; the alternative was to beach the ship on the enemy shore. For the captain there was no question of adopting the latter course. He decided to head for Rabbit Island, 37 miles away, escorted by the *Charlemagne*. As a precautionary measure, all non-essential personnel were transferred to the British destroyers *Mosquito* and *Chelmer*. Shortly afterwards, Admiral Guépratte came aboard to support Captain Briard in his fight to keep the ship afloat. On several occasions offers of a tow were refused. By 15.20 the waterline was one metre below the hawsepipes. The *Gaulois* exited the straits at 16.10, and the stokers, who had water up to their waists, were asked to make one final effort to give the ship sufficient headway to be beached on a sand bank located northwest of Drepano.

At 17.55, the ship's bow ploughed into the sediment of

The Gaulois, *down by the head, makes her way slowly towards Drepano Island.* (Henry Landais collection)

The battleship in difficulties following the explosion of a large-calibre shell close to her bow. (DR)

a relatively sheltered creek. Guépratte disembarked at 18.04 and communicated his thanks to the crew of the *Gaulois*. Without delay, British divers began their investigation of the damage, and repairs were organised using shoring timbers, Makaroff mats and concrete. At 12.03 on the 22nd, the *Gaulois* was refloated and moored between the islands of Mavro and Phido. Three days later at 10.00, the battleship, accompanied by the *Suffren*, left for Toulon via Malta at a speed of 8 knots. Off Sigri, the *Suffren* briefly left the formation to discharge her guns, which had remained loaded since 18 March. On the 27th, the two ships passed the *Armée Navale*, which greeted them with enthusiastic cheers. At around 23.00, having rounded Cape Matapan, they were met by a sea running from the southeast and a rising storm. The temporary repairs quickly displayed their inadequacies. At 02.30 the situation became crtical and it was decided to head for Navarin at 4 knots. The bow of *Gaulois* was again almost submerged and a telegramme was sent to the *Armée Navale* as follows: 'Gaulois to C-in-C.-Urgent- Please send torpedo boats immediately. Position at midnight: 36°32 N, 18°58 E. Course 25 E, speed 4 knots.'

At about 04.00, the wounded ship was joined by the armoured cruiser *Jules Ferry* and the torpedo boats *Cavalier*, *Fantassin* and *Bouclier*. Finally, at 08.00, the formation arrived in the Bay of Navarin, and the ship's divers began work straight away. Repairs took more than 60 hours; shoring was put in place, and it was then necessary to let the concrete harden before the ship again regained her normal trim. The *Gaulois* departed at 02.00, set her speed at 8 knots, and arrived without further incident at Malta 48 hours later. As soon as she was at her moorings coaling began. Her departure was then delayed by an unfavourable weather forecast. On 9 April the *Gaulois* left for Bizerte, arriving on the 11th. Following the inevitable coaling, the battleship attived at Toulon on the 16th. A lengthy spell in dock was now essential, and the following day deammunitioning began.

The modifications made to the ship during this repair period were as follows: the two masts were lightened, the gunnery platform of the foremast being suppressed; the forward end of the bridge and the overhang of the conning tower were cut back; the after armoured bulkhead of the conning tower was removed, as were the

A pumping vessel and a divers' barge alongside the Gaulois *during the efforts to refloat the ship. (DR)*

The hole made in the quarterdeck by a large-calibre shell. (DR)

One of the rare photographs of the Gaulois *without the screens to her after superstructure. Note the lighter foremast and the armoured shields on her 100mm guns; note also the prominent side 'caisson' fitted for stability during her last refit.* (DR)

screens around the after superstructure; and two of the 100mm guns and six 47mm guns were disembarked. Finally, in order to improve stability a prominent external caisson of broadly square cross-section was added just above the waterline; it extended from the bridge to the after superstructure.

The Loss of the Gaulois

On 8 June the *Gaulois* again headed for the Dardanelles; she reached Malta on the 11th and arrived at Lemnos at 17.00 on the 15th. On 27 July, she would replace the *Saint Louis* at Kephalos. No particular mission had been assigned to her and she reentered Moudros on the 30th. On 11 August, the *Gaulois* conducted a bombardment against a Turkish battery near Achi-Baba, moored 1000 metres off shore. Without warning a 100mm shell in the after part of the ship was detonated by splinters, and almost set off the other ready-use ammunition nearby. The sailors calmly extracted the shells from the blaze and heaved them over the side. When she returned, the ship grounded at the entrance to the Kephalos anchorage. Despite the assistance of a tug, *Gaulois* had to disembark a large part of her ammunition before she could be refloated on the 21st. During several weeks of inactivity she was used as a base for submarines such as the *Turquoise* and *Mariotte*.

On 9 September, at Kephalos, Generals Bailloud and Hamilton, and Admirals de Robeck, Nicholson and Dartige du Fournet were accommodated on board for meetings with Admiral Boué de Lapeyrère in which the situation in the Eastern Mediterranean was discussed.

The *Gaulois* left for Moudros on 19 November, and would be joined by the battleship *République* on 6 January 1916 to cover the evacuation of Gallipoli. In need of a major refit, the ship headed for Brest on 20 August. During the immobilisation of the *Gaulois* in dock, her CO, Captain Mourache, stated in October to the Director of Naval Artillery that his ship could no longer take her place in the line unless the range of her 305mm guns could be increased by 4000m. As the ship had been in the dockyard since 26 July Mourache, not unreasonably, felt that these modifications could already have been completed weeks ago. With engagement ranges increasing, the question arose as to whether the *Gaulois* was to be disarmed and serve as a military barracks.

On Sunday 25 November, at 10.00, the bell summoning the crew to 'harbour stations' rang out in all the passageways of the *Gaulois*. The latter sortied from Brest at midday and set her course to the west into an Atlantic swell. She rounded Cape Finisterre three days later, and the four forward 138mm casemates had to be evacuated because they were constantly flooded in the heavy seas. The battleship arrived at Gibraltar at about

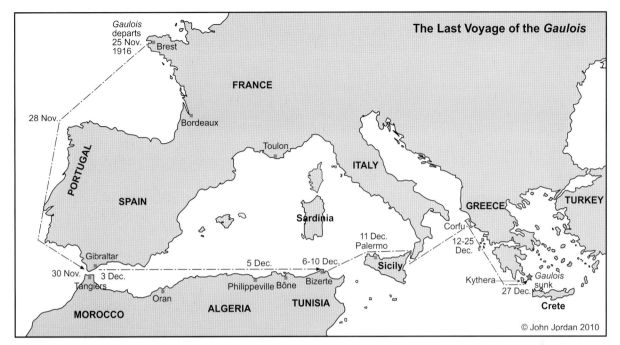

09.00 on the 30th and took on 500 tonnes of coal the following day. The *Gaulois* left the Rock on 3 December at 17.30, almost colliding with a British trawler which was patrolling that sector. At 13.00 on the 5th she was off Philippeville, at 17.00 off Bône, and she called in at Bizerte the following day. After taking on 420 tonnes of coal the ship again sailed at 15.50 on the 10th, and headed east at a speed of 14 knots. She was off Palermo on the morning of the 11th, and off the Lipari Islands at 11.00. After passing through the Strait of Messina the *Gaulois* made a visit to Corfu 12-24 December. The crew took advantage of these few days of inactivity to replenish the ship and to conduct gunnery exercises.

On 25 December, at 08.00, the *Gaulois* departed Corfu escorted by the destroyer *Mousqueton* and by two seaplanes which conducted a reconnaissance of her route to the south. The battleship was off Navarin at about 22.00. She passed Cape Matapan at 01.00 on the 27th, at which point the *Mousqueton* left her. At 03.00 she altered course to the north. The destroyer *Dard* joined her and at 07.30 she attempted to pass a line across. Unfortunately the latter wrapped itself around one of the *Dard*'s propellers and she had to heave to. The *Gaulois* turned a circle at reduced speed while the crew of the destroyer attempted to free the propeller. Both ships then continued on their original course. At that moment the armed trawlers *Rochebonne* and *Marie Rose* appeared. At 08.35, when the course had been resumed and the *Dard* was one mile ahead, a cry rang out: 'Alert to starboard, aft!'. The track of a torpedo had been spotted, and the latter struck the battleship slightly abaft the mainmast. The torpedo hit was the work of the German submarine *UB47*.

Built by A G Weser of Bremen, *UB47* was a coastal submarine of the UB II type and entered service in July 1916. She was subsequently assigned to the Pola Flotilla in the Adriatic, and transported over land in several sections to the Austro-Hungarian base; technicians from A G Weser then reassembled her. From her Mediterranean debut on 16 August 1916 up to

The German submarine UB47 *at Pola.* (Bilddienst).

Lieutenant Wolfgang Steinbauer, the commander of UB47. (DR)

27 December of the same year, she had sunk twelve steamers and damaged another, which beached herself to avoid loss. Her commander was *Oberleutnant zur See* Wolfgang Steinbauer, then aged 28.

UB47 had been in the Ionian Sea since 20 December, and attacked a transport, unsuccessfully, on the 24th. On the 27th, in the early morning, Steinbauer came upon a large vessel escorted by a torpedo-boat and two trawlers east of the Island of Kithira. He decided to shadow what he had identified as a large warship while submerged. Following various manœuvres, he found himself in a good firing position and launched a single torpedo at 08.35. After a few minutes, an explosion confirmed that he had hit his target. Steinbauer assessed and reassessed the situation using his periscope, but the aggressive activities of the escorting ships forced him to remain submerged without being able to make a further attack. Finally he moved away, unaware of the fate of his target.

On board the *Gaulois*, stability was maintained for some time, but the ship then suddenly took on a heavy list to starboard. During this time, certain of the crew claim that a second torpedo passed within fifty metres of the stern. The initial explosion claimed the lives of QM electricians Pierre Marie Arzel and Yves François Marie Eleouet. In an attempt to repel the aggressor, the light guns unleashed a heavy fire against what might have been a periscope, while the *Dard* actively sought out the submarine. The engines were stopped, and the captain gave the order to evacuation stations. The boats were then set down on the water, but cutter no.1 remained suspended by the bow and the men were hurled into the sea. Seamen 1st and 3rd Class George Paul Raymond Vérelle and Tanguy Menguy were drowned during this dramatic episode. All the rafts, supplemented by deck planking, were thrown into the water to help the men in the water stay afloat. On the starboard quarter the *Marie Rose* came alongside to embark members of the crew, and the *Rochebonne* executed a similar manœuvre to port. Raymond Lestonnat would give an account of the exemplary behaviour of the senior officers: 'One after the other the officers reported to the captain that the men under their command were safely off. The ship was sitting deeper in the water and the list was increasing. The command centre was moved first from the after bridge to the forward bridge, then to the forecastle. Suddenly the situation became extremely dangerous and it was time to abandon ship. The cellular compartments to starboard were now underwater; this was the critical point at which the ship would capsize. The trawler *Marie-Rose* stood off. The captain addressed his officers thus: "Gentlemen, it is time to leave." A few officers and members of the crew who had remained with their commanding officers now made their way carefully aft and embarked on the *Rochebonne*, followed by the First Officer and the staff.' Captain Mourache refused to leave his ship, but an officer and a seaman returned to the battleship, and led him forcefully on board the *Rochebonne*, which immediately reversed engines. At 09.00 the battleship was on her side, and five minutes later she capsized, disappearing beneath the surface at 09.11 to shouts of 'Vive la France' from her crew. The two trawlers now busied themselves rescuing the survivors; the last survivor boarded the *Marie Rose* at about 09.30.

The *Gaulois* sank on 27 December 1916 in the position 36°15 N, 23°42 E, 30 miles to the east of Cape Malea, in depths varying between 480 and 500 metres. Only the four members of her crew mentioned in the previous paragraphs were lost.

One of the surivors, Evans Maillard, wrote an account of what happened to them after their rescue by the trawlers:

> Headed Milos, arrived 15.00. We were fed straight away. The crew was shared out among the various ships in the bay. Blankets were distributed. One thing which stood out was the warm reception we received from the crew of the *Henry IV*. On 28 December, after a good rest period, the crew of the *Gaulois* was called together at 07.00. The boats of the *Henry IV* were to transfer us to the destroyers *Cavalier* and *Carabinier*, due to sail for Salamis. We arrived in the Keratsini anchorage at 15.00 after an uncomfortable crossing during which many of us were frozen due to our lack of clothing. A hundred of us then embarked on the *Justice*, where we were given a somewhat frosty wel-

At 08.52 on 27 December 1916, the Gaulois *is sinking while the armed trawler* Rochebonne *is embarking part of her crew.* (L'Illustration)

The Gaulois capsizes at 08.57; the hull will disappear beneath the waves at 09.11. (L'Illustration)

come, and equipment purchased in Greece was distributed. After the evening meal we were given bedding, and the remainder of the crew was divided between the battleships *Patrie* and *Démocratie*, and the cruisers *Jules Michelet* and *Victor Hugo*.

Still on patrol off the Island of Kythera, before returning to base *UB47* would have time to sink the liner *Ivernia*, 14,278 tons, and to damage the *Huntsend* of 8,826 tons. In recognition of his exploits 4 July 1916 – 28 October 1918 Steinbauer would be awarded the Iron Cross 1st and 2nd Class and the prestigious 'Pour le Mérite'.[6]

Footnotes:

[1] The Gauls were a Celtic people who lived in Central Europe and who, around 1500 BC, occupied a territory which embraced modern France, Switzerland, Belgium and Northern Italy. In 50 BC Gaul was entirely under the yoke of Rome following the Gallic Wars and the Battle of Alesia, in which an army commanded by Julius Caesar defeated a confederation of Gallic tribes under Vercingetorix.

[2] The full line-up was as follows: *Durandal, Hallebarde, La Hire, Cassini, Fleurus, Dunois* (1st line); *Flibustier, Forban, Amiral Tréhouard, Bouvines* (CA Mallarmé), *Pothuau* (CA Maréchal), *Galilée* (2nd line); *Cyclone, Chevalier, Iphigénie, Aquilon, Mangini, Masséna* (VA Ménard), *Bouvet* (VA Gervais), *Brennus* (VA Fournier), *Bruix* (3rd line); *Jauréguiberry, Gaulois, Charlemagne, Charles-Martel* (CA Roustan), *Jemmapes* (4th line); *Amiral Duperré, Amiral Baudin, Carnot, Formidable* (CA Touchard), *Valmy, Chanzy, Latouche-Tréville* (5th line); *Du Chayla, Dupuy de Lôme, D'Assas, Cassard, Lavoisier, Linois, D'Estrées* (6th line); *Saint Louis, Hoche, Foudre* (7th line).

[3] The French Lieutenant-General Rochambeau landed troops in support of George Washington's Continental Army at Newport, Rhode Island, during the American War of Independence.

[4] Admiral Fournier was greeted at Cape Henry by the US North Atlantic Squadron commanded by Rear-Admiral Higginson. The squadron comprised the battleships *Kearsage* and *Alabama*, the cruiser *Olympia* and the torpedo-boat *Porter*.

[5] The ships present were the *Queen Elizabeth, Inflexible, Agamemnon, Lord Nelson, Prince George, Triumph, Majestic, Swiftsure, Ocean, Albion, Irresistible* and *Vengeance*.

[6] *UB47* was at Pola when hostilities ended and was ceded to France in 1920. She was broken up the same year at Bizerte. During the war she sank twenty merchant ships and two warships totalling 87,645 tons. Wolfgang Steinbauer died in Köln on 27 January 1978.

THE CRUISER FAMILY *TALBOT*

Intended primarily for trade protection, the protected cruisers of the *Talbot* class were designed and built at the end of the Victorian era and went on to serve during the First World War. **Keith McBride** looks at the origins of the design and assesses its merits and deficiencies.

The Naval Defence Act of 1889 provided for the construction of, among other ships, a number of second-class cruisers of the *Apollo* class, of about 3,400 tons Navy List displacement, intended for both Fleet scout and commerce-protection duties. Like most British cruisers of the period, they were 'protected', relying on an armoured deck at about waterline level, and without side armour. They were armed with two 6in guns fore and aft and six 4.7in guns, three on each side, and were generally highly regarded. Several were sheathed and coppered for service on distant stations. They were followed by the slightly larger *Astraea* class, of 4,360 tons, carrying an additional pair of 4.7in guns. It was generally felt that the increase in armament was not enough to justify the increase in size, and that something distinctly better was needed.

Consequently, when the big Spencer Programme of 1893 was drawn up, it included twelve more second-class cruisers, which became the *Talbot* class. The first of these, the *Talbot* herself, was completed in 1896. Unfortunately, in spite of the efforts of the National Maritime Museum Draught Room, the *Talbot* cover cannot be found, which

Venus in full pre-1903 livery, showing the original mixed 6in and 4.7in armament (National Museum of the Royal Navy)

Diana, with the 3rd class cruiser Tauranga *in the background.* Tauranga, *begun as* Phoenix *under the Imperial Defence Act 1887, spent her active career in Australasian waters. The photo was probably taken in an Australian port in 1900, when* Diana *was serving as a troopship.* (National Museum of the Royal Navy)

makes it difficult to follow the detailed thinking behind the design. However, it is clear that a considerable increase in armament was required, even at the cost of a further increase in size – 28%, to 5,600 tons Navy List. By late-Victorian standards, this almost brought them into the 'First-Class' category; the *Edgar* class of 1889 were only 20% larger. There is a minute by Sir William White, the Director of Naval Construction, setting out his instructions to his staff, pretty much on the lines of the ships as built.

At that period, a vast amount of effort was being put into producing the ideal commerce raider – the *Rurik*, *Minneapolis*, *Châteaurenault* and others of various shapes and sizes – and it seems likely that commerce protection had high priority in the *Talbot* design. Speed was moderate: 18.5 knots at natural draught on an 8 hour trial, but radius of action was high and endurance at the economical speed of 10 knots over 30 days, which was adequate for ocean patrol.

It should be mentioned that the Admiralty took a long time to work out how it intended to carry out the commerce protection role, a solution not being worked out until after 1900, by which time the invention of wireless had revolutionised the situation. Convoy was regarded as out of the question, and opinion varied between advising all merchant ships to stick to definite routes where protecting cruisers could find them, and spreading them out as much as possible, to give commerce raiders the thinnest possible pickings. In either case, the lonely patrolling cruiser would have a task to perform, though as suspected at the time and proved in two World Wars, it was very much a 'needle in a haystack' task.

The low maximum speed was open to criticism, but it was probably felt that in practice the *Talbots* would be as fast as the opposition, and their copper sheathing would enable them to maintain their speed during long periods without docking.

The increase in armament was substantial: against the *Astraea*'s two 6in and eight 4.7in, they carried one 6in in a shield on the forecastle, two aft in separate shields, two more abreast the bridge and six 4.7in, three on each side. There were eight 12pdrs: two right forward, two aft and the remainder alternating with the 4.7in. Six 3pdrs were placed three in each fighting top, and for ultra-close work there were four .45in Maxims, which could be placed either on cone mounts or in the larger of the ships' ten boats. Three 18in torpedo tubes were fitted: two in a submerged flat and one above water behind armour aft. Its presence possibly explains why there were two 6in aft and not one on the centre line as in the preceding ships.

The armoured deck was 2½in on the slopes and was placed to give cover from 6in above the waterline to 5ft below it. The armoured glacis rose above it to protect the cylinders of the triple-expansion engines. These were of the usual three-cylinder variety and drew steam from eight cylindrical boilers at 155psi, to produce 8,000ihp.

TALBOTS: BUILDING DATA & CHARACTERISTICS

Name	Builder	Laid down	Launched	Competed	Fate
Minerva	Chatham Dockyard	04.12.93	23.09.95	04.02.97	Sold 5 October 1920 to H Auten for breaking up
Eclipse	Portsmouth Dockyard	11.12.93	19.07.94	23.03.97	Depot and accommodation ship Devonport 1915-1919; sold August 1921, G Cohen
Talbot	Devonport Dockyard	05.03.94	25.04.95	15.09.96	Laid up 1919; sold 6 December 1921, Multilocular Shipbreaking Co.
Juno	Naval Construction & Armaments Co. Ltd, Barrow	22.06.94	16.11.95	16.06.97	Sold 24 September 1920 to Earle, resold to Petersen & Albeck
Venus	Fairfield, Govan	28.06.94	05.09.95	09.11.97	Sold 22 September 1921, Cohen, broken up in Germany
Diana	Fairfield, Govan	13.08.94	05.12.95	15.06.97	Sold 1 July 1920 to S Castle, Plymouth
Doris	Naval Construction & Armaments Co. Ltd, Barrow	29.08.94	03.03.96	18.11.97	Depot ship, Aden, 1917; sold 2 February 1919, Bombay
Dido	London & Glasgow, Govan	30.08.94	20.03.96	10.05.98	Coast Guard ship Hull, 1903; depot ship Harwich & Portsmouth 1912-1926; sold 16 December 1926, May & Butcher, Maldon
Isis	London & Glasgow, Govan	30.01.95	27.06.96	10.05.98	Sold 26 February 1920, Granton Shipbreaking Co.
Hyacinth	London & Glasgow, Govan	27.01.97	27.10.98	03.09.00	Sold 11 October 1923, Cohen, Swansea
Hermes	Fairfield, Govan	30.04.97	07.04.98	05.10.99	Seaplane carrier May 1913; sunk by *U.27*, 31 October 1914 Dover Straits (44 killed)
Highflyer	Fairfield, Govan	07.06.97	04.06.98	07.12.99	Sold 10 June 1921, Bombay
Challenger	Chatham Dockyard	01.12.00	27.05.02	03.05.04	Sold 31 May 1920, Ward, Preston, for breaking up
Encounter	Devonport Dockyard	28.01.01	18.06.02	21.11.05	Transferred to RAN 5 December 1919, receiving ship, renamed *Penguin* May 1923, depot ship, scuttled off Sydney 8 September 1932

Characteristics: 1st group

- **Displacement:** 5,600 tons
- **Dimensions:** 350ft pp, 373ft oa x 53ft 6in x 20ft 6in (106.7m, 113.7m x 16.3m x 6.3m)
- **Machinery:** two shafts, 3-cylinder inverted triple expansion engines; 8 single-ended cylindrical boilers, 8,000ihp = 18.5kts natural draught, 9,600ihp = 19.5kts forced draught (20kts on trials, light condition); coal normal 500 tons, maximum 1,075 tons
- **Armament:** 5 – 6in QF, 6 – 4.7in QF, 8 – 12pdr QF, 2 MGs, 3 – 18in torpedo tubes (1 stern above water, 2 broadside submerged) (All except *Eclipse* re-armed 1903-1905 with 11 – 6in, 9 – 12pdr, 7 – 3pdr)
- **Armour:** 1½in – 3in deck, 6in CT, 3in gun shields, 6in engine hatch
- **Complement:** 450 officers & men

Characteristics: 2nd group

- **Displacement:** 5,650 tons
- **Dimensions:** 350ft pp, 372ft oa x 54ft x 20ft 6in (106.7m, 113.4m x 16.5m x 6.3m)
- **Machinery:** two shafts, 4-cylinder triple expansion engines; 18 Belleville boilers (1902 *Hermes* refitted with Babcock boilers), 10,000ihp = 20kts (8 hour full power trials: *Hermes* 20.5kts at 10,500ihp, *Highflyer* 20.1kts at 10,334ihp, *Hyacinth* 19.4kts at 10,536ihp; on later trials all reached around 21kts); coal normal 500 tons, maximum 1,100 tons (consumption about 6 tons per hour at 7,500ihp, 8¾ tons per hour at 10,000ihp)
- **Armament:** 11 – 6in QF (200 rpg); 9 – 12pdr QF; 6 – 3pdr QF; 2 – 18in submerged torpedo tubes (7 torpedoes) *Hermes* as seaplane carrier: 8 – 6in, though incl. two aircraft)
- **Armour:** 1½in – 3in deck, 6in CT, 3in gun shields, 5in engine hatches
- **Complement:** 450 officers & men

Characteristics: 3rd group

- **Displacement:** 5,880 tons
- **Dimensions:** 355ft pp, 376ft oa x 56ft x 21ft 3in (108.2m, 114.6m x 17.1m x 6.5m)
- **Machinery:** 2 shafts, 4-cylinder triple expansion engines; *Challenger* 18 Babcock boilers, *Encounter* 18 Dürr boilers; 12,500ihp = 21kts (trials: *Challenger* 21.09kts at 12,806ihp, *Encounter* 21.3kts at 13,000ihp) ; coal normal 500 tons, maximum 1,225 tons
- **Armament:** 11 – 6in QF (200 rpg); 9 – 12pdr QF; 6 – 3pdr QF; 2 Maxim guns; 2 – 18in submerged torpedo tubes
- **Armour:** 2in – 3in deck, 6in CT, 3in gun shields, 5in engine hatches
- **Complement:** 475 officers & men

Highflyer *in the later all over grey colour scheme; in August 1914 she sank the German raider* Kaiser Wilhelm der Grosse *in Spanish waters off Rio de Oro. When paid off in 1921,* Highflyer *was the last active cruiser of the White era.* (National Museum of the Royal Navy)

As mentioned above, 18.5 knots was expected on the 8 hours trials at natural draught – about two knots more than the contemporary battleships of the *Majestic* class; not really a sufficient margin for fleet work. On the 4-hour trial, with moderate forced draught, 19¼ knots was hoped for from 9,600ihp. Crew was 436, for whom 13 weeks' provisions were carried, and the coal supply was 1,100 tons, though as usual only half of this was included in the Navy List displacement. There was the usual supply of ammunition: 200rpg for the 6in, 250 for the 4.7in, 300 for the 12pdrs, and 500 for the 3pdrs – which do not appear to have been fitted in the *Talbot* herself, at any rate at the outset. There were ten torpedoes for the three tubes, presumably four apiece down below and two aft. A curious point was that a limited amount of sail was still provided for. Metacentric height was about 3ft, with maximum stability at 48 degrees, with a range of 90.

The *Talbot* herself was sent to the West Indies for her first commission and was just completing this when, in mid-1896, the Admiralty began considering what improvements could be incorporated in the final three ships of the class. (Incidentally, this was a rare example of some practical experience being available before work began on the Mk.II version!) There could be no question of exceeding 5,600 tons; however, the first ships of the class had come out very well, proving strong, reliable, good seaboats and free from vibration. Above all, they had handsomely exceeded their designed speed, by something like ¾ knot under all conditions. Despite these virtues, opinion seems to have turned against the *Talbots* by the time they entered service; they were regarded as too big, too weakly armed and too slow. Compared with the ships of various foreign navies and the Elswick cruisers, fast and bristling with guns, which were emerging from the Tyne at frequent intervals, they seemed and looked rather stodgy. Something had to be done.

It so happened that the Admiralty had decided to put the 4in gun (31-pound shell) into future construction instead of the 4.7in (50pdr), as the latter had proved a bit too big for sloops and other small vessels. With the 4.7in going into limbo, which lasted until 1917, it was logical to replace those in the *Talbots* by the next gun up, the 6in, thereby securing a 150lb increase in broadside and simplifying ammunition supply. The DNO and DNC discussed and agreed this change in about August. There was weight available; despite the engines having come out 30 tons overweight, there was still 180 tons unused of the 210-ton (3.75%) margin included in the 5,600 tons. This armament change added 100 tons up top.

A further improvement related to the machinery. At this time the 'Battle of the Boilers' was raging with great fury, with blowups, breakdowns, Parliamentary Questions, Royal Commissions, etc, but by 1896 Sir William White and Sir John Durston, the Engineer in Chief, decided that the case for the water-tube boiler had convinced technical opinion far enough to justify putting it into the last three *Talbots*. Eighteen Bellevilles were to replace the eight old boilers. At the same time, four-cylinder triple-expansion engines (one high, one intermediate and two low-pressure on each engine, giving 10,000ihp natural draught, were adopted). This would save about 70 tons and, the new engines being much lower, would permit the abolition of

A fine study of HMS Challenger in tropical white and buff. After peacetime service on the Australian station, she spent the years 1915 to 1919 operating in East Africa and the Indian Ocean. (National Museum of the Royal Navy)

the armoured glacis, with a further saving of weight. It was hoped that another ¾ to 1¼ knots would be gained; 20.5 knots on moderate forced draught was hoped for, though only 20 knots was specified. After much discussion, the half load of coal was left at 550 tons, giving a Navy List displacement of 5,600 tons at 20ft 6in draught against an actual 5,420 tons for the *Talbot*.

Naturally a price had to be paid: crew went up to 470, with provisions and stores, and metacentric height went down to 2ft, which was considered acceptable. The revised machinery caused the new ships to have three funnels instead of two, which left the *Hermes*, *Hyacinth* and *Highflyer* to be regarded as a separate class. The design was prepared in September-October 1896 and submitted to the Board of Admiralty. It is interesting that the First Lord, by then George Goschen, would have preferred a heavier armament, but reluctantly accepted that this was impracticable. He also refused to agree to water-tube boilers until a satisfactory explanation was furnished of a burst steam-pipe in the *Powerful*, which he saw mentioned in his morning *Times*!

The three ships were laid down in 1897 and completed two years later; they seem to have run into a lot of trouble; the *Hyacinth* could only make 19.4 knots until her propellers were changed, and the *Hermes* had total breakdowns on trials and again on passage from Bermuda to Halifax, when she had to be towed in, which caused some red faces. Such troubles were not uncommon in the early

Juno *after repainting in the grey colour scheme; all 4.7in QF guns have been replaced by 6in. (World Ship Society, Abrahams Collection)*

days of the water-tube boiler, and were eventually cured. The Admiralty felt sufficiently fond of the type to have a further try with the *Challenger* and *Encounter* of 1902; these were 5ft longer at 355ft, 280 tons heavier, and had a further 2,500ihp for a further knot. They also thought it worthwhile to have the *Talbots* up-gunned to the *Hermes* armament over the years, though this was never done to the *Eclipse*. Incidentally, the above water stern tube was omitted at the construction stage – the danger of above water tubes was emphasised at Santiago.

That, however, was the end of the line. Construction of medium-sized cruisers virtually stopped in the early 1900s, and they had no place in Lord Fisher's thinking – except as possible victims. Not until after 1908 did the same idea re-appear in the very different form of the 'Towns'. The ships themselves continued their unobtrusive work, on distant stations for the most part. The *Hermes* served briefly as a seaplane carrier. By 1914 they were in a position which could be compared to that of the 'C's and 'D's in the Second World War, though they came off more lightly. The *Highflyer* demolished a German commerce raider, though not very gloriously. At the outset, the *Hyacinth* had a run for her money after *Königsberg*; the more modern German ship, got away, but her engines later gave trouble, which may be significant. The *Hermes*, always unlucky, succumbed to a U-boat in the Straits of Dover. Other ships of the class put in a lot of hard, unspectacular work in the Mediterranean and elsewhere. The *Juno* was sent to escort the *Lusitania* but was recalled. Since she could by then manage only 16½ knots, while the liner, even in wartime form, could do 21, it is difficult to see what help she could have given (though it is interesting to ponder on the possibilities if *U-20* had fired at her instead of waiting for something better!). The rest were all disposed of soon after the Armistice.

The *Talbots* never had much of the limelight; they were never the biggest, fastest or most glamorous; even the life of their designer hardly mentions them. They spent much of their lives on routine 'showing the flag' or commerce protection duties. The First World War came at the end of their lives, and they were soon discarded. The war only showed up their obsolescence. What crippled them as cruisers was their low speed, which was due to size and cost restrictions.

Incidental intelligence: some years later White referred to the Russian *Diana* class as being 'an imitation of our *Talbots*'. Armament was:

Russian: 8 x 6in (87lb shell), 22(!) x 3in
British: 5 x 6in (100lb shell), 6 x 4.7in, 8 x 12pdr.

He also mentioned 'our *Talbot*, all particulars of which were obtained by the Russian designers'. The *Oleg*, *Askold* and *Varyag* were intended to go one better. It is clear that the *Talbot* designers had a lot of trouble getting the engines and boilers into a fairly small hull.

Acknowlegement
Thanks to Ian Sturton for additional help with this article.

Talbot had a busy career, including being fired upon by American forces in the West Indies during the Spanish-American war, and rescuing survivors from the Russian ships Varyag *and* Korietz *defeated by the Japanese and scuttled at Chemulpo in 1904. She is seen here engaged in bombarding enemy forces at Suvla Bay – a task very different from that for which she had been designed. (National Museum of the Royal Navy)*

THE BATTLECRUISERS OF THE *KONGÔ* CLASS

Hans Lengerer examines the origins of the first IJN battlecruiser to be built abroad, and the extent of the technology transfer on which the order depended.

Following the decision to build the armoured cruisers (later battlecruisers) *Kurama* and *Ibuki*, the Navy Technical Department (NTD) drew up more than 30 sketch designs of battlecruisers before a building contract for the *Kongô* was concluded with the British Vickers Co. on 17 October 1910; Vickers' technology was considered superior compared to that of Armstrongs, and the Imperial Japanese Navy (IJN) was also influenced by the award for the contract for the Royal Navy's *Princess Royal*, the second of the *Lion* class battlecruisers, to Vickers.

The Japanese wanted a ship whose characteristics were superior to the *Lion* class, but of equal importance was their desire to upgrade Japanese warship building technology to the latest British practice. The following contractual stipulations were therefore made:

- The IJN was to be permitted to send naval architects, machinery and weapon production technicians, engineers, assistant engineers and senior shipyard workers to supervise construction and to study the production process.
- The IJN was to have free access to all drawings of the hull, armour, guns, main engines and auxiliary machinery and to be permitted to utilise them for the building of sister ships in Japan.

With the decision to order abroad, the IJN:

- aimed for an all-round upgrade of domestic shipbuilding, engine and weapon production technology to bring them up to the current practice of a leading British shipyard;
- relied for technology transfer on the same methods already successfully adopted at the end of the Bakumatsu period (ie after the opening of the country by Perry in 1853/54), and practised throughout the Meiji era: the dispatch of selected personnel abroad to study latest practice in their particular field of expertise, together with the hiring of foreign specialists to work alongside Japanese shipyard workers and engineers in Japan.

Domestic design had centred around vessels displacing about 18,000 to 19,000 tons, with speeds of 25/26 knots and an armament of eight to ten 12in guns arranged as in

Kongô on the slipway at Vickers: view forwards, showing the extension of the double bottom up to the armour belt shelf. The floors, longitudinals and frames are partly in place. (Vickers, courtesy of the author)

the latest British, American and German capital ships. The adoption of a ship displacing 27,000 tons meant a radical departure from existing designs. Even though the broad characteristics of the ship were based on Vickers' draft plan, the Naval General Staff (NGS) insisted on the incorporation of particular requirements based on Japanese strategic considerations and operating conditions, some of which were at variance with British tradition and practice. Japanese and British technicians worked closely together to find acceptable solutions and Sir George Thurston, who was head of the Warship Design Division of Vickers Co., introduced many improvements compared to the *Lion* class. Responsibilities for the design were therefore as follows:

- The draft design of *Kongô* was drawn up in the Draft Design Section of the Shipbuilding Division of the NTD on the basis of a detailed investigation of the proposed design and in cooperation with British technicians.
- The legend design was drawn up by the Warship Design Division of Vickers Co., which also instructed the Drawing Section to execute the working drawings.

It is therefore appropriate to characterise the design of the battlecruiser *Kongô* as a joint venture between Japan and Britain, with much greater influence of the former than had been the case with the capital ships ordered before the Russo-Japanese War.

An Important Change in the Calibre of the Main Guns

When the construction of armoured cruisers of about 18,000 tons had first been contemplated, the main gun calibre was within the standard range adopted in the early 1890s; discussion focused primarily on the length of barrel, namely 45-calibre or 50-calibre, and the latter figure was eventually adopted because a gun with these characteristics was already under construction. The adoption of a larger calibre than that of the *Lion* class was also proposed for the new ships, but was rejected after heated discussions because Vickers had no ready-made design. The contract therefore stipulated the mounting of eight 12in (304.8mm), 50-calibre guns in four twin turrets.

However, Cdr Katô Hirohasu Kanji, who would later rise to a prominent position in the IJN, investigated the armament of current British capital ships and obtained confidential information about the result of comparison firings between the 12in/50-cal and the 13.5in/45-cal guns, the latter scheduled for installation in future capital ships. According to these data the latter was superior in most key respects such as barrel life, dispersion and hit probability. This suggested that if the Kongos were completed with their projected armament they would be inferior to the *Lions*.

Katô's reaction was a request to Navy Minister Admiral Saitô Makoto to change the calibre to 14in (356.6mm), and he supported his arguments by providing the confidential British data. When he did not receive an answer, he dispatched one of the supervisors of the construction of *Kongô* to Japan via Siberia. The latter obtained permission to discuss informally with Vickers a change of calibre, because the official adoption of the 14in gun had of course to depend on the results of the trial firings. The design and trial construction of the new gun was ordered by Vickers at the expense of the IJN, and the company completed the gun in a comparatively short time. In view of the urgency, the firing trials were made on the Royal Navy's proving ground at Shoeburyness[1] because the Vickers firing range was unsuitable for this calibre. The trials began 8 March 1911 and were successfully completed before the end of the month. Representatives of both the IJN and the RN were present at the trials and the results were shared between both navies. On 29 November 1911 a formal decision was made to adopt the larger calibre gun.

The decision to move from 12in to 14in was not a simple one; it required numerous alterations which included barbette and roller path diameter, turntables, turrets, shell and propellant hoists, magazines and shell rooms, as well as structural reinforcements to absorb the stronger forces generated by the firing of the larger calibre gun and protective measures against the stronger blast. Displacement would also have to rise to take account of the additional weight of the turrets. However, Vickers' Detailed Design Division was a very efficient organisation. Even though the keel of *Kongô* had been laid down on 17 January 1911, all the alterations to the working drawings were made quickly; there were no delays in the construction process and none of the sections already completed had to be broken up.

TABLE 1: A COMPARISON OF THE 12IN/50 AND 14IN/45 GUNS

	12in/50-cal (*Kawachi* class)	14in/45-cal. (*Kongô* class)
Calibre	304.8mm	355.6mm
Length of barrel	15.659m (51.4cal)	16.469m (46.3cal)
Weight of the barrel	69t	84.69t
Weight of AP shell	400kg	635.03kg
Weight of propellant*	95.38/139.95kg	136.5/150kg
Barrel pressure*	2760 /2933 kg/cm^2	??/3050 kg/cm^2
Muzzle velocity*	820/865m/s	800/845m/s
Chamber volume	?	283.5l
Life of barrel	200-250 rounds	250-280 rounds
Number of grooves	72 (1 turn in 28 cal)	84 (1 turn in 28 cal), depth 3.05mm

* First figure = standard; second figure = strong

Construction

The beginning of construction was marked by the dispatch of technicians from Japan to ensure the highest degree of technology transfer.[2] Specialists from each field were despatched to Vickers: not only officers belonging to the shipbuilding, engine and weapon production branches, engineers and assistant engineers but also foremen and workers scheduled to form the cadre of the Japanese workforce. These men studied all the technical processes related to warship construction, particularly those which took place on the slipway and in the engine and weapon production factories. The fitting-out committee also consisted of more members than usual.[3] Each of the secondments lasted around 18 months; after that period there were changes in the personnel. Among those to arrive were Cdr Gôtô Takuo – subsequently head of Kure NY (1924),[4] Cdr Noda Tsuruo, naval engineers Hata Chiyokichi,[5] Yokota Eikichi, Uruno Shihei and the shipbuilding Cdrs Shinjo Suekurô, Fukui Jumpei, Yoshida Yasushi.[6] All these people were later in charge of building the capital and other ships of the Eight-Eight Fleet Programme.

Besides naval officers and navy officials there was a large contingent of civilian workers from the Mitsubishi Shipyard, Nagasaki, and the Kawasaki Shipyard at Kobe. Among them were the chief of the Shipbuilding Division of the Nagasaki Shipyard, Shiba Kôshirô, and engineers Abe, Tamai, and Ogawa,[7] while Kawasaki Kobe sent engineers Yoshikunimera, Katayama and others. The personnel from these private shipyards also studied gantry crane and slipway building techniques, and launch technology. Kawasaki's excellent launch technology originated from these observations at the Vickers yard.

More than 100 selected men were dispatched to Britain during this period, and if supervisors, superintendents, fitting-out and trial committee members are added the total rises to about 200. These were the men who upgraded the design and construction capabilities of the IJN and the private shipyards. By about the middle of the First World War, the IJN had become fully independent of foreign assistance and had acquired the confidence to produce its own modern designs.

The dispatch of engineers and construction workers from Japan's largest civilian shipyards was part of a program to involve selected private facilities in the construction of large warships and to expand this branch of heavy industry. Until the Shipbuilding Encouragement Law of 1896 the civilian shipyards did not develop on a notable scale, but afterwards state assistance was given to develop certain enterprises, among them Mitsubishi Nagasaki and Kawasaki Kobe. The IJN began with orders for torpedo boats, destroyers, gunboats and submarines (at that time a speciality of Kawasaki) followed by small (light) cruisers which gave the shipyards the opportunity to learn to design and build more technologically advanced and sophisticated types of warship. With the orders placed with Mitsubishi and Kawasaki for two sisters of Kongô, the IJN wanted to kill two birds with one stone, namely:

– to establish the capacity for the construction of four

The forward part of Kongô *on the slipway, showing the framing and the deck beams for the protective deck.* (Vickers, courtesy of the author)

THE BATTLECRUISERS OF THE KONGÔ CLASS

TABLE 2: BUILDING DATA & CHARACTERISTICS

Name	Builder	Laid down	Launched	Completed
Kongô	Vickers	17.01.11	18.05.12	16.08.13
Hiei	Yokosuka NY	04.11.11	21.11.12	04.08.14
Haruna	Kawasaki Kobe	16.03.12	14.12.13	19.04.15
Kirishima	Mitsubishi Nagasaki	17.03.12	01.12.13	19.04.15

Note: *Haruna* was named 14 December 1913, other ships on 5 June 1911.

Characteristics (*Haruna* as completed)

Length:	199.19m pp, 211.96 wl, 214.58m oa
Beam:	28.04m
Depth of hull:	15.53m
Draught:	8.22m mean
Displacement:	27,384 tonnes normal
Horsepower:	64,000shp
Speed:	27.78 knots
Fuel:	4,200t coal, 1,000t oil
Endurance:	8,000nm at 14 knots
Armament:	8 – 36cm/45-cal. (4xII)
	16 – 15cm/50-cal. (16xI)
	4 – 8cm/40-cal. HA (4xI)
	8 – 53cm TT (u/w)

TABLE 3: WEIGHT DISTRIBUTION AS BUILT

	Kongô	Haruna	Kirishima	Mean Percentage of Displacement
Displacement:	26,624	26,951	26,739	100%
Hull:	8,083	8,098	7,972	30%
Fittings	1,366	1,408	1,451	5%
Protection	6,343	6,549	6,502	24%
Machinery	4,460	4,409	4,438	17%
Armament	4,332	4,283	4,159	16%
Equipment	941	1,104	976	4%
Coal	1,100	1,100	1,100	4%
Margin	0	0	139	

Source: Fukuda, *op. cit.*, p.58

capital ships simultaneously, and – to assist these and other private shipyards in enduring the recession which followed the Russo-Japanese War.

With the completion of the battlecruisers *Kirishima* and *Haruna* at Mitsubishi Nagasaki and Kawasaki Kobe respectively, these shipyards had succeeded in upgrading their facilities, design and construction techniques and management system to international standards. They subsequently received successive orders first for the battleships *Ise* and *Hyuga*, then for the battleships *Tosa* and *Kaga*. They were also selected to build the battlecruisers *Takao* and *Atago*

The after part of the ship; the hull is complete to level of the protective deck. (Vickers, courtesy of the author)

The bow of Kongô, with the imperial chrysanthemum just visible, on 18 May 1912. The ship is ready for launch. (Vickers, courtesy of the author)

TABLE 4: STABILITY

Data for *Haruna* as completed:

	Light	Normal	Full
Displacement:	24,668t	27,384t	32,306t
Draught:	7.54m	8.22m	9.42m
KG:	9.85m	9.46m	9.03m
GM:	1.65m	1.75m	1.87m
OG:	2.31m	1.25m	−0.39m
Range:	N/A	N/A	N/A
Max. GZ:	N/A	N/A	N/A

Source: Fukuda op. cit., p.76

before the Washington Arms Limitation Conference ended the construction of Japan's 'dream fleet'.

Other, lesser shipyards were also encouraged by the IJN and matched the progress of these two shipyards, although on a much smaller scale. They too upgraded their techniques, facilities and management to be able to build warships up to light cruiser size, thereby taking the former position of the 'Big Two'. With the construction of the battlecruisers of the Kongô class, not only were warship design and construction techniques developed in Japan to a level which matched the latest practice abroad, but these advances also paved the way for the building of the Eight-Eight Fleet.

Armour Plate Technology[8]

The armour of the Kongô class was composed of Krupp cemented (KC) and Vickers cemented (VC) armour plates. Krupp cemented was used for the waterline and upper belts, while Vickers cemented was used for protection within the hull. Horizontal protection was Nickel steel (NS) and high-tensile (HT) steel, with thicknesses ranging from 3in (76mm) to 1⅝in (41mm).

During the final decade of the 19th century the IJN had purchased ships from abroad with a variety of armour types, and had been particularly impressed by the Vickers Ni-steel KC 9in (229mm) armour of the battleship *Mikasa*. When the battleships *Katori* (Vickers) and *Kashima* (Armstrong) were ordered from Britain, the Steel Production Division (*Seikô-bu*) of Kure Navy Yard despatched naval weapon production engineers to both companies. Vickers was unwilling to reveal the secrets of its armour plate production, whereas as at Armstrongs the Japanese were permitted to inspect the production process. However, Armstrong armour was considered by the Japanese to be inferior to the Vickers plates.

Between 1904 and 1906 the manufacturing capabilities of the Steel Production Division were greatly expanded by the addition of two blast furnaces, a new rolling mill, an 8,000-ton hydraulic press, three heating furnaces, oil and water pits and a sprinkler plant, ready for the production and repair of armour plates. In 1905 the production of KC armour plates 8in (203mm) thick was begun, and the first 7in (178mm) plates for the armoured cruisers *Tsukuba* and *Ikoma* were tested in April 1906. On 18 and 24 Decmber 1907 two 9in (229mm) plates for the battleship *Satsuma* were tested with 12in shells, and in 1909 12in (305mm) armour plates for the battleships *Kawachi* and *Settsu* were successfully tested. All these plates were produced based on the Krupp face-hardening process as KC armour.

Capped armour-piercing (APC) projectiles were first used for armour plate proving trials between November 1908 and August 1909.

However, despite these advances, domestic armour production capabilities were still insufficient with the result that the IJN continued to import armour plates. German KC and British VC plates were competitive in terms of quality and price, but the contract to build the battlecruiser *Kongô* at Vickers included a stipulation that Japanese engineers and technicians would be instructed in armour production over a period of almost one year beginning in 1911. A group of specialists, headed by Engineer Yokota Eikichi, was duly dispatched to Vickers. When they returned to Japan they produced some plates 9in (229mm) and 6in (152mm) thick applying the methods they had learned during their stay in Britain. Proving trials demonstrated that these plates had the same qualities as plates produced by Vickers. Comparative tests were made with Krupp, Armstrong, Hadfield (UK) and the Bethlehem Steel (US) plates, which confirmed the superiority of the Vickers plate. This result was recognised as a major leap forward in the production of armour plate in Japan.

These undeniably impressive achievements came too late for the *Kongôs*, however, and all the VC armour for the three ships that were built in Japan was imported from Vickers. According to the notes of Technical Vice-Admiral Noda Tsuneo, the following quantities of KC armour were supplied by Kure *Kôshô Seikô-bu* for these ships:

Hiei:	4,407 tons
Haruna:	4,430 tons
Kirishima:	4,417 tons

The *Kongô* class was the last to have a mix of KC and VC plates. For subsequent ships the IJN adopted British armour plate production technology almost exclusively, with New Vickers cemented (NVC) plate being produced from October 1916 and New Vickers non-cemented (NVNC) being added from 1925.

Protection

As with other battlecruisers of the period, the thickness of the vertical armour was insufficient to resist a projectile of the calibre of the ship's own main guns at long range. The battlecruiser prioritised speed, and it was believed that it would enable this type to accept or decline battle depending on the enemy ships encountered. The design of the *Kongô* was completed about six years before the Battle off Jutland, which highlighted the danger of projectiles fired from longer ranges than previously thought probable. Consequently, horizontal protection was totally inadequate against plunging shell.

The waterline belt had a thickness of 8in (203mm) over the machinery and magazines, tapering to 3in (76mm) at its lower edge. Above it were two strakes of a shorter belt 6in (152mm) thick which ended abaft No.3 main gun barbette and extended to the upper deck, the upper strake

A photo of the stern, taken on the same day as the view of the bow. The wood backing for the armour belt, comprising planks of hardwood approximately nine inches wide fixed longitudinally to the inner plating, is in place; the armour, secured by heavy bolts with a diameter of 3 inches, will be fitted after launch. Note the twin rudders. (Vickers, courtesy of the author)

protecting the secondary guns. Fore and aft of the waterline belt were strakes of armour 3in (76mm) thick of differing heights. At the bow the height was the same as the belt but at the stern, where it protected the steering compartment, height was reduced. The barbettes of the main guns were protected by 10in (254mm – some sources give 9in/229mm) of thick armour above the upper deck and 3in (76mm) below, the upper side belt providing additional protection over the lower part of the barbette. The turrets had faces 10in (254mm) thick with 9in sides (229mm – some sources give 10in/254mm); no reliable data has been found for the turret rear.

The lower end of the waterline belt was connected to the lower end of the slopes of the protective deck and it was here that the strake of 3in (76mm) armour previously mentioned provided some underwater protection. At that time no consideration was given to underwater shell trajectories; it would be some twelve years before the problem was recognised by the IJN.

A longitudinal bulkhead, formed by two layers of 1in (25mm) and ⅞in (22mm) thickness respectively, provided a degree of underwater protection outboard of the machinery spaces and magazines. It was located some distance inboard of the double bottom, which extended

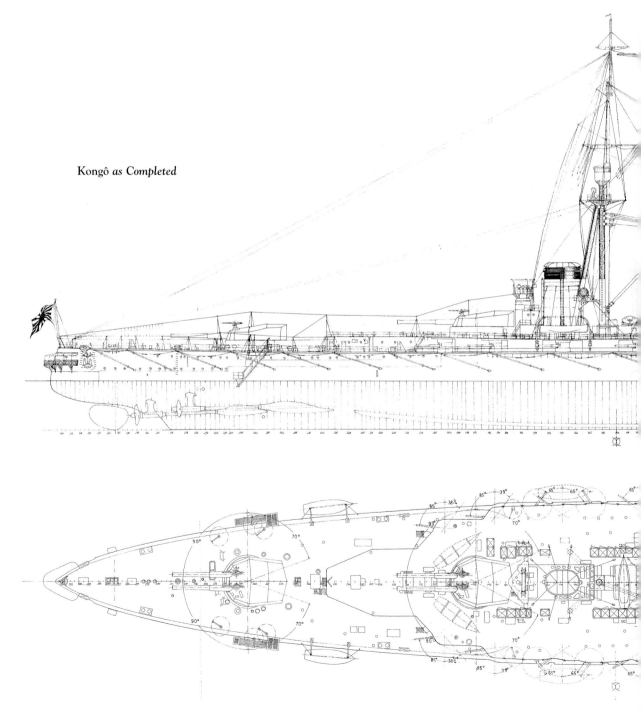

Kongô *as Completed*

THE BATTLECRUISERS OF THE KONGÔ CLASS

to the lower edge of the waterline belt.

The boiler room uptakes were protected by gratings 6.5in (165mm) thick – an impressive figure for the period. The protection of the conning tower is uncertain; some sources state 9in (229mm).

At the time of design and construction, horizontal protection was largely neglected. The lower ('protective') deck over the machinery spaces and magazines was ¾in (19mm);[9] the upper and middle decks were 1in (25mm) and ¾in (19mm) respectively. The roof of the main turrets was of armour plates 3in (76mm) thick, and it is stated that the roof of the conning tower was of a similar thickness. The steering compartment was protected only very lightly by ¾in and 1in (19/25mm) plating.

Machinery

Improved Parsons Turbines of *Kongô*, *Hiei* and *Kirishima*

The turbines of *Kongô* and *Hiei* were ordered from Vickers Naval Construction Works, Barrow-in-Furness; those of *Kirishima* were manufactured by the builder of the hull, Mitsubishi Nagasaki.

(Drawn by Michael Wünschmann)

General Arrangement Plans of Kongô as Completed

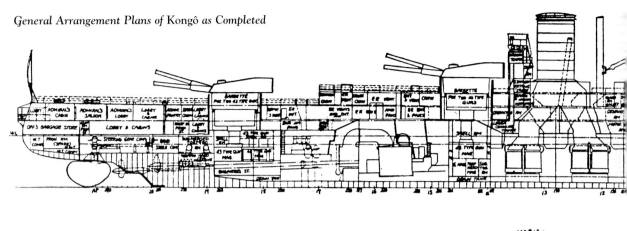

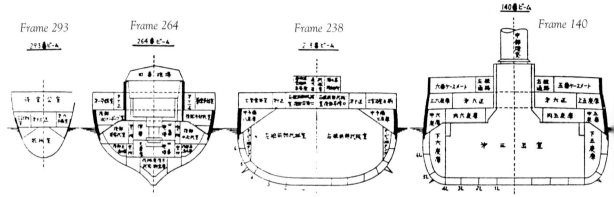

The launch, attended by the shipyard workers and management of Vickers; the Japanese supervisors were also present. (Vickers, courtesy of the author)

THE BATTLECRUISERS OF THE KONGÔ CLASS

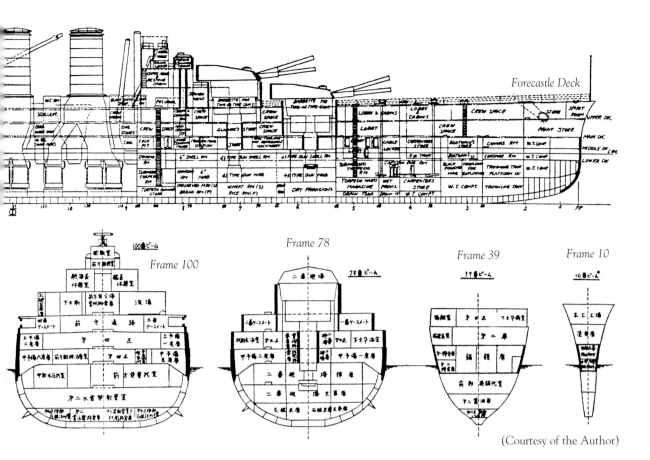

(Courtesy of the Author)

Kongô afloat after launch. Note how little water she draws at this stage of the process. All the heavy items of equipment have yet to be embarked and fitted. (Vickers, courtesy of the author)

The design specified 64,000shp at 290 rpm for 27.5 knots and the propulsion machinery comprised two sets of double-expansion improved Parsons turbines arranged in two compartments separated by a longitudinal bulkhead at the centreline. Each set of turbines comprised a high-pressure (HP) and a low-pressure (LP) turbine; the former drove the outer (wing) shaft and the latter was coupled to the inner shaft. The HP and LP astern turbines were incorporated into the after end of the casings of the corresponding ahead turbines; this arrangement meant that all four shafts were working when going astern.

The improved Parsons turbine was a combination of impulse and reaction type turbines. This principle was adopted only for the HP ahead and astern turbines; the two LP turbines used the reaction principle throughout. The combination of the impulse and reaction systems eliminated the disadvantage of the earlier Parsons turbine, in which steam pressure had to be reduced by passing through a control valve when steaming at lower speeds; instead a Curtis impulse wheel was located at the high pressure end of the turbine. Each wheel carried a single stage of impulse blading comprising four rows of rotating blades with their corresponding guide-vanes. The nozzles (Curtis stage nozzles) were arranged in groups so that high initial pressure could be maintained by shutting off the supply of steam from one or more of these nozzle groups when the turbines were working at reduced power. Following the impulse blading there were seven stages of reaction blades in the case of the ahead turbines, and two short stages of reaction blading in the astern turbines.

Considerable attention was given to the design of the impulse blades and the means by which they were attached to the rotors, and also to the selection of the material from which they were made: a special nickel-coated mild steel, except for the last row of rotary blades which were made of brass. The blades were welded on to sectional function rings of mild steel and the latter were dove-tailed into grooves on the wheel-rim, to which they

TABLE 5: ENGINE TRIALS OF KONGÔ & HIEI

	Kongô	Hiei
Horsepower (shp):		
designed	64,000	
closed ventilation, 10/10	78,275	76,127
open ventilation, 10/10	?	69,973
astern full, designed	32,000	
astern full, actual	24,712	26,790
RPM:		
designed	290	
actual	300.6	295.95
Speed (knots):		
closed ventilation	27.54	27.72
open ventilation	?	27.03
Steam consumption (kg/HP/h):		
designed, main machinery	5.21	
designed, auxiliary machinery	0.91	
10/10 (full speed)	5.16	5.38
8/10	5,67	5.83
6/10	5.70	5.99
4/10	6.20	6.71
2/10	7.28	7.67
`1/10	9.23	9.58
10 knots	13.54	12.57

Note the high steam consumption at low speeds, which illustrates the poor fuel economy of direct-drive turbines.
Source: *Nippon Kaigun Kikan Shi*, Vol. II, p.464ff, particularly pp.470-71.

Kongô *inboard of the British battlecruiser* Princess Royal *soon after her launch; the latter is in a much more advanced state of completion.* (Vickers, courtesy of the author)

THE BATTLECRUISERS OF THE KONGÔ CLASS

Kongô nears completion at the Vickers fitting-out quay. The photo was taken on 14 April 1913; the ship would soon undergo her sea trials. (Vickers, courtesy of the author)

were fixed by brass packing caulked into one side of the groove.

The primary considerations in the design of the turbines were the maintenance of high fuel economy in all service conditions, and uniformity of the turbine load; the power of the LP turbines was therefore increased by 10% compared to the HP turbines. The combined HP ahead and astern arrangement, together with the introduction of impulse wheels and a two-stage cruising element in one casing necessitated exceptionally large dimensions. These features were a departure from the usual practice in high-powered marine turbines. Great care therefore also had to be taken with regard to the detailed design of the rotors and casings. Forged steel was employed for most elements such as rotor drum, spindles, impulse wheels, casing, and shafting to ensure sufficient strength and freedom from distortion under all steam conditions.

The arrangement of all elements of the machinery, including steam and exhaust pipes, feed, drain, and oil lubricating systems, was designed to ensure the independence of the port and starboard turbine sets and to allow either set to be worked when the other was disabled in the event of damage. Particular attention was paid to the fixing

TABLE 6: POWER TO WEIGHT RATIOS

	Haruna	Kongô	Hiei	Kirishima
SHP	80,476	78,275	76,127	79,680
Weight (kg)	4,376.8	4,459.6	4,524.8	4,438.5
SHP/Weight	18.27	17.6	16.8	17.95

Source: Fukuda *op. cit.*, p.151

of steam and other pipes with regard to expansion. Provision was also made to permit free expansion in valves.

Four condenser units were provided, two for each pair of turbines, and located in two condenser rooms separated by the centreline bulkhead. The diameter of the exhaust pipe was 2.13m. Considerable care was taken with the fixing of the pipework to the hull and the penetration of the after bulkhead between the engine room and the condenser room. The condensers were of the Uniflux type, with graduation of the diameter of the tubes between 24.6mm and 38.1mm (upper part 24.6mm, middle part 26.2mm, lower part 38.1mm), thereby ensuring rapid movement of the steam and the condensed water passing through the cooling tubes and improving

Brown-Curtis Turbines (Haruna) *Improved Parsons Turbines (Kongô, Hiei, Kirishima)*

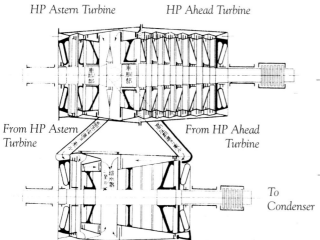
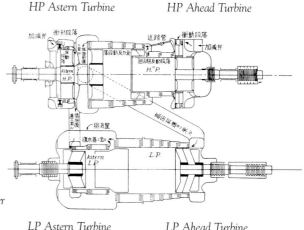

(Source: *Kaigun Kikan-shi* Vol.2, p.467 & p.476)

efficiency.[10] This resulted in a considerable reduction of the cooling area. The tube casings were built up of steel plates and angles, and the end covers were made of cast iron to prevent corrosion. There were 9,065 tubes, cooling area was 1,347m^2 and the flow volume was 6,595 tonnes/hour. The treated steam volume amounted to 101.6 tonnes/hour.

In the past, vacuum pumps and water circulation pump had generally been used, as with the adoption of the turbine it became evident that an increase in vacuum would bring major benefits. However, the vacuum pump proved unsatisfactory and was replaced by a Weir dual-type air pump which had one air and one water barrel. In the *Kongos* one independent air pump of the Weir type was fitted for each condenser, but instead of the dual type, *Hiei* mounted a single-expansion type.

The four circulating pumps for the main condensers were of the centrifugal type driven by two-crank engines with forced lubrication. There was also one auxiliary condenser in each condenser compartment to take the exhaust steam from the auxiliary machinery and for these two air and two circulating pumps were also provided.

Brown-Curtis Turbines of *Haruna*
Haruna was the first ship of the IJN fitted with this type of turbine. The principal differences between the Brown-Curtis turbine and the conventional Curtis turbine were:

– The rotor (Shadô-bu) was placed next to several wheels (Yokusha) and the rotor had neither diaphragm (Shikiri) nor nozzles (Funkô) but impulse blades (Shôdô-yoku). Pairs of stator blades (Seidô-yoku) formed one unit of

Kongô leaves Barrow for Belfast on 20 April 1913. (Vickers, courtesy of the author)

THE BATTLECRUISERS OF THE KONGÔ CLASS

Kongô *at Yokosuka in 1914. She now has a light grey livery; the funnel caps and upper legs of the tripod masts are painted black. When Japan declared war on Germany 23 August 1914* Kongô *was the flagship of the Third Division of the First Fleet.* (Kure Maritime Museum, courtesy of the author)

the impulse stage and the stator blades functioned as nozzles against the moving blades (Dô-yoku).
– The astern turbine (Kô-shin) also consisted of wheels (Yoku-sha) and a rotor (Dô-sha).

The general layout of the turbines in the engine room was the same as in the other three ships of the class; there were HP and LP ahead turbines on each side of the ship, and the astern turbines were incorporated into the casings at the after end. The HP ahead turbine had six stages, of which the first had four rows of blades and the others three; the rotor had 15 rows. The LP ahead turbine had no stages, only a rotor with 38 rows of blades. The HP and LP astern turbines comprised a single stage with four (14) rows of blades and the rotor had ten (12) rows.

The structure of one set of turbines is shown in the figure, and the comparison with the figure showing that of the modified Parsons turbine reveals the main differences.

Boilers

All ships except *Hiei* were fitted with 36 Yarrow large-tube boilers in eight boiler rooms, four on each side of the centreline bulkhead which extended throughout the whole length of the machinery spaces. Steam pressure was 19.2 bar in the boilers and 14.3 bar at the turbine inlet.

Hiei *leaves her builder, Yokosuka N.Y., on 23 March 1914 for Kure N.Y. There she will enter no.3 dock on 31 March in preparation for her trials. Note the raised forefunnel which distinguishes her from her sister* Kongô *as completed.* (Author's collection)

The boilers were designed to work under forced draught with closed stokeholds. In order to burn oil fuel as well as coal a complete installation of pumps, heaters, filters, and collectors with all connections was provided. Electrical indicators for regulating the firing of the boilers were fitted in the boiler rooms, the furnaces being numbered to correspond with numbers which were periodically displayed on the indicator dials.

Five steam-driven air compressors were fitted for cleaning the boiler tubes externally by air jet.

Forced draught was supplied by 34 fans of which two were of the double-breasted type, while the others were of the single-breasted type. The fans were driven by compound steam engines fitted with forced lubrication. The steam and exhaust piping arrangement was arranged in such a way that the turbines could be supplied by steam from any of the eight boiler rooms.

Because *Kongô* was the model for her sisters, this arrangement was repeated in *Haruna* and *Kirishima*, but in their case steam pressure at the turbine inlet was 17.1 bar (the boilers had still the same pressure rating). *Hiei* was fitted with 36 Kampon watertube boilers manufactured by Yokosuka NY and having the same working pressure as the Yarrow boilers. The effect of open versus closed stokeholds (or natural versus forced draught) is well be illustrated in the case of *Hiei*, which developed 69,973shp and 76,127shp respectively in these conditions.

Armament

Main and Secondary Guns

The *Kongô* class as completed were armed with eight 14in/45-cal (355.6mm) guns in twin turrets, arranged as in the drawings The guns were of various models:

– *Kongô* was equipped with eight Type 'B' Model I guns, which had a chamber volume of 283.5 litres. The guns were manufactured in Britain by Vickers, and were mounted during the fitting-out stage.
– *Hiei* was equipped with the same type of gun but of a Model II variant in which chamber volume was increased to 303.2 litres. According to the Annual Report of the Navy Ministry (Kaigunshô Nenpô) four guns were built by the Gunnery Division of Kure NY and four by the Japan Steel Works, the latter using components imported from Vickers.
– *Haruna* and *Kirishima* had the Model III gun with the same chamber volume as Model II, but with a modified Type 41 breech bush and a breech derived from the Vickers models. Seven of *Haruna*'s guns were produced in the Japan Steel Works using components imported from Vickers and one gun was imported direct from Vickers, as were all eight of the guns for *Kirishima*.

Main Gun Mountings

In report O-47(N)-1 of the US Naval Technical Mission to Japan, entitled *Japanese Naval Guns And Mounts – Article I Mounts under 18* the authors made the general statement that 'all Japanese naval turrets and mounts are of sound and practical design and construction, but have no really outstanding features' and 'are all old-fashioned when compared with US and British standards'.. The report explains that the only major calibre Japanese turrets were for 14-inch and 16-inch guns and that 'all of these turrets were built either before, during, or just after' the First World War and states that 'they are similar in principle, and in most details to the turrets built for

36cm Turret
(Kongô 'A' turret simplified)

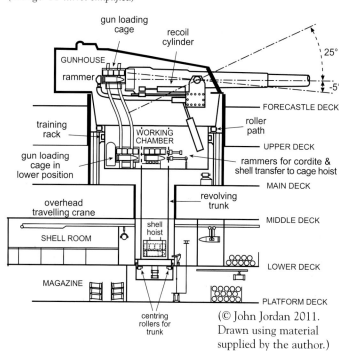

(© John Jordan 2011. Drawn using material supplied by the author.)

In contrast to standard British practice, the shell rooms were above the magazines which, in the fore and after parts of the ship, were separated from the ship's double bottom by store rooms. A bulkhead elevator raised the bags of propellant, which were in quarter charges, to the shell room, in which the handing room was located.

Projectiles in the shell rooms were lifted from the bins and transported to the central ammunition trunk by overhead winches. The shell was transferred to a revolving bogie, from which it was rolled into the lower compartment of the cage when the safety door for the trunk was opened. Simultaneously four powder-bags were lifted from the magazine to the handing room and rolled into the upper compartments of the cage.

The cage was then hoisted to the working chamber, where the shell and propellant bags were transferred to the upper cage hoist. The latter was then raised until it reached the stops of the loading arm, and was locked in this position. Once the projectile was rammed into the breech, a door in the hoist-cage was opened by means of a hand lever, and the four powder bags rolled into the tray ready for ramming. The gun-loading cage was then lowered to the working chamber and locked in the lowered position. Simultaneously the breech block was closed and the gun was ready for firing.

THE BATTLECRUISERS OF THE KONGÔ CLASS

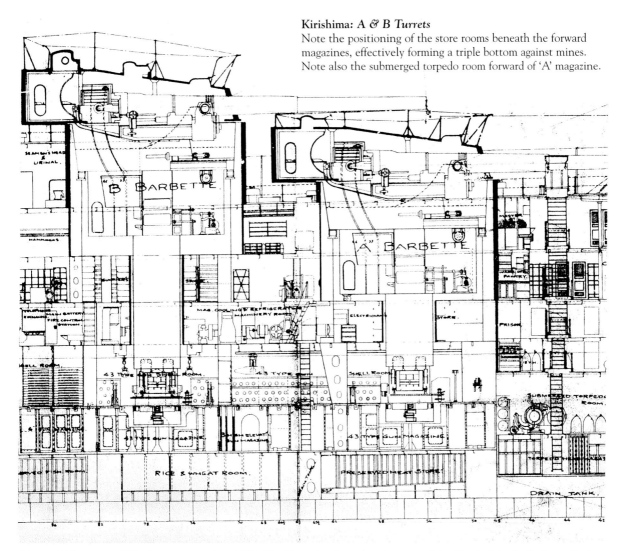

Kirishima: A & B Turrets
Note the positioning of the store rooms beneath the forward magazines, effectively forming a triple bottom against mines. Note also the submerged torpedo room forward of 'A' magazine.

(Original blueprints of *Kirishima* approved in 1915. The blueprints bear the signature of the Head of the Preliminary Design Section of the Navy Technical Department, Vice-Admiral Yamamoto Kaizô.)

Kongô, which in turn are, with the exceptions mentioned later, similar to the 15-inch turrets of the *Queen Elizabeth* and *Royal Sovereign* classes'.

Japanese authors concur with this view and acknowledge that the Vickers turret of *Kongô* was the base-line type, but point out that if details such as (i) structure of the barrel, (ii) type of breech, (iii) diameter of the barbette, (iv) loading system (free or fixed), (v) elevation angle, (vi) configuration of the turret, and (vii) type and mounting of rangefinder are analysed, the IJN used 14 different types in the 40 twin gun mountings of the four ships of *Kongô* class (16 units), the two ships of *Fusô* class (12 units), and the two ships of *Ise* class (also 12 units). Despite these differences all the turrets were known as the Type 43 14-inch twin turret.

The principal differences of the turrets fitted in the *Kongô* class were as follows: those in *Kongô* and *Hiei* were angular in configuration, while those in *Haruna* and *Kirishima* were rounded; and the elevation angle in *Kongô* was −5° to +25°, while in her sisters it was −5° to +20°. Because of the all-angle loading system the diameter of the barbette was 9m.[11] The total complement for each gun turret and its associated magazines, shell rooms and handing rooms was more than 90, of whom 21 were in the gunhouse itself..

The sectional view of the main gun mounting of *Kongô* class shows the general arrangement. Readers interesting in knowing more are referred to Peter Hodges' excellent book *The Big Gun – Battleship: Main Armament 1860-1945*,[12] where he describes in detail the operation of the similar British 15-inch gun mountings of the *Queen Elizabeth* class (p.70ff, also Appendix 3, p.128ff).[13] Like the guns, the mountings were also manufactured in the Gunnery Division of Kure NY and the Nippon Steel Works. Gôtô Takuo, who helped to oversee the construction of the *Kongô* and was later promoted Vice-Admiral, was responsible for the mountings.

Secondary Guns
The secondary guns were 15cm/50-cal. Type 41 guns whose particulars and ballistic data can be found in Tables 7 and 9. Sixteen guns were mounted in casemates and

Kirishima: Q Turret with Submerged Torpedo Room

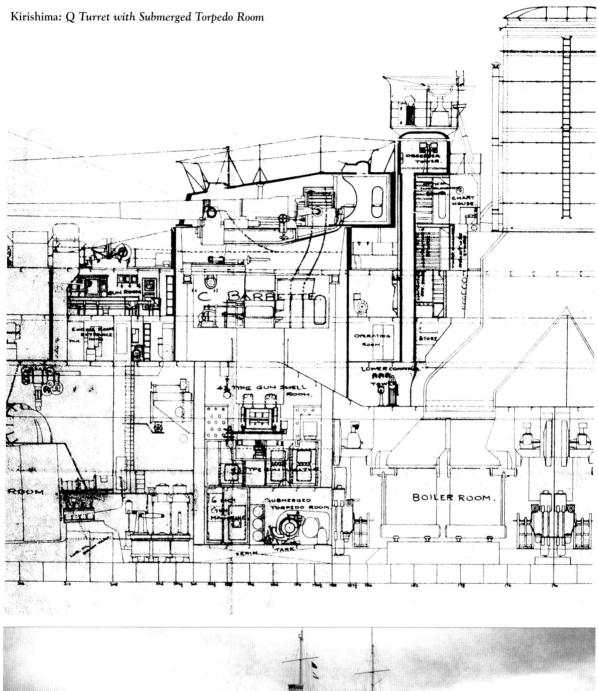

A fine view of Kirishima at Sasebo in late 1915. (Kure Maritime Museum, courtesy of the author)

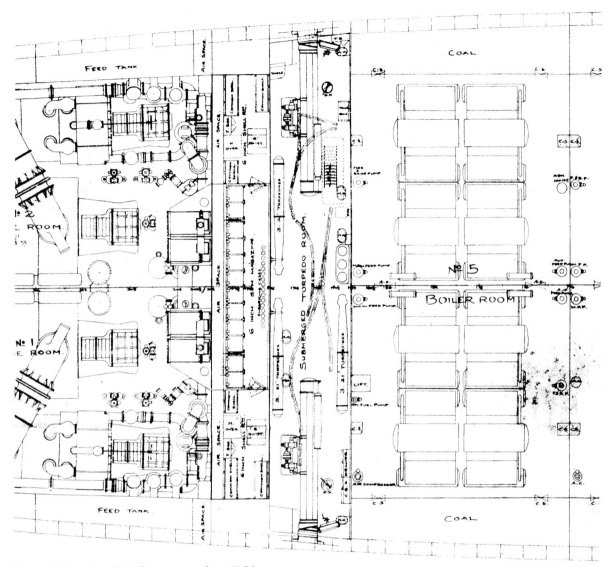

(Original blueprints of *Kirishima* approved in 1915.)

divided evenly between both sides of the ship. The original Vickers gun was adapted by a change in the breech and breech block to the Japanese Type 41.

Footnotes:
1. The Anglo-Japanese Alliance facilitated this concession, but the RN was for its part naturally interested in obtaining first-hand information about the results of the trials. In a conversation with the author the late Rear-Admiral Takasu Kôichi stated that 'joint trial firings took place over 20 days'.
2. Almost seven years had passed since the order of the battleships *Katori* and *Kashima* from Britain. During that period capital ship design had been revolutionised and British building techniques had undoubtedly made great progress. The IJN aimed to make up the ground in one step.
3. When the members of the US Naval Technical Mission to Japan investigated the technical level of Japan at the end of the Pacific War they often stated in their reports that this or that was derived from Vickers technology (cf. the section about the main guns).
4. It was exceptional for a naval architect to become the chief of a Naval Dockyard. Apart from Gôtô there is only one other example, Rear-Admiral Yamamoto Mikinosuke, who became the chief of Sasebo NY in 1933.
5. He belonged to Kure NY Gunnery Division and designed most of the large guns and turrets (including the 46cm guns of the 'super battleships' *Yamato* and *Musashi*). He was widely known as a naval engineer of exceptional ability, and there was a saying: 'With Hata in the IJN, the battleship could be built'.
6. The later Vice-Admiral (constructor) Niwata Shôzô mentions in his book *Do not forget, Yamato!* that he and his colleagues, when working in the Kure NY Shipbuilding Division, were always told by workers and managers about their experiences in England where they had studied the construction techniques of Vickers in building the *Kongô*. He also points out that the people who were involved with *Kongô* were in charge of the construction of the battleship *Fusô* and subsequent capital ships.
7. Yukiko Fukasaku, *Technology and Industrial Development in*

TABLE 7: PRINCIPAL CHARACTERISTICS OF MAIN & SECONDARY GUNS

	36cm/45-cal Type 41	15cm/50-cal Type 41
Calibre: nominal/actual	36cm/355.6mm	15cm/152.5mm
Barrel length:		
breech face to muzzle	16.00m	7.62m
overall / in calibres	16.47m / 46.31	7.88m / 51.68
Weight (incl. BM)	84.69t	8.36t
Construction	wire-wound, liner radially expanded, four layers at muzzle and breech	three layers (tubes), liner radially expanded but older guns wire-wound*
Breech	In contrast to the cylindrical interrupted screw breech of the Vickers type the fore and after parts of the Type 41 were inclined at 5° to facilitate operation. Seen from the side the centre section appears like a bulge. Invented by the later Vice-Ad. (weapon production) Dr. Arisaka Kinzô, the adoption of this breech was officially announced on 21 August 1908 and used from the 8cm gun upwards for nearly all Japanese naval guns as the Type 41 (1908) breech.	
No of grooves/depth & width	84/3.05mm x 8.87mm	72/1.27mm x 7.62mm
Twist	uniform (1 in 28 cal)	uniform (1 in 30 cal)
Length of rifling	13.74m	6.58m
Bore cross section	1,015cm^2	168cm^2
Chamber:		
length	2.007m	0.949m
volume	283.5 to 302.16l	26.14l
Powder container	4 bags (1/4 charges) 132kg	1 bag (1/1 charge) ??kg
Muzzle speed	805m/s	850m/s
Maximum bore pressure	30 bar	28.8 bar
Muzzle pressure	5.1 bar	4.9 bar
Projectile weight	635kg (Type 3 AP) 635kg (Type 3 Common)	45.36kg (Common)
Charge weight	95.38kg to 139.95kg**	12.76kg
Approximate life	250 to 280 rounds***	500 to 600 rounds

Notes:

* The guns built by Vickers for the Kongô class were of the wire-wound type.

** Three types of charges were used, namely full (4/4), reduced (3/4), and weak (2/4). There was also a strong charge (full + up to 20%) but used only for trial purposes.

*** Using equivalent full charges (IJN did not use this term), ie strong charge was calculated as two shells fired, reduced charge as ½ shell fired and weak as 1/16 shell fired

TABLE 8: PRINCIPAL BALLISTIC DATA OF THE 36CM GUN

Elevation/Range	Elev./Angle of descent	Striking speed	Penetration power (AP shell) Vertical (VC)	Horizontal (NVC)
		15,000m /???m/s	302mm	124mm
20° / 22,500m	20° / 31°48'	20,000m / 396m/s	193mm	135mm
25° / 25,800m	25° / 39°06'	25,000m / 403m/s	163mm	157mm

Notes:

VC = Vickers Cemented

NVC = New Vickers Cemented

Note the decrease in penetration power against vertical armour and increase against horizontal armour depending on the range.
Note also the slight increase of the remaining speed due to the high angle of descent.
In the column Penetration power the values are as stated by Fukuda, op. cit. p.159 without specifying the shell.

TABLE 9: PRINCIPAL BALLISTIC DATA OF THE 15CM GUN

Elevation/Range	Elev./Angle of descent	Striking speed	Penetration power
15° / 14,200m	?	?	48.2mm (vertical)
20° / 16,300m	20° / 36°53'	324m/s	negligible
25° / 18,000m	25° / 43°23'	334m/s	?
30° / 19,500m	30° / 49°38'	349m/s	?

Source: Fukuda, op. cit. p.159 and *Umi to Sora* 5/1958

THE BATTLECRUISERS OF THE KONGÔ CLASS

Hiei at Sasebo in 1915; she has the same paint scheme as Kongô following her entry into service. (Kure Maritime Museum, courtesy of the author)

Pre-War Japan: Mitsubishi Nagasaki Shipyard 1884-1934, pp.51-53 and pp.154-57, where fifteen engineers are mentioned. The mission report of engineer Yokoyama Kôzô, who studied mainly turbines as assistant naval inspector for Kongô, is mentioned on p.53.

8. This section is based on the following Japanese sources: *Kaigun Hôjutsu-shi* (History of Naval Gunnery), *Kyû Riku-Kaigun Tekkô Gijutsu-shi no oboegaki* (Notes on the History of the Former Military Steel Technology) and *Kaigun Gijutsu Monogatari* (History of Naval Technique), the latter a series of contributions published in *Suikô*, the organ of the (former) Naval Officers Association.

9. In a refit during the late 1920s it would be strengthened By additional plates 64mm thick.
10. Flow speed was 2.78m/s but two circulation pumps were necessary to transform the exhaust steam to condensed water.
11. In the mountings with a fixed loading angle (5°) the diameter could be reduced to 8.40m.
12. Conway Maritime Press, London 1981.
13. Further data can also be found in various papers of the *Contributions to the History of Japanese Warships* by the author. Readers interested in additional literature may order them via e-mail from 'lars.ahlberg@halmstad.mail.postnet.se' or write to 'milanovich@t-online.de'.

Haruna leaves Kobe 24 April 1915 following the completion of her trials. Note the anti-torpedo nets, which were retained by the IJN long after they were discarded by the Royal Navy. (Author's collection)

THE LIMITS OF NAVAL POWER

The military events of the Franco-Prussian War of 1870-71 had lasting effects for the whole of Europe, but the naval campaign was also relevant. **Colin Jones** examines how it affected the two navies involved.

The saluting guns banged and the bands on board the ships of the French fleet jauntily played the national anthem as they sailed out from Cherbourg on 24 July 1870. But if they had thought at all about the words, they were not 'leaving for Syria', but for the coast of Germany.[1] As things developed, their departure was to be the only good thing to remember. The Empress herself had come aboard the flagship *Surveillante* and read a rousing message from the Emperor. It concluded:

> Go, show our national colours with pride. In seeing the *tricolore* float above our ships, the enemy will know that everywhere it carries in its folds the honour and the spirit of France.[2]

Prussian Chancellor Otto von Bismarck had manoeuvred France in such a way that the Foreign Secretary, the Duc de Gramont, was not prepared to let the opportunity of a crisis slip away. Whether or not Prussia intended to encircle France with its allies, he was to prove the truth of Bismarck's damning indictment that he was 'the stupidest man in Europe'.[3] 'Never', it has been said, 'had an international cataclysm been unleashed over such a futile pretext'.[4] On 15 July 1870 France declared war on Prussia.

When considering in what way the French fleet might be used against Germany, the planners usually envisaged a major landing on the north German coast to open up a second front. In 1867 Rear-Admiral Laffon de Ladebat had studied the scenario and in 1869 the French had practised the manoeuvre, embarking a very large force on their ships at Dunkirk. The manoeuvre had been trumpeted by the theorist Captain Richild Grivel as a key to the defeat of Prussia.

So when war actually came, the strategy seemed self-evident.

In fact, the French had also considered the difficulties of effecting a landing on the German North Sea coast, with its shallows and sandbanks. The only points of entry were the narrow and difficult entrances to the Jade (where the much-desired Prussian fleet base at Wilhelmshaven had just that year had its new docks opened to the sea), the Elbe (Cuxhaven and Hamburg), the Weser (Bremerhaven)

The König Wilhem *was the most powerful ship of the German fleet. Designed originally for Turkey by Edward Reed, she was armed with 18-9.4in and 5-8.2in guns, and when not suffering from engine trouble had a speed of 14 knots.* (Illustrirte Zeitung)

The Océan and the French ironclad fleet at anchor off the cliffs of the British island of Heligoland in August 1870. The Océan was the largest and most modern of the ironclads, with an armament of 4-10.8in and 8-9.4in guns and a speed of 13.5 knots. The ironclads have struck their topmasts. (Illustrated London News, author's collection)

and the Ems (Emden). The Germans, not unaware of the danger, withdrew all sea marks and lightships from the entrances to the Elbe & Weser on 17 July 1870.

The French army was seen as a formidable weapon, able at the very least to march deep into the heart of Germany, but without alliances things might prove difficult in the long run. Austria, so recently defeated by Prussia, would not be drawn in unless there were significant early French victories. For operations against Kiel and Danzig in the Baltic, French preliminary studies had shown need for an alliance with Denmark and an advance base at Køge Bay, next to Copenhagen. The French, it was speculated, would land up to 40,000 men and the Danes would contribute 30,000. In the event, it was all to prove merely academic.

Even before war was declared, the fleets of the two sides were making uneasy moves. The main Prussian battle squadron, ironclads *König Wilhelm*, *Friedrich Carl*, *Kronprinz*, and *Prinz Adalbert*, was on a cruise to Madeira under the command of the namesake of the ship, Prince Adalbert himself. The squadron had made a leisurely trip via the principal British naval arsenals, where the Germans had inspected the latest technology with great interest. At Dover they had been surrounded by excursion steamers with passengers eager to see the fleet that might soon be at war with mighty France. From 1864 to 1870, Plymouth was the real supply base for the Prussian fleet. On 10 July, with storm clouds gathering rapidly over European politics, the ships sailed for Fayal. Knowing the strength of the French fleet, however, it would have been a very unwise move to continue the cruise in the face of the crisis, and so they returned to Plymouth and sailed eastwards on 13 July. Sub-Lieutenant Tirpitz observed that their hurried flight was not without reason, as they carried only 'practice shot (filled with peas) and a fuze which misfired at every opportunity'.[5] Prince Adalbert, although he had been a great advocate of a strong fleet, was to abandon the Navy for the Army during the war so that he would see some action.

French organisation was not seen at its best. Admiral Charles Rigault de Genouilly, the Navy Minister, had attempted to have the fleet mobilised as early as 7 July, but as a result of what has been called 'a disgraceful struggle',[6] he had to give way as chief of the fleet to be sent to the Baltic to the commander of the Channel Fleet, Admiral Louis-Edouard Bouët-Willaumez. The latter had commanded the forces in the Pacific during the war against Mexico, and before that, a squadron in the Black Sea against Russia. The military authorities refused to countenance taking part in an amphibious expedition and pointed to the Navy's ability to use its 12,000 marines. Preparations for their transport and use were dilatory to say the least. Mobilisation, also, was extremely slow and chaotic, and neutral observers were to conclude that the French fleet had sailed for the Baltic at least eight days too late. The army likewise was behind schedule, while the Prussian organisation was running like a well-oiled machine.

As the fleet sailed for the Baltic, Denmark decided to remain neutral, while Britain started to assemble a 'squadron of observation' comprising the frigates *Active* and *Glasgow*.

The French Baltic fleet comprised seven ironclads: the frigates *Surveillante* (brought from reserve and flying the flag of Admiral Bouët-Willaumez), *Gauloise* (flying the flag of Admiral Dieudonné), *Flandre*, *Guyenne* and *Océan* (the last two from reserve) and the corvettes *Thétis* and *Jeanne d'Arc* (the latter from reserve). In fact, Bouët-Willaumez felt far from superior despite the nominal strength of his force, and the reserve crews would need to be worked up to a good standard of efficiency. The Prussian fleet was not insignificant and he wanted to make sure that it was destroyed or totally blockaded before he would venture any landing on the coast. During the early part of August he studied the practicalities, and determined that he would need many shallow-draft vessels of a type that were not currently with his fleet. Also, he lacked the detailed charts that he would need to operate big ships close to an enemy coast. He would also have been aware that the expected march of the main French army into Germany might well render any landing on the northern coast not only difficult but superfluous. Bouët-Willaumez had also considered the strength of his individual ironclads in comparison with the Prussians. His *Surveillante* was definitely inferior in gun power to the *König Wilhelm*, but he hoped to be able to deal with her by the ram. After the enemy warships were neutralised, he expected to have a backup force commanded by Admiral de la Roncière le Noury. It would bring the necessities for coastal attack: gunboats, floating batteries and 30,000 troops under the dashing General Bourbaki.

The cruisers of the Prussian fleet were distributed along the Baltic coast as guard ships, while the French cruisers operated against trade and blockaded Prussian warships on foreign stations.

The French North Sea Fleet had seven ironclads: the frigates *Magnanime* (flying the flag of Vice-Admiral Fourichon), *Héroïne* (flying the flag of Rear-Admiral Jauréguiberry), *Provence*, (flying the flag of Rear-Admiral de Voulx), *Valeureuse*, *Revanche* and *Invincible* (the last three all from reserve), and the corvette *Atalante*. But Fourichon had been held at Oran in Algeria against a possible attack on troop convoys by a non-existent Prussian force and did not sail from Cherbourg until 8 August, the same day on which the Navy Minister abandoned all plans for a landing on the German coast.

Of the other ironclads, the frigate *Couronne* was in the Mediterranean and would be sent north; the corvette *Montcalm* was also in the Mediterranean and would be sent to the Azores; the *Belliqueuse* was in the Levant and the *Alma* was in Japan.

The Prussian commander in the North Sea, Rear-Admiral Eduard Jachmann, wanted all his ironclads together in view of the strong French forces that were being despatched, and so the monitor *Arminius* made a daring escape from Kiel around Denmark to the North Sea. She was able to reach Frederikshavn, near the northern tip of Jutland, on 27 July, mainly due to French unpreparedness. Next day she was chased off Hirstholm by three ironclads and a cruiser, but escaped to Jade Bay. She had unshipped her masts so her profile was very low. Jachmann was a consistent advocate of a strong navy for Prussia and had established a plan to have by 1877 a fleet of 16 ironclads and 20 cruisers. In this war he was to be frustrated by circumstance and by the insistence of Bismarck that no action should be taken against French merchant shipping. In the first week of August he took his ironclads as far as the Dogger Bank, but did not sight the French. The British engines of the *Arminius* were among the best in the Prussian fleet and she was to sortie to worry the French as many as 40 times, thus providing good value to the German public who had subscribed their own money for her purchase.

On 28 July Bouët-Willaumez was received with cheers at Copenhagen.

Every day the newspaper reader could follow the reports of the war correspondents on big printed maps. If the world had been waiting for the outcome of the clash of the armies, it now had its answer. On 6 August there were significant defeats for the French, when General MacMahon's forces were defeated by the Crown Prince at Woerth and the Emperor's 'Armée du Rhin' was defeated by General von Steinmetz at Spicheren. The Prussian army was sweeping forward, but what about the Prussian Fleet? On the German North Sea coast, Fourichon declared the blockade on 15 August.

From the fortified vantage point of Cuxhaven, observers were unable to see that the French fleet was doing very much.

> They lie at their station near Heligoland, do not separate, take a small German merchantman occasionally, now and then stop and send back a neutral vessel, but are content with being 'monarchs of all they survey', and do not go anywhere where their supremacy is likely to be disputed.[7]

Nevertheless, French cruisers were steadily removing German trade from the high seas while their own sailed free of hindrance.

The Océan *with the* Flandre *(drying sails),* Thétis *and* Guyenne *to the left and* Surveillante *to the right, at Heligoland in September 1870. The* Rochambeau *is at the extreme right.* (Illustrirte Zeitung)

THE LIMITS OF NAVAL POWER

The monitor Arminius *engages the* Gauloise *and* Atalante *in the Weser estuary.* (Illustrirte Zeitung)

The Prussians were at a severe disadvantage against the French forces in the Baltic, but they were not going to be merely confined in port. On 17 August the sloop *Grille*, gunboats *Drache* and *Blitz* and paddle sloop *Salamander* engaged in a lively cannonade off Rügen with four French ironclads, a corvette and a sloop. The Germans were able to escape further French attention by slipping back into port, but they had made a point. Three days later the *Grille* took advantage of her 13-knot speed to lead a light French detachment into a gunboat ambush, but the Prussians retired when some French frigates arrived. The French fleet then moved on to Danzig, where it anchored offshore on 22 August. At midnight the following night Captain Johannes Weickhmann took the corvette *Nymphe* to attack the fleet off the port. He fired on the *Surveillante* but escaped after the *Thétis* was sent in pursuit. In each case, the Prussians could challenge the French, but could never face them. The French, in considering their options for action, found them to be extremely limited. At Kiel, for example, the forts were very strong, and other places, likewise, presented difficulties.

> Colberg and Danzig alone can be attacked; but the small effect which will result from these two attempts will be of a nature to deprive the French squadron of the prestige of its force.[8]

The fast aviso Grille *taunts two French ironclads off Rügen on 17 August 1870.* (Illustrirte Zeitung)

The North-German ironclad squadron: from left to right, König Wilhelm, Friedrich Carl *and* Kronprinz. *The first two were British-built; the third was built in France.* (Illustrated London News, author's collection)

Kolberg, despite being unfortified and therefore not officially liable to bombardment, was one of the few places where the water was deep enough for the big ironclads to come close inshore. In the event, rough weather and a fear of Prussian reprisals elsewhere put an end to the idea.

One of the last ships to sail for the German coast was the big ironclad *Rochambeau*, which left Cherbourg on 25 August. She had been built for the US Navy during the Civil War as the *Dunderberg*, but never commissioned as a ship of war until she was bought by the French. She struck bad weather as she sailed up the Dutch coast, rolling heavily, and did not round the tip of Jutland until 29 August. After a brief stop at Copenhagen she joined the rest of the fleet at Langeland on 8 September.

The men of the French fleets off the north German coast, already achieving very little, must have had their morale shattered by the news that reached them during the first week of September. In the simple words of the headlines in *The Times*, a newspaper not usually given to headlines of any size, the true state of France was revealed: 'Total Defeat of Marshal Mac-Mahon', 'Surrender of the Emperor', 'Revolution in Paris'.[9] Even if they missed the newspapers, they could hardly have been unaware of the salutes of 101 guns fired for the victory at Sedan by every German coastal fortress from Pillau to Wilhelmshaven. Bouët-Willaumez went into Copenhagen on 4 September in a frigate to consult with the French representatives, and as a result he decided that the time had almost come to go home.

As for the main German fleet; it was in 1870 as it was to be in the Great War of 1914. It seemed to their men that the warships rusted in port instead of getting to grips with the enemy, however superior he might seem. The Army was in the heat of violent, bloody and victorious action while the fleet stagnated. It was said that the *König Wilhelm* was hampered in steaming by more than 60 tons of mussels on her bottom; there was not as yet any dry dock in Germany big enough to take her. Finally, Jachmann was sufficiently happy with the engines of the *König Wilhelm* and *Friedrich Carl* that he was able to take his ships to sea to meet Fourichon. It was an irony that at this very time the French decided to sail for home so, even as the Germans approached Heligoland on 11 September, the masts of the French fleet sank below the horizon.

It is interesting for a moment to speculate on what might have happened if Jachmann had actually met Fourichon at sea. No doubt the action would have been as confused as that at Lissa in 1866, but fought with equal vigour. Fourichon disposed of eight ironclads against Jachmann's five, but they were not all equal in strength. In their main forces, the French counted seven ironclad frigates, all of similar specification, against the Prussian three, of which the *König Wilhelm* was substantially the most powerful. In a *mêlée* it might have been expected that some at least of the Prussian ships would have been very roughly handled by the superior numbers of the French, but on the other hand, the Prussian flagship could hardly have failed to cause substantial damage, even to the point of sinking one or more of Fourichon's best ships. Perhaps Fourichon was lucky to return to Cherbourg on 20 September, with the majority of his fleet at anchor, still intact, off Calais and Dunkirk. At all events, the passive role of the Prussian Navy was to earn it no credit when the honours were allotted after the war.

In the Baltic, the French fleet cruised off the German coast from 13 to 15 September. The first division then moved back to Danish waters at Køge Bay. As she followed the *Surveillante* at a speed of eight knots, the *Rochambeau* rolled very violently, with waves sometimes breaking right across the sloping sides of the armoured casemate, causing water to pour down into the ship from all available openings. Bouët-Willaumez, observing her difficulties, and noting that his own ship could still have fought her guns, ordered the sloop *Limier* to approach the

THE LIMITS OF NAVAL POWER

Rochambeau so that their rolling could be compared. Although she seemed to roll just as much, she was not nearly as wet. The officers of the *Rochambeau* were saved from the embarrassment of having to leave the squadron by the gradual lessening of the swell nearer to the Danish coast. The ship had just one advantage: because of her relatively shallow draught, she and the corvette *Thétis* were the only ironclads able to transit the Drogden Pass next day, straight from the Baltic to the Sound.

The Danes were very critical of the French fleet as they observed its operations in the Baltic. The *Dagbladet* observed:

> The want of order and foresight, and of settled plans which had been so disastrous to France by land was still more marked at sea... For four years a French man-of-war had never appeared in the Baltic, though a war with Prussia was always in contemplation.[10]

Thus the French were unaware of the conditions they should have to expect, and perhaps as a result of their general unpreparedness, kept their fleet well out of sight of the critical view of the Danes.

It has been estimated that the threat of the French fleet on the north German coast immobilised some 100,000 German soldiers in the region, but the inability of the French field armies to capitalise on the situation made the achievement somewhat academic. By 19 September Paris itself was besieged by the Germans.

As he sailed for home on 26 September, Bouët-Willaumez took the chance to send his two shallow-draught ironclads, the *Rochambeau* and *Thétis* to reconnoitre the entrance to the Jade, but the Prussian fleet was not tempted. The Prussian gunboats which had been supervising trade out of Cuxhaven were nervous at the arrival at Heligoland of the French Baltic fleet on 30 September, but they were just going home.

The Augusta *burns the French steamer* Mars, *caught off the Gironde on 4 January 1871 with a shipment of arms. Built in France for the Confederacy in 1864, she reverted to her intended role as a commerce raider under the German flag.* (Illustrirte Zeitung)

The remainder of the year saw comparatively little in the way of naval action. The Prussian frigate *Arcona* arrived at Lisbon in November and was blockaded by the French for the duration, but Bismarck had at last agreed to allow his cruisers to operate against French trade. The corvette *Augusta* managed to get to sea after the French had withdrawn their forces, on 14 December. Commanded by the pugnacious Johannes Weickhmann, she sailed north around Britain and cruised for a time off Brest and the Gironde from 26 December, hoping to intercept an arms shipment from the United States. He captured two vessels and burned another. After the *Augusta* put in to Vigo on 4 January 1871 she too was blockaded by a pair of French warships. It was a nice touch though, in view of her origin as the Confederate *Mississippi*, that she finally became, however briefly, a raider. Weichmann and his crew never did receive any prize money.[11]

The flagship Surveillante *with the* Océan *and the fleet under way in the Baltic in August 1870. The* Surveillante *and the majority of other large French ironclads had an armament of 8-9.4in and 4-7.6in guns, with a speed of 13.5 knots.* (Illustrated London News, author's collection)

Laying a defensive minefield at Pillau. (Illustrirte Zeitung)

The Prussian warships had been able to do very little, but the powerful and prestigious French fleet had proved to be effectively irrelevant in the war. Fourichon gave over command to Vice-Admiral de Gueydon, who attempted from 21 September to enforce the blockade of the North Sea from bases at Calais and Dunkirk.

Admiral de Gueydon had been set a thankless task. He could stop any German shipping in the Channel, but the entrances to the principal German ports were just too far away. His ships suffered from lack of coal, as well as the lengthening nights and the bad weather at the extreme limit of the season. Coaling in the open sea was difficult enough, but strong west winds soon made it impossible. As he said: 'all efforts would be absorbed in a fight against the elements'.[12] Ironclads such as the *Couronne* and *Invincible* were in poor condition, eating coal and with their speed falling. 'The results obtained from the point of view of the damage caused to commerce are insignificant', he stated.[13] The blockade ended on 20 October and he returned to Cherbourg on 24th.

The German ironclads were caught in the roadstead outside Wilhelmshaven with ice threatening to damage their moorings and the coal barges unable to come out to them. To get into the still-incomplete basins, they had to be lightened and when this was done, on 23 December, their war was over.

In the war against Prussia, it fell to the French battle fleet, ranked second in the world, to give a melancholy demonstration of the limits of sea power. Its critics could say that it was indeed, a 'luxury and vanity'.[14]

The events of the time echoed forward for many years. For France, the future of the Navy was to be subjected to intense scrutiny leading to the adoption of the theories of the Jeune Ecole. It was only the stolid defence of the Parisian forts by the French sailors that saved it from wholesale shame and the political axe. On the German side, a 21-year-old Sub-Lieutenant Alfred Tirpitz, who had spent the war in relative idleness on board the *König Wilhelm*, was to form a firm conviction that Germany in future must have a fleet capable of offensive action. He was to spend a career working towards the goal. Nevertheless, the names of the most prominent German warships tended to celebrate military rather than naval leaders. There were to be, for instance, a *Moltke* and a *Roon* from this war, but never a *Jachmann*.

Sources

Rear-Admiral P H Colomb, *Naval Warfare*, W H Allen (London, 1891).
Clas Broder Hansen, *Deutschland wird Seemacht*, Urbes (Munich, 1991).
Alistair Horne, *The Fall of Paris*, Macmillan (London, 1965).
Michael Howard, *The Franco-Prussian War*, Macmillan (New York, 1962).
Philippe Masson, *Histoire de la Marine*, Tome 2, Charles Lavauzelle (Paris, 1983).
Jean Randier, *La Royale*, Vol 1, Cité (Brest, 1972).
Theodore Ropp, *The Development of a Modern Navy*, US Naval Institute (Annapolis, 1987).
Stanley Sandler, *The Emergence of the Modern Capital Ship*, University of Delaware (Newark, 1979).
Lawrence Sondhaus, *Preparing for Weltpolitik*, US Naval Institute (Annapolis, 1997).
Grand Admiral Von Tirpitz, *My Memoirs*, Vol 1, Hurst & Blackett (London, 1919).
H W Wilson, *Battleships in Action*, Vol 1, Sampson Low Marston (London, 1926).
The Times
Illustrated London News

Footnotes

1. *La Marseillaise* had been supplanted during the Second Empire by *Partant pour la Syrie*, a tune subsequently mocked by Saint-Saens in his *Carnival of the Animals* under the heading of 'fossils'.
2. Randier, *La Royale*, p.23, author's translation.
3. Horne, *The Fall of Paris*, p.6.
4. *ibid.*, p.37.
5. Tirpitz, *Memoirs*, Vol 1, p.6.
6. Ropp, *The Development of a Modern Navy*, p.23.
7. *The Times* 24 Aug 1870. The reference is to Cowper's poem, 'The Solitude of Alexander Selkirk'. Heligoland was still a British possession.
8. Colomb, *Naval Warfare*, p.429.
9. *The Times* 3 & 5 Sept 1870.
10. *The Times* 10 Oct 1870.
11. Weickhmann and Graf von Waldersee (commanding the *Grille*) were, however, the only officers of the German naval forces to receive medals for their actions in the war.
12. Masson, *Histoire de La Marine*, Vol 2, p.127.
13. *ibid.*, p.128.
14. Sandler, *The Emergence of the Modern Capital Ship*, p.60.

WARSHIP NOTES

This section comprises a number of short articles and notes, generally highlighting little known aspects of warship history.

JOHN BROWN'S IN SEARCH OF SOUTH AMERICAN ORDERS

Kenneth Fraser has unearthed further details of projects for South American navies in the John Brown archive.

The number of surplus warships available after the Second World War reduced the market for new ships, but British yards continued to seek orders. Two examples from South America have come to light in the Glasgow University Archives.

In January 1947, the Argentine Government had a major naval programme in mind: an aircraft carrier, a light cruiser, four destroyers, three submarines, a depot ship, a tanker, and a troop transport. The major British yards appear to have been operating as a cartel for this contract, and Brown's were interested most of all in the carrier. Argentina had specifically asked for one similar to the *Unicorn*, but Brown's, pointing out that she was actually an aircraft repair ship with a flight deck, suggested, with the concurrence of the Admiralty, one of the *Hermes* or *Colossus* class; a tender was duly submitted for a carrier similar to the *Colossus* in May. The dimensions given correspond quite closely to that ship, but for some reason the Argentines wanted an armament of 4.7in *low-angle* guns; their number is not stated, but we may recall that the *Unicorn* had 8 x 4.5in dual-purpose guns.

By July, the firm's representative in Buenos Aires wrote that the order was in doubt because its price was much greater than the Argentines had expected. In September Brown's offer was refused, though correspondence makes it clear that modifications were still being made to the design up to that time.

Brown's were also interested in the projected light cruiser. At first it had appeared that Argentina wanted one of the *Jamaica* class, but with 12 x 4.7in HA guns; Brown's did not believe that was feasible. Later it was understood that something similar to the USS *Cleveland* was required, but with 4.7in rather than 5in HA guns. It was believed that this could be managed on a design derived from the *Jamaica* and displacing about 11,500 tons.

A memo (undated but probably from August 1947) reveals why nothing came of these ideas. Argentina was about to attend the Pan-American Conference, at which it was predicted that the USA would offer her ships at a nominal price 'to oust Britain from a market in which she has so far been competitive'; and this is what in fact occurred. However, the Argentine Navy did acquire an aircraft carrier, albeit a second-hand one: the *Independencia* (ex-HMS *Warrior*) in 1958.

Five years later it was Brazil which aspired to a large programme. A letter to Brown's in March 1952 from Captain Diogo Borges Fortes, Brazilian Naval Attache in London, enclosed its particulars, impressively stamped 'Secreto'. The programme programme comprised:

Light cruisers: three, of which one to be built in Brazil.
Displacement: 5,000 to 6,000 tons.
Guns: 6 x 6in/45 in twin turrets (4 ahead, 2 aft);
10 x 3in or 40mm AA in twin mountings;
20 x 20mm AA in single mountings;
4 saluting.
Torpedo tubes: 8 x 21in in quadruple mountings.
Aircraft: 2 helicopters.
Armour: 3in-1.5in side, 1.5in horizontal, 2in-1in turrets, 6in C.T.
Machinery: geared turbines, 4-8 boilers.
Oil: about 1400 tons.
Speed: 32 knots maximum, 14 knots cruising.
[An unknown hand has annotated this 'Dido class', though the armament is more like that of the *Arethusa*. If proceeded with, these would surely have been the last conventional cruisers to be built for any navy.]

Escort carriers [sic]: one, possibly two.
Displacement: about 13,000 tons.
Guns: 4 x 5in/38 HA in twin mountings;
10 x 3in or 40mm AA in twin mountings;
20 x 20mm AA in single mountings;
4 saluting.
Aircraft: 17 fighters and 17 helicopters.
Machinery: geared turbines, 4-8 boilers.
Oil: about 2100 tons.
Speed: over 20 knots maximum, 14 knots cruising.
[Brown's have annotated this ship 'Glory'.]

Fleet destroyers (leaders): six.
Displacement: about 2400 tons.
Guns: 5 x 5in/38 in two twin and one single mountings (3 ahead, 2 aft);
4 x 3in or 40mm AA in twin mountings;
8 x 20mm AA in single mountings.
Torpedo tubes: 8 x 21in in quadruple mountings.
Anti-submarine weapons: [not specified]
Machinery: geared turbines, 3-4 boilers.
Oil: about 560 tons.
Speed; 35 knots maximum, 14 knots cruising.

[Brown's have annotated these ships 'Improved Battles', although the armament suggested is rather different.]

Minelayers: ten.
Displacement: about 600 tons.
Guns: 1 x 3in/45 AA;
4 x 20mm AA in single mountings.
Mines: 30 x 800kg.
Machinery: triple expansion with 2 boilers, or diesels.
Oil: about 170 tons.
Speed: 16 knots maximum, 10 knots normal.
[Brown's have not annotated this ship, presumably because Britain had none of this specification, although Brazil already had several in service.]

No sketches are provided, but the reader who recalls contemporary British designs will be able to form a mental picture of them.

The Brazilian Government hoped (perhaps optimistically) that the destroyers could be completed within 32 months, the cruisers within 36 and the carriers [sic] within 40.

The document goes on to state that the Brazilian authorities would like to know the price of several further ships:

– two surveying vessels similar to HMS *Vidal*.

For the Amazon River Flotilla:

– one small hospital ship with 50 beds; maximum displacement 1200 tons; loaded draught 12ft; maximum speed 16 knots.
– three river gunboats with 2 x 4in guns and 4 x 40mm AA guns; displacement about 850 tons; loaded draught 10ft; maximum speed 16 knots; and carrying a platform for a helicopter.

For the Matto Grosso flotilla:

– three river gunboats, similar to those above but with a maximum draught of 6ft, and maximum length of 42m.

In the case of all these river vessels, Brazil wished 'to receive suggestions about the specifications, according to the experience of the British Navy in the rivers of China and Africa'.

A further letter from Captain Borges Fortes explains that the Brazilian Navy hoped to receive $30 million a year from a special tax on import and export rights, and that this should pay for all the ships in four or five years.

James McNeill, of Brown's, reported this approach to A Belch, of the Shipbuilding Conference, London, on the day it was received. He suggested that the Warship Builders' Committee should inform the Admiralty of it, and obtain permission to quote; but the designs and tenders would involve a great deal of work, and he appears to have doubted if anything would come of the proposal. There is no later correspondence, and we now know that his scepticism was justified. Although Brazil, like Argentina, would acquire in 1956 a second-hand British aircraft carrier, the *Minas Gerais* (formerly HMS *Vengeance*), only a few of the proposed ships would ever be built, and none of them in British yards.

Sources
Glasgow University Archives, UCS1/21/57 [Argentina] and 1/21/70 [Brazil]

HNLMS *SOEMBA*: RADAR-INSTRUCTION & AIRCRAFT-DIRECTION SHIP, 1946-1954

Henk J. Cruijff describes the long and varied career of this Dutch warship, focusing in particular on the period immediately after the Second World War.

HNlMS *Soemba* was commissioned on April 12 1926 as a flotilla leader for the *Indische Militaire Marine* (Dutch Indies Military Navy). She was a 1,457-tonne vessel with a main armament of three 15cm guns and one 7.5cm dual purpose gun. She was capable of a maximum speed of 15 knots. In 1935 the ship was re-classified as a gunboat, without significant changes in appearance. From 1926 until the Second World War *Soemba* saw extensive service in the Dutch East Indies.

After the outbreak of war the gunboat participated in hostilities against the Japanese forces mainly in and around the Sunda Strait before

HNlMS Soemba *in Amsterdam Harbour on 24 May 1947 as a radar instruction ship. The pennant number HX1 was carried from June 1946 until June 1951.* (Dutch Naval Museum)

sailing for Colombo in mid-March 1942. Over the following months the ship was mainly employed on patrol work in the Persian Gulf region before departing for the Mediterranean in May 1943, where she undertook convoy duties and support for the Allied landings at Sicily, Salerno and Anzio. In March 1944 *Soemba* arrived in Portsmouth for a much needed refit which was completed just in time for her to provide support for the landings in Normandy. Finally, in August 1944, the ship was considered unfit for further war duties and was laid up in London, to be used for training duties on a temporary basis. This seemed to mark the end for *Soemba*, but it was not to be.

During the war the Dutch Navy had obtained a number of British warships, and was probably already planning to obtain additional units after the war. Moreover, some of the surviving Dutch vessels had been fitted with British radar, which meant that a proper radar training facility was required. At the end of 1944, the Dutch Navy Staff therefore requested that the Admiralty modify HNlMS *Soemba* in order for her to serve as a radar instruction ship. The request was granted, and the necessary modification was undertaken at Grangemouth between May 1945 and May 1946.

Her original armament was removed and the foremast moved forward against the armoured conning tower, which was retained. The bridge was enclosed and, more importantly, the ship now displayed the entire array of British radar antennae carried by Dutch naval vessels at the time. This consisted of:

The upper part of the mast of Soemba *as a radar instruction ship. Two crew members are scanning the horizon despite the Type 281 display above their heads. Above the Type 281 antenna is a Type 243 interrogator surmounted by a Type 253 transponder. A Type 242 ship interrogator can be seen forward of the mast.* (Dutch Naval Museum)

HNlMS Soemba *as an aircraft direction ship; location and date unknown. The pennant number A891 was carried from July 1951 until final decommissioning in June 1985. The VHF/DF atop the mainmast was not carried at the time.* (Dutch Naval Museum, FT02411)

- a Type 281 antenna fitted to the foremast for long range air warning with a Type 243 IFF interrogator on top of it. This array was fitted to the two ex-British aircraft carriers acquired by the Netherlands Navy after the Second World War (both ex-HMS *Nairana* and ex-HMS *Venerable* were subsequently renamed HNlMS *Karel Doorman*).
- the 'lantern' array of a Type 271/272 surface warning radar on top of the bridge. This was fitted to some of the *Batjan* class patrol vessels as well as HNlMS *Jan van Brakel* and *Johan Maurits van Nassau*.
- a Type 291 air warning antenna on the starboard side of the foremast. This radar was fitted in the Dutch ex-British 'N' and 'S' class destroyers as well as the two ex-'T' class submarines.
- a Type 277 surface/air warning and height finding radar, as fitted to the two carriers, carried forward of the bridge.
- a Type 268 surface warning and height finding radar on the pole mast amidships. The submarines were fitted with this set.
- the antenna for the Type 293 surface/air-warning radar, carried by both the carriers and the destroyers, on the mainmast.

By the late 1940s sufficient radar training facilities were available ashore and HNlMS *Soemba* was decommissioned in October 1949. However, the radar facilities on board were considered sufficiently useful for the ship's life to be extended and for *Soemba* to be refitted as an aircraft direction ship. Work was undertaken at the Royal Naval Dockyard at Den Helder and the ship recommissioned on 1 June 1952. Once again her appearance was changed.

The armoured conning tower was removed. The superstructure was considerably enlarged both forward and aft. The wartime foremast was replaced with a lattice structure, and a lattice mainmast was added. Some of the armament was reinstalled: a single 20mm on either side of the bridge and two single 40mm aft. The radar outfit was adapted for the ship's new role, so only the aircraft-related arrays remained. There was a Type 281 on the foremast, a Type 277 atop the forward superstructure, and a Type 293 on the mainmast. A MF/DF set was added forward of the bridge and a VHF/DF atop the mainmast.

In the course of her operational life as a radar instruction and aircraft direction ship, HNlMS *Soemba* and her sister ship HNlMS *Pelikaan* (ex-HMS *Thruster*) undertook many exercises in the postwar years with her RN equivalent, HMS *Boxer*. The ship also participated in the NATO exercises 'Verity' (1949), 'Factotum' (1951), 'Castanets' and 'Momentum' (1952), 'Mariner' (1953) and 'Haul' (1954).

At the end of November 1954, *Soemba* decommissioned for a third time. This did not spell the end for the ship as she underwent yet another transformation at Den Helder and in 1956 recommissioned as an accommodation ship to serve a further 29 years, making the total span of her career a very respectable 59 years.

Acknowledgements:
The author wishes to thank Henk Visser and Jon Wise for their help in producing this Warship Note.

Sources:
Operational history of the ships of the Royal Netherlands Navy, Dutch Naval Museum, Den Helder, The Netherlands.
Correspondence with former crew-member Mr. Willem H. van Schaik, Veenendaal, The Netherlands.
Norman Friedman, *Naval Radar*, Conway Maritime Press (London 1981).
Derek Howse, *Radar at Sea: The Royal Navy in World War II*, Palgrave Macmillan (London 1993).
Alistair Mitchell, 'The Development of Radar in the Royal Navy', *Warship* Nos. 13, 14 &17, Conway Maritime Press (London 1980-1).
www.dutchfleet.net

HMS *CURACOA* – WHAT'S IN A NAME?

In the first of a pair of Warship Notes, Assistant Editor Stephen Dent looks into the perennial confusion over the correct spelling of the name of this Royal Navy ship.

On 2 October 1942, in one of the worst maritime disasters of the Second World War, the liner RMS *Queen Mary*, being used to transport troops across the Atlantic, accidentally rammed and sank the escorting cruiser HMS *Curacoa*. While this much is pretty well agreed (though at least one web site lists the year as 1943!), a while back, while working on a new Conway book on the great liner ('RMS *Queen Mary*' by David Ellery, Conway, 2006), *Warship*'s Assistant Editor was struck by the wide discrepancies in the published figures for the casualties sustained by the cruiser's crew in the incident, both in books and on the newer medium of the internet. Attempts to arrive at a definitive figure instead revealed another, rather more surprising area of confusion: the actual name of the cruiser!

Numerous published sources give the ship's name as *Curacoa*, including volume 2 of Roskill's definitive *The War at Sea*, Ross Watton's 'Anatomy of the Ship' on the *Queen Mary*, and Peter Kelly's article on the sinking in *Warship* 1997-1998. Many web sites, such as the important U-boat.net and the well-known but far from reliable Wikipedia do the same. However other books such as Richard Woodman's *The History of the Ship* and Philip Dawson's *The Liner, Retrospective and Renaissance* spell the name *Curaçao*, with a cedilla on the second 'c'. Elsewhere there is *Curaçao* in Alister Satchell's *Running the Gauntlet*, and *Curacao* in an article in the May 2008 edition of *Navy News* and the television series 'Great Blunders of the 20th Century'. The BBC's WW2 People's War web site gives both *Curacoa* and *Curacao*!

One would expect JJ Colledge to be reliable here, but while in the MacDonald 'Navies of the Second World War' series he calls her *Curacao*, in *Ships of the Royal Navy*, first published by David & Charles in 1969, he spells the name as *Curacoa*. Even a check of some contemporary reference books fails to completely verify things. Two editions of *Jane's Fighting Ships*, one from 1924 when the ship was in service and one from 1944 where she is listed in the 'War Losses' section, both give the spelling as *Curacoa*, but the 1937 volume *Ships of the Royal Navies* by Oscar Parkes gives both spellings – *Curacoa* and *Curacao* – within the same section, while Lt.Cdr. E.C.Talbot-Booth's 1940 *All the World's Fighting Fleets* lists her as *Curaçoa*.

Confronted with all this, and with a publication deadline looming, for the Conway *Queen Mary* book we naturally chose to settle on the name given in Peter Kelly's *Warship* article in 1997: *Curacoa*. Further research shows that this is at once correct, but also actually wrong!

The cruiser, ordered under the 1916 Emergency War Programme, was laid down at Pembroke Dockyard in July 1916, and launched on 5 May the following year: her first log recording that HMS *Curacoa* was commissioned by Captain B E Domville[1] at Pembroke on Wednesday 9 January 1918. Over the following weeks the ship took on crew, ammunition and stores, and during February, once trials were completed, she joined the 5th Cruiser Squadron at Harwich.

She was the fourth ship in the Royal Navy to bear the name; the first being a 5th rate frigate of 1809-1849, named to mark the capture of the Caribbean island and town of Curaçao from the Dutch in January 1807. The action had been notable for the fact that the Royal Navy squadron suffered just three dead and fourteen wounded, while Dutch casualties were nearer 200. The commanding officer, Vice-Admiral James R Dacre, was knighted, and there were numerous other awards for those involved. The island had first been colonised by Alonso de Ojeda in 1499 at the beginning of what became the Spanish subjugation of much of South America during the ensuing century. In 1634, with Spanish power crumbling, it was taken by van Walbeek for the Dutch West India Company, in due course becoming a major centre of the slave trade. In 1815, eight years after capturing it from the Dutch, the British returned it. There are a number of theories as to the origin of the name and this is likely to be where the confusion over the spelling comes from. Although Dutch charts going back to the seventeenth century always give the name as Curaçao, other sources – both earlier and later – deriving from variously Spanish, Portuguese and Italian, use different spellings, including Curacoa.

A view of HMS Curacoa's after funnel following her speed trials. Commissioned in wartime, her trials, which took place off Milford Haven, were brief. Preliminary speed and gunnery trials took place between 09.30 and 15.30 on Wednesday 13 February 1918, and full power trials between 11.00 and 15.00 the following day. During the latter her machinery produced 40,428hp, six tons of coal and 172 tons of oil were expended, and she worked up to a top speed of 29 knots. On 19-20 February she steamed up the English Channel to join the 5th Light Cruiser Squadron at Harwich, where six days later her ship's company was inspected by His Majesty the King. (Photograph courtesy of Ross Watton)

So, while it is quite possible that the incorrect spelling of the ship's name simply came about as a result of the charming Anglo-Saxon habit of randomly mangling bits of other peoples' languages, a more likely explanation is simply the use of a chart with this spelling in 1807. Although there were subsequently discussions as to which spelling the Royal Navy should use, the Admiralty decided to stick to its guns,[2] even though, just to further muddy things, the prescribed 'correct' pronunciation was 'Curer-sower'… (Sailors, on the cruiser at least, chose to confuse matters even more by adopting the affectionate nickname of the 'Cocoa Boat'.) The case of *Curacoa* is not the only instance of getting foreign names wrong when christening ships of the Royal Navy: there have been three called HMS *Hogue*, although there is no such place in France – it is La Hougue.[3] However, the fact of the matter is that the four ships in the Royal Navy have all been called *Curacoa*, even though the second 'c' is meant to be pronounced softly, as if it *did* have a cedilla. Even so, the name clearly carried on causing problems throughout the life of the fourth *Curacoa*, with assorted spellings continuing to crop up – typeset, typed and hand-written – in the various official records of her career and demise.

There remains the question of why the name was not corrected. For a start the appearance and rapid spread of the typewriter in the later years of the nineteenth century can only have served to consolidate this particular mis-spelling, for there is no easy way of reproducing a cedilla on a standard English typewriter. In fact typing errors are reputed to have been responsible for two other unusual and incorrect names of RN ships, both given to destroyers built during the Great War: *Sterling* (1918-1932) should have been 'Stirling', after the ancient Scottish burgh rather than the British currency; and *Whitley* (1918-1940) should have been 'Whitby' after the port in Yorkshire. In the latter instance it was a case of unfortunate timing: the destroyer was built while an important parliamentary committee chaired by the MP for Halifax, JH Whitley (later speaker of the House of Commons), was looking into the setting up of what were to become called Joint Industrial Councils (better known as Whitley Councils) which were made up of representatives of labour and management with the purpose of promoting better industrial relations and in so doing reducing the chances of unrest. With the country at war this was a major issue of the day and no doubt was in the forefront of the mind of many a Whitehall typist, especially as the Civil Service was omitted from the first Whitley Report.[4]

Rectifying such mistakes in the naming of ships was not as easy as it might seem, especially in the rush of high-pressure wartime work. Ship naming was a complicated business, involving the Admiralty's Naming Committee, which only sat intermittently and then only in an advisory capacity for the Third Sea Lord and Controller, who in turn forwarded the names to the full Board, and then finally to the monarch for Royal consent. To alter a ship's name would also mean innumerable items of ship's equipment, stationery, cap ribbons, name boards and so on having to be replaced, again hardly acceptable either in wartime when all effort and expenditure was meant to be directed towards more pressing matters, nor in peacetime with the inevitable contraction of budgets. In addition, retaining a name meant that all mess plate, trophies and the like could be put into store when a ship was decommissioned for disposal, in due course being presented to a new ship when that name next appeared in the Navy List, and thus serving to foster the sense of heritage and continuity of spirit integral to the Royal Navy.

[This Warship Note will be followed with one looking into the even more striking discrepancies in the published figures for the cruiser's crew, casualties and survivors from the time of her sinking.]

Notes:
[1] Later Vice-Admiral Sir BE Domvile. During the early 1930s, as Flag Officer, 3rd Cruiser Squadron, his flagship was his old command, HMS *Curacoa*. His gunnery officer when *Curacoa* was first commissioned was Lt. Cdr. E. N. Syfret, who was to serve with distinction in the Second World War, in particular in the Mediterranean, later becoming Vice-Admiral Sir Neville Syfret, Vice Chief of Naval Staff.
[2] Not always the case – see *Warship* 2002-2003, p.176.
[3] To be fair, the Royal Navy isn't alone in this: the Royal Netherlands Navy for some time having had a ship called *Chattam*.
[4] A second Report, in October 1917, recommended that this should be rectified. Only initially accepted for the government's 'blue collar' workers, it wasn't until July 1919, after a further year of negotiations that the Cabinet and unions finally came to an agreement covering all government employees. The Admiralty, interestingly, had anticipated this and already set up their own body, the Admiralty Staff Conference, which first met in January 1919.

Sources:
ADM53/39086. Log of HMS *Curacoa*. 9 January – 28 February 1918.

Burns, Lt. Cdr. KV, *The Devonport Dockyard Story*, Maritime Books, Liskeard, 1984.
Colledge, JJ, (revised by Warlow, Lt. Cdr. B), *Ships of the Royal Navy*, Greenhill Books, London, 2003.
Dawson, Philip, *The Liner, Retrospective & Renaissance*, Conway Maritime Press, London, 2005.
Hutchings, David, *RMS Queen Mary, 50 years of Splendour*, Kingfisher, 1986.
James, William, *The Naval History of Great Britain, 1822-24* and subsequent reprints.
Kelly, Peter, 'The tragic loss of HMS *Curacoa*', *Warship* 1997-1998, Conway Maritime Press, London, 1997.
Lyon, David, *The Sailing Navy List*, Conway Maritime Press, London, 1993.
Navy News, May 2008, article on wrecks with legal protection.
Nicholls, Jack Phillip, 'Keeping the Peace', *Ships Monthly*, January 1980 (vol.15, no.1).
Paine, Lincoln, *Ships of the World*, Conway Maritime Press, London, 1997.
Roskill, SW, *The War at Sea*, volume 2, HMSO, 1956.
Satchell, Alister, *Running the Gauntlet*, Chatham Publishing, 2001.
Talbot-Booth, Lt.-Cdr. EC, RNR, *All the World's Fighting Fleets*, Sampson Low, Marston & Co. Ltd, London (undated, but 1940).
Thomas, David A, *Battles & Honours of the Royal Navy*, Leo Cooper, Barnsley, 1998.
Warlow, Lt. Cdr. Ben, *The Royal Navy in Focus, 1920-1929*, Maritime Books, Liskeard, 1990.
Watton, Ross, *Anatomy of the Ship: the Cunard Liner* Queen Mary, Conway Maritime Press, London, 1989.
Woodman, Richard, *The History of the Ship*, Conway Maritime Press, London, 1997.

Wikipedia – www.wikipedia.org
U-boat.net – www.u-boat.net
Roll-of-Honour.com – www.roll-of-honour.com
The White Star & Shaw Savill & Albion Lines – www.shawsavillships.co.uk
BBC WW2 People's War – www.bbc.co.uk/ww2peopleswar
Monsters of the Sea – www.oceanliners.com/ships
Maritime Disasters of World War II – http://members.iinet.net.au/~gduncan/maritime-1a.html
Naval-History.net – http://www.naval-history.net

Thanks also to Imogen Dent, Robert Gardiner, David James of the West Wales Maritime History Society, John Jordan, Nicki Marshall, Julie Sowter of *Ships Monthly* magazine, Henk Visser, Ross Watton and Jon Wise.

CHILE'S QUEST FOR AN 8-INCH GUN CRUISER

Kenneth Fraser's note on the John Brown cruiser project for Chile (*Warship* 2011) prompted regular contributor **Jon Wise** to attempt to put this proposal into its broader context, using his recent research into British shipbuilders' relationship with South America.

In 1925 the Chilean naval authorities had first registered their intention to order two, or possibly three cruisers of 8,000–10,000 ton fitted with 'heavy artillery' as part of a comprehensive modernisation programme that also included destroyers and submarines. Although the South American navy was to achieve a substantial portion of its objective over the next three to four years, when six destroyers, three submarines and a large submarine depot ship were all designed and later built in British shipyards, by the mid-1930s its three remaining cruisers, all dating from the last decade of the nineteenth century, had not been replaced.

The impetus for this ambitious naval building programme owed everything to regional disputes with Peru to the north and Argentina to the south and east. Both neighbours were also in the process of ordering new vessels. In 1926 Argentina had authorised an expenditure of 75 million gold pesos to be spent over ten years as part of an extensive naval replacement programme which, unusually for a plan of this kind, was to survive almost intact over the course of the following decade. Ominously for Chile, Argentina took delivery of two, modern 6,800-ton Italian-built cruisers armed with 7.5-inch guns in 1931. This was followed in 1937 by the launching at Vickers-Armstrong in Barrow of the light cruiser ARA *La Argentina* together with seven destroyers, again all constructed in Britain. Although Peru's more modest inter-war programme comprised just four new US-built submarines it was understood that these vessels had sufficient range to enable them to reach the main Chilean naval base at Valparaíso and return to Callao in Peru without refuelling. Moreover battle simulations had shown that Chile's escorts were inadequate in providing anti-submarine protection for the key unit in the fleet, the battleship *Almirante Latorre*.[1] Thus Peru's acquisition led directly to the construction of six *Serrano* class destroyers based on the RN's HMS *Amazon* and *Ambuscade* prototype designs launched in 1926.

According to Victor Cavendish-Bentinck, the splendidly named British Ambassador to Chile, it was the launching of the Argentine cruiser and the destroyers all in the same year which 'aroused the envy of the Chileans', who then set about making stringent efforts to find the necessary money for new naval construction. Details of an international bidding process for the construction of two 8-inch gun cruisers with a displacement of 8,800 tons were confidently announced by the Naval Staff.[2] In terms of dimensions and armament these were to be powerful vessels, similar in concept to the *Deutschland* class 'pocket-battleships' which were entering service with the German Navy at the time.

However, the public utterances of the naval staff at their main base at Valparaíso did not necessarily correlate with government policy in Santiago. No allowance had been made in Chile's 1937 budget for an acquisition of this kind. In the event

Cruiser for Chile: Design B, 1937

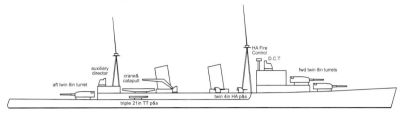

(Drawing by John Jordan, using material supplied by Kenneth Fraser)

the tacit support of the government was subsequently granted, although its real objective was 'to keep the Navy quiet'.[3] The necessary legislation had been passed by both Houses of Congress by January 1938, and there followed an intense nine-month period during which Chile attempted to find a country willing to construct its cruisers.

Although undoubtedly influenced by the progress made with the Argentine cruiser programme, the configuration of the planned Chilean cruisers revealed a quite different set of priorities. Whereas the Italian-designed and -influenced Argentine warships favoured high speed at the expense of more substantial hull structures, conversely the Chilean model sacrificed speed in order to achieve greater protection. At the time of the announcement it was fully anticipated that a British company, most likely Vickers-Armstrong, would be a very strong contender for this contract.

One of the methods subsequently used by the Chilean Naval Staff to try to persuade the RN to its point of view regarding the proposed cruiser design was to bring the latter into its confidence by revealing the tactics it had devised for a decisive engagement with the Argentine Navy in time of war. During the course of a carefully orchestrated 'chance encounter' over luncheon during a visit to Valparaíso by the RN cruiser HMS *Exeter* in October 1937, a senior Chilean naval officer had divulged his country's secret battle-plans to a British staff officer. A hypothetical surface engagement, almost certainly envisaged to take place in the waters south of Cape Horn disputed by Argentina and Chile, had more in keeping with the naval engagements of the First World War. The plan required a holding action by one or two Chilean cruisers of 8,000-9,000 tons with 8-inch guns and good armour protection. High speeds were not required. When it was pointed out that the type of ship described resembled the old-style armoured cruisers, which none of the major naval powers was constructing at the time, it was conceded that the ship would have to be specially designed for the purpose.[4]

Despite this seemingly authoritative discourse on future Chilean strategy, British naval intelligence was aware of a sharp division of opinion within the Chilean establishment about the size and type of cruiser required. A communication from the British Naval Attaché for South America in September 1936 had revealed that while the Director General of the Navy and his staff at Valparaíso favoured the 8-inch gun design, the Naval Secretary in the Ministry of Defence based in Santiago was championing the purchase of a cruiser of 6,000 tons with nine 6-inch guns, a design broadly similar to the Argentine Italian-built cruisers. Unsurprisingly perhaps, the Secretary had been naval attaché in Rome prior to his current appointment. Another faction within the Naval Staff was advocating the acquisition of naval bomber planes instead of cruisers. Quite how a Chilean naval air arm with no previous combat experience might have played a decisive role in a naval battle in the stormy seas south of Cape Horn is not explained.[5]

The signing of the Second London Naval Treaty in March 1936 effectively ended the Chilean Navy's hopes of obtaining such warships from Britain. The ramifications stemming from Britain's determination to uphold both the substance and the spirit of the agreement were to have a serious and lasting impact on Anglo-Chilean naval relations;

the effect was still being felt in the decade after the Second World War.

The signatories to the 1936 London Naval Treaty had ruled that no 'light surface vessels', in this case cruisers, carrying a gun with a calibre exceeding 6.1-inch and no light surface vessels with a standard displacement exceeding 8,000 tons, could be laid down before January 1943. Moreover, Article 22 of the Treaty stated that no warships of this kind could be disposed of 'by gift, sale or any mode of transfer', thus ruling out the possibility of a country such as Chile acquiring a second-hand cruiser.[6] Thus, neither the terms of the Treaty nor its timing favoured the Chilean Navy's cause. The proposed heavy cruiser was precluded at the lower end of the so-called 'zone of no construction' between 8,000-17,500 tons. Of course, the relevant article in the Treaty was not deliberately aimed at a minor naval power such as Chile. It was intended instead to curb the construction of what was described as 'a superior type of cruiser being built in the guise of a capital ship' such as the innovative *Panzerschiffe* of the *Deutschland* class.[7]

The exact wording of the London Treaty itself, and the time taken for its complicated terms to be understood by all parties, inevitably made for misinterpretation. The initial approaches by Chile had coincided almost exactly with the signing of the Treaty. As soon as this was known, it was questioned whether or not a building contract could be completed and signed between the ending of the Washington Treaty date and the commencement of this fresh agreement. This notion was promptly rejected. Nevertheless, in January 1938, with the necessary finances in place, the Chileans invited a number of countries to tender for the contract. The Foreign Office immediately stated that the cruiser could not be constructed in Britain, although it did confirm that building a 6-inch gun ship would not contravene the Treaty.[8]

The Chilean Navy's response that it was 'almost convinced that the ships could be built in the UK, if His Majesty's Government should so desire, in spite of the London Treaty', demonstrated a general lack of appreciation of the significance of the agreement from a country geographically distanced from the international tensions that threatened world peace in 1938. As far as *La Armada de Chile* was concerned, Britain and its navy was its traditional friend and in the past the country had been accorded special favours, for example regarding the training of its personnel.

Once the decision had been taken that it was vital to prevent Chile's 8-inch gun cruiser from being built by any of the Treaty countries including Britain, every effort was made to stop the contract being awarded to a non-signatory nation instead who might have the licence and the capability to construct such a vessel. This was to add a further complication to an already strained state of affairs. Private tenders for the construction of two 8-inch gun cruisers were issued by Chile through agents of shipbuilding firms across Europe and in the United States. Not all of these countries were signatories at the time; there were possibilities that the Scandinavian countries, Sweden, Finland and Denmark and even Japan might also feature as possible contenders. Thus the Chilean Navy proceeded to explore a variety of options to take advantage of this less than watertight international agreement.

One proposal was for the ships' hulls to be constructed in the Netherlands and the armament by Vickers-Armstrong in Britain. For a brief period France, one of the major London Treaty advocates, was suddenly claimed to be an interested party; later speculation circulated about renewed interest being shown by Italy and by the armaments' firm Krupp in Germany.

By July 1938, Chile's remaining options had been systematically reduced to Finland, Sweden and The Netherlands. In the event, none of these countries was prepared to accept the contract. Victory had been achieved through careful lobbying and bilateral negotiations between Britain and the non-signatory nations. The UK's position as a major world power had been utilised to full effect, as this FO letter later admitted:

> Therefore, quite apart from any legal question as to whether or not it is technically proper for the vessels, apart from the guns, or for the guns apart from the vessels, to be constructed in countries which have accepted or are about to accept the provisions of the Naval Treaties, it is inevitable that the influence of His Majesty's Government will be utilised to prevent the construction of such a vessel.[9]

In the meantime the Admiralty, although supporting the FO in its efforts to uphold the Treaty, mounted a strong, technically-based argument suggesting that even if an 8,000 ton 8-inch gun cruiser could be constructed for Chile it would be inferior in terms of rate of fire when compared with a 6-inch gun ship which might still be built to comply with Treaty specifications. It was suggested that the brand-new *Fiji* class design would provide a satisfactory answer to Chilean requirements.[10] Of course, the RN was not driven by altruistic motives in offering the Chilean Navy its latest design of 6-inch gun cruiser. The prospect of a foreign contract was still considered to be important enough to disrupt the domestic naval shipbuilding programme, even close to the outbreak of war, provided that an agreement could be reached on the size and specifications of the vessel. In March 1939, the Controller of the Navy pointed out that 'a ship under construction for a foreign power is potentially available to this country in case of war'. No doubt the Third Sea Lord had in mind the experience of the First World War, when Britain commandeered two 28,000-ton super-dreadnoughts and four large destroyers which were being built in Britain at the time for the Chilean Navy.[11]

However, by April 1939 it was confirmed that the Chileans, having briefly considered the 6-inch gun ship, was once again 'quite definitely' set on acquiring an 8-inch cruiser. The onset of the Second World War effectively prevented the South Americans from pursuing their aims as the major shipbuilding firms became totally preoccupied with wartime construction and repair programmes. Thus their cruiser replacement plans, already some fifteen years old, had to be shelved.

But the matter was not forgotten despite a world war. Throughout the first four months of 1946 there was a succession of enquiries made to the Admiralty by the Chilean Naval Staff regarding the possibility of Vickers-Armstrong either building a cruiser using an existing design, this time a 6-inch gun ship, taking over a partially built warship destined for the Royal Navy or acquiring one that had been recently completed. Each time the approach was rejected. It was pointed out that there were no surplus warships available and no possibility of an order being accepted.[12]

At first sight, such an explanation appears incomprehensible. The warship cancellation rate at the end of the Second World War was predictably high, and historically it had been a primary concern of the Admiralty to encourage continuity of orders so that necessary skill levels could be maintained in this highly specialised sector. For example, the Vickers-Armstrong yard at Barrow was working at 100% capacity in March 1945; by September of the same year this figure had dropped alarmingly to just 60%.[13] In truth the Admiralty's own post-war building plans were in disarray at the time due to the inevitable dislocation caused by the ending of the war, the urgent need to repair existing naval and merchant stock, and delays in the delivery of equipment. Furthermore, there existed a tension between avoiding a drastic cancellation programme, thereby keeping the warship firms active and employment rates high, and building far fewer naval vessels and using the savings accrued on research and development. Therefore, the availability of space on the building slips for export orders depended a good deal on the proposed size and composition of the post-war Royal Navy, and decisions in that regard had yet to be taken.[14]

A little over a year later, with government demands that total spending on defence be reduced to below £800 million per year, the Navy was requested to draw up plans for a budget of £150 million. To achieve this figure would mean scrapping substantial numbers of warships, many with notable war records, among them the light cruiser HMS *Ajax*. News of the Chilean Navy's initial interest in acquiring this 6-inch gun ship, iconic veteran of the Battle of the River Plate, was not to be made public for several months. It was anticipated that there was likely to be a Parliamentary and public outcry if such a sale were eventually concluded. This proved to be correct.

The sensitive nature of the decision to sell this particular warship, and the emerging sovereignty dispute with Chile over Antarctic territories was to form the basis of a controversy, the impact of which was still being felt several years later. In the coming months the Conservative opposition exploited the matter ruthlessly for political gain. At one stage Winston Churchill, addressing a huge political rally at Luton Hoo, declaimed with colourful hyperbole:

> Nothing could do more at this moment to humiliate Britain throughout South America than the sale of this ship to Chile. I suppose that the Admiralty thought that they could get a few dollars more out of the Chileans on that account. It is like selling the shirt that Nelson wore at Trafalgar to General Franco, and getting a little extra for the bloodstains.[15]

In March 1949, following much prevarication, the full Cabinet decided that, in the interests of avoiding 'some political difficulties', *Ajax* would not be sold to Chile but would be scrapped instead. Two years later Chile finally acquired two ageing *Brooklyn* class cruisers from the United States, sold under the terms of the Mutual Defense Assistance Program. Argentina and Brazil also received two identical vessels each. The USA's stated intention was to prevent another South American naval arms race. Sadly, this proved not to be the case, while the North American superpower's true motives bore little relation to Franklin D. Roosevelt's 'Good Neighbor' ideals of the 1930s, being more concerned with its own Cold War hemispheric defence objectives.

Footnotes:

1. Guillermo Arroyo, *Adquisiciones Navales de Chile: Un Estudio Crítico* (Valparaiso: Imprenta de la Armada, 1940), p.3.
2. The National Archives (TNA), (formerly the Public Record Office), Foreign Office (FO) 371/20620, *Chile* (1937). Annual Report, Para. 79, 1 January, 1937.
3. TNA, ADM 116/3920. Letter: British Embassy, Santiago to Foreign Secretary, 21 October 1937. FO 371/21435, *Cruiser for Chile* (1938). Letter & accompanying memorandum: British Ambassador, Santiago to FO, 29 December 1937.
4. TNA, Admiralty (ADM) 116/3920, *Cruisers for Chile: enquiries and proposals* (1936-1938). Report: Commodore, South America Division to C-in-C America and West Indies Station. Enclosure No.2. 'Conversation on 9 October, 1937'.
5. TNA, ADM 116/3920. Letter: Naval Attaché South America to Foreign Secretary, 7 September 1937. Also Emilio C Meneses, 'Maintaining a Regional Navy with Very Limited Resources, 1900-1990', *Defense Analysis*, 7:4 (1991), pp.348-9.
6. Anon, 'The London Naval Treaty, 1936', *Brassey's Naval Annual, 1936*, ed. by Cdr. Charles N. Robinson (London: William Clowes, 1936), pp. 364-71.
7. H.G.Thursfield, 'The London Naval Treaty', *The Naval Review*, 24:2 (1936), 259-77 (p.268).
8. TNA, FO 371/21435. Internal Memoranda & Telegram, FO to Embassy, Santiago, 17 January 1938.
9. TNA, ADM 116/3920. Letter: Foreign Office to Admiralty Military Branch, 15 September 1938.
10. TNA, ADM 116/3921, *Cruisers for Chile and Turkey* (1937-1939). Admiralty Internal Minutes: 9, 20 August, 1 September 1937.
11. TNA, ADM 116/3921. Admiralty Internal Minute: Controller, 13 March, 1937.
12. TNA, FO 371/52008. Foreign Office Letters and Memoranda, 15–27 January, 1946.
13. Cambridge University Library, *Vickers Company Archive*, Works Reports for quarters ending 31 March, 30 June & 30 September 1945.
14. George Moore, *Building for Victory: The Warship Building Programmes of the Royal Navy, 1939-1945* (Gravesend: World Ship Society, 2003), pp. 123-131.
15. TNA, FO 371/68210, *Sale of HMS Ajax to Chile*, (1948). Newspaper cutting: The Times, 'Mr. Churchill's Call: Drive Government from Office', 26 June 1948.

A's & A's

CHINESE COAST DEFENCE SHIPS

In his Warship Note 'Edmund Backhouse's Phantom Ships' (*Warship* 2010, p.176) Kenneth Fraser provided details of two Chinese Coast Defence Ships proposed by John Brown for China. He has now unearthed further evidence of the origins of this design.

A recently discovered reference in the Glasgow University Archives (UCS 1/21/75) explains the origin and date of the specification for Chinese coastal defence ships reported in *Warship* 2010. A letter from Edward L.D. Boyle in Peking to John Brown's, dated 14 January 1913, refers to earlier correspondence (not present) in which the Chinese had been expressing interest in two 'Town' class cruisers. They had inquired about the possibility of fitting these with larger guns, in view of the fact that an unnamed colonial power, evidently the Netherlands, possessed ships with 21cm guns.

Boyle goes on to suggest that, in the light of his discussions with Chinese officials, China might be better served by 'a Coast Defence Vessel with good sea-going qualities' similar to the Norwegian *Eidsvold* and *Norge*. He proposes ships of 5,000-6,000 tons, with two guns of 21cm or 24cm calibre, six 6in guns, some smaller guns, and two submerged torpedo tubes. The speed should be 20 knots, and the ship should be superior to any such vessel in the smaller European navies. He believes that with 6 inches of armour, it would coat £700,000, so that eight could be built for the £5.5 million price of the two cruisers. The ships would not be seen as aggressive by the Great Powers or Japan, and the Chinese could use them to 'show the flag in ports where there are large Chinese communities'. He asks to be sent a complete design and specifications to show the Chinese. Although the previously mentioned reference (UCS 1/21/79) suggests that it may have been produced, it does not survive, and there is no further correspondence on this issue in the file.

RATIONALE FOR THE 45CM MLE 1920 GUN

In their Warship Note on the French 45cm gun of 1920 published in *Warship* 2011 (pp.176-178), John Jordan and Robert Dumas published for the first time detailed characteristics of the proposed trial gun. Since that note was written, further information regarding the choice of the 45cm calibre has come to light.

In a report to the *Commission des matériels de l'artillerie navale* which took place on 24 October 1919, chaired by Ingénieur Général Charbonnier, the following reasons were given as the basis for studies and construction for trials of a 45cm/45-calibre gun:

Calibre
The choice of calibre was determined by the effect of the projectile. The lessons from Jutland were stated to be as follows:

- The high-capacity British shell [CPC] had insufficient penetrating power. It broke up on armour plating; more than 4000 shells were fired and not a single German [battle]ship was sunk. Immediately after the battle the British recognised the inferiority of their shell and developed new ammunition; high-capacity shell was replaced by armour-piercing shell. The lesson from this was that all major-calibre shell should be AP.
- The shell favoured by the Germans was armour-piercing. It had good penetration but damage was localised. With the exception of the battlecruisers whose magazines exploded, all the British ships were able to return to port. Despite sustaining up to 30 hits, these ships were repaired and again ready for action within the month. The main problem for the Germans was that they had no shell greater than 30cm. The lesson from this was that AP shell needed to be high capacity if it was to be destructive once inside the ship

In summary: the lesson of Jutland was that there was a need for the largest calibre shell with the maximum possible range.

In order to build a gun capable of fulfilling these conditions, it was necessary to consider existing manufacturing capability in France. The longest possible barrel length using the available technology and infrastructure was 21 metres. Long range implied the longest possible barrel for a given calibre, but the length of the gun could not exceeed 21m. If the 45-calibre length of existing guns was retained, the maximum possible calibre was 45cm [45 x 0.450 = 20.25m].

Pressure
All things being equal, a high muzzle velocity was related to high pressure in the firing chamber. Current guns were capable of 3000kg/cm^2 maximum. By employing autofretting for gun construction, it ought to be possible to raise this to 4000kg/cm^2. However, in order to avoid possible problems with such a large-calibre gun, it was considered prudent to accept 3500kg/cm^2. Initial velocity was to be 875m/s, for a maximum range of 47km.

Propellant
The studies to be undertaken were outlined in Chapter II of the document [not available to the authors]. In order not to delay construction of a trial 45cm gun it was intended to revert to *Poudre B*, which was slower-burning than the powders currently in use and could be delivered without delay by the *Service des Poudres et Salpêtres*.

Weight of projectile
For an effective projectile it was necessary to adopt a high coefficient without exceeding existing limits. The figure was to be fixed at 16, giving a projectile weight of 1400kg approximately.

Alternative Proposal for a 40cm Gun
Some members of the commission were in favour of building a 40cm gun alongside the 45cm for trials, giving

the following reasons:

- A jump from 34cm to 45cm would be a step into the unknown.
- The 40cm calibre was sufficient for penetration of all existing armour.
- Adoption of a smaller calibre would permit installation of more barrels on a ship of same size, increasing the chance of hits.

These arguments were countered as follows:

- The British claimed no problems at Jutland with their larger-calibre [15in] guns. There was no reason why a 45cm gun should not perform well, provided the existing guidelines for construction were adhered to.
- A key lesson of Jutland was that the ability to penetrate armour was not enough; there was a need to cause more extensive damage <u>after</u> penetration. In this respect the 45cm was superior to the 40cm
- It was better to score fewer damaging hits than to secure a larger number of hits which nevertheless failed to cripple an enemy ship. It was unacceptable that ships which had received 30 major-calibre hits were back in service within a month of Jutland
- A larger number of turrets was a <u>disadvantage</u>. Jutland had demonstrated that turrets were the vulnerable points of capital ships; ammunition handling arrangements could be improved, but only at the cost of undesirable complexity

It was further pointed out that both the 45cm and 40cm would be trial guns; lessons from trials with a 45cm gun would be applicable to a production 40cm model, whereas the reverse was not necessarily the case. Trials would take several years, by the end of which period the 40cm risked being outclassed by foreign guns [it was pointed out that the US Navy was already building 40.6cm guns]. The major lesson of the war was that all parties constantly strove to increase the calibre of their guns. It was therefore important to take advantage of peacetime to experiment with the most powerful guns possible.

The commission concluded that if new battleships were not to be laid down in the near future, the 40cm gun should be put on the back-burner.

Note: The additional information/clarification in square brackets is provided by the authors, who have also underlined words and phrases which they feel to be key to the discussion..

WARSHIP 2011

Reader Charles Shedel of Long Valley, New Jersey (USA) has sent in the following comments about articles/notes published in *Warship* 2011:

Battle at Valparaíso (Colin Jones), p.95

It is quite possible that *Numancia* was not the first ironclad in the Pacific. However, in returning to Spain by way of the Cape of Good Hope, she became the first ironclad to circumnavigate the globe.

Arguably the first Pacific ironclad was the Union *Passaic*-class monitor *Camanche*, which was built by Joseph Colwell Secor in Jersey City, NJ. She was shipped in sections to San Francisco, CA, aboard SS *Aquila*, which sank at her dock on 16 November 1862 prior to being unloaded. The sections of *Camanche* were recovered from the wreck and re-erected by the Union Iron Works. Launched on 14 November 1864 and commissioned on 24 May 1865, *Camanche* served as a training ship until sold on 22 March 1899.

Source: *Dictionary of American Naval Fighting Ships* Vol. III (USGPO, 1963).

The French Fleet Programme of 1920 and the 45cm Gun (John Jordan & Robert Dumas), p.177

Although the statement that 'there are no range benefits beyond 45 degrees' is true in theory, it is not so in practice. Heavy, large-calibre projectiles with low-drag nose profiles actually achieve their greatest range at elevations of 50 to 53 degrees due to the lesser air resistance in the upper atmosphere. This phenomenon was first observed on 21 October 1914 at Krupp's Meppen range. The German Army had requested that Krupp increase the range of their 30.5cm/45 and 38cm/45 naval guns from 24km and 28km respectively to 37km, so that they could be used to bombard Dover if and when the Germans captured Calais. Accordingly, Krupp developed a low-drag profile shell with a projected range of 39km for these guns. When a 35.5cm/52.5 version of this shell was tested it achieved a maximum range of 49km. Analysis indicated that air resistance decreased with altitude, and maximum range would be obtained at 50 to 53 degrees elevation by putting the shell into the stratosphere earlier. This was the elevation used for the German 21cm Paris gun.

Source: Bull, *Paris Kanonen – the Paris Gun and Project HARP* (Verlag E. S. Mittler & Sohn, 1988).

THE LOSS OF HMS *EFFINGHAM*

Following on from Richard Wright's article in *Warship* 2011, the Assistant Editor points readers towards two related accounts.

In addition to Captain Howson's memoirs referred to in Richard Wright's article, an interesting and contrasting first hand account of the loss of HMS *Effingham* appears in the memoir *Dusty Days in the Royal Navy* by Eric Wootten (Avon Books, 1996). Wootten was a young stores rating who had been with the ship since before the war; and as well as describing the actual running aground he also details what happened to himself and the rest of the crew afterwards.

There is also a detailed account of the earlier loss, again by grounding, of *Effingham*'s sister ship HMS *Raleigh*, in *Maritime South West*, no.21, the annual journal of the South West Maritime History Society (SWMHS, 2008, pp.14-24).

ITALIAN AIRCRAFT CARRIERS AND MAS BOATS

Regular *Warship* contributors Enrico Cernuschi and Vincent P. O'Hara have provided corrections and updates to two of their recent articles.

In 2004 we began to publish in *Warship* studies about the Italian navy based on documents available in the Ufficio Storico della Marina Militare (the Italian naval historical branch) and other Italian sources. Because history is a dynamic process, and new documents are still being discovered, we are now in a position to offer corrections and new information to some of our *Warship* articles.

MAS Boats at War
An indication of the many ambiguities that still cloud accounts of Second World War naval actions is supplied by two contradictory sentences, published in the 2009 issue of *Warship*. On page 71 of our article 'Italian Fast Coastal Forces' we wrote: 'Some minutes after midnight on 2 August 1942 MAS 568 charged Balaklava-style the Soviet cruiser *Molotov*. The MAS discharged both its torpedoes from 800m and one struck blowing off 20m of the cruiser's stern.' However, on page 94 of Vladimir Yakubov and Richard Worth's excellent article 'The Soviet Light Cruisers of the *Kirov* Class' the authors state: '[*Molotov*] attacked unsuccessfully by Italian MTBs MAS-568 and MAS-673, attacked by torpedo bombers and hit aft, losing 20m of the stern...' The first statement was based on Italian sources, the second, presumably, on Russian ones. This discrepancy inspired a quest to clarify what really happened to *Molotov* that night.

First, from Italian sources it is easy to confirm that only MAS 568 attacked the Soviet cruiser as its companion, MAS 567 (not 673) had been immobilised an hour before by engine defects. An old book by Admiral Friedrich Ruge published in English as *The Soviets as Naval Opponents, 1941-1945* (Patrick Stephens, Cambridge 1979) states on page 85: 'On their way back [the cruisers] were attacked by German torpedo planes and Italian MTBs. The *Molotov* was hit far forward by a torpedo and lost 60 feet of her fo'c'sle.' A better German source is Rudi Schmidt, *Achtung – Torpedo los! Die Strategische und Operative Einsatz des Kampfgeschwaders 26* (Bernhard & Graefe Verlag, Koblenz 1991). The author, a Group Commander of that same squadron (the only Luftwaffe torpedo bomber unit in the Black Sea during the summer of 1942), based his study on the unit's war diaries and wrote on pages 148-149 and 353 that a dozen He 111s of Staffel 6./KG 26 attacked a cruiser and a destroyer on 3 August 1942, but at noon and not midnight (*mittag*, not *mitternacht*) with no apparent results. The same version was later advanced by Harold Thiele on page 39 of his *Luftwaffe Aerial Torpedo Aircraft and Operations*. The German aircraft attacked two ships in Feodosia Bay which had conducted a shore bombardment 'the previous night'. The air raid from Buzeau (Rumania) was thus launched almost eleven hours after and 90 miles from the night encounter with the MAS boats. Moreover, on 3 August *Abwehr* codebreakers disclosed to the Italian Navy that they had deciphered a Soviet wireless message stating that a Russian cruiser had been torpedoed off Feodosia the previous night. The original despatch is available in the German Navy archives at Aschaffenburg and was quoted in 1981 by Heinz Bonatz in his *Seekrieg im Äther – Die Leistungen der Marine – Funkaufklärung 1939-1945* (Mittler & Sohn GmbH, Herford 1981). Thus, German sources strongly suggest that MAS 568, not the Luftwaffe, should be credited with the torpedo hit on *Motolov*.

The statement on page 68 of the same article that '[MAS boats] patrolled off Tobruk at night [in December 1940 and January 1941] without seeing the enemy...' is not correct. On the night of 17 December 1940 MAS 548 attacked the RN monitor *Terror* off Bardia, launching two torpedoes without result except to defer the shelling of that bay until the next morning.

MAS boats from Augusta (574, 575 and 576), which were attached to the special attack unit, X MAS from December 1941, mined the entrance to Malta's Grand Harbour with five-horned contact mines of the small, spherical Vega 200kg charge type, classified by the Royal Navy with the code name IP between May and June 1942. These fields were much closer than the German minefields, the nearest of which was a mile from the booms. The wooden MAS boats could undertake such a dangerous mission because they did not reflect radar (unlike the much larger S-Boats). Each MAS could carry four of these weapons, which could be moored in depths of up to 25m. On 10 May 1942 they sank the small British tug *C 308* at the Dragut shoal, a cable from the harbour's mouth. However, only 48 Vega mines, manufactured in 1923, were available as the Italian Air Force had discarded that weapon, which it had originally planned to lay with its S.55 floatplanes, in 1926. On 26 May the auxiliary minesweeper *Eddy* struck a Vega mine off the Sant' Elmo breakwater, according to Malta's Weekly Sweeping Reports. On 30 May the similar minesweeper *St. Angelo* met the same fate less than three quarters of mile off the harbour entrance. A subsequent sweeping discovered a line of eleven Vegas.

On the night of 16 June 1942 the British freighter *Orari* struck a mine 400m from the mouth of Malta's Grand Harbour as the surviving ships of the 'Harpoon' convoy were finally completing their costly journey from Gibraltar. Most accounts attribute this casualty to a drifting German mine which had broken its cable, but an hour later the destroyer *Matchless* suffered the same fate and two days later RN minesweepers found two Vega mines in that same location.

After the Navy had expended its stock of Vegas the three MAS were modified in August 1942: the depth charges and the aft 20mm machine gun were removed to enable each to carry one of the more conventional Elia P 145/1930 type mines (British code name IJ). This measure paid a further, small dividend on 15 May 1943 when one damaged the minesweeper *Speedy* just off the Grand Harbour. Sweeping found five weapons of the same type. In any case, in September 1942 the Augusta MAS minelaying section was disbanded and MAS 574 and 575 were sent to the Black Sea to balance the losses suffered in that area, while 576 went to Trapani. On 1943 the Italian navy used MAS squadrons based in Sicily to lay drifting mines of the new Beta (IO) type. The navy of the Confederate States had used such a desperation weapon during the American Civil War with no results; the Italian Navy's experience was similar.

Carriers Revisited
Our article published in *Warship 2007*, 'Search for a Flattop: the Italian Navy and the Aircraft Carrier 1907-

WARSHIP NOTES

Model of the Bonfiglietti carrier project of 1929. (Storia Militare)

2007', discusses the Vian 1932 aircraft carrier project on page 68. The article states that this was the first project undertaken since 1928. New information uncovered by Commander Erminio Bagnasco and published by Storia Militare in April 2008 shows that between 1928 and 1931 a much more advanced design put forth by General Genio Navale (Naval Constructors Corp) Filippo Bonfiglietti preceded the Vian 1932 project. This design carried 40 aircraft. Its specifications were length 220m, beam 30m, draught 6.12m and standard displacement 15,240t. A modified *Trento* cruiser machinery plant was to develop 70,000shp to allow a top speed of 29 knots. Designed endurance was 1,800nm at 29 knots and 3,400nm at 22 knots.

In 1931 the Italian Air Force axed this project, despite an agreement made in December 1927 that a carrier would be deferred for economic reasons but not cancelled, and was to be rescheduled for the 1931-1932 Estimates. The Regia Aeronautica's objections as advanced by the Air Force Minister General Italo Balbo were that the ship had too powerful an armament (four 6in in twin turrets and eight twin 100mm guns) the blast of which would endanger aircraft on the flight deck, and too little protection (a 50-60mm belt, a 40–15mm armoured deck and the Pugliese underwater protection system). The main objection to the program, however, was that the Air Force wanted the ship to be commanded by one of its own officers, as only they would have the necessary air-minded spirit. The Air Force succeeded in having the carrier deferred to 1932. The Italian Navy tried again in 1932 with the much more cramped Vian design, which met with the Regia Aeronautica's requests (except for command of the ship), but the economic crisis of that year scuttled the last true Italian chance for one or, according the orignal 1928-1932 plans, two operational carriers by 1940.

Sources:

Bagnasco, Erminio & Bonfiglietti, Filippo: 'Il progetto Bonfiglietti', *STORIA Militare*, April 2008.

Cernuschi, Enrico: 'Guerra di mine intorno a Malta', *Storia Militare*, January 2009.

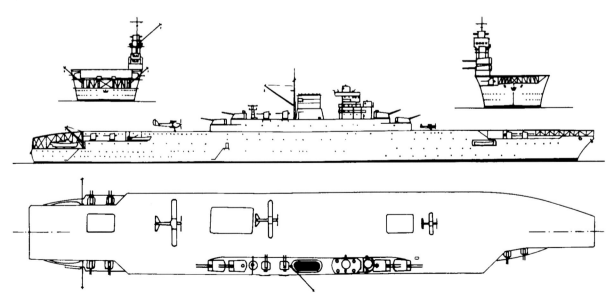

Profile, plan, bow and stern views of the Bonfiglietti carrier. (Courtesy of Erminio Bagnasco, Storia Militare)

PERUVIER

Last year we published an article by Luc Feron on the French armoured cruiser *Dupuy-de-Lôme* (see *Warship 2011* pp.32-47). Luc has written to us to say how pleased he was with the article, but expressed his disappointment that we had been unable to find space for the two photos of the ship at the end of her career, when she was rebuilt as the merchant ship *Peruvier* for the shipping company Lloyd Royal Belge. We are therefore publishing these two very interesting images in this year's Warship Notes. The first photo shows the ship fitting out in the dock of Forges et Chantiers de la Gironde (Bordeaux). Two of the funnels have been removed, new masts fitted, and the hull has been repainted and already bears the ship's new name. In the second photo, the refit is almost complete; prominent in the photo is the new bow, showing how the original ram was plated over to give a conventional, vertical stem.

(Photos courtesy of Luc Feron)

NAVAL BOOKS OF THE YEAR

David Hobbs
The British Pacific Fleet: The Royal Navy's Most Powerful Strike Force
Seaforth Publishing 2011; hardback, 462 pages, many B&W photographs; price £35.00.
ISBN 9781848320482

This is an account of the creation, operational activity and eventual disbandment of the most powerful naval force ever despatched to foreign waters by Britain. However, it is also much more than that; it raises questions about the wisdom of Britain's naval strategy throughout the interwar period, and wider political questions about the supposed 'special relationship' between Britain and the United States.

David Hobbs inclines strongly towards Jellicoe's view that Britain's naval forces in the Far East should have been based on Sydney, Australia, rather than Singapore. And there can be little doubt after reading this book that what Sydney offered in terms of local infrastructure was infinitely greater than a base hacked out of nothing in Singapore. However, the author tacitly acknowledges the major disadvantage of Sydney when he recounts the enormous distances that the BPF had to cover in order to get its carriers to their station off Okinawa. The building of the dockyard at Singapore may have been a relic of the imperial 'coaling station' mentality, but it was ideally placed at the gateway to the Indian Ocean and it was far closer to Japan (Sydney to Tokyo is 4900 miles; by comparison Pearl Harbor to Tokyo is just over 3200 miles!).

Unfortunately, the traditional reliance of the Royal Navy on a closely-spaced network of imperial bases had a negative impact on the endurance built into its ships – even the battleships of the *King George V* class proved to be short-legged when operating in the Pacific – and on the development of underway replenishment, which before the creation of the British Pacific Fleet simply did not exist. British naval aircraft suffered from similar range limitations. The Fairey Barracuda had to be replaced by the Grumman Avenger, while the Seafire had such low endurance it could initially be employed only in the combat air patrol. The ships of the newly-created Fleet Train were generally merchantmen taken up from trade. The tankers had insufficient speed, and the RN still favoured the slow astern replenishment method for its larger ships; stores ships had to be loaded in a completely different way so that pallets were easily accessible for transfer while underway. The RN also failed to anticipate the scale of aircraft losses – attrition rates in one of the early Pacific operations amounted to 25% of aircraft and 10% of pilots – and the pool of replacements proved totally inadequate.

Despite all these initial disadvantages, by the summer of 1945 the BPF had almost caught up with the US Navy in terms of air operations, and new purpose-built tankers and stores ships were arriving to join the fleet train. A network of Mobile Naval Air Bases had been created, dockyard facilities in Australia improved, and support carriers with spare aircraft and maintenance facilities mobilised. One RFA, *Menestheus*, was specially fitted as an 'amenities ship'; she could brew beer from distilled seawater and was equipped with a 350-seat theatre and well-developed catering facilities. Even the Americans were impressed and offered to buy her!

David Hobbs does not skate over the political difficulties between the British and the Americans. (Admiral) Ernest King was resolutely proposed to any incursion by a major British fleet into the Pacific; Nimitz had strong reservations about the ability of the RN to support its fleet without siphoning off his own resources; and Halsey wanted the glory of sinking all the remaining IJN battleships. Their British counterparts Fraser and Rawlings were intelligent men who understood American concerns and susceptibilities and were respected, even well-liked by the US admirals they served alongside. Rawlings in particular chose to adopt US Navy operating procedures and even USN working dress for his crews in an effort to integrate the BPF more closely with American Third and Fifth Fleets. Vian (Commanding 1 ACS), on the other hand, was viewed as 'neurotic' and 'rude' by the American liaison officers attached to him in *Indomitable*, and they criticised his unwillingness to take their advice on air operational matters. British-US political divisions, temporarily submerged during the final operations against Japan, were to surface again in the immediate aftermath of the conflict, when the British attempted to re-establish their prewar position in the southeast Asian colonies occupied by the Japanese and were faced by strong American opposition and, where possible, obstruction.

It is impossible to do full credit to this book in a brief review. The author, as a Royal Navy 'insider', occasionally shows himself to be in thrall to some of that service's mythology, in particular the view that the interwar RN was hobbled by the treaty system rather than by the poor state of Britain's finances. However, his enthusiasm for the Navy's ability to rise to a task that many felt beyond it is infectious, and he argues his case from a base of extensive research and personal knowledge. The book is well-produced on good-quality paper, there are some useful maps (including some striking contemporary US Navy target maps), and the photographic illustration is remarkable. Most of the photos are from the author's collection, and although not all are of the highest quality they provide an unmatched record of every aspect of the operations of the BPF, giving the feel of a contemporary newsreel. The main body of the book is followed by twelve useful appendices, including a full list of the USN pennant numbers under which the British ships served. The first three appendices, which detail the composition of the BPF in January 1945, August 1945 and August 1948 respectively, tell much of the story.

John Jordan

Vincent P. O'Hara, W. David Dickson and Richard Worth (eds.)
On Seas Contested: The Seven Great Navies of the Second World War
Naval Institute Press, 2010; hardback, 352 pages, 29 B&W photographs, 10 charts and 7 maps; price £25.00/$39.95.
ISBN 978 1 59114 646 9

The intention behind this collaboration by an international team of naval historians is to explain how the major navies of the Second World War were organised, how they trained, how they planned to operate, and how they fought. The book delivers a point-by-point evaluation of the United States Navy, the Royal Navies of the United Kingdom and the British Commonwealth, Japan's *Nihon Kaigun*, the German *Kriegsmarine*, the Italian *Regia Marina*, France's *Marine Nationale*, and the Soviet *Voenno-Morskoi Flot*.

The chapters are written to a consistent format; each is divided into major headings such as Backstory, Organisation, Materiel and Recapitulation. Within these headings there is further subdivision: for example, Materiel is divided into Ships, Aviation, Weapon Systems and Infrastructure. It is here where the book goes well beyond the normal lists of ships and actions to what one reviewer has already called 'the invisible elements', such as doctrine, morale, logistics and similar areas, all rarely touched upon elsewhere. While the impact of some of these factors might already be known to those well informed on the subject – for example, the Japanese persistence in using submarines only against warships – other issues were certainly new to this reviewer, such as the inadequacies of the Japanese technological research hinterland. This latter probably goes some way to explain why post-war Japanese industry went on to place so much emphasis on this area.

The section entitled Recapitulation gives a summary of the wartime experiences of each navy, highlighting where the issues described earlier had either helped or hampered the force in question. It is particularly interesting to read, for example, of the *Marine Nationale*'s shortcomings once operating outside of the Mediterranean for which it was mainly intended – lack of range in particular. The lack of a working sonar was equally surprising.

On the down side, it is rather a shame that the presentation of the illustrations is not to a higher standard. The photographs have been reproduced within the text and as a result appear rather flat and grey. A few of them were new to this reviewer, who particularly liked the picture of a German MFP *en portage* between the Seine and the Rhône, a very modern concept! Having said that, the relevance of some of the other illustrations is difficult to understand: for example, a photo of the American Admiral King doesn't really help explain King's importance. It would have been better in many ways to have had a separate photo section on glossy paper, keeping to the theme of the French and German sections of new and slightly unusual photographs.

In searching for a description of this book, the phrase 'comprehensive précis' comes to mind. In its coverage of the major navies of the Second World War it is certainly comprehensive in reach. However, this also means that the contents of each chapter often seem but a précis of the bigger story.

In addition, the practice of using different authors for each navy has produced a somewhat inconsistent style. The chapters on France and Japan are particularly good. In comparison those on the British Royal Navy and the US Navy leave a bit to be desired, although this may be because so much has already been written about these navies. Clearly the authors are to a certain extent constrained by the format. On the whole they have done a good job, but the result is that the book ends up as something of an appetiser for the bigger picture; depending on the reader's main interests, it leaves one either sufficiently enthused to dig deeper, or vaguely frustrated that the book doesn't contain just a little more.

From either view point this is a book that breaks new ground; it is an absolute must for the anyone with aspirations to be a naval historian, and a good read for those simply interested in the navies of the Second World War.

W B Davies

Norman Friedman
British Cruisers: Two World Wars and After
Seaforth Publishing 2011; hardback, 432 pages, approx. 400 B&W photographs and line drawings; price £45.00.
ISBN 9781848320789

This latest work from Norman Friedman is in many respects a sequel to the same author's two books on British destroyers, and those who purchased the latter books will know exactly what to expect: an extraordinarily detailed account of the development of Royal Navy cruisers, beginning with the 'Town' classes of the 1908/09 Estimates and ending with the 'command cruisers' of the *Invincible* class, illustrated with a large number of excellent photographs and line drawings.

In determining the focus and structure of the book the author has made a number of important decisions. The starting point for his descriptions of the development of each of the ships covered is the material held in the various British archives: Admiralty reports, Ships' Covers and Constructors' Workbooks. The profile and plan drawings, by a group of selected artists headed by David Baker III, are generally based on 'as-fitted' plans held in the Brass Foundry. And subsequent modifications (with a particular focus on wartime) are covered by photographs at the end of each section; these have extended captions which not only describe the modifications seen in the photo but give detailed accounts of earlier and later modifications to the ships.

There are advantages and disadvantages in this approach. There will be some readers who feel that the weight accorded to Constructors Workbooks is unjustified (some of DNC's requests to Lillicrap are almost on the level of: 'If we do without the propellers can we have an extra inch of NC on the Admiral's bathroom?'), and that this sometimes serves to obscure the more important considerations in the design process. The line drawings are uniformly of a very high standard, but there are no general arrangement plans for the ships built – a slight disappointment given that much of the discussion surrounding these designs was focused on how to fit the desired equipment (and the required complement) into ships which were limited by cost and displacement. And although the photographs are uniformly excellent, the inclusion of images taken later in the ship's career tends to interrupt the 'design' narrative, while the captions themselves are so detailed that this reviewer opted to read the text of the section first (pausing only to refer to the copious endnotes), and then read through the photo captions.

If the author has a weakness, it is his desire to be 'all-inclusive'; this has resulted in a book which is extremely 'dense', with a complex structure which does not always hang together. However, many readers will find this a strength, and there is no doubting the depth of Dr. Friedman's research. The information is not always easy to locate, but it is all in here somewhere. In between the detailed accounts of the development of the designs, the author shows a perceptive understanding of the tactical and technical considerations which drove British cruiser construction during the period. The quantity (and quality) of the illustration is particularly impressive, and the production values of the book are everything one has come to expect from this publisher. For all its faults this is a towering work, and one which any reader with even a passing interest in British cruiser development will want to own.

John Jordan

James E. Wise Jr and Scott Baron
The 14-Hour War: Valor on Koh Tang and the recapture of the SS *Mayaguez*
Naval Institute Press, 2011; hardback, 320 pages, 28 illustrations and 8 maps; price £22.50/$34.95.
ISBN 978 1 59114 974 30

I was already aware from colleagues in the US Navy that the recapture of the *Mayaguez* was not quite the triumph of US arms that it was painted at the time, and this book exposes the painful truth in some detail. Whilst the name *Mayaguez* probably still strikes a chord with many people, the incident itself has been largely forgotten, and this seems to have been one of the driving forces behind the authors' decision to produce this book.

For those who are not familiar with what happened, the Khmer Rouge took it upon themselves to waylay an American merchant ship, en route from Hong Kong to Thailand, in international waters, and seized the ship and crew. The US decided that having completed their retreat from Vietnam they could not countenance such piracy and set out to recover the ship and crew. The fact that the Cambodian authorities handed both back almost before the fighting began was not made public at the time, with the result that the recovery was used to explain the tragic loss of life sustained by US forces in an armed landing on the island of Koh Tang, off which the *Mayaguez* had been anchored.

The book consists of 12 chapters (or 'parts'), followed by 4 appendices, several pages of notes and an index. Whilst the operations are covered in some detail, by far and away the largest part of the book is given over to recollections of the men involved. Part 12 consists of around 180 pages of personal memories, some clearly still very vivid, some quite painful to read. The preceeding 11 parts relate the events as they occurred and reveal a rescue attempt characterised by a confused command system, the use of marines without combat experience and an almost total lack of hard intelligence about an island which had recently been fortified against possible Vietnamese excursions into Cambodian waters. This was a recipe for disaster, which it seems was to be repeated by the United States in Iran and Somalia! In this case it resulted in some 41 dead on the US side and an unknown number of Cambodians.

A fascinating, if worrying read.

W B Davies

Ian Johnston
Clydebank Battlecruisers: Forgotten Photographs from John Brown's Shipyard
Seaforth Publishing 2011; hardback, 192 pages, maps, plans and 200 B&W photographs; price £30.00.
ISBN 978 1 84832 113 7

Ian Johnston is well known to *Warship* readers for his knowledgeable and informative articles on British shipbuilding during the early part of the last century. While this new publication is essentially a 'picture book', using rare and largely unpublished photographs from the John Brown archive, it is also much more than that, recording in detail not only the construction of the ships concerned (the battlecruisers *Inflexible*, *Australia*, *Tiger*, *Repulse*, and *Hood*), but also explaining the complexities of the Admiralty's contractual procedures, listing the principle sub-contractors for the machinery, armour plate and weaponry of each ship, and touching on shipyard labour issues.

The photographs, which constitute the primary focus of the book, are simply stunning, and are given plenty of space to 'breathe' by the book's designer, another *Warship* regular, Stephen Dent. The author has wisely opted not to include many views of the early stages of construction, which for any warship of this scale are simply an indecipherable tangle of beams and bulkheads, in favour of photographs of the fitting-out process, featuring many close-ups of the installation of the key items of equipment in the ships. These are book-ended by some magnificent photos of the ships on the slipway prior to launch, and others showing them complete and freshly painted, moving down the Clyde to begin trials. The reader is struck by how 'clean' these ships were in their pristine condition, with none of the cluttered wartime modifications which disfigure later photographs. All the pictures are accompanied by informative captions which not only tell us exactly what is going on but point out other equipment and materials on the decks or dockside awaiting installation.

In addition to the informative text there are drawings by the author of the John Brown shipyard and the famous 150-ton hammerhead crane, and appendices which include characteristics and scaled drawings of the ships, graphs of manpower levels during construction, and shipyard monthly reports (peacetime only – the reports for 1914-1918 are thought to have been withdrawn for security reasons). The latter are particularly useful in that they give a blow by blow account of the sequence of hull construction and the embarkation and fitting of key items of equipment before and after launch.

It is a pity that the editing of the book often fails to match up to its contents. There is a misplaced table on p.38, and some of the tables of costings have pound signs while others do not. The incorporation of the numerous Admiralty documents and reports from the shipbuilder into the narrative is also problematic. Although the convention is to render such items verbatim, the sheer number and variety of these make consistency of punctuation and layout difficult, and this issue has not been successfully resolved. Ship names are italicised in the author's narrative but not in the reports, so that the balance is close to 50/50, while there are also numerous inconsistencies of punctuation and capitalisation. This is not an issue simply of 'correctness' but of clarity. The reports are a key part of the book, and would have benefited greatly from more rigorous (and courageous) editing.

These blemishes are, however, minor irritations which are far outweighed by the overall content and otherwise excellent production values of the book. *Clydebank Battlecruisers* has to be one of the outstanding publications of the year, and anyone with an interest in the major ships of the Grand Fleet or shipbuilding on the Clyde will want to own it.

John Jordan

Iain Ballantyne
Killing the Bismarck: Destroying the Pride of Hitler's Fleet
Pen & Sword Maritime, Barnsley, 2010; hardback, 304 pages, illustrated with B&W photographs, plans, maps and diagrams; price £25.00.
ISBN 978-1844-159833

Jim Crossley
Bismarck: the Epic Sea Chase
Pen & Sword Maritime, Barnsley, 2010; hardback, 170 pages, illustrated with B&W photographs, plans and diagrams; price £19.99.
ISBN 978-1848-842502

The seventieth anniversary year has produced further books on the *Bismarck*'s first and only sortie. The six-day episode was conclusive and brutal, with heavy fatalities on both sides. Strategically the British won a clear victory – sea lanes remained open – but the Denmark Straits battle exposed questionable tactics on both sides. For the first time at sea, carrier air power and radar were of decisive importance; the lesson was learnt, and never again would a German capital ship menace Atlantic convoys.

It is difficult to provide fresh insight on a familiar and much researched story. Crossley's book presents a brisk, well-illustrated summary, with additional general information on the *Kriegsmarine* and the naval war. The author, a yachtsman, writes with assurance but has little new to say. The importance of radar is stressed. The influence of ULTRA, stressed on the dustwrapper, was in fact slight. Regrettably, the publisher has not seen fit to insist on notes, references or even a list of sources, only the photos having acknowledgements; there is no preface, foreword or introduction. The description of the *Bismarck*'s anti-torpedo system, including adding the lower strake of the main belt to the anti-torpedo bulkhead, is incorrect, while elsewhere the liner *Britannic* metamorphoses into the *Majestic*, by May 1941 a burnt-out wreck in the Forth.

Ballantyne, an established writer, has provided a much more detailed and thorough book. Developed from material recorded for but not used in his 2009 book on HMS *Rodney*, it is fully referenced and annotated, the sources including archival documents, written evidence and oral testimony. The text emphasises the personal and the immediate, to provide a balanced and very human account, while retaining a technical and tactical overview. It is good to see the contribution of Joseph Welling, a USN observer in *Rodney*, included, as his report of the final battle is often overlooked. The appendices are particularly informative. The results of five expeditions to the wreck of *Bismarck* and one to *Hood* have produced much fresh information on combat damage sustained by both ships, although we will never know with certainty the precise sequence of hits, fires and explosions that caused either to sink. Too much attention is given to a photo apparently taken from *Norfolk* and purporting to show *Hood* in her last moments, and to investigating whether or not *Bismarck* attempted to surrender when *in extremis*. These are minor points; overall, this is an excellent compilation and, if a single publication had to be chosen, the definitive account for the bookshelf.

Ian Sturton

Nicholas Black
The British Naval Staff in the First World War
Boydell, 2011; paperback, 333 pages, 20 figures; price £15.00.
ISBN 978 1 84383 655 1

This book was first published as a hardback in 2009, and was reviewed – very favourably – by John Brooks in *Warship 2011*. Many potential readers will undoubtedly have been deterred by the cover price of £60.00, so we are pleased to be able to announce that the book is now available as a paperback at a fraction of the original cost.

Having read it from cover to cover, the Editor is able to confirm that the book is every bit as good as John Brooks claimed in his review. There is little to add, except that it is exceptionally readable, with none of the polemic or partisanship which colours many histories of this period. The author has an excellent grasp of his sources, both primary and secondary, and treats all of the personalities who figure in his account with sympathy, understanding and no little humour. Finally, it should be noted that this book is not only about the Staff, its personalities and structures, but about the conduct of naval strategy by the Royal Navy during the First World War.

John Jordan

John Peterson
Darkest Before Dawn: U-482 and the Sinking of the Empire Heritage 1944
Spellmount, 2011; paperback, 192 pages, 40 B&W illustrations; price £12.99.
ISBN 978 0 7524 5883 0

This book presents an almost forensic analysis of the sinking of one of the largest ships lost by the British merchant navy during the Second World War, when the *Empire Heritage* from convoy HX-305 homeward bound, off Malin Head, was sunk by *U-482*.

Its ten chapters, sandwiched between an introduction and an epilogue, explain the background, the Battle of the Atlantic, the convoy system, the details of the ships involved, the attack and the aftermath. This is supported by four appendices, a bibliography and a good index. Written by the grandson of one of the survivors of the sinking, the book is the result some serious research into the archives and sheds new light not just on the attack in question, which took place early in the morning of the 8th September 1944, but also on the tactics and final loss of the U-boat in question.

U-482 was one of the first Type VIIC boats to deploy with a schnorkel and her commander, Kapitanleutnant Hartmut Graf von Matushka, a young German Count, was on his first operational mission. His success seems to have been a mixture of sensible tactics, good use of the schnorkel and careful placement of his craft in shallow waters, together with a fair bit of luck, as it was never to be repeated. This success did however encourage Admiral Dönitz to send more boats into British coastal waters, with almost completely disastrous results for the crews involved.

The research into the German archives suggests that the sinking both of the large *Empire Heritage*, a converted whale factory ship, and then the rescue ship *Pinto* was not the cold-blooded war crime it was painted during Dönitz's trial: the submarine's CO simply did not believe that the first ship had sunk in the three minutes or less it took, and so put another torpedo into the visible silhouette, the unfortunate *Pinto*. The survivors were eventually picked up by the trawler *Northern Wave*, whose crew were quite rightly commended for their efforts.

U-482 was herself lost on her very next deployment, although this in no way compensates for the very significant loss of life from the two convoy ships. However, her loss went unclaimed until recently, and then only thanks mainly to the research by the author. In diving on one U-boat wreck, researchers found it to be one claimed sunk by HMS *Ascension* some way off to the north of Scotland. If not her, then which one had *Ascension* really sunk? By a process of elimination it has to have been *U-482*. (By a quirk of fate this reviewer has in his possession the diary of Cdr Moore, *Ascension*'s CO and the father of a late friend, in which he describes the successful attack!)

There is a slight concern over the translation of the German War Diary which seems to confuse sonobuoys and sonars from time to time. Apart from this (and the rather melodramatic title) this book represents both a labour of love and a very detailed report on research carefully carried out. The coverage of the subsequent enquiries, the resulting changes in tactics by the RN, and the awards and censures handed out makes for genuinely fascinating reading. Thoroughly recommended.

W B Davies

David Murfin
Directory of British Cruiser Designs 1860-1960
Croft Books, Haverfordwest, Pembrokeshire, 2011; soft cover, 160 pages, 110 ship tables, 15 profiles and silhouettes; price £16.00.
ISBN 978-0-9569522-0-2

Warship historians have paid scant attention to the design side of British cruisers. After Admiral Ballard's legendary *Mariner's Mirror* series *Cruising Ships of 1875*, there has been little of significance until *British Cruisers of the Second World War* by Raven and Roberts (1980), and very recently Norman Friedman's *British Cruisers: Two World Wars and After*.

This very unusual and original compilation is therefore particularly welcome in providing data for all known British cruiser designs, whether built or not, from the *Inconstant* of 1868 to the last gun designs of 1954. The author has selected lower/upper displacement limits of 2000 tons and 20,000 tons, with proposals primarily armed with missiles excluded. Projects, proposals and actual ships built for foreign navies, from the Chilean *Esmeralda* (1883) to *La Argentina* (1937) and post-WWII commercial proposals, are also covered. Information is presented almost entirely in data tables, text being limited to an introduction and linking pages.

In addition to published sources, Admiralty papers in the National Archives, Ships' Covers from the National Maritime Museum, designers' notebooks and constructors' workbooks have been trawled for authentic data. Each design is assigned a column in a table. Using the 1930s 'Town' class as an example, five preliminary post-*Arethusa* studies lead to *Southampton* and *Liverpool*, then ten more to *Belfast*. Data is carefully presented; legend, normal, standard and deep displacements are distinguished, as are the different figures for length. Where available, all-important statements of weights are included. Armament arrangements are meticulously codified and explained, taking account of deck level, enclosed and open mountings, single, twin and triple mountings, casemates, double casemates, sided guns and en-echelon turrets.

Although space constraints have restricted line drawings to those not previously published elsewhere, the reader is guided to appropriate books or articles. The very complete list of sources therefore constitutes an invaluable guide for researchers. The special sections on scaling up and down and on ship stability, while useful, apply to all warships, and seem out of place; this reviewer would prefer to have seen the space devoted to additional drawings. Such quibbles aside, the book merits a place on every enthusiast's bookshelf, and the author's treatment should be extended to capital ships.

Ian Sturton

Miroslaw Skwiot
German Naval Guns 1939–1945

Seaforth Publishing, 2011, hardback, 400 pages, over 1000 illustrations in colour and B&W; price £40.00.
ISBN 978-1-84832-080-2

The author's claims for this book are ambitious: to illustrate thoroughly and tabulate the data for 'every German artillery piece mounted afloat during the Second World War', with text describing their operation both in terms of detailed descriptions of their mechanisms and replenishment arrangements, and which ships used which guns in which theatres of war. In general terms the book succeeds admirably in this endeavour.

The superb illustrations contribute very largely to its success. A well chosen range of photographs make good use of the large page format and very sharp reproduction to provide not only details of all the guns covered, but views of the ships on which they were mounted, the progress of construction in factory and

dockyard, and life on board around the guns from harbour to the ice-bound Arctic. The photographs are supplemented by detailed plans and drawings of the main types of gun and mounting, and by computer-generated illustrations from all angles, including some in which the shields or turrets have been rendered transparent, providing an unusually clear impression of the working space (or lack of it!) therein. These illustrations are in colour and include renderings of the badges mounted prewar on some individually named turrets. The photos and artwork are backed up by very complete data tables

The Introduction sets German naval gun development, particularly of the heavy guns, in the context of the Versailles Treaty and the subsequent interwar naval arms limitation treaties, which influenced German thinking even though Germany was not a signatory to them. Thereafter, the text focuses on those technical details of the structure and operation of the guns which cannot be gleaned solely from the study of plans and photographs. Excluding photograph captions the text accounts for some 10-15% of the available page space, It is clear, concise and well written, with hardly a hint of the Polish origins of the earlier bilingual publication.

The original edition comprised four softback volumes, corresponding to the four major sections of the current edition. Each cost a significant fraction of the price of this edition, with the earlier volumes already seemingly confined to suppliers of second hand books. The publisher is to be congratulated on putting the information into a single volume between durable covers. Moreover, the already good quality of the illustrations has been improved, though some are a little smaller. Omitting the Polish text not only provides most of the space for the change but improves the layout, making the book easier to read. The coverage of the colour drawings of shells is improved and all the computer illustrations are 'the right way up', removing the need to turn the book 90° to view them. The addition of an index is not just an improvement, but is made essential by the necessary separation of the coloured artwork from the data page to which it relates.

Readers who already have Campbell's *Naval Weapons of World War Two* will find little new (or different) information. The gun data (here entirely in metric units) is identical to Campbell's, although it is more complete and includes details of the weight breakdown of the mountings – always difficult to find. Locations of ammunition stowage seem to have come from another source, with no obvious key to tell where the zones VI, X, etc. are placed in the various ships. The lack of citation of source material has to be regarded as an important omission, given the book's (valid) claim to be the standard reference on its topic.

There are a few errors and omissions. The 28cm turret data table for *Deutschland* repeats that for *Scharnhorst* despite the (correct) statement that the latter were more heavily armoured (and carried somewhat more powerful guns) – Campbell gives 580 tonnes for the rotating weight of *Deutschland*'s turrets, 750 tonnes for *Scharnhorst*. There are also confusions, omissions and imprecisions regarding the designed armament and fate of the *Hipper* class cruisers, and a number of technical errors in the captioning of the destroyer photographs. However, these errors (which have been carried over from the original books) are remarkably few in number considering the scope of the book and its illustration. The reviewer did hope for some details of the few guns intended for ships never built: the 53cm Gerat 36 ordered in 1938; more on the the 33cm and 35cm guns mentioned in the Introduction as considered for *Scharnhorst*, and the 190mm suggested for the *Hippers*; the 128mm KM41 for a late war destroyer design; and the 5.5cm Gerat 58 automatic gun. Presumably their omission was justified on the grounds that none of these guns went to sea.

This book is essential reading for any student of naval guns, while anyone interested in the wartime German Navy will find a photographic record of the ships of the Kriegsmarine which rivals that in any other publication. Those same photographs should sway the balance for anyone who has Campbell's book and thinks they can manage with that. Those who already have all four parts of the Polish/English bilingual edition may hesitate, but the hardback will certainly outlast them, and for its size the book is very reasonably priced.

David Murfin

Andrew Lambert
HMS Warrior 1860: Victoria's Ironclad Deterrent
Conway, 2011; 224 pages, many colour and B&W photos, ships plans and drawings; price £30.00.
ISBN 978-1844861286

Built to reinforce Victorian Britain's supremacy at sea and launched in 1860, HMS *Warrior* was the Royal Navy's first iron-hulled ocean-going armoured warship. Saved from the breakers in 1979, she was subject to an ambitious restoration programme in Hartlepool, and has been open to the public at Portsmouth Historic Dockyard since 1987. To mark the occasion a young naval historian wrote his first book; not only to document the ship and her service career but also to record the skills and devotion that went into the renovation. Almost 25 years on the book has been reissued to coincide with the 150th anniversary of the ship's commissioning.

In this edition, author and now acclaimed naval historian Professor Andrew Lambert combines the polish and visual appeal of a coffee-table picture book with the easy to read but scholarly writing that has become his trademark. Lavishly illustrated, original plans, archival illustrations and photographs are reproduced in high

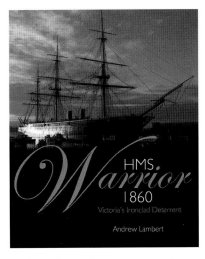

quality alongside numerous photographs of the restored ship today. The narrative gives a comprehensive account of the ship's design, construction and service, the strange twists of fate that enabled her to survive into an age when her significance is at last fully recognised, and her meticulously researched reconstruction. There are exhaustive descriptions of her hull, armour, guns, machinery and rigging, and a useful appendix details the original specification of the ship.

The narrative is substantially unaltered from the first edition, a mark of the quality of the original, although it has been updated and refreshed to reflect the passing of time and to fill in the years since the ship's arrival in Portsmouth. The most significant change from the original is the illustrations. Picture quality is significantly improved, modern reproduction techniques mean the photographs are crisper, and many of the original monochrome images of the restoration are now reproduced in colour. Whilst some of the original photos have been excluded, a wide array of contemporary images has been added; these show how the ship benefits from the decision to display her as built with the minimum of signs or notices, thus giving a clear representation of how she would have looked on her first commission. It is the line drawings that benefit the most from the update, with the sometimes indistinct originals replaced by sharper versions, or in many cases by colour reproductions of the original, tinted, as-fitted drawings – each a masterpiece in its own right.

Unfortunately, with the removal of the names of those who took part in the restoration at Hartlepool this book is no longer a tribute to the restoration, but there is still sufficient new material to make the book a must for anyone with an interest in this important ship. The original book concluded that the longevity of the ship was at risk. The release of this new edition is a fitting tribute to the foresight of those who initiated the project. Some concerns remain, but the increasing interest in the Victorian age, steam engineering and technology must give hope for the future; *Warrior* is quite simply the first and the last of the ironclads, a unique survivor from a golden age. This book is an excellent read and a fitting tribute to a magnificent ship.

Philip Russell

Rif Winfield
First Rate: The Greatest Warships of the Age of Sail
Seaforth Publishing, 2010; hardback, 168 pages, 192 illustrations in colour and black and white; price £45.00.
ISBN 978 184832 071 0

This book has a slightly misleading title, as the First Rates of navies other than the Royal Navy are only mentioned where they were captured or destroyed in combat. That said, the author has provided a feast of illustrations of the Royal Navy's ships from 1610 to 1850, many in the glowing colours of the original paintings.

The book is divided into eleven chapters, the first eight of which cover specific periods of history in the development of the Navy, the other three dealing with fixtures and fittings, ship structure and finally the few captured First Rates to see service with the Royal Navy. The book is topped and tailed by the author's introduction and acknowledgements, plus a single page index.

The book covers the main eras of the age of sail, starting with the Caroline navy, through Commonwealth, Restoration and the French and Napoleonic wars, and culminates in the steam-powered wooden battleships of the Victorian era. Examples of First Rate line of battle ships are described in some detail, covering the advances in design and construction and the final addition of steam power. The longevity attained by some of these later ships is astonishing; they were so well built that several survived for over a hundred years!

Each chapter is illustrated with well chosen paintings, etchings, photographs, mainly of the Admiralty models of the period, and wherever possible Admiralty drafts of appropriate ships. The design and careers of individual ships are briefly described with particular highlights covered in more detail. There are also numerous two-page spreads on related topics. This is one area where the generally high production standards seem to have faltered; sometimes these spreads have the effect of breaking the flow of the main text in rather awkward places.

The reproduction of the illustrations is, without exception, superb; clearly a lot of effort here has gone into getting the colour reproduction as close to the original as possible. The *pièce de résistance* is a superb four-page fold out of the draft of HMS *Victoria* of 1863; a full-colour reproduction, replete with detail. There is a minor problem with duplicated captions on pp.19 and 20, but both refer to the same vessel and probably the same artist so there may not be much lost here. These slight blemishes aside, this is a book to be recommended to anyone with an interest in these ships, which arguably constituted mankind's greatest technological achievements during the 300 years or so that they reigned supreme.

W B Davies

Battleship Yamato: Japan's Secret Fleet
History Films in association with Pen & Sword Digital; double DVD, 136 minutes total running time; price £19.99.
Catalogue no: 4260110581493

As advertised, this two-DVD set claims not only to tell the story of the *Yamato* class battleships and of their predecessors, but also to provide a 'History of the Japanese Fleet'. According to both the box insert and the press release accompanying the review copy, the discs contain archive footage which it had been impossible to show for decades, due to 'the strict secrecy of the Japanese'. Anyone expecting remarkable new film of the *Yamatos* themseves will, however, be sorely disappointed, possibly to the extent of wanting their money back. There is, quite simply, none at all, only a few blurred images taken from attacking American aircraft. Besides these, all we get are some well-known still photographs, a set of images of a model of *Yamato*, and some straightforward but dull computer graphics imaging. The majority of the footage in the hour-long main film features earlier Japanese battlships, battleships of other nations (especially Britain), other ships of the IJN, and ships of other navies as well. Much of this footage is new to this reviewer, and it may well be that it is indeed material that has long remained, if not actually secret, then certainly little-known outside Japan. The lack of any detailed background information here is therefore a great pity.

The story told is straightforward and basic, the footage not always relevant (Tsu-shima is illustrated by a splendid bit of film of British Rendel gunboats blasting away on some exercise or other!) but generally good to look at. However the sound track voice-over is dire: clunky of language, easily betraying its origin (translated first from Japanese into German, then German into English); patchy in its coverage, frequently subjective, and littered with errors. This is hardly unique to the medium, but irritating nonetheless. The DVD interface is generally slow and unweildy.

The second disc is better. The IJN film consists of some 22 minutes of footage of Japanese ships both at sea and in harbour, and of their crews going about their duties, all set to music, with no irritating and/or inaccurate commentary. Presumably some at least comes from propaganda or recruiting films – again there are no details as to source – but it certainly does give an impression of the IJN at the zenith of its power. Accompanying this is a 28-minute compilation of US propaganda films, mixing footage of pre-war exercises and of wartime combat, accompanied by the sort of patriotic commentary that is probably best turned off, plus a short film covering the first few months of the Pacific war, and assorted galleries of (again mostly well-known) still photographs.

Overall, this package is a disappointment. The IJN footage of the second disc apart, it will be of little interest to most readers of *Warship*.

Stephen Dent

James C. Bussert & Bruce A. Elleman
People's Liberation Army Navy: Combat Systems Technology, 1949-2010
Naval Institute Press, 2011; Hardback, 256 pages, 14 photos & 30 tables
Price: £23.50.
ISBN 978-1-59114-080-1

Andrew S. Erickson, Lyle J. Goldstein & Nan Li (editors)
China, The United States and 21st-Century Sea Power: Defining a Maritime Security Partnership
China Maritime Studies Institute & Naval Institute Press, 2010; Hardback, 568 pages, 3 maps, 20 charts & tables
Price: £35.00.
ISBN 978-1-59114-243-0

Andrew S. Erickson & Lyle J. Goldstein (editors)
Chinese Aerospace Power: Evolving Maritime Roles
China Maritime Studies Institute & Naval Institute Press, 2011; Hardback, 544 pages, 4 maps
Price: US$52.95.
ISBN 978-1-59114-241-6

Toshi Yoshihara & James R. Holmes
Red Star Over The Pacific: China's Rise and the Challenge to U.S. Maritime Strategy
Naval Institute Press, 2010; Hardback, 312 pages
Price: US$36.95.
ISBN 978-1-59114-390-1

One notable side effect of the steady rise in the power and importance of China's People's Liberation Army Navy (PLAN) has been the significant growth in the number of books devoted to its analysis. Nowhere is this trend more apparent than in the United States, where a desire to gain a better understanding of this new maritime phenomenon is equalled only by uncertainty as to whether to respond by treating the PLAN as a likely future adversary or as a potential ally. The influence of these various factors is present in these four US Naval Institute Press books which, combined, represent nearly 1,700 pages of analysis published in the course of just ten months.

Messrs Bussert and Elleman's *People's Liberation Army Navy* is, perhaps, the book most likely to appeal to the majority of *Warship*'s readership. Providing authoritative, in-depth technical analysis of the ships and equipment fielded by the PLAN from its formation to the current day, it demonstrates how a combination of imported technology and indigenous progress has produced an increasingly advanced though as yet untested fleet. The two expert authors shed considerable light on PLAN design progression and clear up several previous misconceptions about Chinese naval capabilities whilst not being entirely free from one or two questionable assertions of their own. A more significant criticism, however, is the impact of NIP's rather puritanical production style: the scarcity of illustrations leaving the reader with little other than a number of tables to aid absorbing quite a technically demanding text.

China, The United States and 21st-Century Sea Power and *Chinese Aerospace Power* are, respectively, the fourth and fifth volumes in an impressive series of 'Studies in Chinese Maritime Development' published jointly with the US Naval War College's China Maritime Studies Institute. Bringing together a collection of essays produced by distinguished contributors in their chosen fields, they provide a wide range of interesting perspectives grouped by theme that can be read either selectively or sequentially. Both books examine their subjects from a broadly strategic perspective but *Chinese Aerospace Power*, particularly, also provides some informative technical insights. For example, the various discussions contained within its section on Chinese anti-ship missile (ASBM) capabilities provide much information on a technology that could have a significant impact on the balance of power in the Pacific.

China, The United States and 21st-Century Sea Power looks at areas of possible cooperation, and is notable in containing contributions from several Chinese academics.

Toshi Yoshihara and James R Holmes are also both established contributors to the series and some of the material covered in these books is also key to their analysis in *Red Star Over The Pacific*. They present a broad-ranging study of both the strategic and tactical objectives underlying the rise of Chinese sea power, drawing on the ideas of theorists such as Alfred Thayer Mahan, Sun Tzu and Mao Zedong to inform their assessment. Whilst suggesting that the speedy rise in PLAN military capabilities that has surprised so many external commentators needs careful attention, they also stress the commercial and political imperatives behind current Chinese thinking. An interesting aside for a European reader is their assessment of the contrasting fortunes of Asian and European naval power as the latter focus largely on constabulary duties: 'As one civilization vacates the oceans, another is crowding the seas and skies with ships and warplanes that bristle with offensively oriented weaponry.' Certainly, the capabilities of the major European fleets seem to be increasingly regarded as a sideshow to mainstream naval analysis as underlying economic changes reinforce focus on the maritime consequences of the so-called 'Asian Century'.

Conrad Waters

Steve Backer
Grand Fleet Battlecruisers
Seaforth Publishing / Classic Warships Publishing; hardback, 128 pages, illustrated with B & W and colour photos, drawings and ship colour schemes; price £25.00/$42.00.
ISBN 978-1-84832-104-5

This excellent book is one of the 'Ship Craft' series aimed principally at model-makers. It contains a wealth of information about the origins, operational employment and appearance of the Royal Navy's battlecruisers between 1914 and 1919, however, which makes it into a more general reference work on the subject. The sections on development and operations are well-researched and illustrated, giving a positive view of this major warship type which saw a considerable amount of successful action in the First World War but which had its reputation tarnished at the battle of Jutland. All classes including the two 'R's, *Furious*, *Glorious* and *Courageous* are included in the period from their completion to 1919.

About half the book is devoted to a survey of the model products available and there are colour photographs of component parts and finished models. Models of all the Grand Fleet battlecruisers are available, many of them in a variety of different scales. Builder's models are included and the background story about the haggling between the Australian War Memorial and John Brown & Co over the purchase price of an unusual 1/64 scale model of HMAS *Australia* is fascinating. Whilst this section gives modellers examples and encouragement to achieve excellent results, it also gives more general readers an insight into the construction and detailed appearance of these ships that is simply not available in any other published work the reviewer is aware of.

The last section of the book lists alterations and additions so that an individual ship's appearance at any particular time can be worked out. Line drawings by John Roberts show how the older ships changed to incorporate new technological developments as the war progressed, and there are a large numbers of excellent photographs showing ships, armament and structure. Aircraft operating arrangements in all the ships that had them and especially those in HMS *Furious* up to 1919 are included in this section. Lastly, the constant scale plans and side elevations by George Richardson give an excellent idea of the growing size and complexity of these remarkable warships.

In summary this is an excellent source book for anyone interested in making a model of a Grand Fleet battlecruiser to any scale and is highly recommended for that purpose. It is much more than that, however; it is also a first class reference work full of detail, with well-sourced drawings and photographs that complement the text.

David Hobbs

Robert J Moore and
John A Rodgaard
A Hard Fought Ship: The story of HMS Venomous
Holywell Publishing, 2010; 384 pages, soft covers, many B&W photos and line drawings; price £18.99.
ISBN 978-0-9559382-0-7

A revised and significantly expanded edition of a book first published in 1990, A Hard Fought Ship chronicles the career of the British Royal Navy's modified 'W' class destroyer *Venomous* during both peace and war between 1918 and 1948. Initially written by the commanding officer of TS *Venomous*, Loughborough's Sea Cadet unit, work on the updated volume was completed by John A Rodgaard, a US Navy Captain, following the original author's death.

Adopting a broadly chronological approach, the book tells the destroyer's story largely from the perspective of the sailors that served in her. The authors have gone to considerable lengths to obtain a wealth of recollections from former crew members of all ranks and the result is a compelling read that vividly presents life onboard. Inevitably, the major area of focus – encompassing around three quarters of the book – is *Venomous*' service during the course of the Second World War. The evacuation of troops from continental Europe in 1940, convoy duties in the North Atlantic and Arctic, as well as a variety of duties in the sunnier climes of the Mediterranean are all described in considerable detail. The ship's role in the events surrounding the loss of the depot ship *Hecla* and crippling of the destroyer *Marne* at the hands of Germany's *U-515* on the night of 11/12 November 1942 is especially well documented. Whilst nearly three hundred lives were lost in this tragedy, many more were saved through *Venomous*' rescue efforts.

The wide array of hazards faced by a wartime destroyer and her crew is clearly portrayed. *Venomous* saw action against submarines, aircraft and land-based forces, faced ongoing dangers from mine-laying activities and suffered real risk of loss from both collision and storm. Indeed, given her original design role it is, perhaps, an instructive lesson in the dangers of mission-specialisation that the only threat she never faced was action with enemy major surface units. Crew member accounts of these various challenges are supported by a large number of illustrations, many previously unpublished. As well as portraying the ship's various operations, these also serve to depict the ongoing changes in wartime appearance through the process of progressive modification.

Rigorous design and production values means that images are reproduced clearly to a high standard, and the overall book has a quality feel in spite of its paperback format.

A Hard Fought Ship does not pretend to be a technical history. Accordingly, detail in this area is relatively sparse and reliant largely on secondary sources. A few historical assertions of questionable accuracy also fail to live up to the book's generally high standards of scholarship. However, neither of these points detracts from the authors' achievement in presenting a portrayal of life on a wartime destroyer with a depth and insight that is possibly unequalled by any previously published work.

Conrad Waters

Barry Gough
Historical Dreadnoughts: Arthur Marder, Stephen Roskill and Battles for Naval History
Seaforth Publishing, Barnsley 2010; hardback, 366 pages, illustrated with B&W photographs; price £35.00.
ISBN 978-1-84832-077-2

This very thorough and eminently readable book is the story of the lives and interactions of the two great writers on twentieth century British naval history, the successors to the legendary Alfred T Mahan and Julian Corbett. Professor Arthur Marder and Captain Stephen Roskill wrote between 1940 and 1980, and in combination provide us with the definitive account of the Royal Navy's policy, strategy, tactics and leading personalities from 1900 to 1945.

Marder, the American outsider and professional historian, started earlier, using a mixture of guile and bland innocence to gain privileged access to Admiralty documents normally out of bounds to historians and completing the *Anatomy of British Naval Policy 1880-1905* before he was thirty. Intensely energetic and enthusiastic, he went on to edit Lord Fisher's letters before writing the standard account of the Fisher years and the First World War in the five-volume *From the Dreadnought to Scapa Flow*.

In contrast, Roskill was the cerebral naval officer, familiar with the system. Perennially unpopular with his superiors for speaking or writing his mind, he was sent in 1941 to HMNZS *Leander* in the supposed backwater of the South West Pacific, and was instrumental in saving the ship when she was torpedoed. Invalided out of the service because of the delayed effect of injuries, he was a late choice for writing the *Official History of the War at Sea*, the responsibility of the Cabinet Office. The writing was delayed by clashes with higher authority, in particular with Churchill (at one or two removes, through the formidable Secretary of the Admiralty) over the PQ 17 convoy and other controversial episodes.

Literary jousting began in the 1960s. There was disagreement over a verbatim quotation from a letter of Lord Hankey (Roskill was writing Hankey's biography, with complete control of his papers, Marder wanted to use a short quotation – ultimately just 25 words – from one of his letters). Marder wished to finish *From the Dreadnought to Scapa Flow* with the June 1919 scuttling of the High Seas Fleet, while Roskill preferred him to stop at the armistice, when the latter's *Naval Policy between the Wars* would begin. Finally their studies began to overlap, with Roskill's *Churchill and the Admirals* going over the same ground as his rival's *From the Dardanelles to Oran*, giving rise to strong differences of interpretation and opinion.

The academic spats enlivened correspondence columns in newspapers and learned journals, and contributed to acid footnotes in their later books. Marder, for instance, commented that *Naval Policy between the Wars, Vol.1*, was 'badly organised and somewhat of a jungle of facts in places', while Roskill observed that Marder claimed 'to know better than I (Roskill) what I did when serving on the Naval Staff in 1939-40'. Their personal relationship deteriorated from amicable to frosty, and good humour was never restored. After Marder's death, Roskill's final years were soured by a costly dispute with the trustees of the second Earl Beatty over use of the Beatty papers.

A book about naval historians and their differing approaches to writing history might be dry and dull, but in the author's capable hands (as a Canadian, he is neutral in the dispute) makes a fascinating read. It is a naval book with a difference and one that cannot be too highly recommended for the bookshelf.

Ian Sturton

Ian M. Malcolm
Life aboard a Wartime Liberty Ship: The story of life on a Liberty cargo ship during World War 2
Amberley Publishing, 2011; paperback, 265 pages, 51 B&W illustrations; price £16.99.
ISBN 978 1 4456 0020 8

Morris Beckman
Flying the Red Duster: A merchant seaman's first voyage into the Battle of the Atlantic 1940.
The History Press, 2011; paperback, 160 pages, 21 B&W photographs; price £12.99.
ISBN 978 0 7524 5900 4

These two books present two very different ways of telling the same story; both covering the authors' first voyages as junior radio officers on merchant navy ships during the Second World War.

The first is by a (then) young man from Dundee, the second from an equally young man of Jewish extraction from London's East End. Both authors have been responsible for several books before writing these two, but clearly they had both been moved by recent attempts to get the merchant mariners' efforts during the Second World War recognised more widely.

Ian Malcolm writes with a sort of endearing naivety that makes the story seem very fresh, almost as if it only happened yesterday. I can only suppose that he took copious notes whilst at sea. They must have been very good because at times, the narrative being so fresh, the reader cringes with embarrassment at some of his more unworldly moments. It is hard to believe that the author is now in his 87th year!

Morris Beckman, on the other hand, writes with a more easy rhythm and whilst equally new to the world of the sea, he seems to have entered it with a slightly more cynical approach, the difference perhaps between the Calvinist Dundee and the cosmopolitan East End. Whilst Ian Malcolm continued to serve at sea after the war, Morris Beckman's narrative ends with the information that one of his companions had died on his very next voyage.

Both stories reveal the stress of wartime convoys, the alarms, the torpedo attacks, and the horrors of the treatment meted out to Britain's merchant marine, not only by the enemy, but perhaps more frequently by the shipowners, their fellow countrymen, and by history itself. The tradition of paying off a seaman when he left a ship was carried over to those forced to abandon ship, presumably financially convenient for the owners, but a dreadful reward for services rendered.

Whilst these two stories go a long way to putting the record right by highlighting these iniquities, one is left with the feeling that the average merchant seaman, of whatever nationality, gave a lot better than the nation deserved and certainly much better than he got.

W B Davies

Scott W Carmichael
Moon Men Return: USS Hornet and the Recovery of the Apollo 11 Astronauts
Naval Institute Press, 2010; hardback, 237 pages, 16 photographs; price $36.95/£25.00.
ISBN 978-1-59114-110-5

This book tells the tale of one of the more unusual missions to have been carried out by the US Navy. Everyone knows the outcome of the story, but what makes *Moon Men Return* such an engrossing read is the amount of detail that Carmichael has unearthed and skillfully worked into his narrative, from official and unofficial sources, as well as from numerous eyewitness recollections, resulting in not only a vivid reconstruction of the actual recovery mission itself, but also a portrait of life on board a major USN vessel in the 1960s.

The mission was essentially a straightforward search and rescue, but it was one with a few slightly unusual aspects, such as the presence of the President of the United States on board, the fact that some three-quarters of the world's population would be tuning in, and the nature of the mission the three men being rescued had just performed. With so much at stake, there was a lot of practice in the period leading up to the recovery itself, sometimes in the harshest of conditions. All the while the daily routine of the ship continued as normal, for example with a ferrying run to San Diego, while three helicopter pilots completed their qualification on the way from there to Pearl Harbor. This is one of the striking features of Carmichael's narrative: the juxtaposition of the historic with the totally mundane.

The USN regarded itself as technically advanced, but the arrival of NASA brought innovations such as microwave ovens, velcro, and the installation on board *Hornet* of a very early digital IFF system. In contrast, when the carrier's searchlight turned out to be broken, a replacement was simply stolen from on board a sister ship in the same dockyard. When President Nixon required a specific leather couch for his television appearances, the same technique was used to acquire one from the officers' mess on Ford Island. Indeed something that comes across strongly is that there was as much concern on board *Hornet* about the President's visit than the recovery of the astronauts. His secret service detachment, after checking the backgrounds of every member of the carrier's crew, demanded that a considerable number of them be locked in the brig for the duration of the visit. *Hornet's* captain refused, and eventually a compromise was reached whereby the men in question were all confined to the sick bay.

The thing that *really* had everyone worried was the fear of contamination by 'moon germs' that might have come back with the astronauts. This may seem bizarre today, but at the time it was taken very seriously indeed: it resulted not only in procedures such as the carrier approaching the ditched Command Module from upwind, but also contingency plans to quarantine the entire ship and everyone on board, including the President! Other dangers were more real: quite apart from the possibility of technical malfunction, there was the fear the astronauts might end up being eaten by sharks. In fact the worst thing that happened was that the weather caused a late change in the location for splashdown, necessitating a high speed dash on the part of *Hornet* to get into position in time.

Unfortunately the book's editing is not all it might be. There is a great deal of repetition, and the insistence on referring to all participants in the drama by their full name, title and even nickname nearly every time they are mentioned comes over as pedantic and irritating. Sometimes the ship's name is in italics, sometimes not, while occasionally Carmichael lapses into US (or USN) colloquial expressions which may be unfamiliar to the British reader. A map or two would also have been useful. However, overall these are minor complaints about what is fundamentally a quite fascinating read.

Stephen Dent

Norman Polmar and Michael White
Project Azorian:
The CIA and the Raising of the K-129

Naval Institute Press, 2010; hardback, 276 pages, illustrated in colour and B&W; price £21.95/$29.95.
ISBN 978 1 59114 690 2

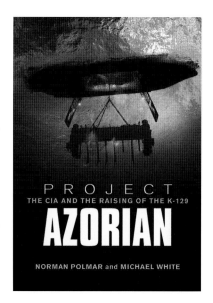

When first completed, the advanced technical capabilities of the seabed mining vessel *Hughes Glomar Explorer* were the subject of much discussion and debate. Sea bed mining was, and to a certain extent still is, seen as the way forward for the extraction of some of the rarer minerals such as manganese, and a more perfect cover story would have been hard to imagine. In fact the ship was purpose-built, at great cost, solely as a heavy lift ship, in order to recover part of a sunken Soviet submarine, the *K-129*. It was only after this that the *Explorer* tried her hand, unsuccessfully as it transpired, at seabed mining, and today she is used as a deep water drill ship by the oil industry.

In this book the authors, both of whom have a good track record for thorough research, set out to tell the true story of the CIA's covert project, from the fatal accident to *K-129* in February 1968 to the recovery of one small part of her in August 1974, laying to rest the many conspiracy theories that have surrounded these events. Whilst some names and details remain classified to this day, the story presented here is clearly believable and logical – logical, at least, if you are prepared to accept that at the height of the Cold War the US intelligence services were prepared to pay out vast sums of money to fund 'black' operations such as this.

The book's twelve chapters are arranged chronologically to the point where the project was formally concluded, after which there are two assessments, firstly of the actual cause of the loss of the submarine and then briefly of the project as a whole. These are followed by eight separate factual appendices ranging from the *K-129*'s crew list to the details of the *Explorer* and major recovery system components. The book concludes with a bibliography and reading list.

The technological achievement represented by the ship and the lifting gear described in the main chapters was finally recognised by the award of the American Society of Mechanical Engineers' Historic Mechanical Engineering Landmark status in July 2006, proving, in their words, that 'the impossible is indeed possible when talented engineers with courage to take prudent risks are provided an incentive to stretch the state-of-the-art'!

Apart from the stunning technical achievements, one of the most telling parts of the book is the discussion on the real cause of the submarine's loss, and this illustrates graphically the risks inherent in taking the early strategic weapons to sea in such a confined space as a conventional submarine. Unlike the modern SSBN the three missiles in *K-129* were arranged vertically in the extended fin (or sail in US parlance), but their launch tubes were sufficiently long to stick out of the bottom of the pressure hull. Naturally this was capped with an extension to the pressure hull, but to any engineer this alone would be a worrying weakness, never mind the several tonnes of highly volatile fuel in the missiles themselves. It was the accidental firing of two of these missiles that the authors conclude was the cause of the loss, a conclusion borne out by the published photographs.

A very interesting book, particularly recommended for students of the Cold War era.

W B Davies

Geoff Puddefoot
Ready for Anything:
The Royal Fleet Auxiliary 1905–1950

Seaforth Publishing, 2011; 224 pages; 36 B&W photos; £25.00.
ISBN 978-1-84832-074-1

Studies in naval history over recent years have demonstrated a welcome broadening in perspective to encompass such matters as shipbuilding, armament, administration and infrastructure. However, the role and progressive development of the Royal Fleet Auxiliary has been something of a neglected subject. Geoff Puddefoot has attempted to address this, first with the publication of *The Fourth Force: The Untold Story of the Royal Fleet Auxiliary since 1945* (2009) and now with this 'prequel' which covers the first half of the 20th Century. Sadly, on the evidence of this book, we shall have to wait a while longer for a thorough-going study which does justice to the subject.

The book describes the origins and creation of the service, through the Great War, the interwar years, the Second World War (seven chapters), and the years up to 1950. The immediate problem here is the very lengthy time-span and, particularly during the world war years, the increasingly complex issues relating to the organisation of the RFA, the roles undertaken by the ships themselves, the technical aspects of their operations and the historical events of the various periods covered. The result is that none of these matters is addressed adequately, the author meandering through the years, not always on a chronological basis, with a seemingly haphazardly focus on one theme or another. In the two chapters devoted to the First World War there are passing references to the primary functions undertaken by these auxiliaries, namely the fuel and store freighting tasks, while a further short section describes the over-complex management structure under which the vessels were operated, a tediously repeated mantra which seems to suggest that the modern-day streamlined organisation of the RFA should have emerged magically overnight in 1905. However, much more space is devoted to what are described as 'specialised' (marginal) roles such as 'dummy battlecruisers that later became RFAs', 'vessels used as kite balloon ships that later became RFAs' and defensively equipped merchant ships, some of which became RFAs. There is also a lengthy digest of four years of war on all fronts, together with a detour to examine the development of refuelling at sea methods in the US Navy.

The second problem is that the subject matter is inadequately researched, as the scant reference section at the end of the book reveals. Many of the author's secondary sources are very dated. Surprisingly, he relies heavily on Captain Sigwart's 1960s work which, admirable though it is, was never intended to be a definitive history of the RFA. Smith and Adams' much later Centenary work, on the other hand, with its strictly chronological approach, seems to be largely ignored. Use of primary sources seems also to have been limited and selective.

There are some irritating errors, such as the assertion that Jutland was 'the last major fleet action fought between steel warships' or that the Battle of Coronel in November 1914 was the only major clash between the British and German navies outside the North Sea – the Battle of the Falkland Islands took place the following month. Elsewhere, there is evidence of sloppy proof-reading which reflects badly on the otherwise respected Seaforth imprint.

Ready for Anything is a disappointing attempt to condense the history of the Royal Fleet Auxiliary over the first forty-five years of its existence into a single, fairly slim volume. Consequently, we are left little the wiser regarding the very subject which is meant to be focus of this study.

Jon Wise

Gary Staff
Battle on the Seven Seas: German Cruiser Battles 1914-1918

Pen and Sword Maritime, 2011; 232 pages; 43 B&W photographs; 28 maps; £19.99.
ISBN 978-1-84884-182-6

In his introduction the author states his purpose as being to provide an accurate and informative 'narrative' of the German cruisers in action during the First World War. In addition to the official German history *Der Krieg zur See 1914-1918*, Staff has sourced contemporary combat reports and war diaries. Often these first-hand statements were written by survivors following the loss of their ships and therefore lend an immediacy which is absent if accounts are written after several years have elapsed. The argument given for lending weight to such accounts is that the approach offers a clearer view 'before later political meddling and influence' can take effect.

While the operations of the High Sea Fleet were confined to the North Sea, German trading and colonial interests in China and East Africa and her close affiliations with Turkey meant that a number of her cruisers were already stationed in the Pacific, Indian Ocean and the Mediterranean at the outbreak of war. Several chapters of *Battle on the Seven Seas* deal with the naval engagements which resulted from these deployments. The Battle of Coronel in November 1914, The Battle of the Falkland Islands the following month, and the skirmish in November 1914 which ended the brief odyssey of SMS *Emden*, all stemmed from the decision by the German Admiralty to order the East Asiatic Squadron to return home shortly after the commencement of hostilities. Two separate chapters describe the battle between the *Goeben* and *Breslau* and Imperial Russian forces in the Black Sea in November 1914, and nearly four years later between the same German cruisers and Royal Navy ships near the entrance to the Dardanelles in January 1918. The events leading to the destruction of the East Africa station ship, SMS *Königsberg*, in the Rufiji Delta are also described.

Other chapters relate to the engagements which took place in the North Sea. In addition to Jutland (or 'The Skagerrak Battle' as it is referred to in this book), the two battles in The Helgoland Bight (1914 and 1917) and The Battle of Dogger Bank (1915) also receive attention. Finally, Staff gives an account of the clash between German and Russian forces off the neutral Swedish town of Östergarn in the Northern Baltic in July 1915. While many of these events will be well known to readers, others, such as the last named, are refreshingly unfamiliar.

It is the author's contention that the German version of events, upon which the majority of the book is based, has greater integrity and is unfettered with bias compared with equivalent British accounts. Unquestionably, the eye witness statements constitute the most fascinating and absorbing parts of the narrative. The quotations chosen, despite being unnecessarily lengthy in places, graphically portray the quite terrifying experience of being within the confines of a steel warship under sustained, heavy fire. The author also succeeds in conveying the pride and dedication of the crew members as they continued to fight, usually against a superior enemy, often in the sure knowledge that their ship was doomed.

By his own admission, Staff has dedicated a great number of years to the study of the Imperial German Navy. His enthusiasm and admiration for their cruisers is evident; he is at pains to point out the efficiency of the German gunnery, the durability of the warships, which in turn is a testament to their construction, as well as the strategic significance of the cruisers in terms of the national war effort. His research among German archival material and also Russian sources provides not only a fresh perspective on some familiar naval engagements but also highlights the lesser known battles and brings to our attention the truly global nature of the war at sea.

One significant omission is any discussion of the strategy and tactics which guided the course of these battles. By concentrating on individual ship movements, which were often a bewildering succession of brief gunnery exchanges amidst the mists and smoke of the North Sea, it is easy to lose sight of the overall course of the action and the decision-making involved unless one has detailed prior knowledge. The maps help, but only to an extent. Nevertheless, there is much to admire in *Battle on the Seven Seas*. For those readers who are drawn to this first, great test of twentieth century naval technology, the vivid and often poignant eye-witness accounts from German and Russian perspectives are brought to life for the first time to English-reading audiences through the author's diligent and skilled translations.

Jon Wise

Tim Parker
Signalman Jones: Based on the Recollections of Geoffrey Holder-Jones
Seafarer Books, 2010; paperback, 135 pages, over 50 B&W photos and drawings; price £9.95.
ISBN 1-906266-21-9

Born in 1915, Geoffrey Holder-Jones joined the RN Volunteer Reserve as a boy signalman at his father's suggestion, as relief for his humdrum life as a hat salesman in 1930s Liverpool during the Depression. His description of pre-war summer training cruises on capital ships evoke a Royal Navy of a bygone era, and are in stark contrast to his later wartime experiences on small ships. Mobilised at the start of the Second World War, he survived the mining of the cruiser minelayer HMS *Adventure* in the Thames estuary on 13 November 1939. He was subsequently awarded the Distinguished Service Medal for bravery when detailed off to provide support for 'two experts from *Vernon*' in dismantling a recovered German magnetic mine. Commissioned shortly afterwards, he spent the rest of the war serving in the Atlantic, mostly in converted trawlers and whalers. He was within fifteen miles of HMS *Hood* when she was sunk by the *Bismarck* but did not hear the explosion. After two years' continuous service in the North Atlantic he returned to Portsmouth, where he acted as a pilot for the D-Day landings before being given command of the trawler HMS *Guardsman* in March 1945.

There have been many published personal accounts of wartime experiences, but what sets this book apart from the myriad of other autobiographical narratives is the successful splicing of personal account and wider historical context. The narrative proceeds at a brisk pace, and is punctuated by personal experiences and amusing anecdotes. The time spent with the escort squadron based in New York is particularly well observed, with the austerity Jones left behind in the UK providing a poignant contrast to the abundance of delights and the generous hospitality available in a nation only just getting onto a war footing.

Much of the historic background will be familiar to readers. However, Jones' personal experiences also cast a welcome light on several lesser-known operations. The extent of the support the Royal Navy gave the Americans in combating the U-boats off their eastern seaboard is one; the tension involved in escorting a floating dock from Boston to the Caribbean at a painfully slow 3.5 knots through hostile waters another.

Well illustrated with over 50 photographs, this book is an enjoyable read and is thoroughly recommended.

Philip Russell

David K Brown
Warrior to Dreadnought
The Grand Fleet
Seaforth Publishing, 2011; paperback, 224 & 208 pages, pprox 250 photographs and line drawings; price £16.99 each.
ISBNs: 9781848320864 & 9781848320857

These two books, first published as hardbacks in 1997 and 1999, have been reissued as paperbacks. In the intervening decade, both have become established (along with *Nelson to Vanguard*, already similarly treated) as parts of a classic history of British warship design and development. Though their titles suggest concentration on battleships, this was far from the case. All types of warship were considered, along with weapons development, and perhaps most importantly, the development of design techniques through the efforts of skilled and distinguished technologists. The author's background (the late David K Brown was a Deputy Chief Naval Architect as well as author of the history of the Royal Corps of Naval Constructors) enabled him to make such difficult topics accessible to the general reader. The books are based on primary sources and call for careful reading, for such topics as the work of the Froudes on model testing of the speeds of warships, and on stability, are not easy. *Warrior to Dreadnought* dispels the myth of a technically backward Victorian navy, explaining the many rapid technological changes adopted over half a century, while *The Grand Fleet* paints a clear picture of a navy predominant not only in numbers of ships, but in technical development, emerging from the challenges of the First World War ahead of all rivals in the new fields of submarines and naval aviation.

The new editions are repeats of the first, the main change being a smaller page size. Therefore a few errors of detail remain (chiefly in the completeness of references in the notes) and no attempt has been made to avoid some limited overlap in content (the evolution of HMS *Dreadnought* being treated in both books to differing extents.) The change in format means that details are a little harder to see in some of the excellent collection of photographs, while the reduced print size makes reading harder for older eyes, especially with the chapter notes. These criticisms aside, the publishers are to be thanked for making these essential books once again available at a very reasonable price.

David Murfin

Eric Dietrich-Berryman, Charlotte Hammond & R E White
Passport Not Required: US Volunteers in the Royal Navy, 1939-1941
Naval Institute Press, 2010; hardback, 187 pages, 29 photos;
price $27.95/£19.99.
ISBN 978-1-59114-224-9

This book tells the stories of twenty-two US citizens who between September 1939 and November 1941 crossed the Atlantic (usually via Canada) and volunteered for service in the Royal Navy. They come across as a disparate bunch, from all manner of backgrounds and with a variety of reasons for embarking on such an unusual and hazardous venture. One volunteered because of his hatred of 'Roosevelt, communists, and socialism'; a collection of motivations which he must have had plenty of cause to ponder during the years that followed. Several were simply taking an opportunity to escape from deeply unhappy financial or personal circumstances. When America became 'properly' involved in the war quite a few of the volunteers returned home to serve in the US Navy; vastly better rates of pay seem to have been an important factor. Two lost their lives while serving in the RN, including John Parker, at 51 the oldest among them. One of those who came through unscathed was Peter Morison, son of the renowned naval historian Samuel Eliot. Several then went on to impressive and successful careers post-war, though a number also died in sad circumstances.

Most seem to have fitted in well with their new British comrades (seven acquiring British wives), but one or two appear to have been less popular, their careers stagnating or even going into reverse, in part no doubt because of the inevitable clashes of cultures and attitudes. The author has a tendency to gloss over such parts of the story, and as it remains easy enough to read between the lines it is difficult to resist the feeling that the reader is being given a rose-tinted version of events. It is clear that a few sticks got inserted into the spokes of the British class system (not least by the young Morison), yet these wider, deeper issues are almost entirely ignored.

The book had three authors before its publication (White sadly died during the course of working on the book). As a result *Passport Not Required* lacks a truly coherent structure and at times is more than a little confusing. In addition the policy of citing each source in brackets as it is used throughout the narrative can become thoroughly irritating to the reader.

This is social, rather than operational or technical naval history. It is an important and in many respects a fascinating story, featuring some remarkable individuals; it is simply a pity that the book's faults tend to detract from its undoubted virtues.

Stephen Dent

Iain Ballantyne
Warspite: From Jutland Hero to Cold War Warrior
Pen and Sword Maritime, 2010; paperback, 224 pages, illustrated with many B&W photographs, line drawings and reproductions of paintings;
price £14.99.
ISBN 978 1 84884 350 9

The original hardback edition of this book (2001) was inspired by the author's attendance at the 1999 reunion dinner of the HMS *Warspite* Association. He subsequently interviewed five members of the association and obtained permission to use material from its newsletter and from its members' published and unpublished accounts and journals. Further reminiscences came in following an appeal in the magazine of the Royal British Legion, while the author also consulted the papers and recordings of crew members that are now held in the Imperial War Museum, as well making use of a large number of photographs taken over the years by those who served in the battleship. The book is also illustrated by line drawings from the journal of Midshipman J G Corbett and by specially-commissioned paintings by Dennis C Andrews; the latter are of limited historical value and are only reproduced in black-and-white.

The book begins with a short description of earlier ships named *Warspite* and of the origins of the *Queen Elizabeth* class of fast battleships, and ends with brief accounts of the careers of the other ships of the class and of the eighth *Warspite*, the nuclear attack submarine. But the heart of the book is the extraordinary career of the seventh *Warspite*, from her first action off Jutland in 1916 to the bombardment of Walcheren in 1944. The author has made good use of the material that he assembled, though it is regrettable that the linking passages contain a number of minor technical and historical errors, especially in the earlier chapters.

The chapter on Jutland incorporates, amongst a number of others, the vivid accounts of Surgeon Lieutenant Gordon Ellis and the battleship's Executive Officer, Commander Humphrey Walwyn, although it does not seem to have made use of the despatch of Captain Edward Phillpotts. For the inter-war years, it is surprising to find no mention of Captain Stephen Roskill, who was *Warspite's* gunnery officer from 1936 to 1939 and responsible for the commissioning of her new armament after her comprehensive rebuilding. The best chapters are those covering the battleship's distinguished service during the Second World War and which incorporate many interesting reminiscences from those who served and fought in her. Some are not what might have been expected; if the pilot of her spotting aircraft remembered correctly, her famous long-range hit at the Battle of Calabria was achieved only after rather timid spotting corrections. This is a reminder that recollections recorded only long after the event have to be treated with caution; however, unless they conflict directly with contemporary, preferably written, accounts, they still have value, especially in capturing the reality of life at sea in wartime.

By the end of her second World War, *Warspite* was in a seriously dilapidated condition, which would probably have ruled out her preservation, even if it had been given any serious consideration. Admiral Cunningham's 'Old Lady' ended her days, accident-prone to the last, on the rocks of Prussia Cove. The photographs of her awaiting the ship breakers provide a link to her past; they were taken by retired Surgeon Captain Gordon Ellis, who had tended her wounded during the Battle of Jutland.

John Brooks

Jean Hood (ed.)
Carrier: A Century of First-Hand Accounts of Naval Operations in War and Peace
Conway 2010; hardback, 448 pages, 40 B&W photographs; price £20.00.
ISBN 978184861118

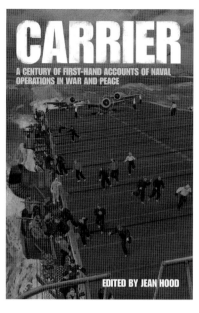

Compiled from eyewitness accounts by aircraft carrier crews and their embarked naval air squadrons and taken from interviews, correspondence, archived memoirs, published autobiographies and official reports, this book is a follow-up to *Submarine*, also edited by Jean Hood and reviewed in *Warship 2009*. Coverage begins with the earliest seaplane carriers and concludes with a chapter on the Falklands war and subsequent carrier air operations. Each of the chapters begins with a general introduction written by the editor and setting the scene for the recollections which follow; these are not entirely free of error (*Furious* completed her full 'through-deck' conversion in 1925, not 1922) but are generally well-researched and well-written. There are two plate sections with a selection of monochrome photographs which illustrate the ships, the aircraft and life aboard.

Like all books of its kind, *Carrier* is to a large part dependent on the quality of the individual recollections. Some of these are too brief to be of great value, some are written transcriptions of oral evidence. Many of the recollections, while purporting to describe life on board a carrier, could equally well be about life on any large surface ship. And some of the recollections relating to the well-known battles of the Second World War are disappointing simply because the perceptions of individuals in these situations are necessarily fragmentary and often inaccurate, although many of the more serious inaccuracies are corrected by the editor. For the period up to the end of the Second World War the book is also dependent on material which is archived and readily accessible. This creates a problem of balance: the British and America national (and independent) archives have preserved a considerable quantity of both oral and written testimony; the Japanese very little. This means that although the editor has made a conscious attempt to gather recollections from all corners and to provide balanced coverage – the modern period, for example, has recollections from French and Indian aviators – for the IJN she has been compelled to rely on the few memoirs published in English (notably Fuchida, whose account of air operations at Midway has been proved to be unreliable). This gives the first half of the book a particularly Anglo-Saxon bias.

That said, there are some real strengths in the book. Some of the people whose recollections are recorded here can really write. The final contribution of the introductory chapter, 'Permission to come aboard', has a wonderfully evocative description of a night take-off aboard the US carrier *Saratoga* during the First Gulf War. And the contributions to Part 3, 'Postwar to Vietnam', are almost uniformly excellent. Unlike some of the earlier sections this one really does focus on carrier operations, and in the process we learn much about the introduction of jet aircraft, angled decks, high-power catapults and landing mirrors and the impact of those developments on the flyers. Over Korea air strikes were contested not only by anti-aircraft fire but by enemy pilots in MIGs, and we learn what it is like to land a fast, heavy jet with a damaged undercarriage on a relatively small length of steel flight deck.

If the reader is prepared to accept the limitations inherent in this sort of book there is much to commend itself here.

John Jordan

David Mearns
The Search for the Sydney: How Australia's Greatest Maritime Mystery Was Solved
Harper Collins 2009; hardback, over 200 illustrations in colour and B&W.
ISBN 9780732288891

On 19 November 1941 a fierce battle, unprecedented in the annals of naval warfare, took place in the Indian Ocean, far from the coast of Western Australia. Both ships involved, the cruiser HMAS *Sydney* and the German raider *Kormoran*, were lost. All 645 officers and men aboard *Sydney* perished, while 315 out of *Kormoran*'s crew of 395 were rescued, subsequently to be held in prisoner of war camps. At the time of her demise, *Sydney* was the most famous warship in Australia because of her outstanding performance in the early battles for control of the Mediterranean. For 66 years, the loss of *Sydney* remained Australia's greatest maritime mystery and generated some extraordinary conspiracy theories which, thankfully, have been fully debunked in this superb book. David Mearns, who is one of the world's foremost shipwreck hunters and has successfully located dozens of wrecks in deep water, accepted the challenge of finding *Sydney* in 2002. However, as he has so ably demonstrated, this required meticulous research into archival material over several years before he could put his skills as a detective, engineer, marine scientist and navigator to the test.

After just 43 days at sea, the author found both *Sydney* and *Kormoran*, which was a stunning vindication of the quality of the research which underpinned his sea search in 2008.

The prologue, written by Lieutenant John Perryman RANR, outlines *Sydney*'s career up to the time of her sinking, while the introduction contains an account of the encounter between the cruiser and the *Kormoran*. This is followed by ten chapters, the first of which describes the original search for *Sydney*, the origin of the controversy, the West Australian and Murchison interrogations, the Eldridge Report and postwar historical reassessments. After describing the results of his search through various archives, his interaction with other groups and individuals trying to solve the mystery and the trials and tribulations of actually mounting the search, the author explains how the wreck of *Kormoran* was found and then used to find *Sydney*. Thereafter, both wrecks are described and illustrated with a fine array of excellent colour photographs before the author addresses the two issues of how *Kormoran*, a converted German cargo ship with an inferior armament, could have sunk a cruiser, and why 315 of the *Kormoran*'s crew of 395 survived while there were no survivors from *Sydney*. One crucial question remains unanswered: why did *Sydney*'s captain negate the advantage of his ship's superior armament by getting so close to the German raider? Clearly, the only people who could have answered that question were killed in the final action, but the author has compiled a credible scenario to explain what happened on that fateful day. The end result is a book which is not only a fitting tribute to those who died, but is also one which makes a significant contribution to naval history. This beautifully-produced book is lavishly illustrated and includes some rarely seen photographs plus a most impressive four-page colour foldout showing *Sydney* in great detail. Highly recommended.

Richard Osborne

Erminio Bagnasco & Augusto de Toro,
The *Littorio* Class:
Italy's Last and Largest Battleships 1937-1948
Seaforth Publishing / Naval Institute Press, 2011; hardback, 320 pages, profusely illustrated with plans, colour artwork, and B&W images;
price £45.00/$85.00.
ISBN: 9781848321052 (9781591144458)

Not since Naval Institute published Marc'Antonio Bragadin's *The Italian Navy in World War II* in 1957 has a major Italian work about the Regia Marina appeared in English translation. Fifty-four years is a long time and helps account for the generally one-sided tone of the English-language literature of the Mediterranean war. At least *The Littorio Class: Italy's Last and Largest Battleships 1937-1948* by Erminio Bagnasco and Augusto de Toro justifies the wait.

Erminio Bagnasco, editor of *Storia Militare* magazine, is widely regarded as the doyen of Italian naval historians. He has authored or co-authored many works, including two which have appeared in English, and his photographic collection is outstanding. His reputation breeds great expectations and this translation of the 2007 Italian edition does not disappoint. The translation itself is functional: there are a few 'Italianisms', but it accomplishes its major goal of rendering a complex and technical subject into easily-readable English.

The Littorio Class is structured into six chapters covering the background to the ships, a detailed technical description, operational history, and finally comparisons and conclusions. There are also appendices covering movements, damage sustained and performance characteristics of the heavy and medium guns

The photographs and drawings are clear and comprehensive, and the captions short and to the point. Drawing and photos have been placed in such a way as to support the text, and the book maintains a flow that very long captions and discursive footnotes would have interrupted.

In sum, this is a magnificent volume. It is also a welcome, long-needed and important addition to the English literature of the naval war. The English reading audience can ask for nothing better, only more of the same.

Vincent O'Hara

[Note: the original Italian-language version of this book was reviewed in detail by the Editor in Warship 2008. This review of the new English-language version has therefore been edited to avoid duplication.]

Books in other languages

Patrick Maurand & Jean Moulin
Les Avisos A69
Marines Editions, Nantes 2011; hardback, 221 pages, many line drawings and colour/B&W photographs; price €45.00.
ISBN 9-782357-430853

This large format monograph, the latest in a long line from Marines Editions, celebrates the service careers of the A69 sloops, the workhorses of the French Marine Nationale since the completion of the first of class, *D'Estienne d'Orves*, in 1976.

Conceived in the late 1960s as a replacement for the American PC type, classified as a 'coastal escort' (*escorteur côtier*) in French service, the A69 evolved into the 'low' end of a US Navy-style 'hi-lo' mix, with the anti-submarine frigates of the *Georges Leygues* class, which with their 30-knot speed could operate as carrier escorts, becoming the 'high' end. The utility of these relatively basic craft, whose armament originally comprised a single 100mm gun, four anti-submarine torpedoes and an A/S rocket launcher, together with a general shortage of frigates following the failure of the ambitious *Plan Bleu* of 1992, resulted in a number of modifications, notably the fitting of Exocet MM38 and MM40 SSMs and a more capable communications outfit, which would increasingly feature long-range satellite comms. Following these modifications the ships were increasingly deployed on overseas patrols which took in the French West Indies, the Indian Ocean and Pacific territories, West Africa and the Lebanon. Due to be deactivated by 2009, the later ships of the class will now serve for up to 35 years, with decommissioning between 2014 and 2019.

The book by Patrick Maurand and Jean Moulin covers all of the above aspects, from the initial conception of the design through the later modifications, to the service history of the seventeen ships of the class. It is well illustrated by line drawings showing the general arrangements and the external appearance of the various ships at the different stages of their careers. In the earlier 'technical' section the key features of the ships are also illustrated by photos taken on board, many by Jean Moulin. The 'historical' section is illustrated by a mix of colour and black and white photos of the ships in service, reproduced a little on the small side by the standards of contemporary Anglo-Saxon publishing, but always with clear and informative captions. There are also particularly complete data tables and tables listing all deployments.

For any reader interested in the modern French Navy this is a thorough, comprehensive treatment of a long-serving (and hard worked) class of ships. The illustration and data tables alone would justify purchase; those able to read French will gain even more from the book.

John Jordan

Robert Dumas &
Gérard Prévoteaux
Les Cuirassés de 18 000t
Lela Presse 2011; hardback, 200 pages, maps, many plans and B&W photographs; price €48.00.
ISBN 978 2 914017 62 6

Laid down more than six months after the completion of HMS *Dreadnought*, the six ships of the *Danton* class, with their powerful mixed armament of four 305mm (12in) and twelve 240mm (9.4in) guns all in twin turrets, have long been regarded as an anachronistic curiosity by English-language naval historians. This new book by *Warship* contributors Robert Dumas and Gérard Prévoteaux goes a long way towards setting the record straight. These ships were in no way anachronistic; in terms of their design philosophy they were, in effect, 'anti-dreadnoughts'. They were built in the full knowledge of developments abroad, but they responded to a conviction that the proponents of the 'all-big-gun' ship had taken a wrong turn, and had learned the wrong lessons from Tsushima. The French Navy of the period continued to believe that a hail of fire from medium-calibre guns, at a 'decisive range' of no more than 5000m, would disable an opposing capital ship more quickly than a smaller number of slow-firing heavy guns.

Of course, as we now know with the benefit of hindsight, it would be the French who would ultimately turn out to have pursued the wrong course. Within two years of the laying down of *Danton* it was becoming apparent that future naval actions would take place at much greater gun ranges than had been previously thought possible (or desirable), and France would lay down the first of her own dreadnought battleships. However the *Dantons*, each of which took some four years to complete, remained the Marine Nationale's premier front-line battleships when war broke out in August 1914, and three of the six continued in active service until 1930.

The obsolescent design of the *Dantons* has been much exaggerated. One of the aspects which comes over strongly in this book is the degree of influence exercised by friendly contacts with Britain and the Royal Navy. They were the first French ships powered by turbines, and this form of propulsion was adopted following visits to British turbine builders and much informed debate. Unfortunately the British companies were more interested in selling their own machinery to the French than in any form of (unpaid) technology transfer, and the French had to learn the hard way that turbines subjected to higher steam temperatures and pressures on board ship than in the factories tended to strip their blades if insufficient allowance was made for expansion between rotors and stators. However, the French learned quickly, and the reliable high-speed steaming made possible by the adoption of turbines was much appreciated, even if the consumption of coal at cruising speed was enormous compared to the reciprocating engines of the preceeding 15,000-tonne ships.

The book begins with a detailed account of the origins of the ships. This is followed by an equally detailed technical study and a particularly interesting account of the technical problems experienced on trials and in service. It concludes with a full service history, which becomes effectively a history of the French *Armée Navale* in the First World War. Unlike the older battleships deployed to Gallipoli, the more modern units spent most of their time swinging at anchor off the Greek islands, awaiting a sortie by the Austro-Hungarian Fleet which never materialised. There are a number of useful annexes, the first of which is an account of the loss of the nameship *Danton*.

Whilst this book will be of most interest to those who can read French fluently, the clear and comprehensive data tables and the quality of the illustration make it a valuable purchase for any enthusiast of the Marine Nationale of the period, its ships and its weaponry. There are many detailed plans, some from official sources, others drawn specially for the book, and the photographs, if not always of the highest quality, provide an impressive historical archive of the ships and their operations.

John Jordan

H. Visser
De Koninklijke Marine: foto's en feiten 1950-1975
Lanasta Publishing, 2010; 120 pages, numerous b&w and colour photographs and colour artwork, [available in UK via Warsash Nautical Books & Mainmast Books]; price £20.00.
ISBN 978-90-8616-083-9

The Royal Netherlands Navy has a long and proud tradition. Although its 'heyday' as a naval power occurred more than three centuries ago it remains to the present time a highly effective, technically advanced organisation capable of global, blue-water operations despite a succession of wounding defence cuts resulting from the end of the Cold War. Interest in De Koninklijke Marine remains strong in a maritime nation such as The Netherlands, and is evidenced by the steady stream of high quality publications about this navy which are produced on a regular basis. It is disappointing that these works remain little known outside the country.

Henk Visser's book, simply entitled 'The Royal Navy: photographs and facts', is the second volume of the author's study of the Dutch Navy covering the middle years of the 20th Century. Each page features at least one photograph or an example of J.Henneveld's evocative artwork. The illustrations are supported by the author's knowledgeable text in the form of extended captions. Naturally, the warships themselves predominate but the selection includes close-ups of armament and other technical equipment together with glimpses into the personal and social life of the Dutch sailor, a subject of particular interest to the author.

The years covered in this volume, 1950-1975, document the renaissance of the navy following the ravages of the Second World War. Thus the early pages feature vessels which will be instantly familiar to many readers: British War Emergency Programme destroyers, the carrier ex-HMS *Venerable*, *Cannon* class DEs, Australian *Bathurst* class mine-sweepers. However, by the middle of the 1950s, the indigenous shipyards had recovered sufficiently for the distinctive *Holland* and *Friesland* class destroyers to be constructed in The Netherlands, followed in the 1960s by the *Van Speijk* class frigates based on the RN *Leander* design. In the meantime, the technical ability of the Dutch home electronics industry was evident in the radar and sensors carried in increasing numbers not only on the new escorts but also on the carrier *Karel Doorman* and the two older cruisers of the *De Zeven Provincien* Class. By the end of the period covered, the distinctive profiles of the *Tromp* and *Kortenaer* Class frigates and the *Zwaardvis* Class submarines, albeit bearing evidence of the ongoing technology exchange between The Netherlands and Britain in particular, all carried distinctive hallmarks of being thoroughbred Dutch warships.

For those not skilled in languages, the text will naturally present some difficulties. However, the subject matter is familiar enough for some measure of guesswork to be used. Henk Visser's intimate knowledge of the topic and his own professional eye for detail means that a little persistence can be immensely rewarding.

There is a danger of becoming Anglo- or US-centric in one's understanding of postwar naval history given the wealth of relevant English language publications currently available. This beautifully produced and meticulously researched book serves to redress the balance at least with respect to this small, historic and highly proficient navy.

Jon Wise

Michele Cosentino
Le Portaerei Italiane

Albertelli Edizione Speciale, Parma 2011; hardback, 248 pages, 8 fold-out plans, 410 drawings and B&W photographs; price €60.00.
ISBN 9-788887-372960

The Italian Navy's failure to build an aircraft carrier prior to the Second World War, despite being permitted an overall figure of 60,000 tons for this category of warship by the Washington Treaty, has been the subject of much debate and controversy. However, the relatively recent discovery of numerous models and plans based on projects evolved and developed by the some of the Regia Marina's most forward-thinking engineers and constructors has made it clear that the aircraft carrier was never far from the navy's thoughts during the period.

This new book by Michele Cosentino, written with the encouragement and support of the prominent naval historian Erminio Bagnasco, attempts to tie all these disparate threads together and to create a coherent history of the development of Italian naval aviation from the early days to the completion of the new V/STOL carrier *Cavour*. Given the piecemeal nature of the evidence from the interwar period, this is no mean achievement. For example, the series of carrier designs by Constructor-General Filippo Bonfiglietti, which could hold their own against any foreign contemporary and in many respects anticipated the French *Joffre* and the German *Graf Zeppelin*, were only 'discovered' in 2008, when his family made available plans and a model of the ship. Navy archive material for this and other significant projects was completely lacking, so Cosentino and others have had to extrapolate technical data from the models and the plans. However, Cosentino has been able to unearth considerable material from the navy archives relating to the detailed discussions which took place between Mussolini and the naval staff during the 1920s. At a key meeting which took place in 1925 there was a marked lack of enthusiasm for the aircraft carrier among the senior Italian admirals, most of whom pointed to the experimental nature of developments abroad and to the high cost of a carrier and its aircraft (20-25% more than a treaty cruiser) at a time of financial stringency. It is clear from this and subsequent discussions that opposition to organic naval aviation was by no means limited to the Regia Aeronautica.

The book is a large-format publication similar to that of Erminio Bagnasco's previous work on the battleships of the *Littorio* class. It is particularly well illustrated with black and white and (for the *Cavour*) colour photographs, including an extensive series showing the *Aquila* under construction, and there are many line drawings and reproductions of plans of both ships and aircraft. Particularly prominent are large pull-out plans of the four major designs which proceeded to the construction stage: the seaplane carrier *Giuseppe Miraglia* of the mid-1920s, the aircraft carrier *Aquila* of the Second World War, and the two V/STOL carriers completed post-war, *Giuseppe Garibaldi* and *Cavour*.

This will almost certainly become the standard reference source for Italian carrier design for the foreseeable future. It is a credit to the author and the publisher.

John Jordan

[Note: The Bonfiglietti carrier design is the subject of a Warship Note in this annual (pp.180-81) – Editor.]

WARSHIP GALLERY

After The Falklands War

This year's edition of *Warship* is published on the thirtieth anniversary of the Falklands War. No doubt the occasion will be celebrated/commemorated extensively elsewhere using stills and video footage of the time taken by official Navy photographers and the big news corporations. The photos in this year's Gallery were taken by **John Jordan** in the aftermath of the war, using a modest 35mm Praktika camera. The quality of the photos is variable, as was the weather in Portsmouth during the summer of 1982, which encompassed the dull and drizzly, the hot and hazy and – on occasions – even the bright and clear. However, this selection attempts to give a flavour of the period following the conflict, when ships returned from the South Atlantic bearing the scars of action damage or, more often, with their paintwork badly weathered by the elements, to be greeted by flag-waving crowds lining the walls and towers; when ships recently completed or emerging from refit were hurriedly worked up ready for deployment, sporting new low-visibility paint schemes and hastily-welded platforms for short-range AA guns and additional chaff launchers purchased from the USA; when morale in the fleet was at an all-time high, and a blind eye was sometimes turned by authority to the over-exuberance of the ships' crews.

The Type 42 missile destroyer Glasgow returns on a drizzly afternoon 19 June 1982. Although of mediocre quality the photo, which was taken from the Gosport side of Portsmouth Harbour, shows clearly the patched-up hole (see inset) made by the bomb which penetrated the after engine room just above the waterline and exited the other side of the ship, fortunately without exploding. After undergoing temporary repairs at sea Glasgow continued to provide area air defence for the Task Force with her Sea Dart missiles, before being relieved by HMS Cardiff.

The burnt-out hangar and port-side GWS22 fire control director of the guided-missile destroyer HMS Glamorgan. The ship had been struck by a land-based Exocet missile on 12 June while conducting a bombardment off the Falklands. The missile gutted the hangar, destroying the Wessex anti-submarine helicopter, and penetrated into the galley below, killing 13 men. The photos were taken during August Navy Days of 1982, when the ship was still in dock for repair.

The Type 42 destroyers Exeter *and* Cardiff *returned from the South Atlantic on 28 July. Exeter had deployed from the Caribbean to replace HMS* Sheffield, *lost to an Exocet missile strike early in the conflict;* Cardiff *joined the Task Force with the 'second wave' led by HMS* Bristol *on 26 May. Both ships claimed to have shot down aircraft with their Sea Dart area defence missiles. The photos were taken from the beach close to the Round Tower at Portsmouth (the tower itself being too crowded for comfort!). Note the broad black stripe down the centre of both ships, painted as a recognition feature so that they could not be confused with the two Argentine Type 42s,* Hércules *and* Santísima Trinidad. *The paintwork of* Cardiff *in particular has taken a battering in the severe South Atlantic weather. Note the differences in the main air surveillance radars:* Cardiff *has the distinctive Type 965 'double-bedstead' of the earlier units of the class, while* Exeter *was completed with the more advanced Type 1022. The haste with which the Task Force was assembled meant that there was no time to fit additional close-range weapons.*

Cardiff's Sea Dart launcher boasts one firm (black) kill and two (red) possibles. Despite the configuration of the aircraft icon, which appears to be that of an Israeli-built Dagger delta-wing fighter, the firm kill is now known to have been an obsolete Canberra bomber, the last Argentine aircraft to be shot down in the conflict. The 'tally board' of the carrier HMS Hermes, painted on the starboard side of her island, is even more impressive. Kills by her Harrier jump-jet aircraft include Daggers, Pucarás, Skyhawks and Canberras, while the helicopters destroyed include several Pumas and a Chinook. No fewer than 26 bombing sorties appear to have been undertaken by the ship's aircraft.

One of the lessons of the Falklands War was the need for enhanced 'last-ditch' capabilities against sea-skimming missiles such as Exocet, which popped up over the horizon too late for the Sea Dart area defence missile to engage with a guarantee of destruction. As an interim measure the Royal Navy purchased large numbers of modern 30mm and 20mm guns from the British company BMARC and installed them in the Type 42 destroyers on specially-built platforms abeam the funnel and the after Type 901 missile FC radome. These close-ups, taken at Navy Days in August 1982, show the newly installed Oerlikon 30/75 on a GCM-A03-2 twin mounting and the Oerlikon 20/85 KAA on its GAM-BO1 single mounting aboard HMS Glasgow during the repairs undertaken in Portsmouth Naval Dockyard. The 30mm weapons would later be replaced by Phalanx 'gatling guns' purchased from the USA on all Type 42 destroyers.

One of the more surprising features of the Falklands War was the speed with which the Royal Navy was able to mobilise its reserves. This is one of three frigates of the 'Tribal' class which were reactivated at Chatham during May and June. The photo was taken from the Round Tower at Portsmouth during late July. The ship's name, Ghurka, is just visible on the stern, but the ship otherwise has an all-over 'low-visibility' light grey livery, with the pendant number and the black funnel caps painted out; the mast and boats are also painted a uniform grey, giving the ship a 'ghostly' look which would have blended in well with the mists of the South Atlantic.
(Note: in the background can be seen the giant floating crane Tog Mor, preparing for the raising of the wreck of the Mary Rose, which took place in October.)

Even after the Argentine surrender there was still a perceived need for a strong military presence in and around the Falklands. Some of the ships which had been hurriedly prepared for deployment to the South Atlantic were deployed after the conclusion of the conflict to relieve the ships which had taken part. The destroyer Southampton had just completed her trials when she deployed, and is shown here returning in September. Note the battered paintwork on the lower hull and the added platform for a 20mm gun: not one of the modern BMARC, which were delivered too late to be fitted for this deployment, but an old 20/70 Mk II of Second World War vintage. Symbolic of the Navy's new-found confidence is the 'smiley face' painted on the fibreglass dome covering the Type 901 missile control radar. In a similar vein the carrier HMS Illustrious, which entered service too late to see action in the Falklands War but subsequently relieved her sister Invincible off the islands, is seen here moored at South Railway Jetty on 20 December after her return to Portsmouth late in the year. The radome of her newly-installed Phalanx 'gatling gun' has been suitably decorated in the lead-up to Christmas.

The damaged Glasgow *and* Glamorgan *would be quickly repaired. In the case of* Glasgow, *repairs to the hull and engine room took only a couple of months, and the dockyard took full advantage of this short period on unavailability to fit her out with new close-range guns. The photo was taken from the Round Tower during August 1982, and the new guns are clearly visible on their platforms abeam the funnel (BMARC 30mm twin) and the after radome (BMARC 20mm single). Note that she now has the standard overall light-grey livery (cf. Photo 1) and still has her pendant number painted out. The damage to* Glamorgan *was more extensive and took several months of work in the dockyard – as a non-Sea Dart ship she was in any case less of a priority. The photo shows her entering Portsmouth on 26 May 1983. She has her full outfit of Exocet SSM launchers (forward of the bridge) and her pendant number has been repainted, but she is otherwise in the overall light grey livery which characterised the post-Falklands period. Note the new platform for US Super RBOC chaff launchers (not yet fitted) abeam the forward superstructure; she retains her original British Corvus model abeam the fore-funnel.*